Women and Revolution in Viet Nam

Arlene Eisen

This book is dedicated to my sons, Biko and Tongo. I hope they will join generations of children who will be as fierce in their respect for women as they are in their hatred for oppression and in their determination for all people's liberation.

Women and Revolution in Viet Nam

Arlene Eisen

Zed Books Ltd., 57 Caledonian Road, London N1 9BU

Women and Revolution in Viet Nam was first published by
Zed Books Ltd., 57 Caledonian Road, London N1 9BU
in 1984

Copyright © Arlene Eisen, 1984

Copyedited by Rosamund Howe
Typeset by Wayside Graphics
Proofread by Louise Hoskins
Cover design by Lee Robinson
Cover photo courtesy of John Spragens Jr.
Other photos courtesy of Arlene Eisen, Hanoi Museum of
  Revolutionary History, Peggy Herod, Sara Rosner,
John Spragens Jr., Viet Nam News Agency.
Printed by The Pitman Press, Bath

British Library Cataloguing in Publication Data
Eisen, Arlene
    Women and revolution in Vietnam.
    1. Women in politics – Vietnam
    2. Revolutions – Vietnam
    I. Title
    322.4′2′09597   HQ1236
    ISBN 0-86232-175-1
    ISBN 0-86232-176-X Pbk

US Distributor
Biblio Distribution Center, 81 Adams Drive,
Totowa, New Jersey 07512.

Contents

Tables

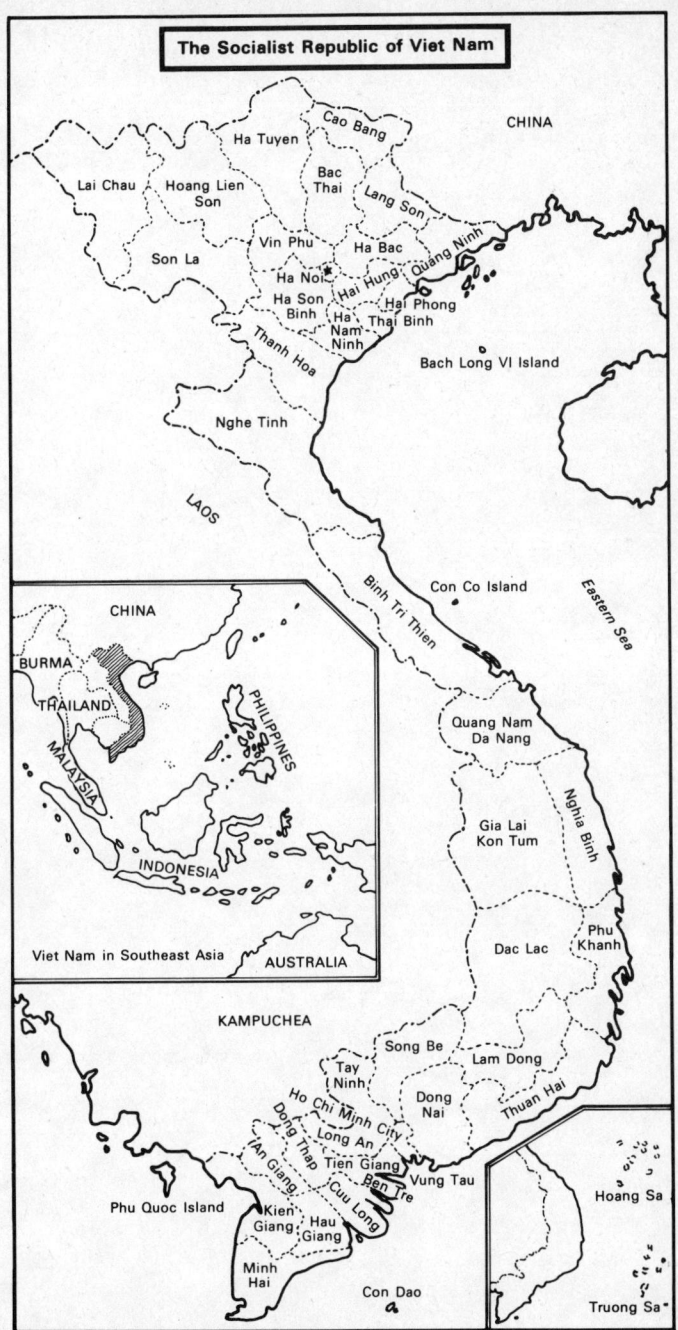

The Socialist Republic of Viet Nam

CHINA

Cao Bang

Ha Tuyen

Lai Chau

Hoang Lien Son

Bac Thai

Lang Son

Vin Phu

Ha Bac

Son La

Quang Ninh

Ha Noi

Hai Hung

Ha Son Binh

Hai Phong

Ha Nam Ninh

Thai Binh

Thanh Hoa

Bach Long VI Island

Nghe Tinh

LAOS

Binh Tri Thien

Con Co Island

Eastern Sea

CHINA

BURMA

THAILAND

PHILIPPINES

MALAYSIA

INDONESIA

Viet Nam in Southeast Asia

AUSTRALIA

Quang Nam Da Nang

Nghia Binh

Gia Lai Kon Tum

Dac Lac

Phu Khanh

KAMPUCHEA

Song Be

Lam Dong

Tay Ninh

Ho Chi Minh City

Dong Nai

Thuan Hai

Long An

Dong Thap

Tien Giang

An Giang

Cuu Long

Ben Tre

Vung Tau

Phu Quoc Island

Kien Giang

Hau Giang

Hoang Sa

Minh Hai

Con Dao

Truong Sa

Appreciation

Many people joined in creating and nurturing this book. It is a pleasure and an honour to express my appreciation to them.

Special thanks to Tran Thi Hoan, Duong Thi Duyen, Vu Thi Lien and many other members of the Viet Nam Women's Union who were my hosts, teachers and friends in Viet Nam. They worked tirelessly and graciously to arrange interviews, visits and travel – offering me all the precious resources at their disposal to make this book as accurate as possible in reflecting the experience of Vietnamese women. Our continuing correspondence has been a valuable source of information for this book. I am moved and honoured by the confidence they've expressed in this project.

Many friends and co-workers supported my most recent visit to Viet Nam by suggesting questions and areas of research or by donating money towards the travel expenses. Thanks to Aiko, Nance Barrett, Judy Clavir-Albert, Carole Colum, Cita Cook, Bernadine Dohrn, Gail Dolgin, Bea Eisman, Bill Eisman, Donna Flutterman, Deborah Gerson, Judy Knoop, Meridel Le Sueur, Pia Moriarty, Essie Mormon, Jane Norling, Sandra Richards, Deborah Rosenfelt, Peter Rubin, Paul Rupert, Magali Sarfatti Larson, John Spragens Jr and the South East Asia Resource Centre staff, the late Elsa Knight Thompson, Jo Tucker, Martha Williams and members of the Association of Vietnamese Patriots in the US. And thanks to my parents, Sylvia and Jack Eisen, who made a generous financial contribution to the project.

After I completed an early draft, a diverse group of people – friends active in the women's movement and women's studies; North Americans who have studied and visited Viet Nam; members of the Association of Vietnamese Patriots in the US; and others active in progressive movements – studied the manuscript and made thoughtful suggestions for improvement. They shared their time and knowledge generously, often engaging me in difficult struggle over complicated issues. Their commitment to the book was an essential source of information, as well as encouragement. Thank you to Manija Ajanaku, Tran An, Nance Barrett, Cathy Boudin, Judy Clark, Judith Clavir-Albert, Ann Froines, Joel Gordan, Kathleen Gough-Aberle, Murray Hiebert, Penny Johnson, Lisa

Manning, Meridel Le Sueur, Van Mai, Carole McCrae, Carli Numi, Sandra Richards, Sara Rosner, Susan Schlacher, John Spragens Jr, Tran Khan Tuyet, Alice Vanderslice, Jayne Werner and Martha Winnacker.

Thank you to the staff of Friends of St Francis Childcare Center and the other people who became second mothers to my children while I worked on the book. Thanks to Jean Miller, Stephanie Sunshine and Martha Williams for giving their time to reproduce copies of the manuscript. I also appreciate the personal support of Miranda Bergman, Mosi Rahema, Rosalyn Grossman and my co-workers at the San Francisco Women's Centers who understood the pressures on a single working mother trying to finish a book.

I deeply appreciate the commitment of Zed Press Co-operative – especially Robert Molteno. From the earliest stages, they struggled to convince me to write this book. Thank you to Anna Gourlay, also of Zed, and Rosamund Howe, for their careful copyediting. And another thanks to my friend, Adrienne Lauby, who painstakingly combed the manuscript one more time, struggling with me to make the style more direct and to clarify the content – especially on the difficult issue of sexuality.

Finally, there are two women whose example and firm support have been a life-giving source of inspiration to this project. My loving appreciation to Meridel Le Sueur and to Bui Thi Me, who, nearly ten years ago, welcomed me to a liberated zone in South Viet Nam with the words: 'We are part of the worldwide family of militant women. The oceans cannot dampen our feelings of solidarity and love.'

Arlene Eisen
San Francisco, October 1983

Glossary

Political Geography

Viet Nam
The Vietnamese people, the Geneva Accords of 1954 and the Paris Peace Agreements of 1973 all recognize that Viet Nam is one country extending from the border with China in the north to the Gulf of Thailand in the South. Between 1954 and 1976 the nation was temporarily divided at the 17th parallel. It was formally reunified in 1976.

DRV (Democratic Republic of Viet Nam)
Ho Chi Minh became the first President of this Republic, proclaimed in 1945. The DRV comprised all of Viet Nam until 1954. Between 1954 and 1976, it comprised only the area north of the 17th parallel.

PRG or PRGRSVN (Provisional Revolutionary Government of the Republic of South Viet Nam)
The coalition government formed in 1969 that adopted the political programme of the National Liberation Front. On 30 April 1975, it became the government of the Vietnamese people living south of the 17th parallel. Before April 1975, areas governed by the PRG were known as liberated areas.

SRV (Socialist Republic of Viet Nam)
Name given to reunified Viet Nam in June 1976. The capital of the SRV is Hanoi.

Republic of Viet Nam, RVN, Saigon regime or Thieu regime
The state originally decreed by Diem in 1955, in violation of the Geneva Accords. This government occupied South Viet Nam's cities and parts of the countryside in southern Viet Nam and was supported militarily, politically and financially by the US. After 30 April 1975, it was dissolved. It's president, Thieu, fled the country.

Ho Chi Minh City
Since June 1976, it is the administrative district that includes old
Saigon, Cho Lon and surrounding rural areas.

NEZ (New Economic Zone)
Areas that were destroyed during US occupation or were previously
uncultivated. Since 1975, they are being resettled by former residents
of Viet Nam's cities.

Democratic Kampuchea
The government headed by Pol Pot that ruled Kampuchea (formerly
Cambodia) between April 1975 and January 1979. During that period
an estimated three million Kampuchean people died.

People's Republic of Kampuchea
The current government of Kampuchea (formerly *Cambodia*),
headed by Heng Samrin. The People's Republic of Kampuchea has
begun to reconstruct the country's economy, health and education
systems after they were destroyed by Pol Pot.

Political Organizations

Cadre
A member of a revolutionary organization or a full-time political
worker.

ICP (Indochinese Communist Party)
Founded in 1930 to organize the fight to abolish feudalism and
French colonialism and to build socialism in Viet Nam, Cambodia
and Laos.

Lao Dong (Workers') Party
Formed in the DRV in 1951 to continue the work of the ICP in Viet
Nam alone.

Viet Nam Communist Party
The fourth national congress of the Workers' Party, in December
1976, decided to rename the party Viet Nam Communist Party.

PRP (People's Revolutionary Party)
Formed in 1962 as the southern branch of the Lao Dong Party.

The Party
When this term applies before 1951, it refers to the Indochinese

Communist Party; between 1951 and 1976, it refers to the Lao Dong Party; and after, 1976, to the Viet Nam Communist Party.

Viet Minh (Front for the Independence of Viet Nam)
Coalition of organizations formed in 1941 to fight for Vietnamese independence against the French and Japanese.

National Liberation Front (NLF)
Coalition of organizations, including the PRP, dedicated to overthrowing US domination in South Viet Nam. Also referred to as *the front.* Western press often called members of the NLF, "Vietcong".

Khmer Rouge
Name given by the former Prince Sihanouk of Cambodia to his left-wing opposition. After the US-sponsored coup that installed Lon Nol in power in 1970, the Khmer Rouge fought to establish a revolutionary regime under the leadership of Pol Pot, Leng Sary and Khieu Samphan.

Khmer United Front for National Salvation (FUNSK)
Coalition of Kampuchean forces formed in December 1978 to oust Pol Pot's regime from power. It succeeded, with decisive Vietnamese support, in January 1979.

Armies

ARVN (Army of the Republic of Viet Nam)
The troops who were trained and financed to defend the pro-US regime. They surrendered on 30 April 1975.

PLAF (People's Liberation Armed Forces)
Army organized by the National Liberation Front.

VPA (Viet Nam People's Army)
National Army of the Democratic Republic of Viet Nam and now of the Socialist Republic of Viet Nam. It originated in 1944 as the Viet Nam Armed Propaganda Unit for National Salvation.

Militia
People who are not full-time soldiers but defend their homes and work-places.

PART I: Roots of Women's Oppression

1. No Going Back

> None of the women are prepared to yield what they have gained from the revolution: neither the women who have chosen independent careers after being freed from concubinage, nor the girls at school discussing equal rights.
>
> *Cam Thanh, writer and Women's Union activist*

A small Vietnamese woman, barely five feet tall, holds her bayonet steady as she leads a hulking US bomber pilot – her prisoner – to local authorities. She is proud. The pilot's head is bowed in shame.

The picture originally came from a news photo of a militia woman defending her home in Ha Tinh Province against US bombs. The Vietnamese national poet, To Huu, wrote a poem about her. Her image soon appeared on a Vietnamese postage stamp commemorating the 2,000th US plane shot down over Viet Nam.

Before long, the picture of the Vietnamese woman and her North American prisoner reappeared in magazine articles, posters, banners and leaflets around the world. She became a symbol that fuelled the conviction that a small, technologically primitive nation could resist and defeat the most sophisticated military power ever unleashed. That conviction became a reality in April 1975, when all US personnel were forced to withdraw from Viet Nam.

There were many Vietnamese women who came to symbolize not only the strength of national liberation movements, but also the potential of women. They inspired women both in the Third World and in the West who were demanding an end to the subjugation of women. The Ha Tinh militia woman; an anonymous woman wearing a conical hat, baby in one arm, rifle in the other; Nguyen Thi Dinh, who was illiterate until she was 17, but became a general commanding the liberation army in South Viet Nam; and Nguyen Thi Binh, the schoolteacher who became the Foreign Minister of the Provisional Revolutionary Government of South Viet Nam. During the war, they were guerrillas and generals, village leaders and national leaders, workers and factory managers, anti-aircraft gunners and engineers. What happened to them after 1975?

In 1975, I wrote a book, *Women of Viet Nam*, that began to tell the story of women's liberation in Viet Nam. In the book's conclusion, I wrote, 'Vietnamese women have moved closer to their emancipation than women anywhere else on the planet . . . .' I expected the gains women had made during the war would be expanded in peacetime.[1] Others predicted the marriage between national liberation and women's liberation would dissolve after the war was over. They expected that once in power, socialists would abandon their commitments to women.[2] I was eager to return to Viet Nam in 1981, after a seven-year absence, to find out what the Vietnamese women thought about this issue. I was also anxious to see the legacy of the war first hand and to learn from their experience of grappling with the problems of transforming Saigon society – once described as 'a huge American brothel' – into an environment where women's liberation might flourish. This book details what I found.

My Itinerary

Duong Thi Duyen, Tran Thi Hoan and Vu Thi Lien – from the Foreign Affairs Department of the Viet Nam Women's Union – met me at the airport outside Hanoi. I had briefly met Duyen – the Chairperson of the Foreign Relations Department, in 1977, when she visited the United Nations in New York. I had corresponded with Hoan, the Vice-Chairperson, but had never met her or Lien, the interpreter, before. They were to be my travelling companions during my stay in Viet Nam and they also took responsibility for arranging the numerous interviews and meetings I requested. I would have to wait until our visit to Ho Chi Minh City before I could talk with old friends whom I had known from my previous visit to Viet Nam. Unlike my hosts in 1974, Duyen, Hoan and Lien did not ply me with questions about the anti-war movement in the US, nor did they take advantage of the drive into Hanoi to point out the landmarks of destruction by US bombing raids. Rather, they marvelled over my 15-month-old son, cuddled and played with him until he fell asleep.

Our Women's Union van inched its way toward downtown Hanoi through a snarl of traffic – thousands of people on foot, with carts or on bicycles – punctuated by an occasional overcrowded bus, jeep or truck, heaving with people. Once we arrived at the hotel, we sat in the lobby, sipping lemonade and discussing my itinerary. My hosts from the Women's Union graciously accepted my proposals to use Hanoi and Ho Chi Minh City as bases for meetings and interviews and also to visit a rural commune in Ha Son Binh Province, west of Hanoi.

They made some additional suggestions. They thought I should also visit Lang Son, one of the provinces invaded by Chinese troops in 1979, and An Giang, a province west of Ho Chi Minh City, that had been repeatedly invaded by Pol Pot's troops between 1975 and 1978. They thought that speaking to women in Lang Son and An Giang would give me a concrete appreciation of the conditions that have been pivotal in recent years in determining the priorities and prospects for women's emancipation in Viet Nam. I agreed.

The next morning at 6 a.m., we embarked on a hectic itinerary which usually included at least three or four meetings and interviews a day. On most days, I took advantage of the midday rest time to go for a walk, alone with my son. During these walks, Vietnamese people, fascinated by the foreign faces in the familiar picture of mother and child, would invariably strike up conversations that demonstrated the enormous respect mothering enjoys in Viet Nam. At other times, a childcare worker, Thoa in the North and Ngoc Suong in the South, joined our entourage – always ready to take care of my son when I needed to concentrate on a meeting or take notes.

In the coming days, the van took us to Lang Son and Ha Son Binh. We were on the road for a total of three days, averaging perhaps 30 to 40 kilometres an hour over mountainous, often unpaved roads. After completing our work in Hanoi, we flew to Ho Chi Minh City. Vo Thi Thang and other representatives from the Ho Chi Minh City Women's Union greeted Hoan, Lien and my family at Tan Son Nhat airport. Thang looked familiar. Then I recognized her as the woman in a poster, who, when she was sentenced to 20 years in prison by the Saigon regime smiled defiantly, and said, 'Your regime won't last that long.' Tears welled up in my eyes. She was the first of many women I would speak with in the South whose memories of US occupation were still very fresh and whose experience in the new society made them optimistic.

Romance and Reality

While I did not meet anyone who felt women had been betrayed by the revolution, I did learn that my earlier image of Vietnamese women and their progress towards liberation had been idealized. Some of us who participated in the anti-war movement tended to romanticize aspects of the Vietnamese revolution. We created an image to meet our own needs. Neither the Vietnamese people nor their leaders are responsible for any misrepresentation, or for any failure to live up to a promise they did not make. The Vietnamese talked not only about the Ha Tinh militia woman; they also talked about the mother who lost all her children in the war and spent her time knitting socks for the soldiers. We, however, chose to emphasize the first experience and not the second, because the illusion that the woman capturing the pilot was typical of *all* Vietnamese women – the illusion that they virtually overthrew all sex roles – met our own need to confirm and legitimize our feminist goals. This was not the goal of Vietnamese women.

The tendency to idealize also blinded us to the enormous difficulties people face every day in a war-torn, economically backward country. Women with carrying poles across their shoulders became symbols of exotic heroism. We gave little thought to the callouses on their shoulders and feet – how hard it is to get your crop to market when there are not enough carts or oxen, let alone cars or trucks. Women's status in relation to men may be an abstract issue to women who are preoccupied with the decreasing rice ration and the skin disease spreading over their daughters' bodies. While their status, in fact, has changed remarkably, they still have trouble meeting the nutritional requirements of their children.

Without adequate nourishment, 50% of nursing mothers cannot supply enough milk to their infants. They also found that undernutrition forces many nursing mothers to abandon breast-feeding, with a result that many infants suffer from malnutrition.[3] The Vietnamese Institute of Nutrition reported in 1982 that 40% of the children living in regions devastated by chemical warfare are still malnourished.

This book tells the stories of many Vietnamese women. Some like Tran Thi Ngoc Minh, who was dependent on her husband's meagre salary when he was a minor civil servant under the Thieu regime. Now she is the director of a handicraft co-operative where her husband is employed. You'll read about women who defended their villages against repeated invasion, first by US bombs and then by Chinese troops. You'll read the testimony of a woman at her divorce trial. You'll visit childcare centres and a maternity hospital. You'll read the testimony of former prostitutes and women whose husbands are still in re-education camps. You'll hear Nguyen Thi Dinh, President of the Viet Nam Women's Union and former general in the Liberation Army, speak frankly about her views on the obstacles which women face in assuming leadership roles in society. And you'll hear other Women's Union officials discuss their ideas on strategy for winning women's liberation.

When Vietnamese women speak, we hear women who have survived feudalism, defeated French colonialism, expelled both US and Chinese invaders, and women who have begun to build socialism. The understanding of a woman like Anh Tho, the writer, for example, is based on experience extending from her birth as a daughter of the first of five wives under feudalism, through her participation in the wars against the French and the US, to her position as a leader of the Writers' Union of the Socialist Republic of Viet Nam.

Ngo Ba Thanh, a Columbia-educated lawyer who was often in prison during Thieu's rule but helped to draft Viet Nam's current Constitution and is now a Vice-President of the Women's Union, marvelled at the experience Vietnamese women draw from when they are asked to talk about transformation: 'We have a heritage of Confucianism, feudalism and capitalism. We have fought two revolutions. No generation could change this quickly. But conditions have pushed us very hard and very far.'[4]

Asking Questions

Through these women and many others, we learn how Vietnamese women, once powerless, timid and valued primarily as beasts of burden, became a strong force in society. How have they made progress towards their liberation in the constant presence of poverty, war and death? Why did Minh Khai, a founder of the Women's Union, speak for so many when she said, 'Revolution is our way of liberation'?

After the war with the US ended, what happened in Viet Nam? What is the experience of women living in the southern provinces, once occupied by US troops, now building a socialist society? How do they organize for change? How do women who once identified with the US troops they serviced, transform their consciousness and recover their dignity? Is it possible for certain roles to maintain their status as 'women's work' without being oppressive to women? Can the patriarchal family evolve into a democratic one under socialism? What priority do socialists place on women's liberation? Does recognizing the tenacity of patriarchal traditions become an excuse for accepting the status quo? How does the Vietnamese experience compare with the experience of women facing wartime conditions without socialism? Or of women in colonizer, rather than colonized, countries? These questions haunt the pages of this book. While I could not provide conclusive answers to most of them, I hope to provide the facts to illuminate an ongoing discussion of these issues.

Before my most recent departure for Viet Nam, I met with friends, activists in women's organizations, community organizations and with teachers, writers and artists – all women concerned with women's liberation and national liberation. From our discussions, I compiled a list of questions to ask as I travelled in Viet Nam. I wrote each question on an index card and once I was in Viet Nam, I reshuffled, reorganized and picked from the stack of cards in preparation for each meeting or interview. With each new meeting and interview, the stack of cards shrank. In some cases, I eliminated cards because the questions had been answered. But sometimes I would pass over a card because the question on it no longer seemed so relevant. I would have felt awkward asking it. For example, before I left for Viet Nam, friends who are health workers in San Francisco urged me to enquire about the influence of men in higher levels of administration of health care for women. When I met women who were doctors and administrators of hospitals and health institutes in Viet Nam, they spoke of their achievements and their problems, especially the scarcity of trained personnel, equipment and medicines. Amidst the data on the problems of trained doctors leaving for France and birth defects caused by Agent Orange, I had enormous difficulty in asking these women if their male colleagues had more influence than they did.

Before 1975, the focus of Vietnamese effort was to win the war that would rid them of US intervention. I found that in the 1980s women again join the rest of the Vietnamese people in focusing their energies on winning a war – albeit another kind of war: a war to build Viet Nam's economy so the nation is no longer chronically threatened with famine. US policy – in alliance with China – to continue to bleed Viet Nam, forces Vietnamese women and men to exert even greater efforts. One cannot overestimate the dangers and privations that the people face. I discarded some of the questions I had intended to ask which ignored the pressures of war and poverty.

For example, I met a woman who was very proud to have won an award for her silkworm breeding. She explained how the money she earned from the new variety of silkworm enabled her to move from a thatch house to a brick one. When I asked her how her life had changed since 1975, she displayed her new clock, radio and bicycle – material wealth which was way beyond her reach during the war. She sadly noted that her husband was still away, defending the country – this time at the China border. I felt too awkward asking her some of the questions on my card probing marital and sexual relationships, and put the card with my questions on sexuality aside.

Women's Liberation Is Giai Phong Phu Nu

Women's liberation translates into Vietnamese as *giai phong phu nu*. So does women's emancipation. Vietnamese women tend to use phrases like 'women's liberation', 'women's emancipation', and 'women's equality' interchangeably. Their definition of women's liberation focuses on economic security, the right to work at a job that won't break your back, health, education, the opportunity to rest, equal rights and freedom from polygamy and other patriarchal traditions. Their concept of women's emancipation also incorporates a struggle to end the ideological and psychological subordination of women, which they usually identify as holding women in contempt. Vietnamese women do not believe they have achieved full emancipation as they define it.

They also believe that the obstacles women face in Viet Nam have much more to do with living in a country ravaged by colonialism and war than with women's status relative to men. Although women in Viet Nam would agree with the President of the Women's Union, Nguyen Thi Dinh, when she stated, 'Women have always been the most oppressed . . . ,'[5] they do not use terms like male power. Rather, they identify their oppressors as feudalists, colonialists and imperialists.

Because this book is about women, I do not document the oppression of the vast majority of Vietnamese men. But it is important to remember that, as colonized people and as poor peasants, Vietnamese men also have had an enormous stake in revolutionary change. For example, the famine of 1944–45, in which two million people died, respected no male privilege; nor did US bombardment. The traditional Confucian belief in the importance of education – 'an untaught child is not a person' – was combined with an élitist mandarin system that denied education to 90% of the people. This meant that the overwhelming majority of Vietnamese men were also objects of society's contempt.[6] And now, problems of economic underdevelopment and bureaucracy frustrate all efforts at change, not simply those that women aim for.[7]

The concept of women's liberation implicit in this book attempts to bridge the historical and cultural gaps between Vietnamese women's experience and consciousness and those of women in the West – particularly those who have not been members of colonized peoples or nations. I assume women achieve liberation when: (1) they have won control over their bodies, including the freedom to enjoy or reject motherhood, the right to adequate and respectful health care, freedom to live without the threat of rape, battering or any other violence, and the freedom to live without being used as prostitutes or any other kind of sex object; (2) when they are able to choose their partners freely and there is democracy within the family, including equal sharing of domestic responsibilities; (3) when they have gained equal access to jobs and political leadership in society, enjoying equal pay, privileges and respect; (4) when society's popular culture respects 'feminine' qualities, rather than assuming they are inferior, weak or 'good only for certain things'.

This concept of women's liberation does not incorporate goals that I find difficult to define across cultures – like the texture of relations between women and men; determination of one's own sexuality, including the freedom to choose lesbianism as Western culture defines it; the ideals of matriarchy or androgyny. While I believe these goals are important, they may not be universal. It seems neither sisterly nor anthropologically sound to impose my Western values on Vietnamese women, whose concept of sexuality is different as well as intensely private. Therefore the concept of women's liberation I use in this book attempts to reflect the concerns of feminists, while basing itself on the issues found in Vietnamese women's consciousness and experience.

When I speak of Vietnamese women's consciousness and experience, however, I do not mean to give the impression that I believe all Vietnamese women share a common point of view. Also, the experience of a peasant woman may have been very different from the experience of the daughter of a general in the Saigon army. A woman raised in Saigon on a steady diet of Voice of America will not easily agree with a woman raised in Hanoi, listening to Voice of Viet Nam. Of course, members of the same class, even members of the same Executive Committee of the Women's Union, may disagree. Despite a tendency to present Vietnamese reality as if it were the result of a determined plan implemented by a monolithic, well-oiled machine, it is very important to bear in mind that every strategy, policy and indication of progress towards women's liberation is the product of concerted – often difficult and fierce – struggle.

Many of the struggles, both implicit and explicit, are documented in this book. But I want to be frank about the limitations of my enquiry. I did not speak with a representative sample of all Vietnamese women, nor do I give equal weight to all points of view. I rely heavily, but certainly not exclusively, on Vietnamese sources who participate actively in building a new society. I respect the Viet Nam Women's Union, its leadership, testimony and self-criticism. In the pages of this book, I sometimes question their logic, the strength of their arguments and their political perspective – but not their sincerity. I understand that they tended to present to me the accomplishments of exemplary – rather than ordinary – women. Sometimes they may underestimate the difficulty of implementing an official policy favourable to women. But, I believe, these mis-estimations indicate the direction of change in Viet Nam and, in that sense, reality is not misrepresented.

Journalists and commentators create a formidable arsenal targeted on Viet Nam. Many people who supported the Vietnamese in their struggle for liberation are confused by stories of 'boat people', war in Kampuchea, war with China – stories calculated to win a moral pardon for US aggression and to justify continuing hostility toward the Socialist Republic of Viet Nam. I believe the facts presented in this book demonstrate that officials in Viet Nam join with the majority of the people in a heroic attempt to build a more humane society. They are not building a utopia – simply a place where, after exhausting work and furious struggle, women can be confident that they travel the path which will some day arrive at their liberation.

The first section of this book, *Roots of Women's Oppression*, provides the historical context for understanding why Vietnamese women have chosen certain paths toward their liberation rather than others. The next section, *Seeds of Emancipation*, includes chapters analyzing the conditions that make women's liberation possible in Viet Nam. The final section is a portrait of the progress the Vietnamese people have made in achieving women's liberation. From their own words wherever possible, I hope to show how the continuing struggle for women's emancipation has been shaped by incalculable hardships, twists and turns. It requires enormous unity, organization and vision to defend and expand what has been won.

Notes

1. Arlene Eisen Bergman, *Women of Viet Nam* (San Francisco: Peoples Press, 1975), pp. 244–53.
2. For recent statements that socialists and communists betray their commitments to women's liberation see: Batya Weinbaum, *The Curious Courtship of Women's Liberation and Socialism* (Boston: South End Press, 1978), and Christine White, 'Viet Nam and the Politics of Gender' (Mimeo: University of Sussex, 8 November 1981). Maxine Molyneux argues that socialist countries are 'permanently deficient' in their progress towards women's emancipation. See her article, 'Socialist Societies Old and New: Progress Towards Women's Emancipation?', *Monthly Review*, Vol. 34, No. 3, July–August 1982, pp. 56–100.

3. Tu Giay, 'The Present State of Nutrition in Viet Nam', *Bulletin of the US Committee for Scientific Cooperation with Viet Nam*, Vol. 1, No. 2, Fall 1982, p. 10; Beatrice Tisman, 'Focus on Nutrition', *South East Asia Chronicle*, No. 87, December 1982.
4. Interview by author with Ngo Ba Thanh (Ho Chi Minh City, 8 September 1981).
5. Interview by author with Nguyen Thi Dinh (Hanoi, 4 September 1981).
6. Alexander Woodside, *Community and Revolution in Modern Viet Nam* (Boston: Houghton Mifflin, 1976), p. 102.
7. Speeches at the fifth national congress of the Viet Nam Communist Party repeatedly targeted bureaucracy in their criticisms. See for example, Le Duc Tho, 'On Party Building', 27 March 1982, translated by Foreign Broadcast Information Service, United States Department of Commerce (Washington DC, 8 April 1982).

2. The Feudal Yoke

One hundred women are not worth a single testicle.
Confucian proverb

Although the feudalists have been overthrown . . . these deep-rooted ideologies and practices have not been totally eradicated. These backward ideas have acted as a brake on the progress of women.
Xuan Thuy, Secretary of the Central Committee of the Viet Nam Communist Party at the 50th anniversary of the founding the Viet Nam Women's Union, 20 October 1980

For the last 20 centuries, Confucianism reigned in Viet Nam. It was a way of life and system of beliefs that defined women as beasts of burden and objects of contempt. Confucianism ordered that each woman accept her place as a subject to be ruled by her father, husband, eldest son and king.

No one knows for certain how to date the beginning of Vietnamese history or how long Viet Nam existed as a nation before the Chinese invaded in 111 BC. Archaeologists have found Stone Age relics that were left by people living in Viet Nam several hundred thousand years ago. A rich Bronze Age civilization, the Dong Son culture, flourished 2,000 years before the birth of Christ.

Legends tell us that in earliest Vietnamese society, women played the dominant role. These legends portray women as giants, both stronger and more capable than men. One tells th story of Nu Oa, for example. When Tu Tuong proposed marriage to Nu Oa, she challenged him to compete with her in building a mountain. Nu Oa created a mountain far superior to the one formed by her suitor. She easily destroyed Tu Tuong's mountain with several kicks.[1]

Another popular legend tells that a couple founded Viet Nam: the wife (Au Co) and the husband (Lac Long Quan). He was a dragon, suited to living on the coastal plains. She was a fairy who wanted to live in the mountains. They agreed to part. Fifty sons followed their father and reigned over the kingdom bordering the South China Sea and 50 sons followed their mother to govern the northern part of Viet Nam. Before

12

separating, they pledged mutual respect and aid in time of crisis. The equality between wife and husband in this legend stands in contrast to Confucian teachings brought by the Chinese invaders. While it is risky to deduce historical reality from legends, the absence of daughters in this story may reflect the beginning of the struggle to establish patriarchy at the time of the Hung kings, 200–300 BC.[2]

Other legends rooted in the remote past show that from the dawn of Viet Nam's history, people organized themselves to bring chronic flooding under control with an elaborate system of dikes. States, even embryos of kingdoms, appeared as early as 2000 BC. In some mountainous regions, pre-state tribal societies persisted, while the kingdoms developed on the plains. Some say slaves built the dikes. Others say they were constructed by communal labour. In any case, an ethnic and cultural community developed long before the Chinese arrived. The Vietnamese people lived by growing rice in flooded fields. Many of the women lacquered their teeth black, as is the custom among older Vietnamese women today.

The Chinese invaders oveturned the remaining communalism and consolidated the destruction of matriarchal life. They left an indelible mark on Vietnamese history and culture. The Chinese ruled Viet Nam for a thousand years, until AD 981. Most Vietnamese kings and feudal lords continued to practise Confucian ways even after they expelled the Chinese.

Feudalism

Feudalism is an agricultural system in which a small minority of landlords control the economic and political life of the majority because they control the only means of survival – the land. During the Chinese reign, and for much of Viet Nam's later history, all land officially belonged to the king, who made grants to nobles and favourites.

As in many other feudal societies, the only way for the landless peasants to survive was to work for these aristocrats – more or less as slaves. Back-breaking labour kept the vast majority of people at the barest level of subsistence, always on the brink of starvation. There were no machines to lighten the burden of work. The king allowed communal villages to rent land not controlled by the aristocracy. In addition to paying rent and taxes, peasants were required to work periodically on the king's roads, dikes and canals, without pay. They were also conscripted into military service.[3] Local notables controlled every important aspect of village life. They organized rotation of communal lands, had judicial power to settle disputes, ran local finances, imposed taxes and demanded forced labour. Of course, only men were notables – usually those with the largest landholdings.

The overwhelming majority of Vietnamese women were poor peasants. Although their labour in the fields was essential to the economy, they had no hope of becoming economically independent. While the

Chinese ruled, and for several centuries afterwards, women were not allowed to own land. But in the 16th Century, wealthy women gained new rights. A reformist dynasty allowed women to share inheritance with men or to inherit the entire family fortune if there were no male heirs. In some areas, an unusually enterprising woman who did own land could exert some economic influence based on her endowment or control of market trade. Three hundred years later, another dynasty snatched these rights away from women. Second-rank wives and concubines never had any economic rights. Generally men were considered the only ones capable of controlling the means of survival.

'Men are to be respected, women despised.' This Confucian principle laid the basis for the sexual division of labour in the countryside. Women did all the domestic tasks, tedious agrarian tasks and all the manual labour which society held in contempt. Women did jobs even some poverty-stricken men would hesitate to do: plant seedlings, carry heavy loads, work on the docks and in small-scale trade. We do not know whether women took on tasks which were already despised; or whether the tasks became despicable after being identified as women's work. In either case, the more rigidly women were segregated in certain jobs, the more contempt both women and their work received.

Confucian Marriage

Marriage itself, and particularly polygamy, in which one man takes more than one wife, was an institution designed to exploit women's labour. Buying a wife or concubine proved cheaper than paying the wages of a servant for life. While a woman's labour made a substantial contribution to her husband's estate, she had the right to none of it. She had no legal claim to her children either, even after her husband died. While the wives of well-to-do men laboured incessantly, folk-songs tell how the husbands spent their time:

'All day long he drinks tea and liquor,
smokes and plays games for money.'[4]

Rich landlords collected concubines by purchasing the daughters of poor peasants who could not afford to pay their taxes and debts. In some areas, the groom presented his new in-laws with a water buffalo to replace the bride's labour. Until the 19th Century, the gifts demanded to marry (sell) a daughter were relatively standardized. But with the arrival of capitalist practices from France, money became more important. Women never freely chose their husbands; rather, they were sold to the highest bidder. While the first wife had certain rights denied to a slave and thought that a higher bride price enhanced her status, she, in fact, had no freedom. A reluctant bride faced two alternatives: she could devote herself to lifelong service to her father and be celibate, or she could commit suicide.

Wife and children resent young concubine

The poor man could not afford polygamy. Often, he could not afford the bride price for even one woman. A poor woman who escaped concubinage, might marry a member of her own class without elaborate bride price or ceremony. This impoverished peasant couple would share their hardship. In practice, this sharing challenged the Confucian notion of man's in-born superiority. But the challenge was only partial. Famine, floods, droughts, plagues and wars were a constant threat to the survival of all poor people – but especially to women. Invariably, during hard times, a daughter would be sacrificed or sold as a concubine, slave or prostitute. At any time, there was little to prevent a mandarin or powerful notable from appropriating the wife or daughter of his tenant.

Wives of wealthy men followed the Confucian marriage manual which taught: 'Even though you sleep intimately in the same bed and use the same cover with him, you must treat your husband as if he were your king or your father.'[5] To conclude the traditional ceremony, the bride prostrated herself twice before her husband, who remained standing over her, nodding his approval.[6]

Until she died, the code of the 'Three Obediences' negated all possibility of a woman's self-determination. As a child, the daughter owed unconditional obedience to her father. When she married, she was supposed to transfer her obedience to her husband. Even her husband's death did not free her, for she was then bound to obey her eldest son.

This rule by men is patriarchy in its purest form. The husband's power in relation to his wife was strongest among the upper classes, it still influenced poor peasants. The peasant wife, on the other hand, sang about following her husband through thick and thin, but made it clear she would share life's hardships with him, and not simply submit to his whim:

'Having pledged eternal love for him,
I will not shun crossing streams and mountains with him . . .
In the way of husband and wife,
Depending on each other is essential to guard against the adversities of life.'[7]

One of the most basic assumptions of patriarchy is that women belong to men as their property. In order to keep their property secure, Vietnamese men, following the pattern of all patriarchs, rigidly enforced rules guarding women's chastity. According to the Gia Long Codes, promulgated in the 19th Century and in force throughout French rule, the unmarried woman caught having sexual relations was punished with 100 lashes.[8] The unmarried mother, even among poor peasants, brought so much shame to her family and villagers, that when exposed, she was forced to undergo a painful and dangerous abortion; and her family had to pay a fine to the village. Apparently, the problem was common enough to find its way into folk-songs:

'The middle part of my body is swelling up:
Mother, I can no longer stay at home.
If I stay, the village will take away the buffalo as a fine,
Therefore, I have to go away in a hurry.'[9]

Upper-class Confucian proverbs urged women to place their chastity above any concern for their own pleasure. A proverb went, 'Chastity is worth a thousand gold coins.' The peasants' folk-song echoes, 'Once deprived of its sweet stamen, a flower is no longer desirable.'[10]

The unfaithful wife faced brutal punishment, even though men were free to take as many concubines as they could afford. In some areas, elephants trampled the wife who violated her husband's demand for fidelity. In others, she had her head shaved and plastered with lime. The laws never mentioned adultery as a crime for which men could be punished. The Vietnamese husband could repudiate his wife easily on such grounds as 'excessive talking'. Repudiation, like divorce, left a woman homeless and propertyless, even though her labour might have been the source of her husband's wealth. Women had no parallel rights to repudiate their husbands. Moreover, widows were supposed to remain faithful to their dead husbands. If a woman was caught making love during the period of mourning for her husband, the law said she should be beheaded.[11]

'If you have a son, you can say you have a descendant.
But you cannot say thus, even if you have ten daughters.'

As the proverb indicated, even though daughters worked hard for their fathers, their value was not acknowledged. Only sons could perform the rites necessary for ancestor worship and perpetuate the family cult and line. Parents considered daughters a liability. They believed that the nature of the female soul – more passionate and corruptible than the male soul – made it harder to raise girls. The resemblance to Judaeo-Christian myths blaming Eve as temptress is striking.

Female children had no opportunity to rise above their inferior status. The Vietnamese followed the Chinese system of education which barred women from learning. Until contemporary revolutionary times, the Vietnamese considered education wasted on women. In feudal society, hardly anyone could advance – either men or women – because only the rich could afford the price of education and the poor had no chance to climb out of their poverty. In wealthy families, with rare exceptions, the only daughters who succeeded in getting an official mandarin education were those who managed to disguise themselves as men.

Layers of Patriarchy

The patriarch is the father who is undisputed ruler. Vietnamese society itself was built as a series of hierarchies modelled on the patriarchal family. At the top, the emperor had absolute authority over all. The root word for 'family' and for 'nation' is the same: *gia*. In the traditional language, the only equivalent for the personal pronoun 'I' was *toi*, which meant 'subject of the king'. A Confucian proverb indicated that no one escaped the king's authority: 'When the wind (king) passes over the grass (people), the grass has no choice but to bend.'[12]

As in any patriarchy, women carried the heaviest burden of the emperor's rule. For example, after Emperor Le Huyen Tong died, in the 18th Century, 300 concubines were sacrificed: they were imprisoned in his mausoleum to keep watch over his tomb for eternity. Peasants contemptuously called him 'the reclining king'.

Mandarins, divided into nine ranks, formed the social layer just below the king. They were the king's representatives and controlled the local notables. Mandarins were an educated élite group of officials who lived on the rents and taxes they extracted from the people in their province, or from the salaries that they received directly from the king. A proverb reflects women's exclusion from the mandarinate and all other public office: 'A woman who meddles in the affairs of court or palace, appears as abnormal as a chicken that crows.'[13] Each mandarin was considered the father of the people in his domain. A domain or district may have included many villages. Within the village itself, it was the local notable who insisted on direct obedience from the peasant. Notables collected taxes and kept some wealth for themselves before they handed their quota over to the mandarins. Notables also drafted soldiers and kidnapped concubines to serve the mandarins and king. Vietnamese revolutionaries, recognizing the patriarchal core of feudalism, had to commit themselves to uprooting patriarchy if they were to be successful in overthrowing feudalism.

Weaker Links in the Confucian Chain

Confucianism grew weaker, the further south one travelled from the Chinese border. Vietnamese feudal lords did not bring Confucianism to Saigon until nearly 1700. Confucianism was also weaker at the village level, especially among the peasants, than at the court level. The need to co-ordinate irrigation and flood control through the system of dikes gave the central government an important economic function. But the Vietnamese village also had a tradition of self-sufficiency. It was in the village that the Vietnamese language survived a thousand years of Chinese occupation. It was in the village that a tradition of co-operation and solidarity developed. It was in the village that patriotism dug its roots in the soil – the same soil where family ancestors rested.

Although 70 to 80% of the Vietnamese people today may practise some Buddhist teachings, Buddhism itself did not seriously challenge the patriarchal codes that Confucianism established. Buddhism taught precepts for spiritual life, while Confucianism guided political and social life. Mahayana Buddhism came to Viet Nam in the 2nd Century AD, but was considered a 'foreign religion' as long as the Chinese were in power.

After the Chinese were expelled, Buddhism became the state religion during the reign of several Vietnamese emperors. Mahayana Buddhists believe that there may be many enlightened ones, not just one Buddha. But this more egalitarian belief did not disrupt the élitist structure surrounding the king. Buddhist clergy enjoyed the privileges previously reserved for Confucian mandarins.[14] During the 14th Century, after 300 years of Buddhist spiritual hegemony, Confucianism again became the official ideology of the Vietnamese feudal regime. It was at that time that Buddhism took root among the common people and became part of the spirit of resistance at the local level.

But even at the village level, Buddhism still helped to maintain women's inferior status. While belief in reincarnation encouraged respect for all life, it also affirmed a fatalistic acceptance of women's subordination in their present life. Moreover, only men could be monks, and Buddhist nuns held an inferior status. Buddhists taught that all passion brings pain, but women seemed to pay more dearly for their passions. Buddhism, like Judaeo-Christian moral codes, considers sex a lower form of animal activity. The ideal is total detachment from worldly concerns, especially sex. The ideal applies to both women and men, but women are considered less clean than men. Even today, when a woman is menstruating, she may be banned from the Buddhist altar.

The greatest challenge to Confucianism has always been a stubborn tradition of peasant rebellion – rebellion in which women played a major role. Vietnamese women were by no means helpless victims. Their tradition of resistance – which one of them called 'riding the tempest' – began with the earliest records of oppression.[15]

Feudal Patriarchy Dies a Slow Death

'It is against the order of heaven for a man to be under the political authority of a woman.' Beliefs like these may have been initially part of a system of myths designed to legitimize and mask the systematic looting of masses of peasants by feudal lords and kings. But once such beliefs become time-worn traditions, habits of thought so deeply rooted in people's consciousness that no one remembers their self-serving origins, they outlive the feudalists whom they once protected. They take on a life of their own that has a pervasive influence centuries after their birth.

For example, Confucian dogma barred women from a mandarin education. The result – a mass of women with no formal education – then proved the 'heavenly assumption' of women's inferiority and impurity. Women were scapegoated as the bearers of misfortune. So if a man met a woman as he left his home, he would return to his house at once because her presence fated his day to failure. Even nowadays, in the Vietnamese countryside, when a woman meets a man on her path, she may automatically step aside to save him the mishap of 'crossing a woman at the outset'. [16]

'A hundred women are not worth a single testicle.' This proverb had economic as well as moral significance. The male child ensured succession. He brought a daughter-in-law, an extra worker to add to the family's wealth. Feeding a daughter, on the other hand, was an unprofitable investment. A folk-song notes:

'A daughter is a child of other people.
Only a daughter-in-law is the true child of her parents-in-law, since they have paid for her.'

As late as 1960, more than five years after the Democratic Republic of Viet Nam had instituted land reform to overthrow feudalism, there were parents who never taught their daughters the trade practised in their village, for fear that, after marriage, they would divulge the secret of the craft to competitors in the in-laws' village. The village of Vong, for example, on the outskirts of Hanoi, is well known for the special way people prepare sticky rice. Only daughters-in-law were allowed to learn how to prepare this special dish. [17]

Xuan Thuy, a high-level official in the Viet Nam Communist Party, denounced the tenacity of feudal ideology in preventing women's emancipation. His 1980 speech still applies:

Some people still wrongly associate women with childbearing and cooking as their only essential tasks; some parents, sticking to their erroneous views, marry their daughters for money; feudal practices regarding marriages and funerals are still existing. Cases in which husbands ill-treat their wives and do not recognize their behaviour as unlawful are not uncommon. However, a great many women, trapped in such backward ideologies, are subject to inferiority complex, passivity, timidity and do not dare struggle against injustice and ill-treatment to gain their rightful positions as workers and citizens equal to men which socialism has reserved for them.[18]

The first time I travelled in Viet Nam, naïve idealism made me assume that if a woman joined the militia and carried a rifle, she would also be consciously committed to women's liberation. It became necessary to remind myself of Viet Nam's millennial patriarchal heritage to cushion my shock when such a woman (or man) would make a remark that assumed women's inferiority.

Feudal ideology not only leaves an imprint of passivity on women. Restriction to menial tasks, isolation in motherhood, constantly trying to make ends meet, narrowed women's interests to the immediate pressures facing them. Discrimination between different family ranks, rivalry between first wives and concubines, cruelty by mothers-in-law against daughters-in-law – these conflicts embittered relationships among women. Deprived of education for centuries, women became prisoners of superstition and dogma. In short, patriarchal feudalism prevented women from making a contribution to the nation's social and political life commensurate with their potential, in addition to locking women into a cycle of submission and servitude. Since the consolidation of patriarchy two thousand years ago, to the eve of the revolution, women were the most downtrodden members of each social grouping. As power changed hands from one ruler to the next, the problems women faced mounted, especially with the French take-over.

Notes

1. This legend and other information about matriarchal traditions in this chapter come from Mai Thi Tu and Le Thi Nham Tuyet, *Women in Viet Nam* (Hanoi: Foreign Languages Publishing House, 1978), pp. 12f. Vietnamese sources refer to legends and folk-tales in which women initiated agriculture and production and, in general, were held in high esteem. They also note that after marriage the husband moved to the wife's family home, that is, marriage was matrilocal; and inheritance was determined by the mother's line, that is, inheritance was matrilineal. Vietnamese authors label these societies 'matriarchal'. Some feminists and anthropologists seriously question such labels. They maintain that technically 'rule by women' never existed. Rather, women were, before the advent of patriarchy, free and equal members of the society, who may have prevailed in certain spheres. We do not have evidence from the Vietnamese experience to take sides in this debate. Therefore, we are using the word 'matriarchy' in a relative sense, rather than a technical one. For details on the issue, see Kathleen Gough and David Schneider, *Matrilineal Kinship* (Berkeley: University of California Press, 1981); Kathleen Gough, 'An Anthropologist Looks at Engels', in Nona Glazer-Malbin and Helen Youngelson Waeher, *Women in a Manmade World* (Chicago: Rand

McNally, 1972), pp. 105–18; Rayna R. Reiter, *Toward an Anthropology of Women* (New York: Monthly Review, 1975); Karen Sacks, *Sisters and Wives* (Champaign, Illinois: University of Illinois Press, 1982). Thank you to Kathleen Gough for calling this issue to my attention.

2. Nha Trang, *The Traditional Roles of Women as Reflected in Oral and Written Vietnamese Literature* (Berkeley: University of California, Asian Studies PhD Dissertation, 1973) pp. 244–5; and Nguyen Khac Vien, *Traditional Viet Nam* (Vietnamese Studies, No. 21; Hanoi: Foreign Languages Publishing House, 1969), pp. 18–9.
3. Nha Trang, pp. 28–30. Vietnamese scholars are now debating whether to call this the 'Asiatic mode of production', and when it evolved into feudalism, in a more technical sense. In this book, I refer to all these pre-colonial systems as feudal.
4. Tu and Tuyet, op. cit., p. 51. In anthropological terminology polygamy refers to either polygyny (more than one wife) or polyandry (more than one husband). We intend the more technical term polygyny, when we use the word polygamy.
5. Nha Trang, op. cit., p. 36.
6. Richard Coughlin, 'The Position of Women in South East Asia' (Mimeo; Yale University: South East Asian Cultural Report Series, 1949), p. 15.
7. Nha Trang, op. cit., p. 170.
8. The Le Codes were more lenient. They gave 50 lashes. Ibid., p. 224.
9. Ibid., p. 164.
10. Both are cited in ibid., pp. 20, 29.
11. Ibid., p. 221.
12. Frances Fitzgerald, *Fire in the Lake* (Boston: Little Brown, 1972), p. 167.
13. Coughlin, op. cit., p. 7.
14. Nguyen Khac Vien, op. cit., pp. 50–3.
15. See chapter 16.
16. Tu and Tuyet, op. cit., pp. 47–8.
17. Ibid., pp. 48–9.
18. Xuan Thuy, 'The Vietnamese Women Continue to Move Onward', *Women of Viet Nam*, No. 1, 1981, p. 3. Maxine Molyneux, a member of the *Feminist Review* collective, bases part of her evaluation of how socialist societies promote women's emancipation on the assertion that recognizing such factors as ideology and psychology and problematizing relations between the sexes 'is virtually absent from socialist states' theory and practice' (p. 71 of her article, 'Socialist Societies Old and New: Progress Towards Women's Emancipation', *Monthly Review*, Vol. 34, No. 3, July–August 1982). Xuan Thuy's speech is only one of many examples presented from the Vietnamese experience that demonstrates the weakness of Molyneux's argument.

3. The French Legacy

Everywhere she [the Vietnamese woman] is exposed to brutalities. In town, at home, in the market, in the countryside, she is exposed to ill-treatment by the administrator, the officer, the gendarme, the customs officer, the railway station employee. She is often called *con di* [prostitute] or *buzu* [monkey] by Europeans. Even at the central market of Saigon, supposed to be a French city, the European guards did not hesitate to use a cudgel to beat native women to make them move on.
Ho Chi Minh, French Colonialism on Trial, *1925*

It took the French armed forces nearly 40 years to complete their conquest of all of Viet Nam. They first appeared off the Vietnamese coast in 1847, trying to force the Vietnamese government to accept unfair trade agreements. They also came to protect Christian missionaries. In 1858, they landed with 3,000 troops and officially began the conquest. Peasant resistance delayed the French take-over. But the Vietnamese king, who was corrupt and more concerned with peasant insurrections than with French domination, kept signing new treaties, granting more and more territorial control to the French. By 1884, the French had stabilized their domination over all of Viet Nam. They exacerbated certain regional differences by dividing Viet Nam into 'three countries' to make it easier to pacify the people.

French colonialists tried to justify their conquest by claiming it was a mission to bring the 'benefits of civilization' to Viet Nam. For the Vietnamese people those benefits meant the price of salt rose 500% between 1889 and 1907. The average amount of rice each person consumed also dropped nearly 20% between 1900 and 1913.[1] French civilization meant additional suffering, especially for women, because the French used the feudal patriarchy as a foundation for their colonial regime. Women now had to carry the burden of French colonists in addition to her patriarchal load. Frenchmen did not try to justify the mounting misery of Vietnamese women. After all, women in France did not win the right to vote until 1945.[2]

Colonizing the Patriarchy

French colonialists boasted about the money they invested in Viet Nam. In fact, they invested only in areas that would make an immediate profit, which they took back to France. They drained the natural wealth of the land by extracting metal ores, coal, rubber and rice, then shipping them to France. They crippled Viet Nam's ability to develop economically by forbidding it to trade with any country but France. The only industries the French built were a few small-scale enterprises to manufacture consumer goods to satisfy the needs of the French settlers and their enterprises. While there was no tax on the business operations or incomes of foreigners, taxes levied on the Vietnamese increased five times. Some 70% of the revenue from these taxes went to pay the police and colonial functionaries.[3] 'The French built more jails than schools, more prison camps than hospitals, more barracks for their colonial army than homes for the people.'[4]

In French eyes, the 'oriental race' was expendable, not worthy of the same rights as the French. The French kidnapped 80,000 people to build a railway to ship their goods to port. Some 25,000 of them died.[5] Conditions in French coal mines were so brutal that Vietnamese people refused to work in them voluntarily. Desrousseaux, Inspector of Mines, wrote a secret report addressed to the Governor General:

> The peasants will consent to go and work outside their villages only when they are dying of starvation. We must therefore arrive at the conclusion that in order to extricate ourselves from the difficulty of recruiting labour, we must see to it that the countryside is plunged into poverty.[6]

The French, therefore, systematically destroyed dikes and flooded villages, leaving peasants no choice but to work in the mines. Fifty thousand men and women died at work in those mines.

The French policy of 'plunging the countryside into poverty' succeeded. At the same time, the French strengthened the hand of the village patriarchs – the feudal notables. They used the feudal notables to collect taxes and demanded that they be paid in cash rather than the traditional payment in crops. Peasants lost their land when they mortgaged it to pay interest rates that ran as high as 3,650%. By 1930, the French had two-thirds of the cultivated land in their control. Most of the peasants were caught in a vicious cycle of debt slavery.[7]

Many Vietnamese novels and short stories portray the misery of peasant women during these times. Until hearing a first-hand account, it is easy to assume that the novels are exaggerated. In one of the most famous documentary novels, *The Light is Out*, a desperate mother is forced to sell her daughter to the landlord for one piastre, the price she must pay to a corrupt official to get an official seal on a document she needs to pay her tax.[8] The author of this novel was, in fact, documenting real events, but placing them in a fictional mask to avoid French censorship.

Slaves in the Fields

Nguyen Thi Dam was 76 years old in 1954, when she was interviewed by an Australian journalist.[9] Her husband had died, leaving her a widow at the age of 30, with two children and a debt to the landlord of 50 pounds of rice and two piastres. The landlord demanded payment of 100 pounds of rice as interest for the first month and another 150 pounds for each additional month she did not repay the debt. Nguyen Thi Dam recalled: 'I tried very hard to work and collect some rice. But every month I was worse off. By six months, it was clear I could never pay. So he took our little plot of land . . .' She continued to recount her next 40 years of work for different landlords: 'I and the children would be fed, but would get no pay. For three years we toiled there and we were all in rags . . . At the end of three years, I could stand it no longer . . . .' She went to look for work in another part of the district, but found nothing, so she returned to her native village and worked for the largest landlord there:

> The work was so hard, I thought I must die. I had to get up at three o'clock in the morning and start pounding rice. It was work enough for three people . . . After that, I had to go to the fields and it was so dark, I would have lost my way except for holding the buffalo by the tail. It was dark again by the time I finished ploughing in the evening and I had to follow the buffalo home again. For that, there was a bowl of rice and a little salt daily for myself and the children . . . Sometimes I would steal a little fish paste – hide it between my thumb and forefinger – and lick it while eating rice. At night, I had to clean up the house and if the landlord wasn't satisfied, he would take his whip to me . . . Myself and the children wore rice sacks . . . I had to carry the manure out to the fields, plough, do weeding, harvesting and everything from three in the morning till ten at night. Once when I begged for something to buy clothes, at least for the children, the landlord brought me 27 pounds of rice. He put it on the floor and said, 'This is what you have earned. And I give it to you. But as I have to feed your children, I must take it back.' And he took it away again . . .
>
> He would invite Japanese or French notables about once a month for a banquet and the villagers had to come and help decorate the house. He had concubines too, but their life was no better than ours. They were starved and whipped.

When her daughter was 16, the landlord severely humiliated her for not gathering enough weeds. He wrenched off all her clothes and flung her head-first into the fish pond. After more years of hard labour and humiliation, Dam could still not afford to pay rent and feed her family: 'My daughter died. She needed rice but I could give her none. There were no clothes, even to bury her in . . . She had scarcely known a moment's happiness in her life. She was beaten by landlords before she even knew who they were . . . .' Her son died of starvation the following year, 1944. Finally, the French bombed her shack, killing her granddaughter.

Nguyen Thi Dam's story is not unusual. A sharecropper had to rent a buffalo at the price of 20% of her or his crop. So it became common for men to hitch their wives and children to ploughs instead of renting buffalo. In 1943, a Vietnamese agronomist observed, 'They hitch to their shoulders ropes padded with pieces of torn matting lest the ropes cut into their flesh. Because of the weight to be pulled, they are unable to keep their balance and must use a bamboo cane to lean on.'[10]

Women Leave Their Bones in the Plantations, Mines and Factories

The French were satisfied with their profitable rubber plantations. Most of the labour on these plantations came from indentured servants who were recruited from the poorest peasant regions. Conditions were so brutal that recruiting agents drugged peasants in order to get them to sign up. The plantations became known as 'hell on earth' and workers who tried to escape were tortured to death. The figures in Table I under-estimate the number who died supplying French industrialists with rubber, because they include only those who officially signed contracts.

Table I
Vietnamese Deaths on French Rubber Plantations (1917–45)

Plantation	Total Employed	Total Deaths
Dau Tieng (Michelin)	45,000	12,000
Loc Ninh and Minh Thanh (Cexco)	37,000	10,000
Terres Rouge	198,000	22,000

Source: Ngo Vinh Long, *Before the Revolution* (Cambridge: MIT Press, 1973), pp. 112–13.

By 1945, the rubber plantations could not recruit enough workers through their accustomed means of deceit. The liberation movement had become too strong. So the French converted the plantations into prison camps and arbitrarily arrested people when they needed more workers. Those who complained were often summarily shot as Viet Minh. By this time, 60% of the workers were women. The French designed a special torture for pregnant rubber workers called the 'upside down pot'. Like African slave women in the US, the victims were forced to dig holes and lie face down with their stomachs in the hole as overseers beat them. Eight out of ten women miscarried. A folk-song expressed the grim reality:

'It's easy to go to the rubber plantations,
But hard to return from there.
Men left their hides, women their bones.'[11]

French industry in Viet Nam was also brutal. While thousands of Vietnamese wore rice sacks, French-owned factories produced textiles for export. A Frenchman named Dupre owned a huge textile mill in Nam Dinh. By 1937, some 14,000 people worked for him – mostly women.[12] Hoang Thi Yen began working for the 'wolf boss' when she was 12 years old. Her mother landed the job for her by bribing an intermediary. Yen recalled:

> It was in 1920. Officially the factory's workday was 15 hours. For most of the women workers, who lived some 10 kilometres distance and went to work on foot, it was, in fact, a day of 18 to 19 hours. I left home before dawn only to come back late at night, broken by fatigue. I could never sleep as much as I needed, or even wash myself, there being no Sundays . . . I ate (a ball of cold rice) in secret at the mill, for no breaks were allowed during work time.

Dupre paid women three-quarters as much as he paid men. All his workers paid fines for lateness, absenteeism, talking, dozing, taking meals during work hours, breaking yarn and breaking shuttles. Workers also had to pay for spare parts and repairs on the machines.

Overseers treated the women at the mill with contempt and competed with each other in manhandling them. Beatings were commonplace. Hoang Thi Yen continued her description of her life as a textile worker:

> I got married at 18 and became a mother at 24. I gave birth to four children, but two of them died for want of care. Each time I was delivered by a village midwife at my own charge . . . There was no maternity leave and every woman had to find someone to replace her during her absence when she was in childbed. Many a prospective mother, compelled to go on working, gave birth to her child at the foot of the machines. After childbirth, young mothers would hurry back to the factory for fear they might lose their jobs. It was the same thing with the sick. The Wolf Boss specified in one of his circulars that the sick who did not come to work should send in their resignations.

There were no safety precautions taken at the factory. Compensation for the numerous maimings was unheard of. Mrs Yen explained why they accepted such outrageous conditions: 'That was horrible. But one had to live. What we feared was neither ill-treatment nor accident. It was the loss of our jobs.' When Dupre's workers finally threatened to strike, he taunted them: 'Listen to this: to recruit 100 dogs is difficult, but I have only to raise a finger and 1,000 coolies of your race will come and replace you.'

In all factories women's wages were consistently lower than men's. In

1930, the average daily wage for a man was 1.50 piastres and for a woman it was only 0.31 piastres. By 1936, during the Depression, the average wage for a man dropped to 1.13 piastres and to 0.17 for a woman.[13]

More Colonial Violence against Women

Increased poverty intensified the humiliation of women. In a famine year, a man could buy a slave woman or concubine for a few pounds of rice. The French commercialized sex and transformed thousands of traditionally modest women into prostitutes. According to Bernard Fall, prostitutes took credit for one-third of all the French posts destroyed by the Viet Minh.[14]

Ho Chi Minh focused one of his earliest articles on exposing the sadistic treatment of Vietnamese women by the French. His 1922 article, 'Annamese Women and French Domination', protested against the rape of an eight-year-old girl and several adult women. In the same article, he urged their 'Western sisters in France' to join a campaign to ease the suffering of women in Viet Nam.

But it was to be a long time before women of colonizing nations could identify with the problems of women under colonialism. Cynical French administrators made jokes about having 'three prisons for every school'. In 1924, out of 600,000 school-age children, only 62,000 boys and 10,000 girls (3%) were enrolled in school. By 1945, some 95% of the women were still illiterate and only a handful were in universities.[15] French administration neglected women's health as much as their education. Thirty per cent of the women who died, lost their lives in childbirth. The infant mortality rate ranged from 30 to 40%.[16]

Racism not only legitimized this super-exploitation and oppression: it also undermined the people's sense of dignity and alienated them from each other. One landowner's grandson admitted his contempt for his fellow Vietnamese:

> The more deeply I entered the French world, the more frustrated I became at the Vietnamese world in which I was forced to participate, the more I could see only the coarse yokel ugliness of people with yellow skins and flat noses, to whom I used to feel I was connected because I also had a flat nose and yellow skin . . . Their simple yokel gestures, like swallowing rice wine fast . . . made me break out all over in goose pimples.[17]

Famine: Two Million Dead

For decades, French policies had reduced the people of Viet Nam to a perpetual state of desperation. Yet they were responsible for unprecedented tragedy during World War II. The French administration, which was friendly to the Fascists, collaborated with the Japanese when they invaded Viet Nam. In order to serve their war machine, the Japanese

Hanoi Museum of Revolutionary History

1886: Political prisoners held by the French

confiscated and burned rice for fuel, forced peasants to plant export crops like jute instead of rice, raised taxes and raided villages, stealing all their valuables. These policies were decrees of mass murder in the countryside where people were already living at bare subsistence level. Two million people starved to death in the famine that began in 1944 and climaxed in 1945.

People continued to work even when they were eating only roots and covering themselves with banana leaves or mats made from hay. Others lay out in the market area waiting to die in hope that some kind-hearted person would notice and bury them. One survivor wrote:

> My village sank deeper and deeper into a morass of hunger and cold. Every day some two dozen people died. Some died digging up their potatoes in the fields; some died on the roads while out begging; some went down to the river to fish and fell in the water . . . .[18]

Parents forced themselves to deny their children food, knowing that if they divided the food equally among the entire family, no one would have enough to live. A French official named Vespy was moved by the mass suffering:

There are old people and there are children. There are men and women, shrunken under the weight of their poverty and suffering. Their bodies are nearly all naked and their bones jut out shaking. Even girls who have already reached puberty and whom one might expect to show some embarrassment are in the same condition. Now and again they stop to close the eyes of those who fall, never to rise again, or to strip off any piece of rag which is left behind on their bodies . . . one feels ashamed of being human.[19]

That same year, in August 1945, after years of anti-colonial organization, a general insurrection swept the country. It became known as the 'August Revolution'. On 2 September 1945, Ho Chi Minh issued Viet Nam's declaration of independence from France. Thousands of people joined the Viet Minh – the independence fighters – as the French tried to maintain their grip on their colony.

Women in the Viet Minh

Anh Tho, now a leading member of the Viet Nam Writers' Union, was one of many women who joined the struggle at that time. She told me why:

My mother was one of five wives. She was the first wife but suffered a lot because she did not give birth to a son . . . some of the concubines would be expelled from the house if they did not give birth to sons. They would starve. Mothers would throw their children into the sea and then jump in after them.

I was deeply moved by the sight of children with eyes blurred from starvation, just sitting listlessly. Sometimes when I opened the door, I would see five or seven people collapse, corpses in heaps . . .

I loved to make poems, but my father didn't think I had the capacity. He held me in contempt and didn't let me study past the primary grades. The best way of making a poem at that time was to act – to make the revolution. Because of the hard life of polygamy, we made the revolution. There was no choice. I joined the Viet Minh because of their women's liberation programme.

Some women like Anh Tho formed collectives to purchase arms and transport weapons. They opened inns and restaurants to finance the movement. They served as liaison, protected other revolutionaries, agitated among enemy soldiers and served as spies.

Women also participated in the earliest armed actions against the French. In 1945, the first all-woman guerrilla unit was formed by Ha Thi Que, who later led the Viet Nam Women's Union and became a member of the Central Committee of the Viet Nam Communist Party – the governing party of the Socialist Republic of Viet Nam. Over a million women actively participated in the anti-French resistance. Chapters 7 and 8 will provide more detail on that participation.

Independence in the North; Betrayal in the South

During the August Revolution of 1945, people throughout Viet Nam joined the general insurrection that expelled both the French and Japanese colonists. The entire nation was freed. People in villages from the Chinese border in the north to the Gulf of Thailand in the south began to elect their own local governments – people's councils. When Ho Chi Minh read Viet Nam's declaration of independence, he spoke for all the Vietnamese people. Emperor Bao Dai, who had co-operated with the French, fled from Hanoi. Ho Chi Minh became the President of the Democratic Republic of Viet Nam – the newly independent republic that represented the entire nation. The French fought back.

In 1950, with US backing, the French set up an artificial country whose capital was Saigon. They reinstated Bao Dai as emperor. By 1954, Bao Dai and his prime minister, Ngo Dinh Diem, represented very few people, but called themselves the official representatives of the 'State of Viet Nam'. After a nine-year war, climaxing in the historic battle of Dien Bien Phu, the Vietnamese people won a decisive victory over French colonialism. It was also a defeat for the US government which, by 1954, was paying for 78% of the French war effort.

After the French defeat at Dien Bien Phu, representatives from the Democratic Republic of Viet Nam, the 'State of Viet Nam', France, the Soviet Union, the People's Republic of China, Cambodia, Laos, the United Kingdom and the United States met in Geneva. The resulting Geneva Accords recognized Viet Nam as one sovereign, independent country. The Accords arranged for the temporary partition of the country to facilitate the withdrawal and disarming of troops on both sides. Viet Minh troops withdrew north of the 17th parallel and French troops to the south. Article Six stated, 'The military demarcation line is provisional and should not in any way be interpreted as constituting a political or territorial boundary.'

The Accords also promised that free elections for a new government of a reunified country would take place in 1956. The US refused to join the other countries in officially committing itself to the Accords; but in diplomatic terms, did 'take note' of the Agreements and declared it would 'refrain from the use of force to disrupt the Agreements.'[20]

The United States began flouting the Geneva Accords before the ink on them was dry. In September 1954, the South East Asia Treaty Organization (SEATO) unilaterally put South Viet Nam 'under its protection'. In November, the US began sending aid directly to the Diem regime. By February 1955, US General John W. O'Daniel took over training the South Viet Nam Army – ARVN's predecessor. That same year, Diem 'dethroned' Bao Dai and declared himself head of the state of the 'Republic of Viet Nam'. In 1956, instead of holding the free elections promised at Geneva, Diem set up concentration camps and began a campaign of terror against all those who demanded enforcement of the Accords. Nevertheless, hundreds of thousands of people demonstrated in the South for the Geneva Accords and against Diem.

President Eisenhower kept Diem in power by financing and training his army. Ike sent the first US soldiers to Viet Nam in 1956. In his book, *Mandate for Change*, he explained why no elections were allowed: 'I have never talked or corresponded with a person knowledgeable in Indochinese affairs who did not agree that had elections been held . . . possibly 80% of the population would have voted for the communist Ho Chi Minh.'[21]

The government of the Democratic Republic of Viet Nam in the North persistently urged Diem to open negotiations for reunification and warned him of the dangers of US domination. At the same time, the people in the North began the tasks of reconstructing the war-torn country, struggling for the power to create a socialist society and moving towards women's emancipation.

Meanwhile, in the South, the people faced mounting problems under a new form of foreign domination: US neo-colonialism. Diem stayed in power by bribing supporters with US-supplied dollars and by arresting and executing as much of his opposition as he could. The *Pentagon Papers* provide overwhelming evidence that the US government created and manipulated the Saigon regime. But even US officials understood that their puppet government could not be successful. In 1960, the US Embassy in Saigon made a special report 'On the Internal Security Situation in Viet Nam':

> The situation may be summed up in the fact that the government has tended to treat the population with suspicion or to coerce it and has been awarded with an attitude of resentment and apathy. The basic factor which has been lacking is a feeling of rapport between the government and the population. The people have not identified themselves with the government.[22]

One effort to establish rapport with the people was the Women's Solidarity League. It was founded by Madame Nhu, Diem's sister-in-law. It was a paramilitary organization ostensibly dedicated to gaining women's rights. In fact, the purpose of the League was to mobilize women to help persecute those who fought for Vietnamese independence. Women who wanted their husbands to keep jobs in Diem's bureaucracy had no choice but to join the League.

In March 1959, Diem declared a state of war against the Vietnamese communists, 'Vietcong', whom Diem defined as anyone who opposed his dictatorship. On 20 December 1960, the National Liberation Front was formed as a political organization that united the following groups: the Radical Socialist Party, representing patriotic intellectuals; the Democratic Party, representing independent businessmen who opposed foreign control; the People's Revolutionary Party (PRP), representing workers and peasants; organizations representing trade unions, women, youth, peasants, students, writers and artists; the Patriotic Buddhists Association; Association of Catholics Devoted to God and Fatherland; Association for the Moral Renaissance of the Hoa Hao Followers; the Movement for the Autonomy of the Tay Nguyen Nationalities; and others. The leading organization in the Front was the PRP, organized as the southern branch of the Viet Nam Communist Party.

They issued a manifesto which explained that the NLF was formed to meet the desires of the Vietnamese people to overthrow the Diem regime and to liberate the nation from US control. They organized the People's Liberation Armed Forces (PLAF).

Many Vietnamese people joined the struggle on the side of the NLF. By 1964, the NLF was close to its goal. The US-supported Saigon regime was crumbling. Massive numbers of US ground troops and bombers came to the rescue. By the end of 1966, about half a million US troops were on Vietnamese soil, attempting to stamp out Viet Nam's drive for independence with massive destruction.

Between 1949 and 1975, the United States budgeted $168.1 billion to maintain control in Indochina. In other terms, it cost the US approximately $168,000 to kill each 'enemy' soldier. The total firepower expended by the US and its allies in Viet Nam exceeds the total firepower expended by humanity in all other wars, before and after the Indochina war.[23] The primary motive for this massive investment in aggression was to teach not only Viet Nam, but all the people of Asia, Africa and Latin America, the lesson that they would pay a terrifying price for resisting imperial domination.

If the legacy of French colonialism left the women of Viet Nam trapped under the yoke of feudal patriarchy and colonial super-exploitation, the genocidal policies of the US government added a staggering weight to the burden they carried – the subject of our next chapter.

Notes

1. Tam Vu and Nguyen Khac Vien, *A Century of National Struggles* (Vietnamese Studies, No. 24; Hanoi: Foreign Languages Publishing House, 1970), pp. 40–5).
2. Nancy Wiegersma, who did her doctoral dissertation on land tenure in Viet Nam, argues that while peasants as a class are increasingly exploited under colonialism and imperialism, 'the peasant women's position relative to the peasant men's may be improved with the breakdown of patriarchal controls in the family' (p. 4). Yet even her data show that the concentration of land

ownership increased with colonialism, resulting in the fact that polygamy was more common in the 1950s in southern villages than in pre-colonial times.

When she refers to the loss of land and power of the 'peasant patriarch' (I suspect he never had much to start with), she is really talking about the redistribution of patriarchal power, rather than the elimination of patriarchal power. She speculates that women's relative power increases once they are able to earn wages or go to a French school.

I believe the data presented in this chapter demonstrate that women working for the French, whether on plantations or in factories, did so only because the destruction of the peasant economy made them desperate. They not only did not *experience* a relative increase in power, they also experienced an increase in the misery of their existence. Also, if 95% of the women were still illiterate in 1945, what could be the significance of a handful of élite women gaining a French education? She concludes that women took leading positions in the liberation struggle because of their central place in the Vietnamese economy and the impact of French-imported capitalism in breaking down Confucian patriarchy. The main argument of this book, I believe, demonstrates that other factors are responsible for women's role in the liberation struggle (see Part II). Quotes from Nancy Wiegersma, 'Women in the Transition to Capitalism: 19th to mid-20th Century Viet Nam', *Research in Political Economy*, Vol. 4, 1981, pp. 1–28. Thanks to Jayne Werner for bringing Wiegersma's work to my attention.

 3. Tam Vu and Nguyen Khac Vien, op. cit., p. 65. Also quoted in Ngo Vinh Long, *Before the Revolution* (Cambridge: MIT Press, 1973), p. 63.
 4. Vo Nguyen Giap told this to Archimedes Patti, who quotes it in his book, *Why Viet Nam?* (Berkeley: University of California Press, 1980), p. 245.
 5. Tam Vu and Nhuyen Khac Vien, op. cit., p. 47.
 6. Ngo Vinh Long, op. cit., pp. 116–17.
 7. Details of this section and many more can be found in ibid., pp. 8–89.
 8. Ngo Tat To, *When the Light Is Out* (Hanoi: Foreign Languages Publishing House, 1960; original edition, 1930).
 9. Nguyen Thi Dam's testimony comes from Wilfred Burchett, *North of the 17th Parallel* (2nd edition; Hanoi: Red River Publishing House, 1957), pp. 119–24.
10. Ngo Vinh Long, op. cit., p. 46. Long writes that in Cochin-China, there was not one peasant who escaped debt.
11. Mai Thi Tu, 'The Vietnamese Woman, Yesterday and Today', in *Vietnamese Women* (Vietnamese Studies, No. 10; Hanoi: Foreign Languages Publishing House, 1966), p. 25.
12. Vu Can, 'With the Nam Dinh Weavers', in *Vietnamese Women* (Vietnamese Studies, No. 10; Hanoi: Foreign Languages Publishing House, 1966), p. 194. The testimony that follows by Mrs Yen comes from pp. 198–202 of this essay.
13. Jean Chesneaux, *The Vietnamese Nation* (Sydney, Australia: Current Book Distributors, 1966), p. 141.
14. Bernard Fall, *Street Without Joy* (New York: Schocken, 1972), p. 141.
15. Chesneaux, op. cit., p. 131.
16. Burchett, op. cit., p. 217.
17. Alexander B. Woodside, *Community and Revolution in Modern Viet Nam* (Boston: Houghton Mifflin, 1976), p. 125.
18. Tran Van Mai, 'Who Committed This Crime?', in Ngo Vinh Long, op. cit., pp. 219–76.

19. Ngo Vinh Long, op. cit., p. 133.
20. For a detailed account of the Geneva Conference and period preceding it from the perspective of a liberal US government official, see Archimedes Patti, op. cit.
21. P. 34.
22. *The Pentagon Papers* (New York Times Edition; New York: Bantam, 1972), p. 72.
23. 'Cost of the Viet Nam War', *Indochina Newsletter* (Dorchester, Massachusetts), No. 18, November–December 1982, p. 12.

4. Megaviolence against Women

> There is peace, but all around is still danger. You must
> walk in my footsteps.
> *Phan Tri Thien, a 19-year-old mine defuser as she*
> *escorted a foreign journalist, 1979*

After years of fighting, in the spring of 1975, the US-sponsored army of
South Viet Nam collapsed. On 30 April 1975, a sea of revolutionary flags
welcomed a column of Liberation Army tanks into Saigon. A young,
well-armed woman hailed and halted the first tank. Nguyen Trung Kien,
18 years old at the time, had been a commando fighter in Saigon. She
climbed aboard the tank to guide it along the shortest route to the
Presidential Palace. Minutes later, the PLAF raised the flag of the
Provisional Revolutionary Government of South Viet Nam over the
Palace. President Thieu had already fled. His replacement, President
Duong Van 'Big' Minh, rose and greeted the first PLAF troops to enter
the Palace: 'The revolution has come. You have come. We have been
waiting for you this morning to hand over power.'

The PLAF officer replied in a gentle but firm voice: 'The revolution
has seized complete power. The former administration has been overthrown. No one can hand over what they have already lost. You must
surrender immediately.'[1]

General Nguyen Thi Dinh, second in command of the PLAF and
President of the Women's Union in the South, explained how local
women's militia units and members of the Women's Union took over
official posts of the Thieu regime in many southern cities even before the
PLAF arrived. She told of a group of women taking over a villa that once
housed two US army colonels and a navy commander. The women
arrived at the villa on 29 April. The US officers fled in the middle of a
meal. General Dinh smiled as she recalled, 'They were very frightened
and left without taking a single needle.'[2]

Like a puppet with its strings cut, the entire Saigon state apparatus
collapsed within hours. The next day, May Day, there was no official
parade, but a spontaneous popular demonstration of joy and relief.
Thousands took to the streets. Saigon was not conquered. It did not fall.

It was liberated. A formal national celebration began on 15 May. In Saigon, two million people packed into the central square waving flags of the PRG and DRV. The celebration included a parade in which women's army and militia divisions marched, proud of the enormous contributions they had made to the victory.

That victory did not come easily. This chapter documents the incalculable sacrifices the Vietnamese people made to defeat the military might of imperial America. Vietnamese women's wounds of war with the US run deep – some of them still fester – demanding prolonged attention and care. Healing is a precondition for women's liberation in Viet Nam.

'There Are Cemeteries of Our Freedom Fighters Everywhere'

Le Thu, Director of Education of the Viet Nam Women's Union, travelled throughout the southern provinces after the victory. She reported,

> There are cemeteries of our freedom fighters everywhere . . . Wherever I visited, mothers whose children had died showed me pictures of their children or their children's diaries . . . You see, the war took away their most beautiful dreams and their most precious loves. Among the survivors, the women suffer the most. When you lose your dearest ones, you never find them again. It's a wound that can never be healed. At one local Women's Union executive committee meeting in the South, all except two out of 15 women were widows.[3]

In the ten years of warfare from 1965 to 1975, over two million Vietnamese people – soldiers and civilians on all sides of the conflict – were killed. A million women were widowed and 800,000 children orphaned. Over three million were wounded, many seriously. Some of the worst wounds were caused by anti-personnel weapons designed in the US to maximize the pain and suffering of human targets – but unable to pierce anything tougher than human flesh. An estimated 90% of the revolutionary cadres who stayed in the South were killed.[4] After 1975, another 10,000 people were killed in fields by the ordnance the US left behind.

The Charlie Company, Third Airborne Brigade, 82nd Division of the US Armed Forces, massacred 504 in the village of Son My on 16 March 1968. It became known as the My Lai massacre. Most of the victims were women and children and before killing the women, GIs raped hundreds of them.[5] Nearly ten years after the atrocity, one of the survivors, Nguyen Thi Doc, aged 73, broke a bitter silence and told a visitor: 'Eleven members of my family were killed: my sons, my daughter-in-law, my grandchildren. Who will take care of my grave? Now, in my old age, I am alone. With no immediate family.' Sobs choked off the rest of Mrs Doc's words. The young woman who tried to comfort her was a veteran guerrilla who had joined the NLF after her family, too, was massacred at Son My. She was 14 at the time. She returned to Son My in 1975, to work as a political cadre, helping to administer the village and organize its reconstruction.[6]

Attack on Future Generations
Doctor Nguyen Thi Ngoc Phuong, Director of Obstetrics at the largest Ob/Gyn hospital in Ho Chi Minh City, asked,

> What should I tell them? Imagine how we feel. Couples who have been separated for many years of war, finally reunite. Some of the women get pregnant. They have been waiting for so long for reunification. Then the newborn child dies because of severe genetic mutations resulting from one of the parents' exposure to defoliants. We have many, many such cases.[7]

Systematic defoliation and saturation bombing of the Vietnamese countryside was a cornerstone of US strategy to deprive the liberation movement of its constituency and strongest base of support – the majority of Vietnamese people who were peasants. A US Senate Subcommittee on Refugees estimated that between 1965 and 1973, more than ten million people were forced to flee their villages.

The US sprayed more than half the territory of South Viet Nam with a chemical defoliant known as 'Agent Orange'. Agent Orange contains dioxin – a chemical unrivalled in its lethal power. Only one gram mixed in one million litres of water is enough to kill a guinea-pig after one swallow. By the end of the war, six pounds per person had been sprayed over South Viet Nam. To make matters worse, dioxin is not soluble in water alone. Vietnamese scientists expect the country's streams, rivers and wells to be contaminated for generations to come.

The total destructive capacity of dioxin is yet to be calculated. Vietnamese doctors have not been able to tabulate the overall damage to the population because they lack the necessary medical and computing equipment to do so. But they have proved that exposure to microscopic doses destroys liver tissue, causes still births, miscarriages, birth defects and cancer.

At Tu Du Hospital, the number of women who miscarried after their second month of pregnancy leaped from little more than 1% in the mid-1950s to 15% in 1967 and peaked at 20% in 1976. Molar pregnancy – a rare mutation of the placenta which kills the embryo and sometimes ruptures the uterus – rose from 0.8% in 1952 to 3% in 1976. The incidence of cervical cancer rose three times between 1952 and 1976 and five times by 1980. Some 65% of female cancer in the South is cervical – a much higher proportion than in the North – because only the South was sprayed with dioxin.

The Institute for Protection of Mothers and Children, a research Ob/Gyn hospital, found that expectant mothers exposed to dioxin have six

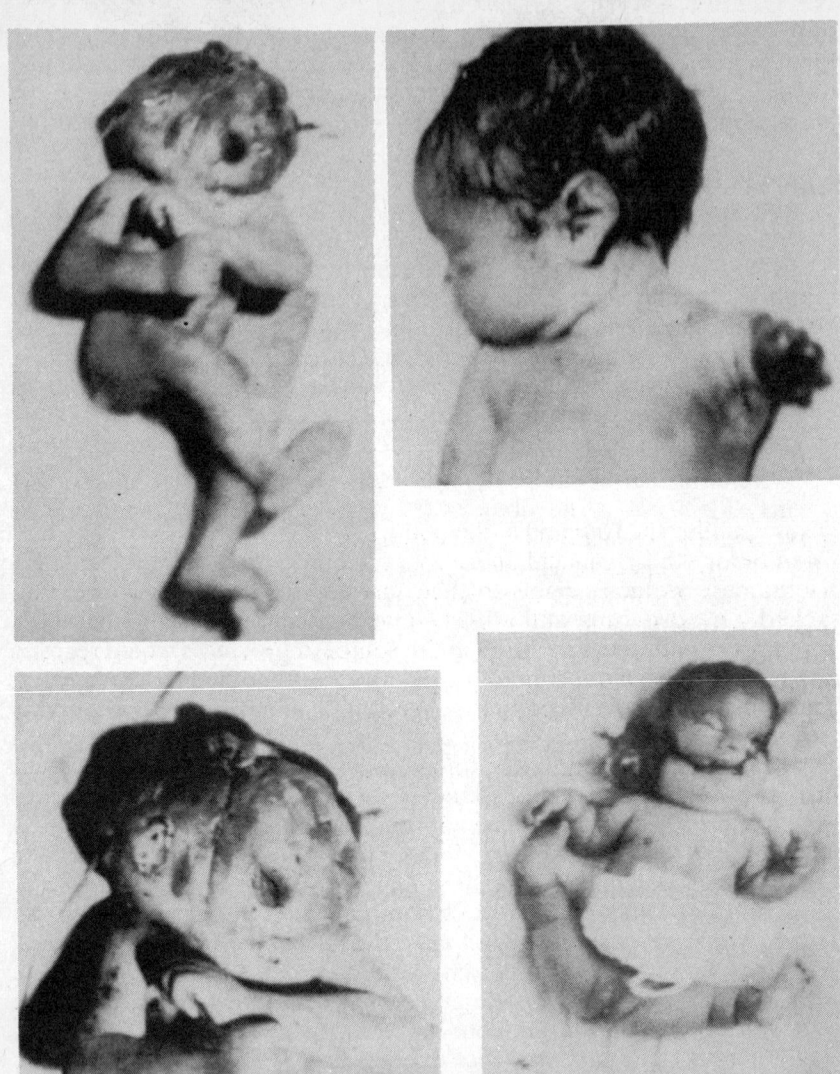

Parents of these genetically mutated newborns were exposed to dioxin
Arlene Eisen

times more chromosome breaks than survivors of Hiroshima. They give birth to babies with flippers instead of arms and legs, babies without tear ducts, babies with two heads, babies without kidneys, and other horrors. No national statistics are tabulated yet. However, at Tu Du Hospital, the number of newborns with fatal mutations rose from 0.01% in 1952 to 0.24% in 1978.[8]

The strategy of forced urbanization left another killer among the Vietnamese population: venereal disease. Most of the ten million peasants who were forced off the land crowded into Saigon, Danang and other South Vietnamese cities. The women had virtually no means of support. Some half a million became prostitutes. VD was not only a problem for the prostitutes. It also infected soldiers, officials and their loved ones. Although the precise figures are not available, the total number of cases of VD in 1975 was estimted at three million.[9] By 1981, all but several thousands of these cases had been treated; but the total elimination of the disease is severely hampered by a scarcity of antibiotics.

Divorce under the Gun and Kidnapping
Even before these genocidal assaults on women's health were launched, Vietnamese women's rights to their families and motherhood were attacked. One provision of the 1954 Geneva Accords stipulated that those who fought with the Viet Minh in the southern provinces would regroup north of the 17th parallel until the country was reunified two years later. Thousands of families separated, expecting to see their loved ones within two years. Instead, Diem's troops arrested and tortured women whose husbands had gone North and forced them to sign forms divorcing their husbands. These women had to remarry within a stipulated time to prove their sincerity. Diem's armed agents would seek them out and rape those who had not remarried.[10] In so doing, Diem was implementing part of a US strategy to keep North and South Viet Nam permanently divided.

In spite of Diem and his successors, family bonds remained strong. During the years that the US enforced the partition of Viet Nam, loyalty to distant family members became a militant defence of one's political principles, as well as an emotional need. A southern woman told police this, when she refused to denounce her husband who had regrouped in the North: 'I could not denounce my husband. He is in my heart. If you want me to denounce him, kill me and take out my heart.'[11]

Years later, in April 1975, the US government airlifted some ten thousand children from South Viet Nam. They were carelessly loaded into cargo planes, unsafe for human transportation. The American press gave 'Operation Babylift' banner headlines, trying to convince the world of its humanitarian intentions. They claimed the communists would kill the orphans. The Vietnamese responded, 'We have struggled and sacrificed for 30 years so that our children's generation could live in peace. This kidnapping is another form of genocide against the Vietnamese people.'[12] On 4 April 1975, more than 150 children died when one of the planes crashed.

Operation Babylift was a last-ditch effort to rally support for a bankrupt policy in Viet Nam. Polls showed that 78% of the people in the US opposed any further intervention in Viet Nam. Congress balked at supporting a loser. President Ford and Ambassador Martin engineered Operation Babylift and persuaded Thieu's Welfare Minister to accept the plan. He explained:

> The US Ambassador stressed that this evacuation along with the millions of refugees abandoning Communist controlled zones will help create a shift in American public opinion in favor of the Republic of Viet Nam. Especially when these children land in the US, they will be subject to television, radio and press agency coverage and the effect will be tremendous.[13]

This politician knew that many of the children were not orphans. Anxious mothers sometimes put children in orphanages to protect them from the ravages of war. Others left their children temporarily in the care of orphanages because they could not afford to feed them at inflated Saigon prices. Some children lived with their parents but had been arbitrarily picked up on the streets by US adoption agencies. Some were orphans who, if they had stayed in Viet Nam, would have been cared for by the community.

Ironically, given the racism rampant in US society, organizers of Operation Babylift claimed they were rescuing children fathered by GIs from the racist hatred of the Vietnamese people. Since the liberation of Viet Nam, the US press gives more space to the supposed discrimination faced by so-called Amer-Asian children than to any other issue regarding Viet Nam. These reports are often fed by a relatively small number of Vietnamese women in Ho Chi Minh City who are drawn to the wealth and comfort of the US. They pin their dreams on emigrating to the 'land of milk and honey' of their children's US fathers and hope their stories of mistreatment will win them safe passage.

An Amer-Asian boy at the Young Flower Orphanage in Ho Chi Minh City told a foreign journalist, 'My name is Tran. I am nine.' Then he sang,
    'The war is gone
    Planes come no more
    Do not weep for those just born
    The human being is ever green.'[14]
I found while travelling in Viet Nam that the mothers of children fathered by GIs are often assumed to have been raped or to have been prostitutes. They are not envied. But their children enjoy the same official rights and privileges as any Vietnamese. Socially, they may inherit some of their mother's lowered status, especially if she was a prostitute who chooses to remain outside the current revolutionary process. If these children are sometimes teased by other children who have not yet learned

the policies of the Socialist Republic of Viet Nam, this social stigma can in no way be compared to the systematic racist oppression which all children of colour face in the United States.

Ecocide and Economic Infanticide

After the massacre at Son My (My Lai), many of the villagers fled, some to join the liberation forces in the jungle, others to find refuge with relatives living in towns. A year later, those who remained were forced into US-controlled refugee camps. Then, the US Army returned to kill the coconut trees. When the trees were dead, bulldozers tore up the earth. Bombs destroyed the sea-wall that kept salt water out of the marshy lands where the people of Son My grew rice. A flourishing village became a wasteland. So did thousands of other South Vietnamese villages.

Over 43% of South Vietnamese plantations and orchards were destroyed. All irrigation networks were subject to repeated bombing. Half the water buffalo – essential for ploughing – were killed. In areas where defoliants were ineffective, the US bulldozed the vegegation, then planted 'elephant grass'. When the grass dried, the US Army doused it with napalm and gasoline, setting off raging prairie fires that consumed everything in the vicinity.

Without the benefit of machinery, people have reclaimed thousands of acres of land, often moving tons of earth by hand in wicker baskets. But as of March 1982, a half million hectares of formerly cultivated land lay fallow and millions of hectares of forest were perhaps permanently destroyed. In one area, there is a layer of coal two metres deep – the remains of U Minh Forest. [15] In central Viet Nam, near the 17th parallel, massive destruction of the forests not only causes chronic flooding and soil erosion; it has also resulted in higher ground temperatures. Without the trees to cool the air as it blows down the mountain, a scorching wind comes roaring down, overheating the rice paddies and blowing sand on to them. [16] With 55 million people and a total cultivated land surface of only 5.4 million hectares – or ten people to every 2.5 acres – it would be difficult to grow enough food to feed everyone, even under normal circumstances. [17] And the circumstances in Viet Nam have been far from normal.

Ten million peasants who were forced to leave their homes also had to let their fields go fallow. So the US supplied 300,000 tons of rice a year to feed the people under its control. [18] When US defeat appeared imminent, they slashed aid: by 30 April 1975, there was only enough rice in reserve in Saigon to feed the city's population for 15 days. Also, widespread flooding in central Viet Nam caused serious crop losses. The combination of these disasters created the threat of famine in the South immediately after liberation. Only huge donations of rice from the North prevented massive starvation in the southern cities. [19]

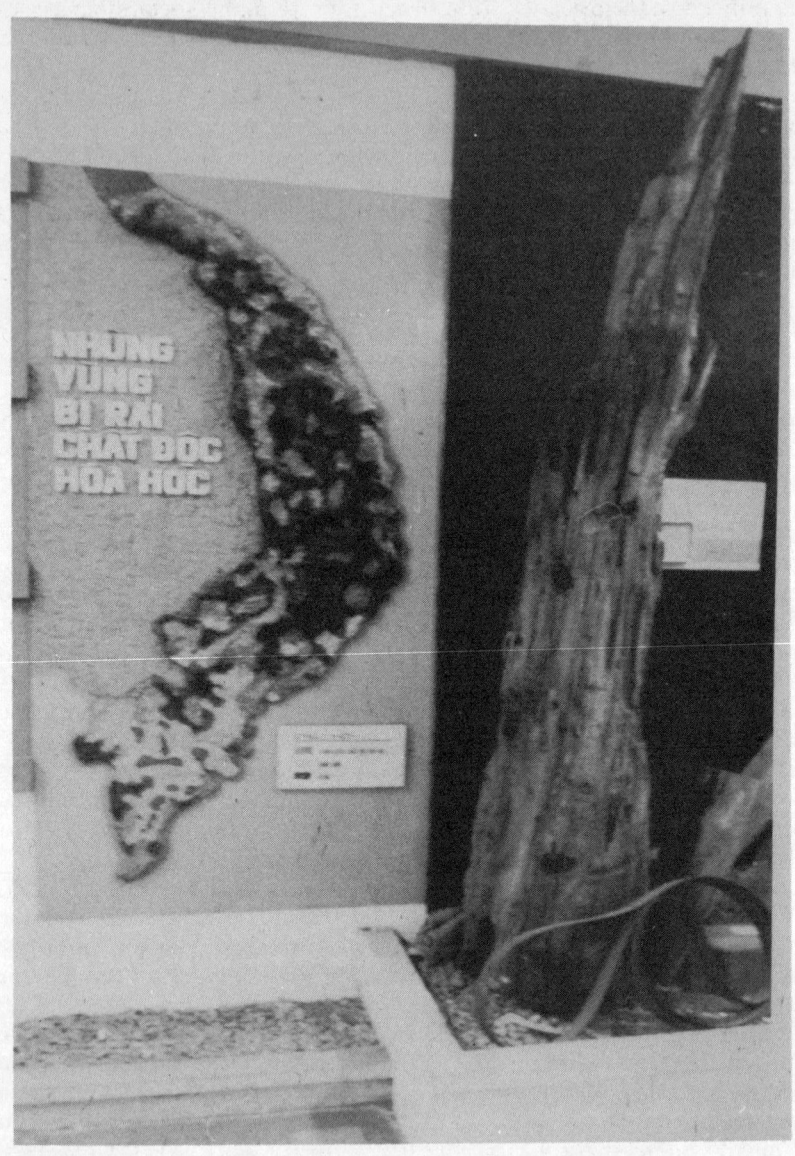

Display at Museum of US War Crimes. Light areas of map indicate areas of Viet Nam subjected to total ecocide. Arlene Eisen

The Price of Glitter
On the eve of liberation, Saigon's shop windows were crammed with Japanese radios, tape recorders and other gadgets. The streets glittered, while hundreds of air-conditioned bars played the latest American tunes. Journalist John Pilger called it the 'world's only consumer society that produced nothing'. In a 1974 report, the World Bank Study Mission concluded that the Thieu regime would need at least $11 billion in aid until 1990 – just to keep from losing ground.[20] A noted Vietnamese commentator, Nguyen Khac Vien, pointed out the price of Saigon's glitter:

> The more bombs fell upon liberated areas, the more goods Saigon received. I don't like to call it a false prosperity because the buildings, cars, goods are not artificial. These things impose themselves, obsess the mind, create an ambiance, a new social order. I would rather say an expensive prosperity, even too dearly paid for. Because if some countries pay for the Mercedes and the Chevrolets, the refrigerators and other gadgets by the sale of oil, South Viet Nam paid for them with flesh and blood.[21]

South Viet Nam's economy was caught in ever rising spirals of dependency, corruption, unemployment and inflation. More than four million former peasants had no work. About six or seven million people lived on wages paid by US dollars – not counting Thieu's army or government administration. In total, 80% of the people depended on the US for their economic survival. United States aid amounted to more than half the gross national product of South Viet Nam. This dependency killed native industry. Any available capital was invested in luxury goods to sell to Americans, to prosperous pimps and prostitutes and to Saigon's generals. Scrap metal – the remains of US planes and other war *matériel* – made up 90% of the exports from the Republic of South Viet Nam.

In 1975, when the US cut off the flood of foreign aid and goods, prices soared. Traders, who numbered in the hundreds of thousands, began hoarding. Prices escalated further. Rumours spread a kind of collective psychosis. Those people who were accustomed to living off the US dole panicked. Sugar mills that imported raw sugar, bottling plants that imported powdered milk, paper mills that imported pulp and hundreds of other enterprises were crippled. With no raw materials or spare parts or foreign technicians, South Viet Nam's Honda-riding generation would have to learn to walk. Many chose not to. They became refugees – not from a communist bloodbath, but from poverty and hard work. In 1978, the per capita gross national product of Viet Nam was estimated at $100 per year.[22]

Crimes Against Women

1. Rape

No collection of veterans' war stories is complete without tales of rape. For example, Sgt Scot Camil, First Marine Division, testified:

> When we went through the villages and searched people, the women would have all their clothes taken off and the men would use their penises to probe them to make sure they didn't have anything hidden anywhere; and this was raping, but it was done as searching.

Sp/4 Joe Galbally of the Americal Division reported:

> We went through the village; it was an eight-man patrol. We entered a hootch (peasant home). These people are aware of what American soldiers do to them, so naturally they try to hide the young girls. We found one hiding in a bomb shelter in a sort of basement of her house. She was taken out, raped by six or seven people in front of her family, in front of us and the villagers. This isn't just one incident. This is just the first one I can remember. I know of ten or 15 such incidents at least.[23]

Ten years later, Viet Nam veterans were still haunted by their crimes:

> I had a sense of power. A sense of destruction. See, now, in the US a person is babied. He's told what to do . . . . But in the Nam you realized you had the power to take a life. You had the power to rape a woman and nobody could say nothing to you. That godlike feeling you had was in the field. It was like I was god. I could take a life. I could screw a woman . . . .

Another remembered:

> You take a group of men and put them in a place where there are no round-eyed women . . . . There are women available. These women are of another culture, another color, another society. You don't want a prostitute. You got an M-16. What do you need to pay a lady for? You go down to the village and you take what you want. I saw guys who I believe had never had any kind of sex with a woman before in that kind of scene. They'd come back a double veteran. Raping a woman and then killing her made a man a double veteran.[24]

It is safe to say that just as no South Vietnamese village escaped the bombs and the napalm made in the US, none escaped the rape. Racism, bred in US society, combined with contempt for women, made rape a convenient tool in the hands of the Pentagon. It was unwritten Pentagon policy to condone, if not encourage, rape as a way of motivating the soldiers. If they couldn't fight for a just cause in Viet Nam, at least they could 'prove their manhood' in the patriarchal tradition of rape.

Rape also served another strategic purpose for US military planners. Terrorism is a classic counter-insurgency tactic against people's war. And rape is a classic act of terrorism which not only assaults and destroys a woman; it also humiliates and intimidates her family and community.[25] In many societies, women who have been raped are outcasts. Patriarchal codes in many Western, as well as Third World, countries assume that a woman provoked her rapist. 'She asked for it.' She is impure. The policy in liberated Viet Nam was to treat women who had been raped as victims of US aggression. Revolutionary cadres actively fought against the traditional shame and prejudice that stigmatized rape victims. Nevertheless, the scars remain. The horror of rape is not forgotten. The mutilation and disease are not easily cured. The child conceived in terror will be loved, in spite of her origin or the burden she brings to the woman who did not plan for her.

Crimes Against Women

2. Prostitution
Officially the Thieu regime maintained that prostitution was illegal. But a Saigon official candidly explained, 'The Americans need girls; we need dollars. Why should we refrain from the exchange? It's an inexhaustible source of US dollars for the state.'[26] At the height of US troop occupation, there were nearly half a million prostitutes in South Viet Nam, almost one for every GI. This amounted to 20 times more prostitutes than the combined total of women doctors and professionals. The prostitute scene fascinated US journalists who often gave the impression that women profited from US occupation. But some described the grim reality:

> There is a woman who directs a group of deaf and dumb prostitutes – most of them 14 and 15 years old, some even younger. They cluster nightly at the corner of Tu Do Street nearest the Continental Hotel, usually just before curfew hour . . . At this time of night, there are prostitutes – among them some who I have watched grow old and tightfaced in the last ten years – standing at street corners all over town, hoping to be picked up by late-cruising customers. At this hour too, pimps haul their girls around on the backs of motorcycles and offer them at bargain prices.[27]

Some prostitutes may have become rich by Vietnamese standards, but all were subject to brutal exploitation. One veteran who had been stationed in Pleiku said that in 'Sin City', which appeared within three months after the base was built, a room in the whorehouse – actually a tent – would have 15 or 20 beds. He remembered, 'They got 300 piastres a lay.' Three hundred piastres were officially equal to three US dollars, but with black market dealers, it came to about one dollar. If the prostitutes tried to get more money, US Military Police would declare their establishments 'off limits'. Similar strips appeared wherever there were US bases. Another strip at Phu Loi, however, operated only during daylight hours because the NLF controlled that area at night.[28]

Among the 500,000 prostitutes, there were many varieties, each suited to the different demands of the clients. In provincial outposts, some provided multiple services as indicated by the following advertisement: 'Car wash and get screwed.' Since many white GIs would not go with women they had seen with Black GIs, some prostitutes learned American habits of discrimination. A GI could 'rent a wife' by the day, week or month. These marriages, resembling indentured servitude, forced the woman to be both sex provider and servant. Many GIs preferred to rent wives because the faithful wife was less likely to catch and pass on VD. In Viet Nam, GIs could live in luxury previously reserved for high colonial administrators: 'Like I had, ah, it sounds kinda strange, but I had a houseboy and at first I had a girl to come in and she'd shine my shoes and make my bed, do my laundry, just anything entailed in taking care of my house for a grand total of $7 per month.'[29]

As GIs left Viet Nam, the prostitutes remained trapped in a cycle of heroin addiction, poverty and self-hatred. Probably a majority were infected with venereal disease. Their Amer-Asian children, although loved, became reminders of their degraded past. As soon as Saigon was liberated, a ban was placed on prostitution and the Women's Union launched an enormous campaign to find housing, food and new skills for thousands of unemployed women. The majority of them returned to the countryside. But thousands remained in the cities, requiring an enormous outlay of social resources to restore their dignity – an effort discussed in detail in Chapter 14.

Crimes Against Women

3. Drug Addiction
Today, the School for New Youth, in a suburb of Ho Chi Minh City, is a centre where a sensitive combination of acupuncture, physical therapy, and political and vocational education helps victims of drug addiction regain control over their lives. A room in the school is devoted to an exhibit showing US responsibility for making heroin addiction epidemic in South Viet Nam. One photo in the exhibit shows a huge GI handing a marijuana cigarette to a small girl of perhaps eight years old.

The French imposed the opium trade on Viet Nam in 1865, but there was little heroin there until 1964. By 1970, there had been a 400% increase in the heroin available. Indochina, with the support of the CIA and its Air America, became the hub of international heroin traffic. The CIA bought the loyalty of many Vietnamese officials with the proceeds from this booming trade.[30] According to documents from the Thieu regime, there were 150,000 heroin addicts in Saigon alone in 1975. Almost 85% of them were under 35 years old. Phan Nguyen Binh,

Director of Education at the School for New Youth, gave a portrait of the scars the drug users bear:

> Besides their addictions, they were infected with VD, tuberculosis and malaria. But their most dangerous diseases were spiritual. Their social personalities were destroyed. They had no confidence in themselves, their families or society. Some were Buddhist, some were Catholic – but whatever their religion, they all believed that drugs were gods. If they dropped their addiction, they were sure the god of drugs would kill them. They suffered severe depression. As late as 1978, some 50% of our students were in thieves' gangs.
>
> Every addict wants to stop but can't do it alone. We work very hard in this centre to restore their confidence. We tell them, 'You are not culpable, you are only the victims of colonialist culture. If you begin today, it's not too late for you to contribute to the country. If you contribute to the struggle against addiction, you're making a big contribution.'[31]

Schools like these require an enormous outlay of resources to feed, clothe, house, care for and re-educate their students. Generally people stay at the school a year before they fully recover their health. Some 20% need more time and 15% of the students are returnees. Thousands have joined productive life permanently. In 1981, Binh estimated that only 5,000 hard-core addicts remain in Ho Chi Minh City. He thought that by 1983, the school would no longer be needed, and would be converted into a factory. Yet when I visited Viet Nam in the autumn of 1981, syringes seemed to be one of the most common items sold openly by petty traders on the streets near the former Continental Hotel in Ho Chi Minh City.

Crimes Against Women

4. Cultural Intoxication and Pornography

The US attempt to 'win the hearts and minds' of the majority of Vietnamese people failed. Yet 20 years of US domination over all legal sources of information and education in Saigon-controlled areas seriously damaged the culture and consciousness of the South Vietnamese people. For 20 years, the CIA, the United States Information Agency, and all the machinery of the US government was mobilized to justify US aggression with stories of communist atrocities, North Vietnamese invasion, bloodbaths and revenge.

The *Pentagon Papers* documented memos by generals, top Pentagon and State Department officials boasting about their psychological warfare campaigns, systematically using lies and other 'dirty tricks'.[32] US control over the education of Saigon's youth meant, for example, that despite her participation in the Viet Minh, Vo Thi The lamented, 'My 4th grade nephew in Saigon learned that Ho Chi Minh sold out South Viet

Vietnamese children on their way to US-sponsored "strategic hamlet"
Viet Nam INC.

Nam to the French at Geneva and Diem returned to save the country.'[33]

A woman who worked as a secretary for a US corporation in Saigon fled to the US as Saigon was liberated because she believed the CIA-sponsored rumours that single women would be forced to marry Vietcong amputees. Even after Saigon was liberated, the psychological war continued. A Women's Union cadre who worked on the campaign to innoculate children explained:

> We began innoculating the children against cholera, tetanus, typhoid and all the other preventable diseases right after liberation. But we had a terrible time getting parents to bring their children to health centres. Rumours raged throughout the city that rather than innoculating the children, we were taking blood from them for transfusions for wounded 'Vietcong' soldiers. All our cadres had to make a big show of bringing their children to be innoculated first, before the rest of the population would trust us. After, we were able to arrest some of the people who initiated the rumours. They made a public apology for their crime.[34]

The US attempt at controlling the political thinking of the Vietnamese people was not only designed to justify US aggression, it was also designed to demoralize and dampen the spirit of resistance. Truong Tuyet Anh now teaches literature at the University of Ho Chi Minh City. She explained how years of anti-communist propaganda had affected her:

> I have known the humiliation of a person conscious of living under foreign domination; but because I did not understand the great history of our nation, I simply suffered, thinking that I belonged to a small, weak and backward people continuously subjected to oppression and foreign domination, and I felt ashamed of being powerless in the face of the enslavement of my country . . . I believed the brutal war in our native land was between the 'dictatorial communist side' and the 'free nationalist side' (although I was well aware at the same time of the dirty, contemptible things being done in the 'free side'), and so I found no way out of the impasse either for my country or for myself. As a consequence, I paid little attention to the political situation under the former regime, closeted myself in my ivory tower of poetry . . . .[35]

Shortly after liberation, a Museum of US War Crimes opened its doors to the public in Saigon. Exhibits carefully documented the genocide committed against the Vietnamese people, as well as the cultural assaults. A US journalist noted, 'The crowds that the exhibit has drawn reflect the fact that many Saigonese know far less about the atrocities of the war . . . than the average American. The old government had censored all hostile or critical reporting in Saigon.'[36]

The US also tried to dampen people's spirit of resistance by glorifying 'the American way of life'. Each GI flaunting his portable radio became a walking advertisement for the benefits which the US economy could provide. They also imposed a white Western standard of beauty. Thousands of Vietnamese women underwent the ordeal of cosmetic surgery to become more appealing to their customers from the US. Rounder eyes, breasts expanded with silicone, hips padded with silicone – all brought higher prices from GI 'johns'. According to an article in *The New York Times*:

> Dr Ban will convert what he refers to as 'natural Asian defects' within an hour. (He has a team of five doctors.) He also said, 'By removing a woman's complexes, we give her confidence and transform her psychology. It's a lot of fun.'
>
> The fashion doesn't stop there (at eyes and breasts). In their eagerness to imitate Europeans, some Vietnamese want bigger noses, dimpled cheeks, cleft chins . . . even fatter fingers. A pioneer in the operation is Mrs Nguyen Cao Ky, the glamorous wife of the former Vice President . . . . Cosmetic surgery is still a risk, contends Doctor Thai Minh Bach who has performed the operation often, but says that he spends half his time patching up the mistakes of other surgeons. [37]

Many of the Vietnamese women who worked as waitresses or walked the streets could not afford to Westernize their bodies. They had to settle for Westernizing their names. *Xuan*, which means spring in Vietnamese, became Ann. *Phuong* (flower) became Fran. Some GIs bragged about how they could entice a woman to bed with a can which the woman thought was hair spray. In fact it was spray starch. Few of the women could read labels. While they spoke quite a bit of English, they remained illiterate in their own language. Even many of the wives of Saigon army officers and administrators, able to dress in expensive Western styles, were illiterate.

For those who did read, the CIA exported more books and magazines to South Viet Nam than were printed inside that country. They ran editorials like, 'What is happiness? No such thing exists. Only acceptance is real. To accept, that's all.'[38] A room in the Museum of US War Crimes features charts and some examples of the pornography exported to South Viet Nam. A guide carefully explains the humiliating function of pornography and challenges any potential voyeurs looking at the exhibit.

When Saigon was first liberated, students and other young people took the initiative in cleaning the streets and painting over signs and billboards that insulted women. They also collected demoralizing and pornographic literature. But six years later, degrading music, literature and other materials were reappearing:

> At the beginning we underestimated the importance and strength of cultural imperialism. Now we've discovered there has been an organized ring promoting music calling for the overthrow of socialism. Their literature is

pornographic and defeatist. It's a plot of cultural intoxification. Our *Hom Thom* campaign aims to combat this new psychological warfare. The people who print and distribute it are punished. Users are considered victims. But it is not enough to forbid it. We must create and popularize a healthier culture. [39]

The literature she is referring to was found in Ho Chi Minh City in 1981, written in Vietnamese, but often published in the US and distributed free. These books draw a gloomy picture of socialist Viet Nam. There were also hundreds of 1981 calendars featuring a naked woman and the striped flag of the former Saigon regime. The caption read, 'Proud as ever to be Vietnamese'.

The music seemed to be more popular than the books. One of the composers is Pham Duy, a defector from the Viet Minh in 1954, who worked for Saigon's propaganda apparatus during the war. His recent songs, taped in the US, are titled 'Farewell Saigon', and 'To Those Who Remain', and others urging people to leave Viet Nam. Voice of America, broadcasting from transmitters in southern China, the Philippines and offshore Viet Nam, features this music.

These unwelcome 'gifts' from the US continue to undermine efforts to reconstruct the country; they promote a psychology of sexual exploitation, cynicism, pessimism and selfishness.

Problems of National Reconciliation

A policy of national reconciliation is the political antidote to the cultural intoxification still plaguing South Vietnamese society. National reconciliation flows from Ho Chi Minh's teaching: 'Viet Nam is one. The Vietnamese people are one.' The policy assumes that there are neither victims nor vanquished among the Vietnamese. The only defeated enemy is US imperialism. Virtually every family had some member on the other side during the war – which accounts for the depth and spirit of reconciliation.

The Provisional Government of the Republic of South Viet Nam began to implement the policy of national reconciliation even before the final victory in 1975. During my visit to liberated areas in 1974, Bui Thi Me, Vice-Minister of Health of the PRG, introduced me to former members of the Saigon Army living peacefully there. The PRG and the Women's Union were taking special steps to educate people in such a way as to encourage reconciliation rather than revenge. Bui Thi Me's explanation relied on a substantial dose of nationalism: 'If we took revenge, we would be falling into the trap of Vietnamization . . . allowing the US government to set one Vietnamese against another. No Vietnamese is our enemy, only the US government. Thieu is not Vietnamese. American blood flows in his veins.' [40]

There were over a million soldiers and officials of the US-sponsored

Thieu regime. Most of them were drafted against their will. But some had committed serious crimes against the Vietnamese people. By early 1976, after varying periods of re-education, 95% of them were reintegrated into society with their full civil rights restored. They voted in April 1976, for the first reunified National Assembly.[41] Reconciliation was only possible because re-education (*hoc tap*) became part of the curriculum of every school. In factories, workers also engaged in *hoc tap*, at meetings where they discussed problems of organization, management and distribution of profits. Street meetings in residential neighbourhoods included lectures on such themes as French colonialism, the struggle for independence, US aggression and war crimes, the Communist Party and the future of the country. The press, radio and TV discussed similar themes. Neighbourhood exhibitions clarified the issues.

For all soldiers, officials and most politicians of the old regime, there was a minimum of three days' obligatory re-education. For the rest of the population, re-education was more casual. A former secretary at a US government agency described her relief:

> I thought liberation would be the end for people like me. When, some days later the call came for everyone to register, I thought, 'This is it.' But it took me 15 minutes in all and so far no one has asked about my work again. In fact, when the soldiers came around to our house, it was only to check if we had enough rice.[42]

There was not one authorized execution of any official of the Thieu regime, regardless of how heinous his crime. De Gaulle spoke in his memoirs of 2,070 French people being executed for having collaborated with the Nazis. French women who had taken German lovers had their heads shaved and were publicly humiliated in the streets. Vietnamese revolutionary authorities took deliberate steps to prevent people from seeking revenge.

Yet reconciliation has not been all smooth sailing. People, especially in Saigon, are often uncooperative at re-education meetings. A British journalist reported:

> Food or lack of it is obsessively discussed; at one neighbourhood re-education session there were muffled complaints about the bureaucracy's poor record of distribution. 'You should not complain,' said a humourless cadre. 'It's better than before when the Americans ate the flesh of your babies!' At this, an old woman leapt to her feet and shouted, 'Rubbish! We all know the Americans only eat out of cans!' The audience burst into laughter and cheering, relishing the moment of rebellion. Re-educating millions of like-minded heretics will not be easy.[43]

Others say, 'You forgive me, but I want to continue to doubt, hoping or expecting the US to return soon.' A few people live on gold they have managed to hoard and thousands live on gifts they receive from relatives overseas. They pack their belongings and wait for the first chance to leave. A tiny minority actively plot to overthrow the government.

The ones remaining in re-education camps as of the autumn of 1981, were those who persisted in counter-revolutionary activities after 1975; those who set fire to Haiphong Harbour; those who planted bombs in the Hanoi railway station in 1979; those who attempted other forms of sabotage with the encouragement of the US or China; and those who, the government fears, would put their pro-imperialist ideals into dangerous practice if given a chance. Special re-education programmes must be designed for these people. Time is also needed for a thorough investigation into their past before authorities can distinguish between those who are ready to become trusted citizens again and diehard counter-revolutionaries who remain a danger to society.[44]

However, thousands, perhaps hundreds of thousands, of people in Ho Chi Minh City and other southern cities who sneer at the revolutionary government pose the greatest challenge to reconciliation. Although some are quite poor, most of them are professionals and small business owners. Rather than actively sabotaging economic and political mobilization, they passively resist. They complain about their deteriorating economic situations, assume they are more civilized and sophisticated than revolutionary cadres and cynically wait for the revolution 'to make them an offer'. They disdain collective work and will not join organizations like the Women's Union. They spread rumours to undermine public confidence in revolutionary cadres and institutions, exaggerate the government's errors and weaknesses and ignore its achievements.

Members of the Association of Vietnamese Patriots in the US, an organization which actively supports the Socialist Republic of Viet Nam, believe that the problems created by these detractors are significant. Nguyen Long's account of his 'escape' from Viet Nam, called *After Saigon Fell*, is a case in point. He had earned a doctorate in political science in the US and returned to Saigon in 1972. He lost his teaching job in November 1975, because he was accused of educating his students in a reactionary manner. Finally, in 1979, he joined the ranks of the boat people, he explained, because his wife feared 'the children would live in poverty as the offspring of a bourgeois intellectual.'[45]

Meanwhile, thousands of people who have little respect for revolutionary policy hustle freely in certain districts of Ho Chi Minh City. They openly attempt to cajole foreigners into illegal currency deals or into buying stolen goods or a prostitute's time. District One, for example, the former red light district of Saigon, seems far from re-educated. Those women who dress indiscreetly by Vietnamese standards may elicit a critical frown from a passing Women's Union cadre born and raised in the North. Yet the two co-exist. At times they struggle. It will probably take generations before they are reconciled.

Whether we look at the lists of war dead, the devastation of the

Vietnamese ecology and economy or the crimes committed directly against women, the wounds of war with the US remain as dangerous obstacles to women's emancipation.

Notes

1. Victory scenes from *The New York Times*, 3 May 1975, and *South Viet Nam in Struggle*, No. 300, 12 May 1975, and Nos. 301–2, 19 May 1975.
2. Associated Press Release, 23 May 1975.
3. Interview with Le Thu by author (Hanoi, 29 August 1981).
4. Statistics from John Cavanaugh *et al.*, 'A Time to Heal' (Washington DC: Indochina Resource Center, 1976); Le Anh Tu, 'Viet Nam: Legacy of War' (Philadelphia: American Friends Service Committee, 1975); John Spragens Jr, 'Food and Will', *The Texas Observer*, 27 February 1981, p. 8.
5. Committee to Denounce War Crimes of US Imperialism, *Crimes Perpetrated by US Imperialists and Henchmen Against Women and Children in South Viet Nam* (South Viet Nam: Giai Phong Publishing House, 1968), p. 13. For a thorough analysis of rape in Viet Nam by US troops, see Arlene Eisen Bergman, chapter 4: 'The Politics of Rape in Viet Nam', *Women of Viet Nam* (San Francisco: Peoples Press, 1975).
6. Martha Winnacker, 'Recovering from Thirty Years of War', *South East Asia Chronicle*, Nos. 56–7, May–July 1977, pp. 5–6.
7. Interview with Nguyen Thi Ngoc Phuong by author (Ho Chi Minh City, 12 September 1981).
8. Information on dioxin from interview with Dr Phuong and from Ton Duc Lang, 'US Chemical War in Viet Nam Has Not Ended', *Viet Nam* (pictorial), No. 267, March 1981, pp. 12–13. See also, *Report from International Symposium on Long Term Ecological and Human Consequences of Chemical Warfare in Viet Nam* (Hanoi: Foreign Languages Publishing House, 1983).
9. Cavanaugh *et al.*, op. cit., p. 11. For more information on prostitution, see Arlene Eisen Bergman, op. cit., Chapter 5: 'Mass Production of Prostitutes'.
10. Wilfred Burchett, *Viet Nam Will Win* (New York: Guardian, 1970), pp. 119–20.
11. 'History of the Vietnamese Women's Movement', *Viet Nam Report*, No. 9, April 1975, p. 9.
12. Unpublished letter from Internews reporter, Linda Garrett, who was in Hanoi, 28 April 1975.
13. Letter of former Saigon Minister of Welfare to ex-Premier Tran Thien Khiem, *The New York Times*, 7 April 1975.
14. John Pilger, 'Back to Viet Nam', *Aftermath* (London: New Statesman, 1982), p. 18.
15. Kathleen Gough, 'An Interview in Hanoi', *US/Viet Nam Friendship Association Newsletter*, Vol. 4, No. 3, May–JUne 1982, p. 4.
16. Ngo Vinh Long, 'View from the Village', *Indochina Issues*, No. 12, December 1980, p. 7.
17. Ibid., p. 1.
18. John Spragens Jr, 'The Way It Was', *South East Asia Chronicle*, No. 76, December 1980, p. 5.

19. 'Agriculture in South Viet Nam Before and After Liberation', *Viet Nam Courier*, No. 57, February 1977, p. 11.
20. Spragens, op. cit., p. 5.
21. Nguyen Khac Vien, 'South Viet Nam: 1976', *Viet Nam Courier*, No. 47, April 1976, pp. 6–7.
22. This statistic is from Jayne Werner, private correspondence, autumn 1982. Nayan Chanda in 'South East Asia Isn't the Monolith the West Anticipated', *The New York Times*, 11 September 1977, says it is $160.
23. Quoted by David Hunt, 'Organizing for Revolution in Viet Nam', *Radical America*, Vol. 8, No. 1–2, January–April 1974, pp. 39–40; and *Winter Soldier Investigation* (Boston: Beacon Press, 1972), p. 26. For a detailed account of the total destruction of one Vietnamese village by the US army, see Jonathan Scell's *The Village of Ben Suc* (New York: Vitage, 1967). Also for more on rape, Chapter 4 of Arlene Eisen Bergman, op. cit.
24. Mark Baker, *Nam: The Viet Nam War in the Words of the Men and Women Who Fought There* (New York: Morrow and Company, 1982), pp. 152 and 166.
25. For a discussion of how rape was used as a counter-insurgency weapon against slaves in the US, see Angela Davis, 'Reflections on the Black Woman's Role in the Community of Slaves', *Black Scholar*, December 1971.
26. Thanh Nam, 'In the Shadow of the American Embassy', *South Viet Nam in Struggle*, No. 164, 11 September 1972, p. 2.
27. *New Yorker*, 15 April 1972, pp. 52–4.
28. Jonathan Schell, op. cit., pp. 108–9.
29. Norma Juliet Wikler, *Viet Nam and the Veterans' Consciousness* (Berkeley: University of California, Department of Sociology: PhD Dissertation, June 1973), pp. 136, 170. For a more respectful view of the prostitutes in South East Asia, see Stanley Goff, Robert Sanders with Clark Smith, *Brothers: Black Soldiers In the Nam* (London: Arms and Armour Press, 1982).
30. See Alfred McCoy, *The Politics of Heroin in South East Asia* (New York: Harper, 1973).
31. Interview with Phan Nguyen Binh by author (Ho Chi Minh City, 9 September 1981).
32. For examples of early psychological warfare techniques, see *Pentagon Papers* (New York: Bantam, 1971), pp. 55–60.
33. Interview with Vo Thi The by Donna Futterman, 22 July 1975 (unpublished notes).
34. Interview with Tran Thanh Tuyen by the author (Ho Chi Minh City, 9 September 1981).
35. Truong Tuyet Anh, 'One Year with the Revolution', *Viet Nam Courier*, No. 57, February 1977, p. 27.
36. Frances Starner, 'The Streets of Ho Chi Minh City', *San Francisco Bay Guardian*, 17 October 1975, p. 12.
37. *The New York Times*, 21 May 1973.
38. Ann Froines, 'The Cultural War: Smack, Pimps and Coca Cola', *University Review*, April 1972, p. 19.
39. Interview with Bui Thi Me by author (Ho Chi Minh City, 8 September 1981).
40. Interview with Bui Thi Me by author (liberated Quang Tri, September 1974).
41. In 1980, Vietnamese authorities maintained that 20,000 remained in re-education camps: 'Written Reply of the Vietnamese Government to Amnesty

International Memorandum, September 1980', in *Report of an Amnesty International Mission to the Socialist Republic of Viet Nam* (London: Amnesty International Publications, 1981), p. 26.

42. Rami Chabra, 'Adjusting to New Life in Viet Nam', *San Francisco Chronicle*, 15 August 1975, p. 4.
43. Pilger, op. cit., pp. 15–16.
44. There has been enormous publicity and controversy on this issue. Amnesty International does not accept the Vietnamese government's view that it has the right to keep these people in re-education camps. See Amnesty International's criticism of Viet Nam's alleged denial of human rights in the above cited report.
45. Nguyen Long with Harry Kendall, *After Saigon Fell* (Berkeley: University of California, Institute of East Asian Studies, 1981). Robert Scalapino, a political science professor who advised the State Department during the Viet Nam war, wrote the foreword for this book.

5. Viet Nam Still Bleeds

Our children still cannot sleep soundly. We are in a state of semi-war, with a half million Chinese troops at our northern border.

Le Thu, Education Director, Viet Nam Women's Union

(This note is too important to leave in a footnote: unlike other chapters in this book, this one does not focus specifically on women. Chapter 5 is an attempt to unravel the confusion created by the US 'cold war' against Viet Nam, the exodus of the boat people, Viet Nam's war with Pol Pot's forces in Kampuchea and China's invasion of Viet Nam. I believe the chapter provides the essential context for understanding Vietnamese women in the post-1975 era. Continued hostilities against Viet Nam, the subject of this chapter, not only act as a brake on women's progress, they also define the boundaries and set the priorities for all women's struggles in Viet Nam.)

The last US official fled Viet Nam on 29 April 1975, only hours before the liberation forces took over the Presidential Palace in Saigon. The US had invested $275 billion to maintain control over South Viet Nam. During the last ten years, nearly 58,000 of the three million US soldiers who did a tour of duty in Viet Nam had died. Another 157,000 had been wounded. And after some 14.3 million tons of bombs had been dropped on Viet Nam,[1] the United States still suffered a humiliating defeat. This defeat transformed international power relations. It exposed and seriously weakened the US system of domination.

Despite the fact that it is nearly a decade since the US Embassy closed in Saigon, the US government is still deeply involved in Viet Nam. The policy guiding that involvement is revenge. The strategic goal is to force Viet Nam to continue to pay in blood and tears for defeating the military might of the US; to continue to teach other Third World countries that might be inspired by the Vietnamese example that the victory may be too costly; to rewrite the history of the war so that Americans can be proud of that shameful adventure and the US government can justify the continuation of its imperialist adventures in other parts of the world.

Because the system of corporate domination must constantly expand if it is to survive at all, the government it controls cannot accept defeat. Whether in Viet Nam, Angola or Nicaragua, the US government persists in its attempts to destabilize and disrupt, if they cannot blatantly overthrow, revolutionary societies. The aim is to weaken socialist development as much as possible, thereby strengthening their own potential for hegemony.

Revenge

In Article 21 of the Paris Peace Agreements, signed 27 January 1973, the United States agreed to help Viet Nam heal the wounds of war. President Richard Nixon specified the nature of that aid in a written promise to Prime Minister Pham Van Dong on 1 February 1973:

> 1. The government of the United States of America will contribute to postwar reconstruction in North Viet Nam *without any political conditions*. (Author's emphasis.)
> 2. . . . the US contribution will fall in the range of $3.25 billion of grant aid over five years. Other forms of aid will be agreed on between the two parties . . . .

Nixon claimed the treaty void. The three presidents who succeeded him each found additional reasons to justify breaking these treaty obligations.

So, while millions of dollars worth of bulldozers, cranes and other construction equipment lie idle beside abandoned construction projects in the US, Vietnamese women dig foundations for new buildings with picks and shovels. They repair bombed-out dikes, carrying earth by the basketful. They search in fields for unexploded ordnance, using crude hand-carved sticks. They perform sophisticated surgery on a liver made cancerous by dioxin, with hand-patched, reused surgical gloves. The US government's thirst for revenge against Viet Nam means pressure on other governments to deny it aid. A US-enforced trade embargo causes chronic shortages of raw materials, spare parts and technical assistance to develop the economy – the same economy that the US spent so many billions to destroy. In 1979, the US government pressured the European Economic Community to suspend powdered milk shipments to Viet Nam.

This economic warfare takes its toll on Viet Nam's already crippled economy. In 1980, when the Vietnamese economy was feeling the worst effects of the US food weapon, the Paediatric Hospital in Ho Chi Minh City was treating 400 severely malnourished children. Doctors had only 10% of the milk needed by their patients. Dr Duong Quynh Hoa, former Health Minister of the PRG and now Director of Research for Paediatrics, recently conducted a survey of child nutrition, using World Health

This woman lived in an underground shelter throughout the war so that she could support the guerrillas. She lost her arm in a US shelling. Sara Rosner

Organization standards. She found 28% of pre-school children in the suburbs of Ho Chi Minh City were malnourished. In a sample from inside the city, she found 38% of the children under five years to be suffering from malnutrition. The parents of these children, Dr Hoa explained, were unemployed, poor workers or low-level government officials.[2]

If nearly 15 million tons of bombs did not break Viet Nam's will, it is unlikely that economic hardship would. Rather than capitulate to the US, Viet Nam tightened its belt, instituted economic reform and sought aid from other countries. By 1981, the stream of Vietnamese refugees fleeing from poverty, known as the 'boat people', dwindled.

Voice of America: 'Calling All Boat People'

According to a report by the US Embassy in Thailand – a report intended to be kept secret – out of 5,000 Vietnamese refugees in southern Thailand in 1981, only 27% left for political reasons and 63% left for economic reasons.[3] Alexander Casela, Asian Section Chief of the United Nations High Commission for Refugees, corroborates this report: 'People are leaving not because they are being persecuted, but to seek a better standard of living.'[4]

The Voice of America broadcasts to Viet Nam, inviting poverty-stricken Vietnamese to emigrate to the US to enjoy a comfortable life. One US official admitted that theirs was more a programme of allurement than rescue and that in 1981 they had more spaces allotted for refugees than they had refugees to fill them. The conservative *Far Eastern Economic Review* speculated, 'If the 7th Fleet sailed into the Indian Ocean and let it be known that those reaching it would be resettled in California, the exodus from the subcontinent would dwarf that from Indochina.'[5] Lionel Rosenblatt, a former staff member of the US Embassy in Saigon and now Refugee Co-ordinator in the US Embassy in Thailand, admitted that US motives in giving sanctuary to Vietnamese refugees were far from humanitarian: 'I feel what we are doing is an appropriate extension of our war in Viet Nam. I think it's important for America to remember its responsibilities in the region.'[6]

Many refugees, once they arrive in the West, tell their hosts what they want to hear: tales of atrocious violations of human rights in Viet Nam. Some admit the truth. For example, before I visited Viet Nam in 1981, I asked a class of Vietnamese who were studying English, what, if anything, they would like me to try to learn during my visit. Their questions demonstrated an overriding concern for living standards:

> How do people earn a living? Are private businesses allowed now? Does electricity still shut down in Saigon? Do people have to wait all day to see a doctor? Is there still a black market? Who is allowed to go to the university? What is the ration of rice? Sugar? Noodles? Vegetables? Does the government have jobs for women? Do they work in the fields? What about childcare? What are the current conditions for granting exit visas?

The questioners had arrived in San Francisco between 1979 and 1980. Three out of four of them were ethnic Chinese – Hoa people. The exodus of nearly half of Viet Nam's three million Hoa people since 1978 gave new fuel to the fire of Viet Nam's critics.

Why the Hoa People Left
The United States and China painted the Hoa refugees as victims of arbitrary racist expulsion. The issue is a complex one. After 1,000 years of colonization by the Chinese, some anti-Chinese sentiment is bound to have deep roots in the Vietnamese consciousness. Viet Nam's fierce national pride was originally forged in its resistance to Chinese feudal occupation. More recently, many Chinese were resented for their relative prosperity – a prosperity gained from their control of the black market in both Hanoi and Ho Chi Minh City. However, while there may be some popular prejudice against Chinese residents in Viet Nam, the first wave of Hoa refugees was not a response to racial discrimination. It was led by the Chinese merchant community of Ho Chi Minh City.

Archimedes Patti, in charge of US intelligence in China and Viet Nam during World War II, explained that when Chiang Kai Shek's allied troops occupied Viet Nam, ostensibly to disarm the Japanese in 1945, his 'commercial and financial agents masterfully laid a solid base in Indochina for an exploitative economic operation that lasted over 30 years. We see them now as the "boat people".'[7]

In March 1978, the Vietnamese government moved to abolish private commercial trade – the traditional hotbed of speculation and hoarding that had contributed to Viet Nam's economic problems. The Chinese merchants, who had operated 80% of the private commerce in Ho Chi Minh City, were hardest hit. Not because they were Chinese, but because that had obstructed socialist reconstruction. Rather than accept a loss in their status, they left Viet Nam. Most of them emigrated to Thailand, Malaysia and other capitalist countries. At the same time, rumours originating in China flooded the Hoa communities. They predicted that war between Viet Nam and China was imminent. One of the rumours most effective in provoking flight was: 'if you stay, and there's war between Viet Nam and China, either the Vietnamese will kill you because you are Hoa; or else the Chinese troops will kill you as a traitor.'

A Hoa woman told me why she thought the rumours were effective:

> People were not well-informed. They had seen that Pol Pot's troops were able to massacre hundreds in An Giang and Tay Ninh. So they thought that anything was possible. It's a short distance from the Kampuchean border to Ho Chi Minh City. Hoa people thought since China was so big, it might win a war with Viet Nam. They remembered that in 1977, Pol Pot killed many Hoa people in Tay Ninh. He didn't distinguish between Hoa and Vietnamese. Survivors came to Ho Chi Minh City with tales of the massacres. These people feared for their lives, so they joined the ranks of the boat people.[8]

In northern Viet Nam, most of the nearly 300,000 Hoa people were factory workers, coal miners, dock workers, fishers and civil servants. A few were small traders in Hanoi and Haiphong. According to Charles Benoit, who interviewed many Hoa refugees, those leaving the North had three motives: 1) fear of their fate in the increasingly likely event of war between China and Viet Nam; 2) sentimental attachment to their nationality that spurred them on to return to the Chinese homeland; 3) erosion of their privileges in Viet Nam after the 1978 clampdown on black-market activities.[9] The abrupt flight of more than 100,000 Hoa workers before 1979 severely disrupted the economy in the North.

After China invaded Viet Nam in February 1979, another surge of Hoa people fled Viet Nam. They had many of the same motives for leaving as the previous refugees. In addition, the Vietnamese government instituted new security measures affecting many of the ethnic Chinese who remained in the North. Often Hoa people who remained near the border acted as fifth columnists, spying for and guiding the Chinese invaders. The Vietnamese government was forced to act quickly. There was no time to investigate all Hoa people. So the Vietnamese government offered those Hoa people who lived in militarily sensitive areas the choice of relocating to New Economic Zones or leaving the country. The government assisted those who chose to leave in arranging departures. Defence requirements motivated this assistance, to expedite a process that many Hoa people might have chosen to prolong.

The departures were less orderly in the South, where there is a relative scarcity of experienced cadres. While there was no official 'exit tax' as the Western media claimed, there were undoubtedly cases of lower- and middle-level officials accepting bribes.

Most of the more than one million Hoa people who remain in Viet Nam are workers and peasants. They officially enjoy the same rights and duties as all Vietnamese citizens: to go to school, to work and be drafted. Those who stayed were fearful at first. But day-to-day reality disproved the rumours that Hoa people would be expelled from school and fired from jobs. Hundreds still belong to the Viet Nam Communist Party. Once they saw the truth, many of the Hoa people who stayed became angry with the Chinese authorities who had lied to them. A group of Hoa women in Ho Chi Minh City told me that those responsible for the persistent racist incidents against Hoa people there are usually children of former officials of the Thieu regime. Some children whose fathers were still in re-education camps would tease their Hoa classmates.

It is probably true that actual persecution of Hoa people is an uncommon event in Viet Nam today. However, I did sense that subtle anti-Chinese sentiments are more common than my Hoa informants cared to acknowledge. On at least one occasion, for example, a Vietnamese cadre from the Women's Union, using standard racist reasoning, told me that she thought Hoa children did not take school seriously because their parents were more concerned with using them to make money in the market. It was obvious that most of the children she was referring to came from poor working-class families. I had no way of knowing how such offensive sentiments find their way into practice, although it is safe to assume there is no systematic history of racist oppression. On the contrary, historically, the Hoa have been a privileged group in Vietnamese society.

Strange Bedfellows
'They may sleep in the same bed; but they have different dreams.' The Vietnamese use this traditional comment on marriages of convenience to describe the alliance between China and the United States. In most such marriages, one party, usually the groom, has a power advantage. In this case, the United States is the groom. According to Viet Nam's Foreign Minister, Nguyen Co Thach:

> The direct enemy of our country, since they invaded in February 1979, is China. But America is behind China. The US is China's biggest supporter. If the US opposed China's invasion, China would not have been able to do it . . . . [In September 1978 Thach negotiated with the US to normalize relations. Everything was settled but then the US suddenly cut off the normalization process.] In December, President Carter welcomed the Chinese Premier Deng Xiaoping to the US and approved when Deng threatened 'to teach Viet Nam a lesson'. Two weeks after Deng returned to China from his visit to the US and Japan, China invaded Viet Nam. The US Secretary of the Treasury, Michael Blumenthal, arrived in China after the invasion and declared the invasion would, in no way, interfere with the normalization of relations between China and the US . . . . Our struggle is now a continuation of our struggle against US imperialism. The skin colour has changed, but behind the skin is the same enemy: the US pushing and encouraging China against us.[10]

While the spectacle of a top Chinese communist leader wearing a cowboy hat and kissing babies in Texas may have come as a shock to many, the alliance between the US and China had been brewing at least since Nixon's visit to China in 1972.[11] As China's leaders came to define the Soviet Union as China's main enemy, alliance with the US gained priority for China. China, no doubt, is also courting US economic assistance.

For years, Viet Nam followed a strategy of trying to resolve its differences with China as quietly as possible, hoping that as long as the problem was kept private, the US would not be able to take advantage of it. This strategy, a dismal failure, made it more difficult for Viet Nam to prepare its own people and its potential allies for defending Viet Nam when war with China did break out.

More recently, however, the US has made no secret of its alliance with China. In 1978, China broke all of its commitments to aid Viet Nam.

Roger Sullivan, member of the staff of the US National Security Council, stated frankly:

> To put it in terms of a Chinese dialectic, the US policy is to squeeze Viet Nam as hard as we can, to force Viet Nam to rely on the Soviet Union: then, when Viet Nam will find that the USSR cannot meet all its needs . . . . If Viet Nam experiences economic hardship, I think that's just great.[12]

And, on 2 June 1981, the Assistant Secretary of State for East Asia and the Pacific went on record with this widely publicized statement: 'We will seek, if we can, to find ways to increase the political, economic, and yes, military pressures on Viet Nam, working with others in ways which will bring about, we hope, some changes in Hanoi's attitude towards the situation.'[13]

The US and China co-operate in providing sanctuary and military and political support for an impressive array of Viet Nam's enemies. Jack Williamson, a USAID official in Laos in the 1970s, now co-ordinates Task Force 80, a special Thai intelligence unit assigned to police the Kampuchean refugee camps in Thailand. In fact, this task force advises and assists Kampuchean operations on the side of Pol Pot.[14] In July 1981, the following forces met in Peking to organize a Pan-Indochinese, anti-Vietnamese united front: Ieng Sary of the ousted Pol Pot regime; In Tam and Son Sann, former right-wing politicians in Kampuchea; Vang Pao, leader of the CIA-sponsored mercenaries among the Hmong people in Laos; Phoumi Nosavan, former right-wing Laotian premier and others.

China has been operating military training centres for various dissident groups from Kampuchea, Laos and Viet Nam. The United States backs them and is channelling $3–4 million a year to anti-communist groups stationed in Thailand.[15]

The US also appreciates the harassment value of Colonel Pham Van Lieu, whose home base is Sacramento, California. With the apparent agreement, if not encouragement, of the US government, Lieu, the former National Police Director for the Saigon regime, openly organizes, recruits and trains a small army of refugees to 'liberate Viet Nam from the communists'. Thousands attend his well-financed public rallies to hear reports of how their 'National United Front for the Liberation of Viet Nam' is supposedly progressing inside Viet Nam.[16]

The Spectre of Viet Nam

During the US-Viet Nam war, a vast gap opened between ideologists defending the US government and hundreds of thousands of anti-war critics. In recent years, various administrations have made a concerted effort to close this gap, so that the US could continue its quest to manage the world with as little internal opposition as possible. The spectre of Viet

Nam will haunt US policy makers until the American public can be made to believe all the wrong lessons.

The required systematic miseducation begins in public school. Consider the pathetic irony of all those people who marched, petitioned and demonstrated against the war in Viet Nam having their children read in school textbooks that 'their country came to the defence of democratic South Viet Nam.'[17] Media in the US rarely mention Viet Nam, except to bemoan the fate of the Amer-Asian children, boat people, MIAs (Missing in Action), political prisoners inside Viet Nam or GIs allegedly tortured while they were POWs. Some people who opposed the Viet Nam war on humanitarian grounds have joined the chorus of Viet Nam's critics. This campaign reached its peak when Joan Baez and others made headlines condemning alleged repression in Viet Nam. When their facts were proved wrong and their sources tainted, when supposed prisoners were found working freely and the dead came back to life, there were no headlines or retractions.[18]

More recently, for example, the liberal *New York Review of Books* published a bitterly critical article called 'The Myth of Liberation' by Truong Nhu Tang, former Minister of Justice of the PRG. In an introduction, the editors insist that Tang is a 'man beyond the charge of CIA complicity'. They did not mention that Tang visited the US for meetings with the State Department and Senate Armed Services Committee, hoping to get support for his anti-communist efforts.[19] A few feminist critics of Viet Nam who mistakenly assert that 'the marriage between women's liberation and national liberation during the war came to an abrupt end at the end of the war,'[20] inadvertently contribute to the cold war campaign against Viet Nam. Their analysis rarely includes much evidence or appreciation for history. (We shall return to this issue in Chapter 17.)

The movie industry contributes heavily to the effort to resanctify the image of the US. Even somewhat progressive movies like *Apocalypse Now* and *Coming Home* – those that expose some of the atrocities the US committed in Viet Nam and note the toll the war took on American society – never portray the Vietnamese people as human, nor their cause of independence as just. It is impossible to find one believable Vietnamese character in US fiction. The most celebrated of the post-war era Viet Nam films is the most vicious attack on Vietnamese people. One reviewer wrote,

> *The Deerhunter*, a Hollywood smash, was designed to appease a sulking American bitterness called 'the new patriotism', to satiate the box office demand for gratuitous violence, to portray the Vietnamese as venal sub-humans and the Americans in Viet Nam as tragic heroes; and greeted by millions of Americans as a mighty purgative for everything they did in Viet Nam. Today, *The Deerhunter* is no longer a lie; it is policy and the policy is revenge . . . . The cover is outrage in the name of the boatpeople. The prize is the China card.[21]

As a result of this propaganda campaign, the huge majority of those who opposed US aggression in Viet Nam until April 1975 are now confused and mute in the face of continued aggression.

Pol Pot and the China Card

Nguyen Thi Cham is the President of the Women's Union of Thoi Son Co-operative in Tinh Bien District, An Giang Province, a few kilometres from the Kampuchean border. She is a sturdy peasant woman. When I met her, she wore an immaculately clean, pressed, white shirt, but her nails were permanently brown from years of labour in the soil. I did not have to ask her many questions. She spoke quickly, as she proudly detailed the role women played in her co-operative in 15 different battles with invading Pol Pot troops:

> People here have had their homes destroyed two times: first by US troops and then by Pol Pot's. We only had peace for five days after liberation from the US. Then the Pol Pot forces began to attack. We fought back and didn't see them again until 1 January 1978 . . . . We organized 400 women to fight back. We killed 29 of the enemy and took many of their weapons. Their rifles were made in China.
>
> During a battle on 18 April 1978, 30 women pulled a mortar up the mountain. We posted ourselves there to attack the Pol Pot troops. The battle lasted five days. We would not allow them to massacre us. Eighty other women dug trenches. We know the enemy burns all, destroys all. We have no choice but to defend our country or be killed. So our women have done tremendous work in combat. I could talk about it for days.[22]

Shortly after the first attacks in 1975, Pol Pot explained to an unsuspecting high-level representative of the Vietnamese government that the incidents happened because Khmer Rouge forces were 'ignorant of local geography'. The Vietnamese attempted to settle the mounting border tensions by negotiation. The Khmer Rouge abruptly adjourned the talks in May 1976. By the beginning of 1977, the Khmer Rouge frequently launched large-scale attacks. In April 1977, the Viet Nam People's Army launched a counter-attack, expelling Pol Pot's forces from Viet Nam. Viet Nam then proposed the resumption of negotiations. The Khmer Rouge rejected talks and the situation deteriorated.

By late 1977, tens of thousands of Pol Pot troops were invading Tay Ninh Province, just north of Ho Chi Minh City. In early 1978, they also invaded An Giang Province further to the west. On 18 April 1978, they massacred more than 2,000 people in Ba Chuc, An Giang Province, committing hair-raising atrocities, especially against women and children.[23] Some 350,000 people had to be evacuated from the areas bordering Kampuchea. These people lost their homes and their harvests. By the

Some of the 2000 massacred at Ba Chuc Commune, An Giang Province, by Pol Pot's troops. Many of the women were raped by the troops who also used poles.
Viet Nam News Agency

time the Vietnamese had ousted Pol Pot's forces from An Giang, more than 4,000 people had been killed.

Why was a negotiated solution between two supposedly friendly neighbours impossible? The answer is complex and involves an understanding of developments inside Kampuchea as well as outside. Pol Pot's Khmer Rouge troops waged a genocidal war against their own people, as well as against the Vietnamese people. This began with the forced evacuation of all Kampuchean cities on 17 April 1975, when even women who had just given birth, still on hospital operating tables, had to join a forced march to the countryside. Thousands died on that march. In the course of trying to 'purify' Kampuchea by ridding it of the corrupt influence of foreigners, intellectuals and other 'parasites', the Pol Pot regime caused the deaths of an estimated two to three million people.

'We Did Not Even Have the Right to Weep'
Pol Pot divided Kampuchean society into three categories: 1) 'old people' were that minority considered loyal to the Khmer Rouge because they were residents of the liberated zones prior to April 1975; 2) 'new people' were those living in Kampuchea's cities or in areas controlled by the US-sponsored Lon Nol regime; 'new people' were suspect, guilty of being foreign agents, corrupt and anti-communist until purified by work in slave labour camps; 3) the third category was 'enemies' – anyone who had served in Lon Nol's army or civil service or had worked for the US government or any foreign enterprise. They were summarily executed.

There was no concept of national reconciliation as in Viet Nam.

Conditions for all the people were so horrible that, as one Kampuchean said, 'We did not fear death (believing in reincarnation), we only feared being reborn in Kampuchea.'[24] Almost the entire population was herded into slave labour camps. 'Old people' could be leaders of work brigades and had some rights. But 'new people' had none. They worked 16 hours a day with no pay, only a bare subsistence ration. There was no school, no religion and no culture allowed that might challenge Pol Pot's authority.

Most of the millions who died succumbed to starvation, exhaustion or exposure. Summary execution was also routine for the most petty offences. Pol Pot's policy assumed that 'it was better to kill ten innocents than allow one enemy to live.' He maintained that the New Kampuchea needed only one or two million of its original eight million population.[25] Women stopped menstruating, their bodies ravaged by heavy labour and hunger. They were not allowed to choose their husbands. Marriages were arranged by the Khmer Rouge administration.

How was it possible for a leader of a national liberation struggle to commit such crimes against his own people? How did he come to power in the first place? William Shawcross, author of an award-winning book on Kampuchea, holds the US responsible: 'There are only two men responsible for the tragedy in Cambodia today: Mr Nixon and Doctor Kissinger. Lon Nol was nothing without them and the Khmer Rouge was nothing without Lon Nol.'[26] Pol Pot had hardly any popular base until the CIA installed Lon Nol in power in 1970. Lon Nol was hopelessly corrupt and incompetent, discredited by his dependence on the US. Ironically, before April 1975, Pol Pot also received decisive military aid from the Viet Nam People's Army.

There had been several tendencies within the Kampuchean revolutionary movement.[27] Pol Pot, representing a national chauvinist tendency, gained ascendancy over the others, using ruthless tactics. His fierce nationalism appealed to some of Kampuchea's educated people who saw their country as a nation shrinking in size, threatened with extinction. Peasants, who had suffered enormously under US carpet bombing – hundreds of thousands were killed and 3,389,000 were made refugees – were also attracted to Pol Pot's militarism. He promised to recover the glory of Kampuchea's past Angkor period by reconquering the Mekong Delta from Viet Nam. Finally, his promises held special appeal for the nation's teenagers.

Once he took over the government, Pol Pot retained control by skilfully manipulating traditional animosities among people of different regions, between peasants and city dwellers and between intellectuals and the uneducated. He also monopolized the distribution of food, all weapons and controlled all movement in and out of work-sites. In the face of growing discontent, he escalated arrests and executions. He counted on national hatred against Viet Nam to offset popular reaction to the ruin he had brought to millions. On a Radio Phnom Penh broadcast, he exhorted, 'So far we have attained our target: 30 Vietnamese killed for every fallen Kampuchean . . . . So we could sacrifice two million Kampucheans in order to exterminate the 50 million Vietnamese and we shall still be six million.'[28]

It is difficult to estimate the extent of China's control over Pol Pot. There is ample evidence that Pol Pot's ideology was strongly influenced by Mao Tse Tung in the early days and that Pol Pot was receiving enormous military, economic and political support from China after 1975. Shawcross noted the dependency: 'Phnom Penh was deserted. None of the apparatus of modern government existed. Every office was deserted . . . . There was no postal system, no currency, no telephone. The main link with the rest of the world was one biweekly flight to Peking.'[29]

Vietnamese Foreign Minister, Nguyen Co Thach, elaborated, 'How could Kampuchea with a population of less than 10 million dare to take on the battle-hardened Viet Nam with a population of over 50 million? . . . The Khmer Rouge are sure they have 800 million Chinese behind them.'[30]

While Pol Pot promised to reconquer Viet Nam, he also claimed that Viet Nam intended to annex Kampuchea and eliminate the Kampuchean race by Vietnamizing it. By defining Viet Nam as enemy number one, Pol Pot was also able to justify his massacres of the internal opposition, whom he labelled Vietnamese agents. Whatever Pol Pot's ultimate goal, his vulnerability made it possible for China to use him to wage a war against Viet Nam. The Vietnamese considered it a war by proxy. Viet Nam launched a decisive counter-attack in December 1978. The Viet Nam People's Army, combined with the Kampuchean forces opposed to Pol Pot, forced Pol Pot to flee Kampuchea by 7 January 1979. Weeks later, China invaded Viet Nam with some 600,000 troops to 'teach Viet Nam a lesson'. Years after, China is still supporting Pol Pot in an attempt to return to power in Kampuchea.

The Unimaginable Happened

'So the thing we could never have imagined, happened. China, who had been our close friend, became the main enemy of our people,' Le Thu, Director of Education of the Women's Union, remarked. She was trying to explain the current obstacles women face in their efforts to rebuild their country and expand their rights. She continued,

> There is a Vietnamese saying: 'Chinese people and Vietnamese people drink water from the same well, graze our buffalo in the same field, collect fire wood in the same forest.' So when the war started, people – especially those who were close neighbours with the Chinese – could not understand it . . . .
> Chinese troops killed and massacred our people. Their crimes were even more barbarous than the US. We defended ourselves and they were forced to withdraw soon, but they still continue their hostilities. They send spies.

They try to sow discontent among our people. They kill buffalo, pass counterfeit money to sabotage the economy. Periodically, they grab bits of our territory. They ambush peasants on their way to the fields and they mine the roads . . . . War could break out at any moment . . . . But it's better now than before because we are no longer surrounded on two fronts. Now we have a friendly government in Kampuchea, and China can only attack us from one side.[31]

China deliberately tried to cripple the economic infrastructure in the region occupied by its troops. In the six northern provinces, Chinese troops destroyed bridges, all factories, power plants, state farms, forestry reserves and mines. Some 1.5 million people had to be evacuated, while 85,000 hectares of rice fields were burned or abandoned. Most of the evacuees' homes were destroyed or damaged. The toll on the health and welfare of women and children was particularly high: 82% of the schools, 99.5% of the hospitals and health centres, and all the day-care centres were destroyed. Some 60% of the buffalo and oxen and 80% of the pigs were killed or looted.[32] When I visited the border city of Lang Son in 1981, nearly two years after it had been invaded, economic and social life in the city seemed to be struggling for rebirth in makeshift open-air market-places and schools. All public buildings appeared to have been levelled and still had to be rebuilt.

Not only the people of the six border provinces suffered when the

February 1979, evacuation of children and older people from border area after Chinese troops invaded   Viet Nam News Agency

Chinese troops invaded. A Canadian visiting Hanoi several months after the invasion observed trenches being dug all over the city. She wrote,

> Fresh mounds of earth all along the sidewalks show the seriousness with which people view the Chinese threat and the cost of preparation . . . . All those people digging up old air raid shelters could be building houses, filling in bomb craters left by the US or running factories . . . .[33]

When I visited Ha Son Binh, west of Hanoi in 1981, I found that 75% of the adult population were women. The men were mobilized to fight in case the Chinese made good their threat 'to teach Viet Nam a second lesson', and invade again. My hosts told me Ha Son Binh was no exception. Viet Nam remains on war alert and expects to be facing a threat from China for years to come. That war alert is an extremely costly one.

The Price They Pay

The legacy of a hundred years of colonialism and the wounds of war with the United States, then with Pol Pot and China, combined with severe flooding and mistakes in economic management, spell cruel economic hardship for the Vietnamese people. Not all these factors have equal weight, however. Nguyen Khac Vien calculated:

> It it had not been for the war with China, by now we would be self-sufficient in food . . . . The rice from the Mekong Delta could be enough for the people there and for the people of less fertile ares. But we have a transportation problem. There's a shortage of trucks and trains and with the threat of war, all transportation must be used for defence . . . . The fuel we use to keep one fighter plane in the air for one hour could feed a family for a year.[34]

So the Vietnamese standard of living remains abysmally low and acts as a strong brake on women's emancipation. Most labour is back breaking, with little aid from machinery. Vietnamese women have to work much too hard: this endangers their health, quite apart from depriving them of the leisure necessary to develop their potential. For example, the law guarantees sanitary facilities to women working at a silk-weaving factory I visited. But the lack of resources means that for the time being, they must use an outdoor stall containing a hole in the ground. Free childcare is the right of all mothers who work or study outside the home. But not all children in the existing centres can be nourished adequately because of food shortages. Toys, except for those made by the childcare workers and children themselves, are a rare luxury. Wome who were once illiterate now read. But their continuing education is limited by a severe paper shortage. The Women's Union publishes an excellent weekly magazine, but they have had to cut back on their circulation, not because of lack of interest but because paper is strictly rationed. These examples could be multiplied by every detail of living.

71

The problems we have been discussing in the last four chapters – feudal patriarchy, French colonialism, war with the US and continued hostilities – not only hinder women's progress. The misery they have created for women became the reason for the existence of a Vietnamese women's movement. They define the conditions and set the boundaries and priorities for all aspects of women's struggles in Viet Nam. When we attempt to evaluate or compare the progress Vietnamese women have made, it is important to remember these roots of women's oppression (and resistance), not only the ideal of women's liberation.

Notes

1. Le Anh Tu, 'Viet Nam: The Legacy of War' (Philadelphia: American Friends Service Committee, 1975).
2. Murry Hiebert, 'The Food Weapon: Can Viet Nam Be Broken?', *Indochina Issues* (Washington DC: Center for International Policy), No. 15, April 1981, pp. 1–2.
3. *Far Eastern Economic Review*, 17 July 1981, p. 7.
4. *Far Eastern Economic Review*, 24 July 1981, p. 6.
5. *Far Eastern Economic Review*, 17 July 1981, p. 7.
6. John Pilger, 'Only the Allies Are New', in *Aftermath*, by John Pilger and Anthony Barnett (London: New Statesman, 1982), pp. 91–2.
7. Archimedes Patti, *Why Viet Nam?* (Berkeley: University of California Press, 1980), pp. 381–2.
8. Interview with Du Hue Lien and Ly Kim Mai by author (Ho Chi Minh City, 13 September 1981).
9. Charles Benoit, 'Viet Nam's "Boatpeople" ', in David W. P. Elliott (ed.), *The Third Indochina Conflict* (Boulder, Colorado: Westview Press, 1981), p. 151; also Murry Hiebert, 'Viet Nam's Ethnic Chinese', *South East Asia Chronicle*, No. 68, December 1979, pp. 21–5.
10. Nguyen Co Thach, interview by author (Hanoi, 1 September 1981).
11. Kathleen Gough Aberle reports that as early as 1976, Vietnamese spokespeople were telling friends in private, 'We were weeping when Nixon visited China.' See her *Ten Times More Beautiful* (New York: Monthly Review Press, 1977), p. 244. For a history of Chinese betrayal of Viet Nam dating back to 1954, see Wilfred Burchett, *The China, Cambodia, Viet Nam Triangle* (London: Zed Press, 1981); and the Ministry of Foreign Relations of the Socialist Republic of Viet Nam, *The Truth About Viet Nam-China Relations Over the Last 30 Years* (Hanoi: 1979).
12. Quoted by John Spragens Jr, 'The Way It Was', *South East Asia Chronicle*, No. 76, December 1980, p. 7.
13. *Far Eastern Economic Review*, 26 June 1981, p. 10.
14. Pilger, op. cit., p. 95.
15. Nayan Chanda, 'Agree to Disagree', *Far Eastern Economic Review*, 24 July 1981, pp. 13–21; John Spragens Jr, 'Viet Nam's Fight to Rebuild', *Guardian*, 10 Feburary 1982, p. 24. Recently, Viet Nam obtained information from captured spies about the return of reactionaries from the US and their attempt to recruit dissidents inside Viet Nam to be sent to China for training; see

Thanh Tin, 'Vo Dai Ton and "Project Z" ', *Viet Nam Courier*, Vol. 18, No. 8, August 1982, pp. 8–11. For background, see Helen Chauncey and Lowell Finley, 'US Policy and the Crisis in Asia', *South East Asia Chronicle*, No. 68, December 1979, pp. 2–9.

16. Steve Talbot, 'Saigon USA' – Special report broadcast on Channel 9, KQED (San Francisco: KQED, 5 January 1983).

17. William Griffin, Robert Knowles and John Marciano, 'Viet Nam and the American Textbook', *Inochina Chronicle*, No. 48, April 1976, pp. 4–14; and for an analysis of the rewriting of history at a higher academic level, see Marilyn Young, 'Viet Nam Rewrite', *Bulletin of Concerned Asian Scholars*, Vol. 10, No. 4, 1978, pp. 78–80.

18. 'Blaming Viet Nam', *Indochina Newsletter* (Indochina Aid and Friendship Project, Boston), No. 8, December 1980–January 1981, p. 1. Also, for an exposure of some early cold war propaganda against Viet Nam, see Arlene Eisen, 'Cold War Against Viet Nam Builds', *Guardian*, 20 October 1976, p. 6.

19. Nayan Chanda, 'Ganging Up with the Exiles', *Far Eastern Economic Review*, 31 July 1981, pp. 11–12. For the original article, see Truong Nhu Tang, 'The Myth of Liberation', *New York Review of Books*, 21 October 1982, pp. 31f.

20. Christine White, 'Viet Nam and the Politics of Gender' (Mimeo: University of Sussex, 8 November 1981), p. 2.

21. John Pilger, 'Revenge on Viet Nam', *Viet Nam Newsletter*, No. 4, July–August 1979, p. 4.

22. Conversation by author with various veterans of the war with Pol Pot (Long Xuyen, An Giang Province, 6 September 1981).

23. The Foreign Ministry of Viet Nam, *Viet Nam Courier* and Viet Nam Press Agency have fully documented Pol Pot's atrocities in Viet Nam. The indictment has been corroborated by neutral sources. See, for example, William Shawcross, *Sideshow* (New York: Simon and Schuster, 1979), p. 391; and back issues of *Far Eastern Economic Review*.

24. Jacques Danois, *The Will To Live* (UNICEF, 1979). Other information on Kampuchea from author's own visit there in September 1981; and Chantou Boua, 'Women in Today's Cambodia', *New Left Review*, No. 131, January–February 1982, pp. 45–61.

25. François Ponchaud, *Year Zero* (Middlesex: Penguin, 1978), pp. 86 and 92.

26. Shawcross, op. cit., p. 391.

27. The following discussion is adapted from Ben Kiernan, 'Pol Pot and the Kampuchean Communist Movement', in Kiernan and Chantou Boua (eds), *Peasants and Politics in Kampuchea: 1942–1981* (London: Zed Press, 1982), pp. 227–317.

28. Broadcast, 10 May 1978, quoted by Kiernan, op. cit., p. 232.

29. Shawcross, op. cit., p. 369.

30. Burchett, op. cit., p. 149.

31. Interview with Le Thu by author (Hanoi, 29 August 1981).

32. Murry Hiebert, 'Waiting in Ruins for the Next Installment', *Far Eastern Economic Review*, 15 June 1979, p. 28; also, 'Remember these Crimes', *Viet Nam* (pictorial), No. 246, June 1979, p. 14; and 'Crimes of the Chinese Troops in Viet Nam', *Women of Viet Nam*, No. 3, 1979, p. 5.

33. Sara Rosner, 'Letter from a Friend in Viet Nam', *Viet Nam Newsletter*, No. 4, July–August 1979, p. 25.

34. Interview by author with Nguyen Khac Vien (Hanoi, 1 September 1981).

PART II:
Seeds of Women's Liberation

6. Liberation, Reunification and Socialist Commitments

> Some foreign friends have asked us: 'Now that the war has ended, will Vietnamese women keep their position in society or will they return to the home, leaving their places to men?' We can tell our friends that the building of a peaceful, independent, democratic, reunified, prosperous and strong Viet Nam will quickly take us women even further.
>
> *Editors,* Women of Viet Nam, *organ of the Women's Union, 1975*

Women's prospects for emancipation, even for survival, may largely depend on who has state power: that is, who controls a country's government and military apparatus. For Nguyen Thi Chau, a South Vietnamese woman who refused to denounce Ho Chi Minh when questioned by Thieu's police, the overthrow of the US-sponsored regime brought the end of torture and imprisonment.

She had been one of the 250,000 political prisoners in Thieu's jails.[1] Nearly half of those prisoners were women. Some had been arrested because they rejected the sexual advances of Thieu's soldiers. Some were arrested when they got caught in indiscriminate round-ups. Some were arrested because they campaigned for peace and because they supported the PRG. Hardly any of these women had trials and none had definite sentences. They lived in a police state. On 29 April 1975, the eve of the liberation of Saigon, the guards at Chi Hoa prison fled. Once free, Nguyen Thi Chau helped organize the new government and became the President of the People's Revolutionary Committee that governs 250,000 people in the 10th District of Ho Chi Minh City.

When the South was liberated, the changes in the lives of other women were not quite so dramatic as in the case of Nguyen Thi Chau. But peace, liberation and reunification have transformed the life of every Vietnamese woman. The following portraits are meant to illuminate the major proposition of this chapter: the commitment of the party and government of the Socialist Republic of Viet Nam to women is a condition that makes women's liberation possible in Viet Nam.

Portraits of Liberation

Dang Thi Ngoc is currently Vice-Director of a college in Ho Chi Minh City that trains childcare workers. Before the liberation of Saigon, she was a teacher. She taught French and civic education to third-grade students. As a member of the anti-Thieu underground, she had to be very careful. She seemed embarrassed as she explained to me: 'I was obliged to teach lies. I had to follow their programme of study. But every once in a while, I found ways to teach the truth. I had to be very subtle.'[2] Now she organizes the education of childcare workers who learn the most effective ways of teaching children to be 'new socialist women and men'.

For Mai, liberation transformed her family life, rather than her occupation. In her early forties, the mother of five children, Mai was still waiting for her husband, Nam, to be released from re-education camp.[3] It was 1979. Her husband, a former high-level intelligence operative for the CIA, had been in the camp since the spring of 1975. Mai complained that he had been kept in the camp too long. Their youngest child, born only a few months before liberation, did not know her father. The two older children had visited him regularly.

When Mai talked about life during the war, it was clear that she had lived well materially and could give her children everything they wanted. But the corruption and mercenary attitude that prevailed in Saigon society had destroyed her marriage and family life. Once a kind and considerate husband, Nam had spent more and more time making the rounds of the bars with his friends, drinking and picking up prostitutes. He took a second wife and increasingly neglected his first wife and children. 'By the time of liberation, I had lost all feeling for him, except as father of my children,' Mai admitted. But life in the camp has mellowed him and made him think for the first time about the kind of life he had been leading and what he had done to his family. He became more humble and wrote loving letters to his wife, thanking her for her loyalty and strength in raising the children alone.' At least the camp has taught him to love his family,' his sisters told Mai.

Some of the relatives felt sorry for the younger children who were growing up deprived of the toys, clothes, good food and fancy holidays the older ones once enjoyed. But the children do not seem to regret the changes. Although her father was in the re-education camp, the eldest daughter was chosen to be leader of the neighbourhood children's group. The other children enjoyed the various games and programmes provided for all the children in the community.

And in the countryside, before liberation, the ethnic minority peoples of the Central Highlands lived in misery, prisoners of beliefs that prevented the full use of their resources. For example, in the district of Tay Son, Phu Khanh Province, if a *cu lan*, a kind of squirrel, crossed the rice field, the villagers would abandon the field in panic, expecting the fury of *giang*, heaven, to descend on them. If they suspected a cow or pig of being haunted by a ghost, they immediately slaughtered it. Frequent offerings to heaven decimated the livestock. Whenever a villager died, the whole community would move elsewhere. Anyone suspected of harbouring *ma lai*, the man-eating ghost, was killed.

Since liberation, people there no longer live in caves. They have built roads and, for the first time, people are learning to read and write and they receive medical care. They are digging wells and latrines and beginning to set up agricultural co-operatives. The district town of Cung Son, which had been totally destroyed by bombs, has been rebuilt and is now a bustling centre with state-run shops, a hospital, factory and child-care centre.[4]

A Glimpse of Socialist Change

Tran Thi Ngoc Minh is the director of the Cua Long Handicraft Co-operative in Ho Chi Minh City. She supervises the work of more than 2,000 people at the co-op and nearly 2,000 more who work in their homes. She is an energetic woman, enthusiastic about her work, although her painted toe-nails, perfume, lipstick and plucked eyebrows set her apart from most veteran cadres. Co-operatives are important institutions in the Vietnamese economy – stepping stones to socialism. Director Minh told me, amidst much laughter, what co-operatization had meant to her:

> Before liberation my husband was a teacher and his income was the most important one. I was a housewife. I did some hat-weaving and other handicrafts on the side to supplement our income. But I earned very little and had to be dependent on my husband. I didn't get any appreciation for my work.
>
> Once, when I was in Ben Tre, I was very disturbed to see two orphans drown. Some merchant had given them a few pennies to throw away his garbage. As they were doing it, they fell in the river. The incident wouldn't leave my mind. Finally, I talked to the nuns who had cared for the orphans and proposed to them that we teach the children to support themselves by making handicrafts. They could sell them to foreign tourists. It would be a lot safer than scavenging near the river.
>
> Many people ordered things from the orphans' exhibition, but we were not allowed to sell them because we did not have the proper licence. I didn't want to sell to an intermediary, because he was demanding too much profit for himself. So I dropped my work in handicrafts.
>
> After liberation, at first I didn't even try to do handicrafts. I assumed that no foreigners would come any more and that the communists would think such work was frivolous. So I sold broken rice in the market. Then on 2 September 1975 (Viet Nam's independence day), I went to a handicraft exhibition and to my surprise, I saw things I had made on display. I was

pointing out my things, quite loudly, so the person in charge of the exhibition came over and said, 'Oh, these are yours. We've been looking for the person who made them. Why don't you do these things any more?' I said that I thought under socialism everyone was supposed to till the land and that there would be no use for handicrafts. He laughed and encouraged me to take up the craft again.

I invited some people from the exhibition to my house and they bought a lot of things I had made. I was so astonished, I forgot to get the address of the man in charge of the exhibition. After some months, I got a visit from the Minister of Foreign Trade. He found me in the market. He asked me if I would like to make hats for export. It began a new life for me. He ordered 20,000 on the stop. I stammered, 'I could only do 20 a day and that would be pushing it.' So he advised me to set up this co-operative and here I am.[5]

Nearly all the workers at the co-op are women, including 60 nuns. The rest of the women are former students, housewives and petty traders. Only 20 of them knew their craft before liberation. The co-op trained them and paid them for their work, even when its low quality made it unsaleable. The co-op not only provides these women with an income so they can be financially independent; it also earns important foreign exchange for the economy, without requiring the investment of scarce resources in machinery.

A workers' committee sets wages according to the quality of the product and the amount of labour time that is required to make it. The director earns only three times as much as the lowest-paid trainee. There is childcare and free complementary education for all workers. Minh herself is studying French and English, so she can be more effective in administering the export end of the business. The most pressing problem the co-op now faces is the scarcity of raw materials, so Minh plans to shift from producing quantity items to more artistic items in smaller quantities.

Once a year, the entire co-op membership meets to decide policy on production plans, costs, investments, salaries, how to spend the social welfare fund and other matters. They also elect a management board to make daily decisions and a control board to keep an eye on management. They have elected Minh to be director of the management board every year. The ongoing struggles to transform power relations throughout the society makes workers' control possible in this co-op.

When peace came to Viet Nam, women in the North also enjoyed the change. Socialist development had a chance to proceed without spending valuable resources on defence. Ta Thi Het is a leader of a production brigade at My Duc silk-weaving factory in Ha Son Binh Province, west of Hanoi. When I asked a group of women if there had been any changes in their lives since the liberation of the South, they all spoke at once. Then Ta Thi Het spoke, as the others nodded,

Many changes. Before 1975, we had war. Our factory was bombed many times. There were so many people hurt, it was difficult to make our production goals during the bombings. Now we don't have to be afraid of the bombs anymore. We can raise the quantity and quality of our production, so our income has improved. So have our work conditions. We always fulfil our production plan. Many of our families are reunited, although there are still many husbands away, gone to defend the Chinese border. [6]

Reunification: No Happier Spring

When Ho Chi Minh was alive, every year he sent New Year's greetings to people all over Viet Nam. In 1969, the year he died, his greeting was, 'Let us fight until the Americans quit and the puppets topple. Forward! Fighters and compatriots, North and South reunited, can it be a happier spring?' On 2 July 1976, Viet Nam was officially reunited on the level of state administration.

Reunification was the fulfilment of the aspirations of most of the Vietnamese people. A member of one of the US charitable organizations in Viet Nam who witnessed liberation commented: 'Even cynics were glad about reunification and were moved to tears when they saw Ho Chi Minh's poetry published in Saigon's newspapers.' [7] When Ho Chi Minh first organized the Indochinese Communist Party in 1930, he unified revolutionaries throughout Viet Nam. In 1954, the Geneva Accords recognized Viet Nam as one, sovereign, independent nation. It was the United States that attempted to divide Viet Nam permanently into two separate nations.

When Quang Tri, the northernmost province of South Viet Nam, was liberated in May 1972, the US plan to divide Viet Nam at the Ben Hai River (17th parallel) was destroyed. Since the day of Quang Tri's liberation, there has been a sign at the river: 'The North and South are kith and kin.'

We must take the slogan literally. Hundreds of thousands of people were forcibly separated when the US sabotaged the Geneva Accords. Towards the end of the war, even before the liberation of Saigon, newspapers in the South were crammed with advertisements by people searching for family members: 'Mrs Pham Thi Duong seeks news of two younger brothers, Giap and Vinh, who followed the revolution from the first day of the coup against the Japanese. They regrouped in 1954 in the North. No word since then.' Another woman from Quang Ngai, on the southern coast, asked for news of her husband, a Viet Minh soldier who went North in 1954. Her notice closed with, 'Our daughter was born eight months after his departure.' [8]

A popular song, heard at a Quang Ngai cafe, before the liberation of that city, also expressed the feelings of the people:

I Shall Go Visiting

When my land has peace, I shall go and never stop.
To Saigon, to the centre, to Hanoi, to the South.
I shall go in celebration and hope that I will forget
The story of this war.

When my land has peace, I shall go visiting.
I shall go visiting.
Villages turned into prairies. Go visiting.

The forests destroyed by fire;
When my people are no longer killing each other,
Everyone will go out into the street
To cry out with smiles . . .[9]

No doubt many of those who sang this song hoped to see relatives in the North. Others were simply refugees, who, when the war was over, were liberated from years of idleness and despair in the US-controlled camps. They loaded everything they owned on to bicycles or into shoulderpole baskets, crying happily to one another, 'We're going home.'[10]

When I first visited North Viet Nam in 1974, half the people present at most meetings appeared to be southerners. One of them was Tran Thanh Tuyen, a cadre for the Women's Union. She wrote to me in the spring of 1975,

> Then I went to the South, reunited with my mother, sister, brother, nieces and nephews. It was perhaps the greatest joy I have ever felt in my life. I felt that the 20-day visit was a short time after nearly 30 years of separation. But I believe that in some months I shall work there for ever beside my dear ones. So I am both happy and sad. Happy because in the long run I will return and work in my native land and sad because I'll be far away from old friends and comrades in the North . . . .

Tuyen has been working in Ho Chi Minh City since 1976. She is one of the thousands of cadres who worked in the North and went South after liberation. The Western press claimed that women like Tuyen were 'northern cadres invading and taking over the South'. But, in fact, they are southern activists going home.

Reunification: A Continuing Struggle
While family reunions gave new strength and support to thousands of individuals, especially single mothers, reunification at the state level also facilitated reconstruction, the initiation of socialist change in the South and the further development of socialism in the North. The Western press tends to exaggerate the conflicts between North and South in an attempt to maintain the myth that the US was defending democracy in the South

against northern invasion. In fact, the differences that exist are not so much a matter of simple geography. While the northern part of Viet Nam was being built as a socialist society, those living in the South, under neo-colonial control, were poisoned with the idea that democracy meant freedom to wear miniskirts and ride Honda motorcycles. These southerners were frightened and suspicious of a 'communist take-over'. The following is one anecdote that became a popular tale dramatizing people's fear and confusion: in one of the meetings called after liberation, a confused market woman was asked by some *bo doi* (liberation fighters) what she thought of liberation. She replied, 'Thank heavens for you *bo doi*. You came in time to save us from the communists. The communists were threatening to shell the city and kill all the people.'

The Women's Union held more than 2,000 teach-ins to try to alleviate the confusion and explain the significance of reunification. Systematic political education, not only in the form of teach-ins, but, more importantly, in the form of opportunities for new experiences, are essential to bridge the gaps between North and South. Sara Rosner, a Canadian teacher, described one problem arising from people's experience with opposing political systems:

> Those who lived under the former (Thieu) regime consider patronage the normal way of life. As regrouped southerners returned from the North, they assumed positions of authority in their home towns. Soon, relatives came to them for favours: to get a son out of a re-education camp or to protect a factory from 'socialist transformation'. When the new official refused, he or she would incur the wrath of all the relatives. I often heard people say, 'In the old days, one official could save 100 relatives. Now they can't even save one.' The same people who complain about corruption among revolutionary cadres curse their own relatives for not doing favours for them. We met one such cadre who had been finally forced by his constituents (almost all relatives) to resign because he would not use patronage to help them.[12]

On the other hand, sometimes it has been difficult for northern-educated cadres to respect and trust southerners. Their training has been somewhat inadequate and the temptation too great. Dr Duong Quynh Hoa, former Minister of Health of the PRG who is still a national official in Viet Nam, explained,

> It is easy to make no demands and be incorruptible when nobody has anything . . . but the Northern cadres saw that in Ho Chi Minh City almost every worker had a refrigerator and they asked, 'Are these supposed to be the exploited? No, these are the exploiters!' So a lot of cadres became suspicious and hostile – or corrupt. They didn't understand that exploitation included dependency . . . .[13]

Women in the North are also coming under the influence of certain southern styles. In comparing my visual impressions upon arrival in Hanoi in 1981 with my arrival in 1974, I saw the most dramatic difference in women's shoes. In 1974, flat plastic thongs or sandals were the only footwear visible on the streets of Hanoi. Seven years later, it seemed that most women, especially the younger women, preferred sandals with a higher heel or even platform. Changing shoe styles may reflect other changes in lifestyle, although it is difficult for a foreigner to understand more subtle changes in attitudes and relationships. Vietnamese friends have told me that after years of denial and self-sacrifice, northerners would greatly appreciate some of the consumer goods which the southerners once took for granted.

Nguyen Thi Binh, a southerner who was PRG Foreign Minister and is now Minister of Education living in Hanoi, drew a general picture of the respect women enjoy in the North and South:

> During the resistance against French colonialism and US imperialism women took part in great numbers. There were liberated zones and temporarily occupied zones. In the liberated zones, people had militant beliefs about the equality of women. But in occupied zones, especially the towns and cities, the consciousness of the people had been poisoned. Since liberation, we have had progress, but the level of consciousness of the people in the two zones is still not equal . . . . So education becomes very important. People will gradually recognize the truth through the reality of their living.[14]

The Women's Union is taking concrete measures to protect women even before a massive transformation of consciousness occurs. Despite great improvements in the North, beating and contempt for women is still a significant problem in the South. So, at a meeting of the State Council in 1981, Nguyen Thi Dinh, President of the Women's Union, proposed amendments to strengthen the Law on Marriage and the Family, to take into account the requirements of southern women. For example, the law prohibits polygamy, but an amendment was needed to provide stiffer penalties to improve enforcement of that provision. Women in the South are beginning to be able to take advantage of the rights that women in the North have been enjoying for years. These rights are, in part, the fruit of a commitment made by the Indochinese Communist Party generations ago.

Early Promises
In 1929, a woman named Minh Khai had to leave her home because her parents forbade her to go out at night. Her father worked on the railway and her mother was a petty trader. They feared their daughter would bring scandal to the family. Repression made it too risky for Minh Khai to explain to them that she spent her evenings doing political work, organizing people to challenge feudal patriarchy and French colonialism. She was a member of one of the revolutionary groups that, following the

leadership of Ho Chi Minh, united to form the Indochinese Communist Party (ICP) in 1930. The ICP set two basic goals: 1) to fight against French colonialism to win national independence; 2) to fight against feudalism to gain land for the peasants. The ICP incorporated the struggle for women's emancipation into its fight against feudalism and colonialism. Experience showed that women's emancipation was impossible under colonial rule and that patriarchy was a cornerstone of the feudal system which it wanted to destroy. Ho Chi Minh often reminded his listeners, 'Women make up half of society. If women are not liberated, then society is not free.'[15]

From its infancy, the Vietnamese revolutionary movement led by the ICP, with a handful of members, hungry and hunted by the French, was committed to women's liberation. The ICP pledged to struggle for equality between women and men in its 1930 founding programme, and so became the first organized national group in Viet Nam to take responsibility for abolishing women's oppression.

From its birth, the party attempted to represent the interests of all workers and peasants in Viet Nam. But its goal has been to recruit as members only those who have proved themselves committed to revolutionary principles and most willing to sacrifice their personal needs for the attainment of these principles. For more than 50 years they have provided leadership in Viet Nam's struggle for national liberation and the building of socialism.

Every six months or year, the party branch of each factory, co-op or other work-place must report its activities to the non-party people there. The non-party people voice their criticism. Also, when someone new is being considered for admission into the party, non-party people are consulted through secret ballots and private enquiries.

Minh Khai and other women affiliated with the ICP founded the Viet Nam Women's Union a few months after the formation of the party. It was the first national women's organization ever to exist in Viet Nam. Many of the leaders of the Women's Union were also members of the ICP. They enthusiastically accepted ICP policy and guidance. ICP policy assumed that women needed their own separate organization in order to concentrate their energy on the struggle for women's rights and to mobilize women for the national struggle. They aimed to include all working-class women in their organization and others who supported their goals.

A year after its founding meeting, ICP leaders formally stated that 'women are the most oppressed element of society', and that women's liberation would require a revolution.[16] In 1935, the party underlined its commitment to women's liberation by sending Minh Khai to represent the ICP at the congress of the Third International – a meeting of representatives of revolutionary organizations from many nations.

There, she gave a sharply-worded speech praising women's contribution to the revolution and also criticizing the ICP and other organizations for not recognizing the importance of women's emancipation:

The women heroes of China, the women workers of Japan and India, the women workers and peasants of Indochina are becoming a real force in the ranks of the Eastern colonies . . . . Dear comrades, I would like to say that work among women is not given proper attention not only in our country but also in many other communist parties. We may see how few women have expressed their view on the important problems discussed at this Congress . . . . What does this show? It proves that work among women workers, peasants, unemployed and housewives in the struggle for a united front has not been carried out correctly. As delegates of the Indochinese Communist Party, we will do our best to apply a new spirit so as to correct and develop our work.[17]

Three years later, in 1938, Nguyen Thi Kim Anh, a revolutionary theoretician and leader of the ICP, wrote a book which explained how feudalism and colonialism were responsible for women's misery. She criticized arranged marriages, polygamy and double standards, demonstrating the feudal origins of institutions that oppressed women. She interpreted Marx, Wollstonecraft and other Western theoreticians and applied them to Vietnamese reality. Her book elaborated official ICP policy on women.[18]

In 1945, the people who began their lives as revolutionaries in the 1920s proclaimed Viet Nam an independent state. The early ICP programme became the law of the Democratic Republic of Viet Nam in 1946. Article 21 of the DRV Constitution stated,

In the DRV, the woman is the equal of man in rights, from the political, economic, cultural, social and family points of view. For equal work, she is entitled to equal pay. The State guarantees women workers and functionaries the right to paid maternity leave before and after childbirth.

The State protects the rights of mother and children, and sees to the development of maternity clinics, creches and kindergartens.

After the defeat of the French in 1954, control over the full resources of the state made more effective implementation of this Constitution possible.

In 1967, the National Liberation Front elaborated its programme and introduced similar rights for women in the areas under its control in the South.[19] The Constitution of the reunified Socialist Republic of Viet Nam, adopted in 1980, maintains the principles of the 1946 document and adds,

The state and society are responsible for raising the political, cultural, scientific, technical and professional standards of women, and constantly improving their role in society . . . . The state and society ensure the development of maternity homes, creches, kindergartens, community dining halls and other social amenities to create favourable conditions for women to produce, work, study and rest . . . . Marriage is based on the principles of voluntariness, progressiveness, monogamy, and equality between husband and wife.

Other articles of the current Constitution give the Women's Union the right to submit draft laws to the National Assembly and give the President of the Women's Union the right to participate in meetings of the Council of Ministers (Viet Nam's cabinet).

Collective Mastery by Women and Men

Before detailing the specific commitments of the party and state to women, it is important to explain the power that all Vietnamese citizens have and their rights to influence and participate in the decision-making process. The foundation of the Vietnamese system of socialist democracy is what they call 'the right of collective mastery'. Citizen participation is not limited to casting a ballot every few years to vote for a candidate who can afford to manipulate public opinion by buying expensive television time. Rather, each citizen may take part in public life on a daily basis in her factory, co-op, local section of the Women's Union, youth organization or residential committee.

The right of collective mastery aims to guarantee all members of society political, economic, cultural and social power. The achievement of this right in practice requires constant struggle. The Vietnamese press frequently criticizes bureaucracy, feudal attitudes, profiteering, and other problems which may obstruct people's free exercise of their right to collective mastery. If women workers, peasants and other traditionally dominated groups are not perpetually on guard and mobilized, their rights are not guaranteed.

The right of collective mastery in the political field is built into the structure of the state where people elect and recall representatives at every level. Mass organizations, like the Women's Union, give their members a chance to propose laws, nominate candidates, stand for election to the National Assembly and other representative bodies. The passage of the 1980 Constitution itself was the result of people exercising their right to collective mastery.

In 1976, a drafting commission appointed by the National Assembly, began its work. By early 1978, cadres, state employees, and members of trade unions, the Women's Union, peasants' co-ops and youth organizations began discussing the draft. In all, some 20 million people participated in these discussions. They amended 138 of the original 147 articles and also added some new ones. Then the Drafting Commission and the party incorporated the ideas expressed in these discussions and wrote a new draft which the National Assembly passed.[20]

Collective mastery in the economic field means that no individual owns the nation's factories, fields, banks or natural resources and that the people manage the production and distribution of the nation's resouces. Management committees, elected by the workers of each establishment, make the daily decisions. No one can be humiliated by a boss or made to feel like a hired hand with no voice at work. The 1980 Constitution also gives the state responsibility for creating the material conditions necessary for all citizens to be able to exercise their fundamental rights. It makes no sense, for example, to guarantee equal rights for women and men, if the state and society do not relieve women of the burdens of childcare. In practice, the Women's Union and other organizations must mobilize frequently to defend these rights against 'old timers' and bureaucrats.

In the cultural field, collective mastery aims to make 'all cultural values the property of the people, and the people become the direct creator of all cultural values.' In practice, this means promoting a culture that encourages co-operation, selflessness, national pride, dignity and confidence in people, challenging pornography and all other forms of degrading culture.

Collective mastery of social relations includes promoting democracy within the family and within the community. The aim is to allow every individual to develop to her fullest potential; and for each person to become conscious and confident that she can make history – that what she does makes a difference to the society.

At the grass-roots level, people exercise their right to collective mastery through their local Women's Union branch or the branch of whatever organization they belong to. Trade unions in all factories, hospitals, offices and state farms organize to protect the rights of workers. Each trade union also has a women's commission that co-operates with the local Women's Union. The women's commissions have responsibility to give voice to women's grievances and wishes, to supervise the implementation of women' rights at the work-place – including childcare and health care. They also help provide opportunities for working women to study. Militant women's commissions struggle daily against patriarchal tendencies to undervalue women's work and neglect their rights.

People's inspection commissions – another institution in which people exercise their right to collective mastery – were organized in the late 1970s. They are local agencies, elected by the people, to control and supervise local organs of state power. Some 60% of those elected to these commissions in Hanoi are women. They have been successful in controlling bureaucratic abuses so that people in their neighbourhoods enjoy improved relations with various officials and a better standard of living. In one case, the commission responded to a complaint about someone's daughter who was arbitrarily denied admission to college. In another case, the commission won a change in shopping hours and electricity services.[21]

Women's Rights

More than 30 years ago, in a message of greetings for International Women's Day, 1952, Ho Chi Minh wrote,

> Many people think the problem of equality between the sexes is a simple one . . . . A serious mistake! What equality really means is a thorough-going difficult revolution, because contempt for women dates back thousands of years. It is deep-rooted in the thoughts and attitudes of everyone. It cannot be done away with by coercion . . . . If this large-scale revolution is to be successful, progress will have to be made in every field: political, economic, cultural and legal. This revolution must involve heart searching by each one of us and must involve the whole people. This is a big task and a difficult one, but our success is certain.[22]

Every party congress – the national meeting that sets the general tasks and goals for Viet Nam for the following period – has affirmed the party's commitment to women's liberation. At both the fourth congress in 1976 and the fifth congress in 1982, party Chairman, Le Duan, gave the most important political report. In 1976 he noted, 'The victory of the Vietnamese revolution has given women access to collective mastery of society. Equal to men in all respects, they have made extraordinary progress in material and intellectual life . . . .' And he recommended,

> Women must be educated in a high sense of collective mastery and a greater will for advancement. Feudal prejudices against women still in existence in society and even among a number of cadres and Party members must be eradicated. Women's cultural level, scientific knowledge, technical know-how and professional skills must be raised; more female cadres must be trained, women's participation in leadership and management must be strengthened and the female component of the work-force must be used more rationally. There must be close cooperation between the organs of state and mass organizations – chiefly the Women's Union – in stepping up the women's movement and in settling matters related to women's interests.[23]

His report in 1982 recommended essentially the same measures but suggested that they be accelerated:

> To continue to step up the cause of liberating women and achieving equality between men and women . . . . Party committees should ensure that the Party's viewpoint and policy regarding work among women are fully grasped in all organizations . . . It is necessary to struggle to eliminate feudal and bourgeois viewpoints in the evaluation of women's forces and capacities, the training and employment of women workers and cadres, and the resolution of concrete matters related to the life of women and children.[24]

Ho Chi Minh encouraged cadre training for women   Viet Nam News Agency

The Constitutional and legal guarantees to implement these policies have already been enacted. There is no public function closed to women – from the local people's councils to the Central Committee of the Viet Nam Communist Party. Women's right to work outside the home is also guaranteed and the Constitution of the SRV also guarantees that no worker – woman or man – will be exploited. A series of laws and Ministry of Labour Codes provide special protection for working women. (See Chapter 9.) Along with political power and economic independence, women have also won the abolition of polygamy and other patriarchal institutions. (See Chapter 11.) The Vietnamese government again affirmed its commitment to women's emancipation when the Council of State ratified the United Nations Convention on the elimination of all forms of discrimination against women. The UN passed the resolution in 1979, but the United States has yet to ratify it.

Theory and Practice
The Vietnamese understand that hundreds of years of sexism will not disappear with the signing of a law or decree. Policy commitments serve, rather, to point the direction for struggle. The former President of the Women's Union and member of the Central Committee of the party, Nguyen Thi Thap, underlined women's responsibility for that struggle:

> When we say the interests of women are bound to the class and national interests, obviously, this does not mean when the revoluton is successful,

and the working class seizes power and destroys the right of private property in production, then the problem of women's liberation will be immediately resolved.

In reality, after the revolution has been successful, women – especially women strongly influenced by feudalism – still have to struggle for true equality with men by raising their political level and knowledge, and taking part in production, the management of society and in the activities of every social sphere.[25]

Ho Chi Minh provided leadership in putting the party's commitment to women's emancipation into practice. In a typical visit to a training session for district-level party members, the first question he asked was, 'How many comrades are attending this class?'

'288, Uncle. Among these, 131 are district cadres,' someone replied.

Then Ho Chi Minh asked, 'How many of them are women?'

The reply: 'Sixteen, Uncle.'

The President looked displeased and insisted, 'This is a shortcoming. The comrades in charge have not paid enough attention to training women cadres. This applies to our Party as a whole. Many people still don't estimate the worth of women correctly, or are shackled by prejudices. They are wrong. At the present, many women are participating in leadership work at the grass roots level and they are doing their jobs well . . . . They are not only zealous, but also competent . . . they are less likely to embezzle and waste or to indulge in drinking and show arrogance than the men. Isn't that true? Speak up if you don't think what I am saying is correct.'

Ho Chi Minh did not let the matter rest after everyone nodded in agreement: 'So I hope that you'll set your biases right vis à vis women. As for the women, especially those who are district cadres, they must fight hard for their rights. Otherwise, those of the men who are prejudiced against women won't mend their ways.'[26]

More recently, at the fifth party congress in March 1982, the party launched a concerted campaign against an epidemic of bureaucracy that sabotages not only the advancement of women cadres, but also all opportunities for collective mastery. Le Duc Tho, one of the party's top leaders, gave a detailed report filled with plans for expelling corrupt and exhausted cadres, training and retraining others and

> eliminating the practice of granting Party membership only to 'yes men'. District and precinct Party committees and basic level committees must find outspoken people who have, out of their concern for the common good, dared to denounce shortcomings and to defend the truth.[27]

Viet Nam's literary weekly magazine also frequently features realistic stories exposing the details of how bureaucrats undermine people's morale, production and democracy.[28]

Nevertheless, the percentage of women assuming leadership roles has not improved recently. We shall discuss this problem in detail in Chapter 15. The problems of promoting women's leadership suggest that party and state commitment alone will not guarantee women's full emancipation. The role played by women to achieve their liberation, and particularly the strength of their organization, may prove to be decisive.

Notes

1. For details on women political prisoners under the Thieu regime see Chapter 7 of Arlene Eisen Bergman, *Women of Viet Nam* (San Francisco: People's Press, 1975).
2. Interview with Dang Thi Ngoc by author (Ho Chi Minh City, 11 September 1981).
3. This portrait of a family in 1979 comes from Sara Rosner, 'Those Who Stayed', *South East Asia Chronicle*, No. 76, December 1980, pp. 26–8.
4. Vu Hong, 'Changes in a Mountain District in Central Viet Nam', *Viet Nam Courier*, No. 5, 1981, p. 30.
5. Interview by author with Tran Thi Ngoc Minh at Cua Long Co-op (Ho Chi Minh City, 11 September 1981).
6. Meeting with author at My Duc Silk-weaving Factory (4 September 1981).
7. Earl Martin, *Reaching the Other Side* (New York: Crown, 1978), p. 267.
8. Quoted by Sophie and Paul Quinn-Judge, 'Viet Nam: Reunification and Reconciliation', *US/Indochina Report* (Indochina Resource Center, Washington DC), 30 April 1976, p. 11.
9. Martin, op. cit., p. 7.
10. Ibid., p. 128.
11. Ibid., p. 263.
12. Rosner, op. cit., p. 27.
13. Erich Wulff, interview with Dr Duong Quynh Hoa, 'Must We Make All the Old Mistakes Again?', *South East Asia Chronicle*, No. 76, December 1980, pp. 20–1.
14. Interview with Nguyen Thi Binh by author (Hanoi, 2 September 1981).
15. This quotation is repeated in nearly every document written about women published in Viet Nam.
16. Mai Thi Tu, 'The Vietnamese Women, Yesterday and Today', in *Vietnamese Woman* (Vietnamese Studies, No. 10; Hanoi: Foreign Languages Publishing House, 1966), pp. 30–1.
17. Minh Khai's speech is on display at the Museum of Revolutionary History in Hanoi.
18. Nguyen Thi Kim Anh's book was called *Van De Phu Nu* (The Woman Question). It has not been translated. Thanks to David Marr for providing a summary translation.
19. For details, see Arlene Eisen Bergman, *Women of Viet Nam* (San Francisco: People's Press, 1975), pp. 186–7.
20. The term 'collective mastery' is the official Vietnamese translation for *Lam Chu Tap The*, which might also be translated 'group control'. The term in

Vietnamese does not imply gender. This discussion of collective mastery is based on the following sources: 'The Main Content of the Socialist Republic of Viet Nam Constitution', *Viet Nam Courier*, No. 1, 1981, pp. 4ff; 'Outline of the Draft Political Report of the Central Committee of the Viet Nam Workers' Party', *Viet Nam Courier*, No. 55, December 1976, pp. 5ff; Le Duan, *On the Right to Collective Mastery* (Hanoi: Foreign Languages Publishing House, 1980).

21. Le Mai Anh, 'Hanoi: One Year of Peoples Inspection Activity in City Districts', *Viet Nam Courier*, No. 66, September 1977, pp. 3–5, 13.
22. Mai Thi Tu and Le Thi Nham Tuyet, *Women in Viet Nam* (Hanoi: Foreign Languages Publishing House, 1978), pp. 171–2.
23. Le Duan, 'Outline of the Draft of the Political Report of the Central Committee of the Viet Nam Workers Party', *Viet Nam Courier*, No. 55, December 1976, p. 20.
24. Le Duan, 'Political Report of the Central Committee of the Viet Nam Communist Party to the Fifth Party Congress', translated by FIBIS (Foreign Broadcast Information Service), US Department of Commerce, March 1982.
25. Nguyen Thi Thap, 'Women and the Revolution', *Viet Nam News and Reports*, No. 14, March 1973, Supplement on Women, p. 8.
26. 'President Ho Chi Minh and the Emancipation of Women', *Women of Viet Nam*, No. 3, 1969, pp. 22–3.
27. Quoted by John Spragens Jr, 'Vietnamese Fiction Tackles the Bureaucratic Plague', *Indochina Issues*, No. 26, June 1982, p. 4.
28. John Spragens Jr, for details of recent stories published in *Van Nghe*.

7. People's War Is Women's War

> The revolutionary potential of women constitutes one of the main forces of the revolution. Without the participation of masses of women in the revolution, the revolution will never succeed.
>
> *Indochinese Communist Party statement, 1930*

As producers, as organizers and as fighters, Vietnamese women have made decisive contributions to Viet Nam's independence and post-war reconstruction. And, as they contributed their harvests and fought in the ranks of the 'Long-Haired Army', they also began to free themselves from their traditional oppression as women. By proving themselves competent and indispensable to the success of people's war, they seriously undermined patriarchal myths that had kept women subordinate. This chapter traces women's achievements from the earliest battles against French colonialism to the most recent campaigns against famine.

Fighting a People's War

General Nguyen Thi Dinh, the woman who was Vice-Commander of the People's Liberation Armed Forces, recently disclosed that she had been arrested several times during the US occupation of Viet Nam. Once, sometime after 1965, when Thieu's soldiers arrested her without knowing her identity, many villagers – aware of her real identity – all went to jail, insisting that she was their relative. When they had convinced her captors of her loyalty to the Saigon regime, she was released.[1] This incident illustrates the fact that a small, poor country can defeat a large, technologically advanced country if it educates, mobilizes and arms the whole population to resist. For these reasons, the Vietnamese call their recent wars 'people's wars'.[2]

In 1951, Ho Chi Minh gave these instructions to Vietnamese soldiers fighting the French:

> We fight for the people. But we are not the 'saviors' of the people. We have the duty to serve the people. All soldiers must gain the trust, respect and

love of the people . . . . When you have not yet arrived, the people are waiting for you, when you arrive the people will help you, and when you leave, the people will regret your departure. To accomplish this, the army must assist and love the people. Each soldier must be a propagandist by his or her own deeds.[3]

The first section of this book, 'Roots of Women's Oppression', explains why women joined this people's war. Their reasons depended on when they joined, where they lived and their individual experiences. Some fought on after 1954 primarily to reunify the country so their families could be together again. Others were enraged by the rape of their sisters and saw that the only way to stop assaults on women was to get rid of the US troops and to convince the Saigon Army to lay down its arms. More joined to avenge the death of people they loved. Thousands joined local militia forces to defend their villages rather than be herded into concentration camps. When peasant women realized that bombs would fall on their homes, whether or not they were resisting, many decided to increase their chances of survival by joining the liberation struggle and learning to operate anti-aircraft weapons.

When Pol Pot's troops invaded An Giang Province in the spring of 1978, many women stayed to defend their homes, rather than follow the children and older people who were being evacuated. Truong Thi Lan, in charge of security for her commune, organized other women to stay and fight because 'We had seen our homes and families destroyed once by the US. Then we tasted the joys of peace and independence. We were not about to give that up so easily.'[4] A year later, when China invaded the six northern provinces of Viet Nam, thousands of women again mobilized to defend their families, homes and country.

Women as a Decisive Force
People's war is women's war because most women have been poor peasants and getting rid of feudal injustices, including patriarchy, has been a primary goal of people's war. The August Revolution of 1945 began to overthrow the feudal regime at the same time as it fought for independence from France. Whenever the people's army drove the French out of a region, they confiscated land owned by the French and redistributed it among the peasants.

Vietnamese revolutionaries knew that their struggle would be protracted because they needed many years to wear down the strength of an enemy who initially had so much more power. They needed strong bases of resistance to sustain the fighters over generations. These bases or 'liberated zones' were relatively free from feudal or colonial domination.

The liberated zone . . . is a place for the armed forces to reorganize, train and rest . . . . It is furthermore the starting point of attacks against the enemy's refuges. It not only satisfies the material requirements of the front, front, but is also the source of revolutionary enthusiasm for our armed forces and population . . .[5]

Because they continued to meet as many of the people's needs as possible, given the hard times and priorities of war, the liberation forces constantly grew. One woman who came from a very poor family in the South wanted to go to school, but could not afford the fees charged by Thieu's government. She joined the liberation forces because she knew that in liberated territory there were free schools that did not discriminate against women. Another woman joined to escape the burdens of a patriarchal household. She explained:

> I considered my serving the Front an escape from all the hardships I endured while I lived with my mother-in-law. She behaved very harshly towards me before I joined the Front. Joining was also an opportunity for me to care for people's welfare and happiness. That is what I liked most.[6]

People's war is also women's war because women's participation is essential for success. The concept that every citizen must become a soldier is a tried and tested tradition in Viet Nam's history of self-defence against invaders. It was first used to defeat the Mongol invasion in the 13th Century. During the people's wars of this century, again, there have been no civilians. A peaceful village one day may become a combat zone the next. The front has been everywhere and everyone was needed to contribute to the battle.

For example, an 88-year-old woman was enraged by the atrocities committed by US troops passing through her village. She insisted that NLF cadres teach her to trigger land mines. She waited six months for an opportunity to kill two US soldiers. Other GIs captured her, but she convinced them that 'she was just an innocent grandmother'. She became known as 'Heroine Eighty-Eight'.[7] Other older women smuggled rice and arms to younger women and men soldiers. Children delivered messages. Students demonstrated. Even Kien, with one leg cut off by torturers, worked in a liberation hospital.

Some liberated zones and all of the territory of northern Viet Nam may not have been subject to US ground invasion, but faced daily battle with invading bomber planes. General Vo Nguyen Giap described the 'ground against air war' as a new kind of people's war in which everyone fights the enemy's air and naval forces, works to ensure communication and transport, engages in production, that is, fights 'to defend the North, while serving the Front in the South'.[8]

The Women's Union launched the 'Three Responsibilities Movement' in the North in 1965 which specified women's indispensable role in this new kind of people's war. The Three Responsibilities were for production, the family and fighting, if necessary. In the course of this campaign, women learned new professions and took over important management roles in the economy.

The decisive victory that forced the US government to flee South Viet Nam is impressive evidence of the strength of people's war. Because of the strength of people's resistance, in 1979 some 600,000 Chinese troops were able to advance only 15 to 20 kilometres into Vietnamese territory and retreated after three weeks. Women were not only essential to these successes, they were also crucial in the war of independence against the French.

Early Battles of the Long-Haired Army
The work of persuading people to join the struggle, organizing protest demonstrations, planning rallies to raise people's spirits and persuading soldiers in the enemy army to desert – all this is called 'political struggle'. The Vietnamese called the movement that waged this political struggle the 'Long-Haired Army' because women took responsibility for most of its activity.

Beginning in 1930, the Women's Union organized hundreds of demonstrations and strikes to challenge the French colonial administration. Their demands reflected the needs of peasants and women who worked in French-owned factories: 'Reduce rents and interest rates! Equal rates for equal work! No dangerous work for women! Two months' fully paid maternity leave! Down with forced marriage! Down with polygamy! Abolish the habit of holding women in contempt!'[9]

During the political ferment of 1930–1, women strikers at a central rubber plantation felled trees to make road-blocks and disarmed local French soldiers. Women who had been raped by French Foreign Legionnaires blinded the rapists with a mixture of lime and ash. In spite of incredible material sacrifices, the workers at Nam Dinh textile mill – mostly women – struck for three weeks. In 1931, in the provinces of Nghe An and Ha Tinh, French repression incited peasants to arm themselves and forced local functionaries to flee. Peasant associations took over local administrative functions, creating an embryonic form of revolutionary government in a territory of 100,000 people.

For the first time in Vietnamese history, lands were distributed to women; women took part in public meetings and political education classes, gaining new control over their lives. The peasant administration, called the Nghe-Tinh Soviets, fell after several months of intensive bombing and shelling by French troops. Although they had power for only a short time, the Nghe-Tinh Soviets made a deep impression on Vietnamese women, moving large numbers of them to join the anti-French struggle.[10] The original Nghe-Tinh armed self-defence unit included 40 women out of a total of 120.

French repression forced the Women's Union to be a clandestine organization. Many activists escaped arrest thanks to peasant women who hid them in their homes. During French colonial occupation, women

Hanoi: 1938   Hanoi: Museum of Revolutionary History

cadres had to find discreet ways of organizing others. They formed mutual aid societies for funerals and weddings because such social gatherings were the only legal form of group activity. At these gatherings, union members would find the most active and energetic women and recruit them into the union. They met secretly, often in darkness, with their faces hidden, using aliases and leaving meetings one by one. This anonymity was an essential protection. If one member was arrested and tortured, she would have little information to reveal.

During the only time the French allowed the Women's Union to function legally, 1936–9, it organized rallies against Fascism and for women's rights. It led strikes and demonstrated for the abolition of arranged marriages and other institutions that held women in contempt. When the Popular Front government fell in France, the colonial system in Viet Nam resumed its repression.

Between 1940 and 1945, the ICP prepared to take political power from the French. It formed the Viet Minh, a coalition of many organizations which united to expel the French and Japanese Fascists from Viet Nam. The Women's Union organized the Women's Association for National Salvation which joined the Viet Minh. The Association mobilized women to demonstrate against high taxes, against the Japanese confiscation of the rice crop and against the press-ganging of Vietnamese men into the pro-Fascist army. Beginning in 1943, French and Japanese Fascists confiscated rice and ordered peasants to plant jute instead. As a result, within the following two years, two million Vietnamese people died of starvation.[11] Women, faced with starvation, picked up sticks and pitchforks to defend themselves. Ha Thi Que, former Women's Union President, described how they organized to recover their rice:

> We organized teams for demonstrations . . . . We came at different times from different directions, so the enemy would not know how strong we were. We made them confused and worried about where all the women were coming from. We set up committees to take the rice away, some to stop the Japanese soldiers, some demonstrated in front of city hall, some cared for those who might be wounded. [12]

Although the Women's Association for National Salvation was illegal, the famine and other French and Japanese atrocities convinced more and more women that their only means of survival was to join the revolutionary movement. Some formed collectives to purchase and transport weapons. They opened inns and restaurants to finance the movement. They served as liaison, protected other revolutionaries, agitated among enemy soldiers and served as spies.

While only a minority of soldiers were women, women's status was not diminished by their concentration on political struggle: in people's war, political struggle has priority. The first unit of the Vietnamese People's Army, formed in December 1944, was called the 'Armed Propaganda Brigade for the Liberation of Viet Nam'. President Ho Chi Minh pointed out the significance of the name: 'The unit showed by its name that greater importance should be attached to the political than to the military side.' [13] Later, General Vo Nguyen Giap explained why political struggle is so important. First, he wrote,

> . . . only by proceeding from solid political organization was it possible to build up solid para-military organizations and to advance towards creation of small guerrilla units closely linked with the revolutionary masses and thereby capable of operating and developing. [And secondly] . . . Political struggle plays a very fundamental role because it is in the political field that lies our fundamental superiority and the enemy's fundamental weakness. [14]

Even former Secretary of State Henry Kissinger grudgingly made the same analysis of the sources of NLF strength. [15] In practice, no matter how strategic a contested area might be militarily, the Liberation Army would not initiate a battle unless it was clear that the people in that area had been involved in a political struggle and would welcome the liberation forces. As we have seen, women played a decisive role in this work.

Three women also joined the original 34 soldiers who formed the Armed Propaganda Brigade for the Liberation of Viet Nam. Then, in 1945, Ha Thi Que organized the first all-woman guerrilla unit. In the following years, some one million women took up arms against the French. Vo Thi Sau was one. She came from a poor peasant family and joined a guerrilla unit when she was only 14. She did spy work and managed to kill 13 French soldiers with one well-placed grenade. Later, she tried to assassinate a notorious French agent but was caught. Despite torture and bribery, she refused to give the French any information. She became the youngest woman to be executed by the French. Thousands of women vowed to avenge her death and aided in the final defeat of the French at Dien Bien Phu in 1954. The French had assumed that Dien Bien Phu was invincible largely because it was a fortress located in a very inaccessible mountain region. Thousands of *dan cong* – people silently carrying supplies on their shoulders by night on a labyrinth of invisible roads – made the siege of Dien Bien Phu possible. Some two-thirds of the *dan cong* were women.[16]

Spreading the Movement Like a Drop of Oil

Bue Thi Me, former Vice-Minister of Health of the PRG and Vice-President of the Union of Women for the Liberation of South Viet Nam, is a veteran of the Long-Haired Army's battles against both the French and the US. She explained how they incorporated women into the movement in the days when possession of a leaflet could doom a woman to arrest and torture:

> We extended our organization like a drop of oil. Little by little. One of us would speak to three others. Each of the three would speak to three more. Before we spoke to anyone, we would study her history, beliefs and feelings – to prevent infiltration. In people's war, it is the people who must make the propaganda.[17]

Revolutionary activists gained the trust of the rest of the people by practising the 'Three Togethers': living with the people, working with the people and eating with the people. Tuyen, a Women's Union cadre, explained how she learned the 'Three Togethers'. She had left home when she was 16 to work in the liberated zone. Her mother had been a shopkeeper near Saigon. Tuyen expected everything in the liberated zone to be perfect according to the revolutionary theory she had read as a student. During the first few months she lived, worked and ate with the people in the countryside, but she often became impatient and angry with people who did not live up to her ideals. She did not trust them and probably they resented her contempt. During the weekly meetings she had with other cadres, they tried to summarize what they had accomplished and to decide on their next tasks. Tuyen's comrades often criticized her methods of work as 'bourgeois idealism'. Tuyen recalled,

> I had a hot temper. They tried to explain to me that no one was perfect. That the revolution would take a while. They were very friendly and gentle. Not heavy-handed. They made clear that they respected me and urged me to be gentle in my criticism of others the way they had been with me.[18]

Another experienced activist explained the advantages of practising the 'Three Togethers'. Hoang Thi Me, now in her early seventies, was a leader in the women's movements against both the French and the US. She reminisced:

> We worked with women in the fields. As we planted, we talked about the issues. The women wanted to be active and were very militant because we were struggling for women's rights . . . . We would make propaganda a long time in advance of demonstrations. But we wouldn't pass the word about the actual time and place of the demonstration until the day before, so the police could not find out. We would pass the word quickly as we met friends on the way home from the fields or market.[19]

The Women's Union often played a key role in such struggles. Over the years, they developed a step-by-step process to organize women's energy and increase their unity. Le Thi Xuyen, a Vice-President of the Women's Union, described five steps, which are often taken simultaneously: 1) study the situation and problems to learn as much as possible about the women involved; 2) make propaganda that explains to women the cause of their problems, gives them confidence in their power when they are united, and a vision of their potential good life. If they are confused about who their worst enemy is, ask them, 'who is most powerful?' If they lack confidence, explain how women in socialist countries have made progress and describe the victories of workers and peasants from our own and other people's history. These explanations are also part of a step-by-step process. 'We do not try to do everything at once,' Xuyen emphasized; 3) organize concrete struggles that focus on gaining a crucial demand. This, in itself, is another slow process that begins with people's consciousness of their own interests but raises a consciousness that demands a larger political solution; 4) choose new cadres from among the most active and militant in the struggle and give them further political education; 5) involve more women in the organization and in the struggle. 'We learn to talk differently to women coming from different social strata: peasants, workers and students.'[20]

Demonstrations Against US Invasion
A huge student demonstration in 1950 protested against the arrival of a US ship in Saigon harbour. This demonstration was the first to recognize US responsibility and support for French colonialism and was a significant show of force against both the US and France. Nguyen Thi Binh, who later became Foreign Minister of the PRG and is currently Minister of Education in Viet Nam, was an active participant in this demonstration.

Ten years later, in Mo Cay, a district of Ben Tre Province, South Viet Nam, during a popular uprising on 17 January 1960, the people seized power from Diem's tyrannical officials. All the insurgents were women and their leader was Nguyen Thi Dinh. The uprising, known as the 'Ben

Postage stamp issued by DRV commemorating Ben Tre uprising, led by General Nguyen Thi Dinh

Tre Uprising', gave the signal for a general uprising throughout southern Viet Nam.

The Diem regime – created by the US – could only prevent reunification of Viet Nam by fiercely repressing the people. By 1960, the people had had enough. From a group of ten women in Mo Cay, thousands of women in the Mekong Delta arose to take part in the insurrections. Uprisings spread from village to village, district to district, province to province. On 20 December 1960, Nguyen Thi Dinh joined with other leaders to form a new political organization to lead the struggle for national liberation: the National Liberation Front of South Viet Nam (NLF). The People's Liberation Armed Forces (PLAF) became the regular fighting army under the leadership of the NLF. Madame Dinh received the rank of general and became Deputy Commander in Chief of the PLAF. (Since 1980, she has been the President of the Women's Union. Her appointment to the Women's Union indicates the importance and high status of that organization.) As Diem's outposts collapsed, US troops were rushed to the rescue. President John F. Kennedy launched his 'special war' in Viet Nam. Women escalated their struggle.

They co-ordinated political demonstrations with military activity to help divert enemy troops away from guerrilla placements. For example, while local guerrillas were in the process of taking over a Saigon garrison, thousands of women demonstrated outside the local governor's office. They demanded that their sons and husbands – many of whom had been forced to serve in the Saigon Army – be given higher pay and less dangerous jobs.

Le Thi Tien's description of how demonstrators stopped troop movements provides a dramatic example of the military skill of these women organizers:

> We in Ben Tre decided to calculate the exact space . . . to know how many people we needed to fill it up. Then we could organize the necessary number from the countryside. This had to be done carefully too, so the exact numbers would arrive from different directions to be in town at 5.00 a.m. Every square yard was occupied by our 'human sea' so the target town would be paralyzed by dawn. In this way, it was impossible to arrest us, because the troops and the police could not move; nothing could move except us. We organized demonstrations of 20,000 – almost all women.
>
> If the authorities were able to call out the troops and they threatened to open fire, we had special spokeswomen . . . . (They would say) 'Sons, you could all be my children. My two lads are in your army. They look just like you. If you shoot at us, it will be just like shooting at your own mother or wife. Why have we come here? To stop people from getting killed. Maybe your mother is in a village being bombarded or your wife being raped by Diem's troops at this very moment.'[21]

Demonstrations like these required high morale, ongoing organization, and leadership capable of effective reaction to enemy counter-attacks. The Long-Haired Army was, in many respects, no different from the regular army. It needed efficient organization of the rear, including food supplies, attention to family affairs and childcare. Older women and men performed most of these tasks. Sometimes demonstrators would occupy an area for weeks. Each village kept a force for political struggle in full readiness.[22] They were prepared to launch a protest against the destruction of their crops by defoliants or enemy bulldozers at a moment's notice.[23]

Women also played a key role in undermining the fighting morale of the Saigon troops and encouraging them to desert. Most ARVN soldiers were conscripted against their will, and resented their officers and US advisers who treated them with contempt and brutality. Some demonstrations – expected to be pro-Vietcong – surprised Saigon troops by displaying banners demanding higher salaries for ARVN soldiers. Once, when a district chief questioned the demonstrators as to why they thought the salaries were too low, the women replied, 'Everyone knows that during raids on villages, the soldiers steal chickens, rice and even cooked fish. This shows they don't have enough to eat, so we're asking for a salary increase for them.'[24]

During the US occupation of Viet Nam, the political struggle never really stopped. Women took advantage of every opportunity, even chance meetings, to undermine the morale of Saigon soldiers. They often turned market-places into political forums. For example, in one village, they secretly organized a number of women to pose as traders who had come to sell their possessions before Saigon troops plundered them. Others who had, in fact, already been plundered would join in these denunciation markets. Anger became contagious.

In the Cities
Immediately after Thieu staged his own one-man presidential election in 1971, students set fire to the US library in Saigon. Leaflets signed by the 'Movement to Drive Out the American Aggressors', told people that a young woman named Vo Thi Bach Tuyet was President of the movement. In the coming weeks, the same group launched a systematic campaign to 'make life dangerous for GIs on the Saigon streets'. Hundreds of jeeps and other vehicles went up in flames.

Also in the cities, women who were members of the PLAF served as secretaries and servants to top officers in Thieu's army. They relayed valuable information to the liberation forces and had the opportunity to plant explosives in the meetings rooms of top brass in Saigon. General Dinh pointed out how their upper-class lifestyle made Saigon officers vulnerable: 'They know we do this, but they have to hire servants.'

The banner reads, "US Imperialism out of Viet Nam"

Women who served GIs, doing laundry, shining their boots, selling them fruit or soft drinks, often worked for the PLAF. During the daytime, they routinely gained entrance to US bases and measured the exact location of targets to be shelled the coming night. The following day, they returned to the base to assess the results of the previous night's mortar attacks. When they found they had missed their target, they would repace the distances, all the while smiling meekly to passing GIs. The second night, the base would be shelled again according to the new measurements. Even General Dinh gained access to US bases disguised as a peasant woman.

In the tradition of Minh Khai, a founder of the Viet Nam Women's Union and a martyr in the struggle against French colonialism, women organized clandestine trade unions under the noses of the Saigon police. All trade unions, along with any public gatherings of non-family groups, were illegal in Saigon. Nevertheless, in 1970, more than 700,000 workers joined in a general strike demanding peace and higher wages. In another strike, some 700 workers of the Con O battery factory in Saigon, most of them women, struck for more than three months. The women provided an inspiring example for all workers in Saigon as they held out in the face of brutal beatings, arrests and threats of starvation.

While they were occupying their factory, other workers came to visit them with donations of food and money. After Mrs Trung Ba Hue, the General Secretary of the union, was brutally stripped and beaten, 18 other unions in Saigon launched a work stoppage to protest against the brutality at Con O. Even some deputies in the Saigon parliament declared their support for the strikers. The Women's Committee to Defend the

Right to Live, an organization opposed to US intervention, also pledged its full solidarity. In Janury 1972, they finally won the wage increases they had demanded and the reinstatement of 17 women who had been fired. [25]

A year later, at another factory, the Eternis Company, workers risked imprisonment to protest against abuses by the company's manager. His sexual harassment of women workers had become routine. The workers insisted that the Thieu regime take measures to protect women's dignity – a demand that could only embarrass the regime. [26]

The Paris Peace Agreements, signed on 27 January 1973, provided for a political end to the war. But both the US government and the Thieu regime never intended to abide by the agreements. By the autumn of 1974, thousands of people in the cities under Thieu's control risked their lives to demonstrate for Thieu's resignation. Buddhist nuns, the Women's Committee to Defend the Right to Live (which was initially organized in outrage at the rape of Vietnamese women) and the clandestine Women's Union spearheaded many of these mass demonstrations. They laid the political foundation for the decisive military victory in the spring of 1975.

Women in Arms Against the US
Women were full-time members and often leaders of the PLAF. Some 40% of the regimental commanders of the PLAF were women. There

105

were also regional guerrilla forces and local self-defence militia. The militia were not full-time soldiers; they fought when their area was attacked, pinned down local enemy forces and kept their posts permanently encircled. A higher percentage of women were in the local militia and regional guerrilla units than in the regular units of the PLAF. The local militia kept villages fortified with trenches, booby traps and spikes. These defences were essential in wearing down the morale of Saigon and US troops.[27]

The Vietnamese still retell stories of women who proved themselves in battle. They hope others will follow the example of women like Ta Thi Kieu. The National Liberation Front's publishing house, *Giai Phong*, printed an entire book (which they translated into English) about her life. The book emphasizes the tremendous odds she had to overcome as a woman in order to gain respect as a fighter. The night before her first attack on a Saigon army garrison, she told herself, 'I must succeed to show men they shouldn't make a mockery of women.'[28]

Some of the men in her unit protested against her participation in the battle because they feared a woman would not be strong enough to carry away the wounded. In the end, Ta Thi Kieu and another woman took the garrison alone. The men had mistimed their actions. When the two women entered the fort, Kieu boldly announced, 'The liberation forces are here!' The Saigon troops took her word for it and surrendered. Ta Thi Kieu, a mother of two children, is currently a major in the regular Viet Nam People's Army, with men and women under her command. She now defends the country against the threat of Chinese invasion.

Nearly all the women in the North were part of the militia and formed self-defence teams in factories, fields, schools and villages against the US air war. The Three Responsibilities Movement established defence as a primary task for women. They became experts with anti-aircraft weapons and took credit for downing hundreds of US aircraft. Women gunner units protected fishing hamlets by sinking US warships which had been shelling them. All women in the North received military training, including hand-to-hand combat.

Relatively few women, however, joined the Viet Nam People's Army (VPA) – the mobile, full-time soldiers who usually travel far from home. If the front is away from home, it has not been general policy to send women there. But few Vietnamese would suggest that women are incapable of becoming full-time members of the VPA. I asked a Vietnamese friend if the VPA discriminated against women and if women had a lower status than men because they rarely fought at the front. Her answer was proud:

> Every country must limit its full-time army because the army cannot be economically self-sufficient. Some people must stay at home to take care of production and the children. Besides, the militia is very important. We could not win the war without village defence. The entire country recog-

nizes the contribution of women in fulfilling the 'Three Responsibilities': production, defence and the family – not just defence. In any case, we do whatever the revolution requires without calculating personal gain.[29]

General Giap, former Minister of Defence, also underlined the importance of the militia: 'Local people's war, self defense militia and regional forces are the firmest and broadest basis of the whole armed struggle and all the people's armed forces.'[30]

Most of the women who are members of the VPA serve in highly skilled, often dangerous, jobs as bomb defusers, medics and liaison workers. These positions are highly respected, but also partially segregated along sex lines. Many women also serve as support troops and supply carriers. They became the heroes of songs and films which praised their 'feet of brass and shoulders of iron'. Members of these units are mostly young women without children.

Women with children, including grandmothers, won recognition for their contribution to the military effort in other ways. In 1974, when I travelled in Quang Binh Province, just north of the 17th parallel, people discussing military achievements invariably referred to Mother Suot. For years, she had defied blizzards of bombs and shells to ferry troops and ammunition across the river near her home. She became a martyr at the age of 60, when a bomb finally hit her ferry. Usually women of her age are active in the Association of Mothers of Fighters, a mass organization of women over 50. Their main task is to encourage the fighters, help disabled soldiers and the families of those who have died in battle.

This division of labour expresses the Vietnamese conviction that raising children is primarily women's responsibility. Many household chores and childcare are shared by society, and when men come home from the front, they are applauded for helping their wives. (See Chapter 10.) But Vietnamese women do not feel that their emancipation depends on the complete elimination of all sexual division of labour. They believe motherhood enhances their dignity. If they choose to fight or study instead of raising children, they have that opportunity. But they have not been drafted into the army.

The image of woman in North Viet Nam has been multi-dimensional. She is a respected mother and a fighter. The national poet of Viet Nam and a member of the Central Committee of the Viet Nam Communist Party, To Huu, wrote a poem about the Ha Tinh militia woman who captured a US pilot.

> The small guerrilla holds her gun at the ready,
> The burly American bends his head low,
> After all, a stout heart is better than a big belly.
> One need have no beard to become a hero.

Magazines and newspapers, especially those for women, carry endless stories of women in combat, giving women new confidence in their ability to take on new tasks and emancipate themselves. One woman who worked as a bomb defuser in the most heavily bombed province just north of the 17th parallel, summarized the experience of thousands of women in Viet Nam: 'We must try to perform things normally considered beyond our capability.'[31] And when women did perform things normally considered beyond their capability, myths to justify their exclusion from high-status jobs or leadership roles began to crumble.

Women's Contribution to Re-education

After the US was defeated, the Long-Haired Army mobilized to find antidotes for the political poison left by the American occupation. Nguyen Thi Phuong Dung, Vice-President of the Women's Union in Ho Chi Minh City, recalled the early days after liberation:

> In the first days after liberation, tens of thousands of women came to our office to learn about our activities. The first thing we did was talk about the policies of the new government . . . . Our biggest problem was cleaning up the town. Women were very eager to establish security and order . . . . Women also played the most effective role in getting rid of prostitution, pornography, delinquency and drugs.[32]

The Women's Union in the 4th District, for example, organized meetings that nearly 25,000 people attended to discuss the problems of the old regime and the changes that the new one should encourage. They explained the policies of reconciliation to the families of people who had been detained for re-education. They convinced worried mothers of sons who were drug addicts that they would be cared for and restored to health, not punished. At the same time, they helped to capture more than 100 pimps, a gang specializing in stealing motorbikes and a group of gold speculators.[33] The 4th District of Ho Chi Minh City is a poor waterfront district with more than 200,000 people crowded into three square kilometres. For decades, smugglers and gangsters had competed to control the waterfront. Thousands of women and children had struggled for survival as small traders at the wharf. The Women's Union took responsibility for encouraging these small traders to switch to production. It was a long and difficult struggle.

First, the Women's Union cadres held private discussions and public meetings with the women to find out what their preferences were. Most of the wealthier traders wanted to continue their businesses under state direction. The smaller pedlars preferred to work in factories or production teams. Others wanted to learn a trade before switching to production or agreeing to go to one of the New Economic Zones.

The first meeting at Xom Chieu market, which had 520 stands and many pedlars, faced serious challenges. Some people still loyal to the old regime tried to sabotage the Women's Union efforts with innuendo calculated to sow suspicion. They grumbled, 'Before liberation, underground revolutionary cadres urged small traders to struggle for the right to sell in the markets. Now, the same cadres are creating difficulties.'[34] Others threatened grenade attacks if the Women's Union persisted in their meetings with the market women. But the Women's Union cadres were not intimidated. As a result, 50 women joined teams that became a sewing co-operative.

In another ward, Women's Union cadres made their first contacts with the poorest women, trying to convince them that their lives would not improve if they stayed in the city. Those who agreed to resettle in New Economic Zones, and became relatively prosperous, would return to the ward for a visit and encourage others to follow their example. In the first few months of 1978, the Women's Union of the 4th District helped 7,218 families to leave for the New Economic Zones, 1,385 women to get jobs in state factories, 1,741 to join handicraft production teams and 712 to return to their native villages.

In the course of this work, Women's Union cadres learned that to be effective, they had to proceed from the interests of the women themselves and help them resolve whatever difficulties might arise from the transition process. For example, when the sewing co-op did not produce enough quality shirts to pay its members a living wage, the Women's Union arranged for the Trade Service to supply co-op workers with food and other necessities until they developed their skill enough to earn their own way. They also learned that they needed the co-operation of other members of the community. For example, Buddhist nuns lent the union a pagoda where the co-op could set up shop and also have enough room for a childcare centre.

The Women's Union in Ho Chi Minh City also publishes its own weekly newspaper. It puts more emphasis on healing the political wounds of war than does the national women's newspaper published in Hanoi. It has published many stories like 'The Road She Chose' which criticizes a revolutionary brother who is too impatient with his sister who was raised under imperialist influence. The story encourages patience, understanding and respect for those who do not yet understand revolutionary ways of life. A severe paper shortage forced the Women's Union to reduce the press run from 50,000 to 25,000 copies. To overcome this limitation, the union organizes newspaper-reading groups. Every weekend, in the evenings, groups of 15 to 20 women get together to listen to articles about a variety of subjects: concerning production, life problems, family affairs, children's education and other issues. After someone reads an article, everyone joins in the discussion. At first, it was difficult to convince women to come to the weekly sessions. Many were ashamed to admit that they were illiterate. But after the literacy campaign in Ho Chi Minh City was successfully completed, the meetings became more popular.

When there are sharp differences of opinion Women's Union cadres take special care to point out the differences between the lives of women workers and the life of the boss in the past. They point out the different opportunities available to the workers' children and the boss's children. They analyse the concept of exploitation and ask the women to calculate their hours and pay – specifically how they were exploited. There are thousands of these groups in Ho Chi Minh City and other cities in southern Viet Nam. The Women's Union also carries on its educational work by reading selected articles over loudspeakers in neighbourhoods and work centres.

Anh Tho, a leader of the Writers' Union who has lived in Ho Chi Minh City since 1975, gave me a detailed picture of how she struggled to persuade a friend of hers to trust the new government:

> My friend was a writer and a Christian. She had eight children and gave up her art in order to work as a hairdresser to support her children. She had a lot of problems under the Thieu regime. The *Cao Daists* burned down her shop and she sold her house to help publish her husband's book, not hers. [Anh Tho laughed] . . . We had been close friends before I regrouped north in 1954, but when she heard I was a 'high-ranking VC [Vietcong]', she refused to meet me again. When we finally met, she asked me if I believed in the soul. When I said 'no', she refused to see me again. I told her she had a right to her beliefs, but I would like to be her friend. She asked me, 'Don't communists want free love, with common husbands and wives?' I responded, 'If you want to know how communists live, come and spend a week at my house.' She came for ten days. When we offered her chicken, she said she heard that in the North, when you kill a chicken, you must make a report. She was surprised we ate chicken without making a report. The flowers on the table also surprised her. She thought we were only allowed to plant vegetables . . . .
>
> I helped her to move to a larger house and also to get a job in a knitting co-op. In the co-op, there are many wives of former officers in Thieu's army. They slander us a lot and do not take their work seriously. They only join the co-op as a pretext to stay in the city. But my friend is now progressive and explains the latest directives to the other women. She challenges their slanders and now they accuse her of being 'VC'. It took many months of struggle to change her mind, but now she says I am her best friend. I told her it is our duty to help people, not just because they may be friends. Now I am helping her to write her memoirs of life under the Thieu regime. They should be very interesting.[35]

New Battles for Heroes Without Beards

With the invasion of Pol Pot's troops from Kampuchea, stories about the heroism of women in defending Viet Nam again appeared in the Vietnamese press. Some of the new heroes were veterans of the war against the US. Ha Thi Sen, for example, worked as an NLF liaison for 12 years during US occupation. After that war, she became Vice-President of the Women's Union in Tan Hoi village, Dong Thap Province, near the Kampuchean border. She was also appointed chief of the militia unit and took responsibility for training both women and men to defend the village.

When Kampuchean troops attacked her village in November 1978, she led the militia while they covered the escape of the rest of the villagers. She commanded six battles against the Kampuchean invaders and is credited with saving her village from total destruction.[36]

At a meeting I attended of women veterans who had defended An Giang Province, also on the Kampuchean border, they explained how they continued harvesting their crops, even as they defended themselves against Pol Pot's invasion. Their willingness to stand and fight, to dig trenches, to take responsibility for supplies, and to protect the homes of those who had evacuated, limited the devastation intended by Pol Pot.

Women's Unions in each of the provinces invaded by Pol Pot's troops called emergency meetings to mobilize women to dig trenches and supply the fighters. They also launched political campaigns to denounce Pol Pot's atrocities and to encourage people to share food and clothing with evacuees and other victims of the invasion. As they helped in the defence of the border, they also encouraged more women to join co-operative movements to protect the harvests menaced by the invasion.[37]

Women also made essential contributions to the defence of the country

Vietnamese women capture Chinese troops who have invaded Viet Nam.
Viet Nam News Agency

111

against the Chinese invasion of 1979. In February 1979, Hoang Hong Chiem became the most celebrated example of women defending Viet Nam against Chinese troops. The Women's Union, in addition to publishing stories of her courage, has also produced a slide show that they present at meetings throughout Viet Nam, encouraging all women 'to work and fight like Chiem'.

Chiem worked at a consumers' co-operative in Po Hen, Quang Ninh Province, close to the Chinese border. On 17 February, the day the first Chinese troops invaded, she and her fellow workers were preparing to move the shop to an evacuation area when a heavy artillery barrage came from the Chinese side of the border. Her fiancé was one of 50 soldiers stationed at an outpost by the border itself. When she heard that 2,000 Chinese troops had surrounded the outpost, she ran there to help. First she brought more ammunition, then she replaced one of the dead soldiers defending the post. Her bravery inspired other soldiers there. Despite her wounds, she continued fighting. The Chinese finally overran the post when she ran out of ammunition. The Women's Union concluded that she was the last survivor and continued resisting even after the Chinese entered because she was found bound and beaten to death.[38]

Photographs of Vietnamese women militia members leading lines of Chinese POWs became commonplace after the Chinese invasion. The press was filled with stories of women snipers and commandos, defending their villages. Women belonging to national minorities in the region received special attention. More than 100 women were honoured with awards for their heroism in armed actions during the Chinese invasion.

Again, the Women's Union in Lang Son and the five other invaded provinces called special mobilizations to supply the men fighting at the front, care for the wounded and share food with evacuees and other homeless. They encouraged women to follow the example of those who 'sacrifice silently', not only those who fight. The silent sacrificers are those women who defy continuing intimidation by Chinese troops. Chinese threats are designed to press border residents to leave their land, so that the Chinese troops can move border markers and expand their territory. Doan Thi Ninh is one of many women praised for their vigilance. She succeeded in detecting five Chinese spies. Since she was unarmed, she invited them to dinner and then alerted the militia to arrest them.

Feeding a Nation
While defusing a bomb or arresting a spy is the more dramatic display of women's capabilities, women's responsibility for production, particularly agricultural production, has been a continuous contribution to Viet Nam's survival. Ha Thi Que, member of the Central Committee of the Viet Nam Communist Party and former President of the Women's Union, gave a speech to the 1976 Party Congress. In it she reminded her listeners of the importance of allowing women to develop their capabilities to the fullest extent:

112

Women make up 60% of the labor force in agriculture, light and food industries, trade, public health, culture and education and over 30% of the labor force in other branches . . . . To which degree the five year plan will be fulfilled largely depends on the level of awareness and abilities of women.[39]

The 1982 Women's Union congress reported women account for 45% of the nation's industrial output.

During the war against the US, there was a banner across the entrance of the Nam Dinh Textile Mill. It read, 'Every metre of cloth is a bullet against the enemy.' The women who worked at the mill understood that the nation depended on their work. When the mill became a favourite target of US bombers, the workers decided to suspend the day shift and try to make up the production at night. Other women had to evacuate their factories and continued working in caves and similarly camouflaged areas. Since rice fields could not be moved, peasant women dug trenches inside their homes, along the way to the fields and along the edges of the fields where they worked. They took rifles with them to the fields and learned to defuse modern US time and magnetic bombs. In the district of Vinh Linh, just north of the 17th parallel, women stubbornly continued work, at the same time as defusing the bombs which fell *every day* for eight years. When the men were at the front, women had to teach themselves to do the work men had traditionally done, especially ploughing. At first, the image of a woman behind a plough aroused disapproval. Some fathers even threatened to expel their daughters from their homes if they learned to plough. But women doing ploughing, harrowing, building dikes, doing masonry and carpentry and repairing farm implements were soon common sights in the countryside in the North. Thousands of short-term courses were organized to teach the women new skills.

After the US war, women's role in peacetime reconstruction, and during the shorter wars with Kampuchea and China, remained as important as it had been during the protracted war against the US. When I asked Women's Union cadres if, by 1981, women had gone back to their traditional roles, Le Thu responded,

Women still do the same work as during the war. There has been no change. We have peace, but we still must be ready for war at any time. The threat from China will not end soon. Actually, women's role in production has expanded because women who worked exclusively in the home as housewives before liberation are now working outside the home. In An Giang Province, for example, before liberation, only 20% of the women worked outside the home; now, 80% either work or study outside the home.[40]

The Vietnamese do not yet have the resources to keep precise, up-to-date figures on the percentage of women in various fields outside the state sector. The following percentages, then, give an approximate sense of women's importance in the economy, rather than a precise accounting.

113

John Spragens Jr.

Women bailing water out of flooded fields

Table 2
Women's Contribution to the Economy

Occupational area	Percentage of workers who are women
Agriculture	63
Crop cultivation	80
Livestock breeding	80
Technical work	45
Dike building	75
Research	45
Light industry	65
Communications and transport	32
Commerce	60
Construction	35
Handicrafts	85
Health care	65
Education	60
Heavy industry	25
Civil servants, cadre and state workers	45
Technicians	42

Source: Duong Hong Dat, 'Women in Agricultural Science and Technique', *Women of Viet Nam*, No. 1, 1981, pp. 11–13; Viet Nam Women's Union, *Women of Viet Nam: Statistical Data* (Hanoi: Viet Nam Women's Union, 1981); and this author's interviews in Viet Nam in 1981.

Both the fourth (1976) and fifth (1982) congresses of the Viet Nam Communist Party gave top priority to the tasks of reconstruction and building the economic base for socialist prosperity. With so much emphasis on the economy, women assume their roles with a new sense of importance and urgency. At the fifth national congress of the Viet Nam Women's Union in May 1982, delegates adopted a programme that made mobilizing women for improved production a primary task. National gatherings, the media and local meetings applaud the achievements of outstanding women workers in the hopes that they will serve as examples to others. Nguyen Thi Kim Nang, for example, received a special award for inventing a method for removing the rust from the factory's damaged supply of needles which had been buried under earth following a US bombing raid. Her invention and her later initiative in designing spare parts helped to maintain her factory's self-sufficiency.[41]

In 1981, the workers of Ho Chi Minh City who had made the most significant contributions to the economy were awarded at a congress of 'emulation fighters'. Fifty per cent of those receiving awards were women. One was Le Thi So. Her husband had been a soldier in Thieu's army, and she had been afraid of what might happen to her when her husband's army was defeated. Nevertheless, she became an outstanding weaver and was nominated 'emulation fighter' for her work for four successive years. Another woman, Doctor Nguyen Thi Ngoc Phuong, was awarded for her work in obstetrics. Her husband, also a doctor, stayed in France after Saigon was liberated and continued to pressure Phuong to join him. But rather than leave Viet Nam, she dedicated herself to her work and also became a Vice-President of the Women's Union in Ho Chi Minh City. Phuong and So's work not only contributes to society, but is also a source of their own independence and liberation as women.

As women work to maintain Viet Nam's security and reconstruct the war-wounded economy, they develop new capabilities and shatter old myths about women's inferiority. Pham Van Dong, Chairman of the Council of Ministers, told the opening session of the 1982 Women's Union congress,

> The process of struggle to contribute in all spheres of economic and social life should be women's process of continuous growth. Let every woman advance . . . and increase their capabilities. Therefore, it is necessary to concentrate on training many more women cadres, including economic management cadres, scientific and technical cadres, educational, health and cultural cadres . . . . With their contributions and maturity, our nation's women will be able to assume and discharge heavier responsibilities in leading organizations. This is the process of achieving equality between men and women in reality and in life.[42]

Thus women's participation in people's war and reconstruction has paved the way for women to assume greater leadership roles and gain respect and full emancipation.

Notes

1. Nguyen Thi Dinh told this story to Jane Fonda in an interview on 19 April 1974. This author read the transcript of that interview.
2. Much of the information in this chapter on people's war comes from the classic statement on the subject by General Vo Nguyen Giap, *The Military Art of People's War* (New York: Monthly Review Press, 1970).
3. Quoted by Tran Van Dinh, 'The Viet Nam People's Army', *Indochina Chronicle* (Washington DC), No. 31, 28 February 1974, p. 3.
4. Interview with Truong Thi Lan by author (Women's Union Office, Long Xuyen, An Giang Province, 6 September 1981).
5. Pham Cuong, 'In the Liberated Area', *South Viet Nam from NLF to PRG* (Vietnamese Studies, No. 23; Hanoi: Foreign Languages Publishing House, 1969), pp. 105–6.

6. Quoted by David Hunt, 'Organization for Revolution in Viet Nam', *Radical America*, Vol. 8, No. 2, January–April 1974, p. 140.
7. Story of Heroine 88 reported by Jane Barton, a medical worker from the US who worked in Viet Nam for two years, to author.
8. Vo Nguyen Giap, 'Revolutionary Armed Forces and the People's Army', *Viet Nam Courier*, No. 3, August 1972, p. 14.
9. Unpublished correspondence from Viet Nam Women's Union, Hanoi, 23 October 1973, to this author.
10. Information on the period 1930–1 from Tam Vu and Nguyen Khac Vien, *A Century of National Struggles* (Vietnamese Studies, No. 24; Hanoi: Foreign Languages Publishing House, 1970), pp. 98–101; and from unpublished correspondence by Viet Nam Women's Union to author.
11. For more information on the famine, see Tran Van Mai, 'Who Committed This Crime?', in Ngo Vinh Long, *Before the Revolution* (Cambridge: MIT Press, 1973), pp. 219–76; also, Arlene Eisen Bergman, *Women of Viet Nam* (San Francisco: Peoples Press, 1975), pp. 47–8.
12. 'History of the Vietnamese Women's Movement', *Viet Nam Report*, No. 9, April 1975, p. 9.
13. Ho Chi Minh, 'Instruction to Establish the Viet Nam Propaganda Unit for National Liberation', in Bernard Fall (ed.), *Ho Chi Minh on Revolution* (New York: Signet, 1968), p. 138.
14. Vu Can, 'The NLF and the Second Resistance in South Viet Nam', in *South Viet Nam from NLF to PRG* (Vietnamese Studies, No. 23; Hanoi: Foreign Languages Publishing House, 1969), p. 40.
15. For quote by Kissinger, see Tran Van Dinh, op. cit., p. 3.
16. Mai Thi Tu and Le Thi Nham Tuyet, *Women in Viet Nam* (Hanoi: Foreign Languages Publishing House, 1978), p. 163.
17. Interview by author with Bui Thi Me (Quang Tri Province, September 1974).
18. Interview by author with Tran Thanh Tuyen (Hanoi, September 1974).
19. Interview by author with Hoan Thi Me (Quang Tri Province, September 1974).
20. Interview by author with Le Thi Xuyen (Hanoi, September 1974).
21. Wilfred Burchett, *Inside Story of Guerrilla War* (New York: International Publishers, 1965), pp. 63–4.
22. Mai Thi Tu and Le Thi Nham Tuyet, op. cit., pp. 186–7; and Vu Can, op. cit., p. 43.
23. For a particularly dramatic account of women's courage in such demonstrations see Arlene Eisen Bergman, op. cit., p. 155.
24. Xuan Vu, 'Flames in the Night', *Vietnamese Women* (Vietnamese Studies, No. 10; Hanoi: Foreign Languages Publishing House, 1966), p. 74.
25. 'An Example of Courageous Struggle', *The Vietnamese Trade Unions*, No. 89, January–March 1972, pp. 27–9.
26. 'In the Cities', *South Viet Nam in Struggle*, No. 199, 21 May 1973, p. 3.
27. David Hunt, op. cit., p. 143. For more information on the woman who was Vice-Commander of the PLAF, General Nguyen Thi Dinh, see her memoirs: *No Other Road to Take*, translated by Mai V. Elliott (Ithaca, New York: Data Paper, No. 102; Southeast Asia Program, Cornell University, June 1976).
28. Phan Thi Nhu Bang, *Ta Thi Kieu* (South Viet Nam: Liberation Editions, 1966), p. 43.

29. Interview by author with Tranh Thanh Tuyen (Hanoi, September 1974).
30. Vo Nguyen Giap, *People's War Against US Aeronaval War* (Hanoi: Foreign Languages Publishing House, 1975), p. 146.
31. Duy Thuy, 'Opening the Road to the Front', *Women of Viet Nam*, Nos 3–4, 1971, p. 37.
32. Discussion by author with Nguyen Thi Phuong Dung (Ho Chi Minh City, 5 September 1981).
33. Mai Huong, 'The Re-education of Thugs and Hooligans', *Women of Viet Nam*, No. 3, 1976, pp. 14–16.
34. 'Motivating Small Traders to Switch to Production', *Women of Viet Nam*, No. 3, 1978, pp. 29–32.
35. From author's conversation with Anh Tho (Ho Chi Minh City, 13 September 1981).
36. Interview with Le Thu (Hanoi, 29 August 1981).
37. Le Thi Lac, 'The Tay Ninh Women Promote Production and Supply the Front', *Women of Viet Nam*, No. 3, 1978, pp. 7–8.
38. 'To Work and Fight Like Hoang Thi Hong Chiem', *Women of Viet Nam*, No. 2, 1979; and author's interview with Le Thu (29 August 1981).
39. Ha Thi Que, 'Speech to Fourth Party Congress', reprinted in special supplement to *Women of Viet Nam*, No. 4, 1976, p. 5.
40. Interview by author with Le Thu (29 August 1981).
41. 'Mrs Nang's Initiative', *Women of Viet Nam*, No. 3, 1978, pp. 14–15.
42. Pham Van Dong, 'Speech to 5th National Congress of Viet Nam's Union', *Nhan Dan*, 20 May 1982, translated by Tran Khan Tuyet.

8. The Viet Nam Women's Union

Since the war against the US, our rights have expanded. This is largely due to the efforts of our organization . . . . If the Women's Union sleeps, the emancipation of women will sleep.

Le Thu, Director of Education and Central Committee member of the Viet Nam Women's Union

I have tried to demonstrate that while national independence and socialist commitment constitute necessary conditions for women's liberation, the labour of women themselves in achieving national liberation and socialism gives birth to women's liberation. But that birth cannot be assured without the organization and political militancy of women. The Viet Nam Women's Union continues to be the indispensable midwife in the bringing to birth of women's liberation in Viet Nam.

From its founding in 1930, the Women's Union has performed a dual function: to mobilize women for the tasks which society needs them to perform and to defend and expand women's rights. Chapter 7 outlined the highlights in the Women's Union history of mobilizing women to defend and produce for the country. In effect, women's contributions to the struggle and the history of the Women's Union are inextricably tied. Without organization, the best intentions of the most talented individuals can yield only scattered results.

A Movement of Their Own

Early attempts to organize a strong women's union, capable of mobilizing and defending women, faced formidable obstacles. In 1930, the ideas of women's emancipation and women's importance to the struggle for national liberation were completely new. Most of the militants of that period refused to acknowledge women's capacities or to believe women were of any importance to the struggle. Unfortunately, after being victimized by patriarchy for centuries, women themselves were often too vulnerable to challenge those who held them in contempt. The Vietnamese women who have written extensively on the subject explain,

Almost all the illiterate peasant women were kept in a state of miserable underdevelopment and the first generation of women workers were still handicapped by their peasant origin. The small number of women intellectuals, civil servants and students lived isolated from the masses . . . . Women found it difficult to free themselves from the trammels of excessive modesty and resignation . . . . Women workers and peasants may have been . . . slower in joining the struggle, but they proved to be more resolute and tenacious in fighting for the revolution. The old society offered them nothing and its perpetuation held no attraction for them . . . . In the first political struggles of 1929 and 1930, none of the slogans concerned defense of women's rights . . . . The plenary session of the Indochinese Communist Party in October 1930, severely criticized these shortcomings.[1]

That same meeting of the newly formed Indochinese Communist party resolved that:

to rally the women of all social strata, women's organizations should be founded to unite them in the struggle for their own rights and for their complete emancipation . . . . At the same time, women must participate in the revolutionary struggles of all peasants and workers . . . for if they do not take part in these struggles, they can never emancipate themselves.[2]

They also agreed to support women's specific demands for paid maternity leave and equal pay for equal work.

In the following decades, the party affirmed its commitment to building a women's organization and training women cadres. In 1959, during a major policy speech, Le Duan, the national Secretary of the party, told a conference of women activists: '. . . *women should not merely take part in the general movement, but also build* a revolutionary movement of their own' (emphasis in the Vietnamese text).[3]

Le Thi Xuyen, a Vice-President of the Women's Union, recalled the early enthusiasm when the Women's Union was able to take advantage of national independence:

A dream, formerly unrealizable, was now coming true. With the revolution, we women lived, in fact, a new life. We had an organization of our own . . . . Taking part in that first meeting (in 1946, after independence) were delegates of working women, country women, intellectuals and other social strata, religious and social assistance organizations, the militia from Hanoi and other provinces. They debated their immediate tasks in their particular social conditions. Never did we feel closer to one another. Never had our collective spirit been so great.[4]

After independence, with the support of the party and the government, the Women's Union was able to increase its membership and raise the militancy of the women's movement to levels that would have been impossible under colonial repression. For example, women were able to gain a new sense of their own power in speak bitterness meetings where – without fear – they directly confronted their former oppressors. Shortly after the Geneva Accords were signed in 1954, about 15,000 peasants gathered in the village of Son Nam, 20 miles south of Hanoi, for a speak bitterness meeting. The Women's Union was one of the main organizers of the meeting.

They flew banners denouncing landlordism and several militia women stood guard as the charges against a landlord named Cac were read. They forced the landlord to stand in a shallow hole, so that he could not look down on his accusers. Then witnesses began to 'recount their sorrows'. One middle-aged woman whose husband had died from a beating inflicted by Cac, moved closer to Cac as she accused him. Her face was distorted with anger and pain as she testified:

> Once, when I was out collecting manure, you came and tried to violate me. I threw manure in your face, but you threatened me with your dagger and you took me. And once when I was coming home, you surprised me at the corner of a rice field and threatened to kill me with your dagger if I did not submit . . . . You killed my husband and then tried to force me to become your concubine.

A 19-year-old woman testified next. She had been sold to Cac by her starving mother 11 years before. As she spoke, she was trembling all over, but her voice was hard and clear:

> You beat me every day for six years [her accusing finger wagged an inch or two from his nose] . . . Once, early in the morning . . . you said I had not learned my lesson and you beat me with fire wood. Then you pulled off all my clothes, took a piece of burning wood from the fire and plunged it into my vagina . . . .

As Cac tried to deny this accusation, another woman got to her feet and pushed her way through the crowd to face the ex-landlord. She was dressed in rags, but she had lost her customary passivity and resignation:

> Cac! You're a savage! I sold my daughter to you when my family was dying of starvation. You beat her almost to death and once you violated me at dagger point . . . nothing but a savage. That's what you are. Now, thanks to the Lao Dong Party and the Women's Union, I can come here and denounce your wickedness . . . you're finished now.[5]

Meetings like these happened everywhere in the Democratic Republic of Viet Nam. At first, revolutionary cadres would organize them. Later, they became so popular villagers would initiate them on their own. About 1,500 of the most brutal landlords were sentenced to death during the land reform of the 1950s.[6] More often, landlords were given a chance to reform and those who refused were given prison sentences. The speak bitterness campaigns dramatized the possibilities and reality of the new self-determination for women and men. The denunciation itself marked the beginning of the battle to abolish all patriarchal power based on feudal exploitation.

Cadre-Training Schools

The Women's Union organized schools to train women to be leaders in liberated areas in the South as well as the North. Bui Thi Me, a former Minister in the PRG and Vice-President of the Union of Women for the Liberation of South Viet Nam, talked about how they overcame women's traditional passivity in such schools:

> When women stayed home all the time, they lost touch with society. Their isolation bred insecurity and, after a while, shyness and passivity seemed like women's 'natural qualities'. The ideology of feudalism became internalized in this way. We work to overcome this problem by struggling against feudalism. Men are also the victims of feudalism, so they join us in the struggle . . . . We also think it is important to struggle everyday with our shyness . . . . We use political courses to help overcome shyness. When the shy ones mingle with women who are confident, little by little they overcome their passivity.[7]

Today, there are two central cadre-training schools run by the Women's Union: one in Hanoi and one in Ho Chi Minh City. They conduct short-term courses for three months and longer-term courses which last two years. The women live and study together at the school, developing skills that will strengthen the women's movement. Each school has a childcare centre and infirmary to care for the students' children.

The curriculum includes: fundamental viewpoints on women's emancipation, the role and duty of the Women's Union in socialist revolution, the international situation, the current situation in Viet Nam, how to build a movement among women and the particular historic achievements of women. Other classes teach modern methods of cultivation, animal husbandry and economic management. Students also learn the laws and policies concerning women's and children's interests, and the psychology and physiology necessary to protect their health and implement family planning.

After each lecture, the women gather to discuss it. They compare what they have done in their villages with what they have studied in class, and learn by criticizing their past practice. Experienced political leaders take special care in training new cadres. They assume if a student has reservations when she leaves a class, she will not be effective later on. Leaders encourage everyone to voice her questions and criticisms. Debate continues until doubts are resolved.

Le Thi Xuyen, Women's Union Vice-President, explained some of the goals of cadre training:

> We try to teach them about the enemy – his weak and strong points. If they learned only about his strong points, they would lack confidence. We explain our programme and strategy for defeating the enemy. We try to foresee the difficulties in advance, while we stress our strong points . . . . In the end, the most important thing for a cadre to understand is that her main task is to develop the capacity of the population because cadres cannot do everything themselves . . . .[8]

In addition to the central training schools, thousands of women have taken advantage of local training courses at the district and province levels.

Current Strength of the Women's Union
Today's Viet Nam Women's Union is a direct descendant of the union founded in 1930. Depending on the level of repression and the demands of the struggle, it has taken various forms and names: Association for the Emancipation of Women, Association of Anti-Colonialist Women, Association of Women for National Salvation, Union of Women for the Liberation of South Viet Nam and Viet Nam Women's Union. Membership in the union is open to all women over 16 years old, to special interest groups and to women's sections within trade unions. Anyone in general agreement with the union's goals may join. Dues are nominal. Until the country was partitioned in 1954, there was one organization. By 1950, it had nearly three million members. After 1954, Diem repressed the union in the South. It re-formed in 1961 as the Union of Women for the Liberation of South Viet Nam, but was handicapped in its growth by its illegal status. By 1975, it probably had close to two million members. By 1975, the Women's Union in the North was at least five million strong.

Both unions were organized at every level: from the commune, district and province to national bodies. Except for workers who belong to trade unions, membership in the Women's Union is direct. Women who work in factories and offices belong to the Women's Union through the women's section of their trade union because they believe the most important rights of women must be defended where they work. In the countryside, where the overwhelming majority of women live and work, the Women's Union is the most important organization representing women.

On 10–12 June 1976, the Central Committees of the Women's Unions from North and South held a conference in Ho Chi Minh City. They decided to merge the two organizations: a move that reflected the new reality of a reunified Viet Nam. The new Central Committee of the organization – or leading national body – included all the representatives of the two pre-existing Central Committees. In May 1982, a national women's congress elected Nguyen Thi Dinh, the former President of the Union in the South, to be President and also elected a new Central Committee of 109 members. In May 1982, the Viet Nam Women's Union included 9,257,048 members; that figure includes the majority of women in the North and hundreds of thousands of new members from the South. Yet thousands of women in the South also choose not to join the union, remaining apathetic to women's liberation and the other goals of the Women's Union.

The national headquarters of the union is in Hanoi, with 200 permanently employed cadres who do political and administrative work, publish the national women's magazine and run the cadre-training schools. By 1982, some 5,000 women also worked full time as paid cadres for the Women's Union throughout the country. The Central Committee represents the leadership from each province, women from various social strata, national minorities and religions. The Central Committee directs the organization between congresses, but, because its members come from all over the country, it meets only twice a year. The Central Committee then elects a standing committee of 25 who assume the day-to-day responsibilities of leading the organization.

The national budget of the organization comes primarily from membership dues and sales of its publications. It is supplemented by a relatively small subsidy from the state. Branches of the union at the local level pay for their expenses out of membership dues and the proceeds of collective labour and other fund-raising activities.

The union represents women to the government and the government depends on the advice of the union to defend women's rights, to design new laws and serve as a watchdog to ensure the implementation of all policies to protect women. A number of leaders of the Women's Union are leaders of the Socialist Republic of Viet Nam as well. The Constitution gives the Women's Union the right and responsibility to propose new laws and have its President sit in on cabinet meetings. A Vietnamese diplomat commented on the political clout of the Women's Union: 'Some mass organizations have more influence on the National Assembly than others. For example, the Women's Union is very influential. The National Assembly spends months discussing its proposals.'[9]

Yet, in official documents by the government and party, the Women's Union is usually mentioned towards the end of a list of organizations, after trade unions, peasant organizations, youth organizations and the 'Fatherland Front', which is a coalition of all mass organizations in Viet Nam. I questioned Women's Union leaders about their strength compared to other organizations. Le Thu, Director of Education, responded:

> We do so much, but we have no one to advertise us outside Viet Nam. We work together with the trade unions, the youth organizations and the Fatherland Front and the National Planning Commission to expand

women's rights. Sometimes we have contradictions with them. But we struggle resolutely, not just to get a law on paper or to draft a constitution, but to implement it as well . . . . We also urge other organizations to have their meetings and publications discuss things like the need for men to share housework. I must say, many men have responded well to our campaigns . . . . But it is not good for us to praise our own importance. Ask others, men included, if it is possible to replace the Women's Union.[10]

Several of the top leaders of the Women's Union, including its President, are members of the Central Committee of the Viet Nam Communist Party. The Women's Union accepts the guidance of the party in setting general policy. For example, it is probably no accident that the fifth national Women's Union congress opened within two months of the fifth national party congress in 1982. But it would be wrong to assume that the Women's Union merely rubber-stamps party resolutions. Party guidelines to the Women's Union are very general, allowing enormous latitude in interpretation and implementation. For example, Le Duan's report to the fifth party congress gave this guideline to the Women's Union:

> The Viet Nam Women's Union must strive to educate and encourage women to bring into play their right to collective mastery, to make even greater contributions to the fatherland and to socialism and to carry on the struggle for the liberation of women and the molding of the new socialist woman. It must cater to the welfare and life of women, afford them conditions for the good performance of their productive tasks, social activities and raising children. It should coordinate with other organizations and propose policies and laws to the state to ensure women's rights and contribute to the implementation of these laws.[11]

It is up to the Women's Union to decide whether to push for stronger enforcement of the Marriage Law or how much emphasis to put on its political education work among women in interpreting a guideline such as 'cater to the welfare of women'.

After two visits to Viet Nam, as a guest of the Women's Union, it seems to me that while men are often in leadership roles in relation to women, Women's Union cadres are self-confident and rarely defer on matters of principle to men representing the party. For example, at one meeting where a male member of the Central Committee was present along with several national leaders of the Women's Union, the man told me, 'Women in Viet Nam are now completely liberated.' Several of the women quickly corrected him, maintaining that although they had made enormous progress towards their liberation, there was still a lot of work to be done and they had to maintain their vigilance to protect the gains they had already made.

Political Orientation of the Women's Union

However, most important in understanding the relationship between the party and the Women's Union is recognizing that they share the same goals and ideology. There is little political basis for challenge. Madame Nguyen Thi Binh, Minister of Education and Vice-President of the Women's Union, explained to me:

> My friends in the Women's Union agree that our first goal is to have peace and independence to ensure the happiness of all our people. Peace and independence are necessary conditions for rebuilding our country. This is the first aspiration of women because only with such conditions can we be free to educate our children and build a better life.[12]

The Women's Union, then, has always made mobilizing women for defence and production its priority. The legacy of continuous war – a crippled infant industry; ecology in ruins; millions killed, disabled and homeless – sets the conditions and priorities for women. For example, if the Women's Union succeeds in educating peasant women on how to raise more livestock in the village of My Duc, the people of that village will meet their minimum protein requirements. If not, they will be malnourished.

In the rare event of a disagreement between the party and the Women's Union, the arena for struggle would probably be private, within each organization. The conflict would be resolved according to the wishes of the majority, with lower levels of each organization deferring to higher ones from villages to the national level.

After defence and production, defending women's rights is the third task of the Women's Union. The Women's Union itself recognizes: 'Our weak point is that we mobilize members to do tasks for the country and not enough to defend our own interests.' When I asked how they planned to remedy this weakness, Le Thu responded:

> In the South, beating women and contempt for women are still a problem. In the latest meeting of the State Council, our President Nguyen Thi Dinh proposed that penalties be more severe for those who violate the Law on Marriage and the Family, to make the law a more useful tool in the South . . . .
>
> We also have to pay more attention to the needs of young mothers: to health and maternity clinics in the provinces . . . . We have to provide more books and scientific materials to teach women how to improve their capabilities . . . . We have to train cadres, especially at the lower level, to grasp the Constitution, so they understand when it is violated and are in a better position to fight for women's rights.[13]

Spokespeople for the Women's Union explicitly reject any suggestion that as long as women have special tasks, as long as childrearing is

CHÀO MỪNG ĐẠI HỘI PHỤ NỮ V.N LẦN THỨ 4

GIỎI VIỆC NƯỚC, ĐẢM VIỆC NHÀ
PHẤN ĐẤU THỰC HIỆN NAM NỮ BÌNH ĐẲNG

Ban Tuyên huấn Hội Phụ nữ Việt Nam và
Xưởng tranh cổ động Trung ương phát hành

In tại Nhà máy in Tiến Bộ

This poster greets the Fourth National Congress of Vietnamese Women and affirms women's capacity to excel in all areas

assumed to be 'women's responsibility', women's interests cannot be fully defended. When I pressed the issue, Lien, the interpreter, insisted, 'We are not like certain feminists in the West. We do not believe that all differences between men and women should be erased . . . . We are proud of our role in society and the family.'[14] Although Lien's statement was more rigid than characteristic statements by other Women's Union leaders, no one present at the meeting attempted to soften her position. This attitude may prevent the Women's Union from being more militant in challenging men's over-representation in leadership positions. We'll return to the problem in Chapter 15.

The fourth task the Women's Union assumes, after defending the country and mobilizing for production and women's rights, is to build and strengthen its own organization. Training cadres is the foundation for building a strong organization. In the South, the Women's Union still needs to recruit many more members to be fully representative of women there. The organization recognizes the need to improve its methods of work. It is self-critical of its tendency towards bureaucracy. The Women's Union aims to close the gap between national leadership and local members by recruiting more peasants and workers into the ranks of the national leadership. National leaders also spend a month each year in the countryside, practising the Three Togethers: living, eating and working with the peasants.

The Fifth National Women's Union Congress

The fifth national congress of the Viet Nam Women's Union, meeting in May 1982, was the first for the reunified Women's Union. More than 1,000 delegates arrived in Hanoi, representing women from all over the country. They included 450 Women's Union cadres, 205 factory workers and state employees, 103 peasants, 26 artisans and 16 members of the armed forces. There were 101 women from national minorities and 92 of all the delegates – roughly 10% – had a college education.[15] The purpose of the congress was to elect new leadership and decide Women's Union policies and programme for the coming period. It had been postponed, once in 1978 because severe flooding made it impossible for women from remote areas to travel to Hanoi and again in 1979, because of the overriding demands of the Chinese invasion.

In the months of preparation for the congress, discussions and elections of delegates stimulated and reawakened a strong consciousness of the particular needs of women. Nearly ten million women participated in provincial, town, district and work-place meetings. Every local branch made reports that were combined into district reports. District-level groups elected representatives to the first round of congresses at the provincial level. At each provincial congress, delegates struggled over the drafts of reports for the national congress, evaluating the growth and achievements of the women's movement, considering party guidelines and making recommendations for future work. They also discussed the report and recommendations submitted by the union's national Central Committee and made suggestions for changes.

The final programme adopted at the congress, after all these pre-paratory meetings, reflected the overriding concern of all Vietnamese to develop their economy, eliminate the dangers of starvation and build the base for socialism. The programme emphasized the need to mobilize women

> to step up agricultural production by making them understand that agricul-ture is now in the forefront . . . . In areas where cooperativization has been completed, the mobilization of women to increase production must be connected with the education and motivation of women to strengthen and perfect the productive relations. (By improving women's understanding of the reformed system of economic management that gives greater material incentives to produce beyond agreed upon quotas.) . . . .
>
> The Women's Union, together with the trade unions, should study the labor conditions and livelihood of women in order to promote, supervise and inspect the implementation of regulations and policies. The Women's Union should intensify its relations with women intellectuals and encourage them to develop their professional skills and make contributions to the cause of liberating women by organizing the study of issues related to women and children and popularizing scientific knowledge among women. Women's Union chapters throughout the country should launch a move-ment to combat theft of socialist property, corruption, conspiracies and the wasteful practice of competing in staging costly wedding and funeral cele-brations and Tet (Vietnamese New Year) anniversary banquets.[16]

The first three points of the programme, which will guide the organiza-tion's work until 1985, detail the ways in which women can work to make the economy viable. The Central Committee report to the congress suggested that the most effective way to motivate women to be produc-tive and abandon petty trade and desires 'to get rich quick' was to educate them so they understand the difference between labour and exploitation. They also aim to teach the advantages of joining co-operatives and how socialism makes the emancipation of women possible. 'We should help women realize that the existence of a private economy is conducive to women's low status in the family as well as in society.' The report noted that the union's education programme requires an understanding of the feelings and thoughts of union members. Based on this understanding, the union 'should devise well-prepared seminars and symposiums on specific issues', rather than 'tedious and formalistic classes'.[17]

The fifth point of the programme aims to strengthen the family planning movement, so that the birth rate will drop to 1.7% by 1985. The sixth point focuses more specifically on other women's issues: urging the improvement of health and childcare services, the building of new cul-tured families in which wives and husbands share household tasks more equally, strengthening the Law on Marriage and the Family and improv-ing reconciliation teams. The report noted,

> The Union must step up propaganda work to win support from the public for progressive actions and criticize illegitimate love, irresponsibility towards the family . . . condemn child marriage or forced marriage . . . concubinage, bullying and ill-treatment of women.[18]

And, after insisting that violations of the law had to be severely punished, the report emphasized that it was the responsibility of the 'Union at all levels to guide women to exercise their right to complain about and denounce breaches of laws and regulations.'

The seventh point of the programme reiterates the organization's commitment to train cadres, especially youth. The Central Committee report expressed concern for politically uncommitted women: religious women, small traders and housewives in the South; and urged serious research on the problems facing these women which 'cannot be solved by old groping methods or on the basis of old experiences.'[19]

The last point affirms the commitment to strengthen the Women's Union's international ties and solidarity among women of socialist countries, the Third World and capitalist countries in order to 'contribute to the common struggle for peace, national independence, democracy and social progress in the world.' The Women's Union frequently sends delegates to international women's conferences and accepts invitations to visit other countries and is an active member of the Women's International Democratic Federation. It also invites delegations of women from various countries to visit Viet Nam.

The Women's Union at Work

After the Women's Congress, the national organization sponsored conferences in each province where cadres responsible for education and propaganda in the villages and districts met to improve their own educational levels, to develop methods for children's education and to exchange experiences to improve their struggle against the survival of US influence in the South.

The national organization also sent delegations to local areas to study two problems: how to frame a more effective law on marriage and the family; and how to improve the life of ethnic minority women in the southern provinces. They also held conferences on how to improve silk production.

Local chapters of the Women's Union hold monthly meetings. In the months after the fifth national congress, local chapters discussed the programme and resolutions passed by the congress and how best to implement them in each local context. Typical meetings plan agendas so that the problems, grievances and aspirations of the membership can be heard and passed on to the provincial and national levels. Usually, local meetings also set aside time to discuss specific topics. For example, one month they will discuss the Law on Marriage and the Family, the next they will discuss international solidarity, then children's education or the history of the Women's Union. Finally, meetings devote time to exchanging experiences on how best to increase production, usually of poultry, fish or pigs.

A closer look at one Women's Union meeting in June 1981, at a village in An Giang Province, shows how the programme and priorities evolve in practice at the local level. Choi, the President of the local Women's Union and I had the following conversation about their most recent meeting: 'Would you please tell me what you discussed at your last meeting?'

'We talked about the problems our children face in school. The schools need repairs after being evacuated to protect the children when Pol Pot's troops invaded. We also discussed the problem of families who need help buying notebooks for their children. There is a terrible paper shortage, so we must share what we have. The next item on the agenda was our plan to build a maternity hospital for our village. We've collected some materials to begin construction, but not enough. So we decided to ask the local authorities for help.'

I asked, 'Have they agreed to supply the materials?'

'Of course,' Choi answered. 'Since we are a mass organization, they expect us to make proposals like this that reflect the needs of our members.'

'But do you have to struggle to have your requests met? Are they ever refused?' I wondered.

Choi's answer was confident: 'No, our proposals are always accepted. I cannot remember a proposal ever being rejected. Of course, we make reasonable proposals. For example, at our last meeting, we also talked about how we wanted more toys and better benches for our childcare centre. The facilities there are really poor. Also, since conditions in our area have been so unstable, with people still returning from evacuation areas, we don't have as many children in the childcare centre as we should. We decided to ask for help from the district government in improving our childcare facilities.'

I could not find out if the incredible lack of resistance to Women's Union proposals at the local level was owing to the Union's self-restraint, or to the community's support of the Union.

Sometimes the Women's Union calls special meetings to discuss a new emulation movement. Emulation movements are favoured vehicles for mobilizing women to work at the various tasks specified in the programme. These are campaigns in which the group decides what criteria a woman must meet in order to be awarded the title 'New Woman Building and Defending the Country', for example. Local chapters decide the most appropriate ways women can win the title. In Ho Chi Minh City, there may be more emphasis on encouraging people to resettle in New Economic Zones or on exposing illegal business dealings. In a rural area of the

North, the campaign may focus on awarding women who have excelled in silkworm production. After six months, the group meets again to nominate the women who have been most successful in meeting the criteria of the emulation movement.

Since 8 March 1978, the movement for the 'New Women to Build and Defend the Country' has been the primary emulation movement. But there are also others: 'The Movement to Build the New Cultured Family' encourages neighbours to nominate families whose parents share housework, whose children are well educated and whose members maintain good relations with their neighbours. There are also more specific movements to greet an important national holiday or meeting by increasing production; to meet a specific disaster, such as a flood, by raising food and making clothing for the victims; or to celebrate the liberation of Viet Nam by setting up classes to train childcare workers. Awards bring prestige to the winner, especially because emulation movements receive focused publicity in the media, but they offer little material reward.

The Women's Union also lobbies for women's rights at the local, provincial and national levels. While a local chapter may press the People's Council in a district for childcare facilities, the national organization makes proposals that expand women's rights to various ministries and the National Assembly. For example, the Women's Union recently proposed to the National Assembly that the forthcoming labour code contain a special section on women's labour, and the establishment of a 'super-agency' with state power to supervise the resolution of special problems women face.[20]

Once the laws or resolutions are passed, the Women's Union works for their enforcement. It checks with Women's Commissions at various factories and work-sites to make sure industrial safety laws for women are enforced. The Women's Union intervenes directly in enforcing women's rights outside the work-place.

One woman responsible for defending women's rights is Ngo Thi Nguyen, a member of the Executive Committee of the district branch of the Women's Union just north of the 17th parallel. She is a 64-year-old peasant and has been active in the Women's Union for 36 years. Before the August Revolution in 1945, she was completely illiterate. Now she has a sixth grade education, which includes a month-long cadre-training course she took in 1960. Nguyen has five children, all of whom are either soldiers or students. For years, she has not lived with her retired husband because her duties as a full-time Women's Union cadre require that she travel to three or four villages each month. In each village, she stays in the home of a local family, sharing the work. She tries to learn what the women are doing, what they are feeling proud of, what their grievances, problems and achievements are. She explains the current Women's Union programme and gives people a sense of the national political situation.

Nguyen, a small woman by Vietnamese standards, seemed to derive most pleasure from her responsibility for enforcing laws against holding women in contempt. Her eyes glistened and she laughed proudly, as she told me,

> It should not be necessary for a wife to have to seek help. It is the responsibility of the Women's Union to go to her. For example, there's a man named Hoang Tu who used to curse and sometimes beat his wife. I went to their home and tried to explain to him in a personal talk that his wife is also a human being, she has a right to be treated equally and the revolution has been fought for everyone. He said he agreed but did not really change his bad behaviour. So we invited him to the Women's Union headquarters to give him a collective criticism of his behaviour. That convinced him he must abandon his feudal ways. We also tried to give his wife more confidence to struggle with him. In some cases, women don't know all their rights, so we try to teach them. We use the same step-by-step procedure to get men to share in the housework or to allow their wives to go out at night. We work with other organizations too to help us. When a man continues to flout the law and ignores us, he gets punished by the law. We take him to court.[21]

Women like Nguyen also organize reconciliation teams – groups of Women's Union activists responsible for resolving family conflicts in a way that protects women's rights and also tries to avoid divorce if children are involved. In a typical case, the Women's Union intervenes when a husband is being unfaithful to his wife. They try to convince the man and the 'other woman' that everyone would be better off if he did not 'behave like a feudal polygamist'. If the problems between the husband and wife are, in fact, irreconcilable, then the Women's Union helps the woman to seek a divorce in court. They refer to this continuing struggle against feudal ways as the 'inner struggle'. A representative explained, 'The struggle is not a clash between men and women, but between institutions and ideologies, and between the new government and old customs.'[22] In other words, while the Women's Union challenges individual men who cling to the privileges inherited from feudalism, it holds the old institutions, and not the individuals, responsible. At Women's Union meetings and other activities, in trade unions, schools, youth organizations and in the home, groups of people meet together to evaluate their past work and plan their future work. After each task is complete, they try to help each other understand their strengths and weaknesses. They call this process *kiem thao*, self-criticism/criticism. Mutual respect and solidarity is a necessary base for self-criticism/criticism and the process, in turn, strengthens solidarity. A member of a women's gunner unit told me,

> It is natural that we have errors and disagreements, but self-criticism/criticism helps us to keep our unity and to create greater love among us. We never use heavy pressure. If the error is one of principle, we struggle to the end. But if

the error is one of personality, we usually let it pass. In any case, no one is ever pressed into the mud. We try to struggle in the spirit of love.[23]

After an initial personal discussion to warn a person he will be criticized, the group will discuss the problem. Then, the man who has been 'behaving like a feudal lord' will try to show he understands the problem by talking about ways to solve it. The process breaks down traditional patriarchal relationships and gives the group collective responsibility for the problem, so no woman has to struggle alone for her rights.

Cultural activities also counter women's isolation. The Women's Union organizes monthly cultural meetings, where women have a chance to express themselves in poetry and song. They also hold forums on books, do sketches, show slides and films. The clubs are especially popular in the countryside, where access to other cultural events is limited. At these events, women gain new self-confidence and learn to speak in public in a friendly atmosphere.[24]

The Women's Union has its own publishing house, magazine and television and radio programmes to support its activities. Since 1975, they have produced a daily 15-minute radio programme called 'The New Woman'. The weekly *Phu Nu Viet Nam (Vietnamese Woman)* is the second largest circulating magazine in the country. It is the central organ of the Women's Union, so women regularly discuss articles from it in their local chapter meetings. The magazine frequently exposes violations of women's rights and interests. It also sends cadres to investigate and resolve women's problems and then sums up the experience in the pages of the magazine. Each month, the editorial board receives thousands of letters from readers – not counting letters addressed to the popular 'Heart-To-Heart Talk' advice column.

Recognizing Their Own Problems

The Women's Union is a presence in the life of millions – the majority of Vietnamese women, but it has not been able to reach all. Even in Hanoi, for example, one woman, an interpreter, was being pressured by her family and fiancé to marry and have a child immediately, while her supervisor wanted her to delay. He was afraid she would have to resign once she became a mother, because her job required travel. She was confused, hesitating to make the difficult choice, apparently unaware that she need not choose between career and motherhood and unaware that she could receive advice and support from the Women's Union.[25]

In a self-criticism, the Women's Union recognizes its limits. After criticizing both its bureaucratic tendencies and its failure 'to relate fully to the feelings and aspirations of masses of women', a 1974 Women's Union report continued:

> The machinery of the Union and its cadres are not yet equal to their tasks. Its executive committees at various levels cannot yet claim to be truly

representative of the broad masses of women . . . . They (cadres) must be fully conscious of their responsibility towards the cause of women's emancipation, strive to overcome all obstacles, ceaselessly seek to raise their standards, be modest and learn from the masses . . . . To strengthen the organization from top to bottom, so the Union will know the wishes and opinions of its members . . . a given policy should always be accompanied by measures . . . to get it carried out.[26]

At the fifth national congress of the Women's Union in 1982, the Central Committee focused a serious self-criticism on other failures in leadership:

The Union's activities . . . usually lack the spirit of initiative, are too ambitious and are mainly focused on motivating women to do urgent immediate tasks. We have not given women a substantial and systematic education in socialism, and have not made them fully aware of their rights and responsibilities in the struggle between the two paths: socialism and capitalism. The movement for fostering new-type socialist woman lacks concrete content. The method of educating women mainly through political studies has proven tedious and arid and does not suit women of different strata, ages and localities.

The Union leadership does not know how to make use of the Constitution, laws, orientations and policies of the State . . . . Much remains to be desired . . . in protecting the legitimate rights and interests of women and children. While production and the people's life still meet with numerous difficulties, and the women's minds are perplexed, the Union has not concentrated on studying realities so as to propose to the State and Party appropriate solutions to urgent problems.

There is a lack of firmness, continuity, concreteness and close coordination with other branches in organizing and guiding the movement for building a new cultured family. The Union's activities in some places tend to be administrative in character with a lot of meetings, papers and exhortations, instead of giving concrete direction aimed at obtaining practical results. The Union's style of work is still limited to the framework of its hierarchy, with little coordination with other branches and not many forms of motivating women in other branches to serve the women's movement. . . . In many localities, the Union's grassroots organizations are still weak, their activities scattered and lack practical content . . . .

Members of the Union have not been given the basic groundings in economic and social management as well as social sciences. As a result, they are at a loss to change the content and mode of Union activity to suit the new situation. The Union has not studied and proposed to the Party and the government the appropriate policies towards women cadres, hence the great difficulties in selecting and training women and caring for their life.

These shortcomings for which the Central Committee of the Union is mainly responsible are experiences we should sum up to improve our work in the coming period.[27]

These self-criticisms are impressive for their severity and demonstrate the Women's Union's sincerity and commitment to thorough-going internal change – change that will hasten the achievement of women's emancipation.

The responsibilities the Women's Union bears are formidable and its weaknesses are significant. But with its political commitment, with its active membership of nearly ten million women, with its more than 50 years of experience and battle-tested leadership and with its organizational resources and support from the party and state, its potential to meet its responsibilities is promising. The Women's Union does have 'an irreducible area of influence over policy formation in areas directly affecting women'. It does mobilize women to confront 'interpersonal relations that subordinate women'. Most important, rather than taking a 'satisfied stance that would encourage conservatism',[28] it recognizes that the struggle for women's emancipation is far from over. Therefore, the Women's Union provides a powerful vehicle for Vietnamese women to define their goals and fight for them.

Notes

1. Mai Thi Tu and Le Thi Nham Tuyet, *Women in Viet Nam* (Hanoi: Foreign Languages Publishing House, 1978), pp. 114–16.
2. Quoted in ibid., pp. 116–17.
3. Le Duan, 'We Must View the Women's Question from a Class Standpoint', *On Socialist Revolution in Viet Nam*, Vol. 3 (Hanoi: Foreign Languages Publishing House, 1967), p. 114.
4. Le Thi Xuyen, 'The Early Days', *Viet Nam News and Reports*, No. 14, March 1973, Supplement on Women, p. 9.
5. Speak bitterness testimony quoted by Wilfred Burchett, *North of the 17th Parallel* (Hanoi: Foreign Languages Publishing House, 1957), pp. 126–34.
6. US officials tried to justify intervention in Viet Nam by citing fraudulent evidence of bloodbaths during the land reform of the 1950s. Former US President Richard Nixon claimed that half a million were killed. For a definitive and reliable refutation of these lies, see D. Gareth Porter, 'The Myth of the Bloodbath: North Viet Nam's Land Reform Reconsidered', Interim Report No. 2, International Relations East Asia Project (Ithaca, New York: Cornell University, 1972).
7. This section on cadre training is based on: interviews by author with Bui Thi Me (Quang Tri Province, September 1974); Nguyen Thi Lan, 'Cadre Training: An Urgent Task', *Women of Viet Nam*, No. 2, 1979, p. 27; and Doi Minh Tinh, 'Twenty Years Development of the Central School for Women Cadres', *Women of Viet Nam*, No. 1, 1981, pp. 7–8.
8. Interview with Le Thi Xuyen by author (Hanoi, 29 September 1974).

9. Xuan Oanh, official from Vietnamese/American Friendship Committee, in an interview with Heidi Kuglin, April 1976. (Thanks to Heidi Kuglin for providing me with her unpublished notes.)
10. Interview by author with Le Thu (Hanoi, 2 September 1981).
11. Le Duan, 'Central Committee Political Report to the Fifth Congress of the Viet Nam Communist Party', reported by Foreign Broadcast Information Service, Department of Commerce, Washington DC, March 1982.
12. Interview by author with Nguyen Thi Binh (Hanoi, 2 September 1981).
13. Discussion at National Women's Union Headquarters (Hanoi, 2 September 1981).
14. Ibid.
15. 'Fifth Vietnamese Women's Congress', *Viet Nam Courier*, No. 6, 1982, p. 9.
16. 'Program of the Viet Nam Women's Union, 1981–1985', *Nhan Dan*, 21 May 1982.
17. 'Report of the Central Committee of the Viet Nam Women's Union to the Fifth National Congress of Vietnamese Women' (unpublished mimeo furnished by Women's Union to author), May 1982, pp. 28–31 and 34. Hereafter cited as 'Report'.
18. Ibid., p. 39.
19. Ibid., p. 53.
20. Nguyen Thi Dinh, 'Vietnamese Women Enthusiastically Help in the Establishment and Enforcement of Socialist Legality' (speech given by Women's Union President to first session of 7th National Assembly), *Women of Viet Nam*, Nos. 3–4, 1981, p. 2.
21. Interview with Ngo Thi Nguyen by author (Vinh Linh, September 1974).
22. Kathleen Gough Aberle in personal conversation with author (December 1982).
23. From interview by author with member of Women's Gunner Unit (Ngu Thu Village, Quang Binh Province, 23 September 1974).
24. Cecilia Molander, *Women in Viet Nam* (Stockholm: Swedish International Development Authority, 1981), pp. 28–9.
25. Thanks to Kathleen Gough Aberle for this example in unpublished correspondence with author, 16 June 1982.
26. 'Report from Central Executive Committee of Viet Nam Women's Union' (unpublished mimeo), March 1974, p. 59.
27. Report, pp. 23–4.
28. The phrase 'irreducible area of influence over policy formation in areas directly affecting women' is Maxine Molyneux's. She posits it as the minimal criterion set by Western feminists for an organization to qualify as an 'autonomous women's organization'. The Viet Nam Women's Union certainly does not conform to Molyneux's sweeping generalizations either about the conservatism of women's organizations in socialist countries or their lack of concern with ideology and interpersonal relations. See Maxine Molyneux, 'Socialist Societies Old and New: Progress Towards Women's Emancipation', *Monthly Review*, Vol. 34, No. 3, July–August 1982, pp. 71, 93–4, 98.

PART III: Progress Towards Women' Emancipation

9. Women Working Outside the Home: A New Independence

To liberate themselves and become really equal to men, women must not only acquire a sufficient political level and cultural knowledge, but also have a legitimate occupation to sustain themselves without relying on others . . . . This problem has been basically solved in the North, but in the South, the union will have to carry out intensive activities to make women fully understand and solve this problem.

Xuan Thuy, Central Committee member of Viet Nam Communist Party in speech to 1976 meeting of reunified Women's Union

Moving from the position of hired hands to that of masters of the factory, we feel somewhat perplexed, but also elated.

Nguyen Thi Hue, head of production team at Pharmaceutical Factory No. 4, Ho Chi Minh City

As long as a woman must depend on her husband for her subsistence, her home will be his castle and he will be her master. As long as her labour is hidden in the household and family fields, she has no chance to gain equal rights, let alone full emancipation. Economic independence for all women, or what the Vietnamese call 'collective mastery in the economic field', is the foundation of women's liberation. In Viet Nam, a country in the process of building socialism, the right to work outside the home is guaranteed. It is also the self-evident duty of every citizen.

While the majority of Vietnamese women, peasants, have always toiled in the fields, their harvests belonged to their fathers or husbands. Now, women receive their pay according to how much work they do, independently of their fathers or husbands. In 1961, only 20% of the waged labour force in North Viet Nam was female. By 1982, women constituted more than 45% of the labour force of all Viet Nam, including the armed forces. Today, in the North, nearly all women between the ages of 16 and 55 either work or study outside the home. Since liberation in 1975, the percentage of women working outside the home in the South has leaped from 20 to 80 in most regions.[1] As the problems of scarcity of raw materials, technology and transportation are resolved, unemployment and underemployment of women will disappear.

New Opportunities in the Countryside

In the past, peasant women did only the most back-breaking labour, followed their husband's or landlord's orders and received only bare subsistence in return. In 1945, 62% of the peasants in all of Viet Nam owned no land and worked as sharecroppers. Land reform in the northern countryside eliminated the huge concentrations of wealth that had forced women into concubinage and slavery. The landlord system, which once extracted unfair rents and taxes, has been abolished. Peasants have new power based on collective work and collective ownership of land and tools. Everyone is paid according to the work she or he does for the co-operative.

After 1954, land reform was the basis for the socialist transformation of the Democratic Republic of Viet Nam. The defining features of a socialist economy are that economic decisions – what to produce, how to produce it, and whom to produce it for – are made by the producers themselves or their representatives. As socialism develops, the political and economic power of individual or corporate owners of factories, fields, mines or other sources of the nation's wealth is gradually eroded. Organizations of workers, peasants, and intellectuals plan their work after extensive discussion about productive capabilities and how to meet the people's needs. Under capitalism, on the other hand, factory owners make decisions for workers, agribusiness tells farm workers what to do, and the publishing industry decides what writing will sell the most books. All decisions have one goal: the unending expansion of individual or corporate profit. In Viet Nam, concerted struggle has largely eliminated profit making from the labour of others, once the source of gross inequalities. In Viet Nam, one does not hear people say, 'I am poor.' Rather, people repeat, 'Viet Nam is poor.'[2]

Yet precisely because of its poverty, Viet Nam's socialist transformation is still in its very early stages. There are still a million and a half small traders in Viet Nam.[3] Many people eke out a living selling cigarettes and trinkets on the street corners of Ho Chi Minh City and even Hanoi. Not all of them are die-hard capitalist merchants. Many of them would like to work in factories or other socialist enterprises, but because of the underdeveloped state of the economy, no such positions are available. Agricultural co-operatives in the countryside, then, are only the beginning of socialism for Viet Nam.

In the Bui co-operative, Ha Nam Province, for example, after 1954, every landless peasant received a plot of land and then decided to join

John Spragens Jr.

together to work it collectively. By breaking out of their traditional isolation, they were able to repair dikes, and save the crops from floods. A Vietnamese proverb explains the increased prosperity in the Bui co-operative and others like it: 'In hell, people starve because their hands are chained to six-foot-long chopsticks – too long to bring rice to their mouths. Heaven is the same – only there, people feed each other.' The co-operative freed the women from the patriarchal family economy and challenged centuries of sex-defined roles. For the first time, women of the Bui co-op guided buffalo, drove ploughs, learned to use mechanical pumps and began fish breeding. Women leaders have responsibility for the co-op's seed selection, storehouse, animal breeding and technical innovation as well as for finances. The chairperson and 11 of the 15 members of the co-op's managing committee are women.[4]

Jayne Werner, a US scholar specializing in Viet Nam, reported similar developments in the Yen So co-operative, which she visited in 1980.

In the Yen So cooperative south of Hanoi, female participation in the agricultural labor force rose to 80% of the work force during the war. The deputy manager, Nguyen Thi Tuyen, age 33, had held the elected position since she was 20 years old. The two other top posts in the village, Party Secretary and Chairperson of the Peoples Committee, are also held by women. Women comprise 35% of the Party members . . . . The great

143

improvement in women's status occurred from 1965–75. There was also substantial improvement in village livelihood during this period . . . . By the end of the war, women had gained economic independence and control of village work. Male villagers returning to Yen So, according to the deputy manager, were unlikely to undermine this female authority because women have shown that they can take charge and make great progress without men.[5]

She concludes that wartime needs and the withdrawal of men from agricultural production gave women a chance to challenge the traditions that had kept them in the most menial jobs.

However, she says, 'socialist transformation made these gains possible.' Under feudal ownership, the landlord kept all the surplus for his own use. When the co-op earns a surplus, the earnings stay in the village where the people can use them for building childcare centres, health stations, schools, libraries and investment in more efficient tools and fertilizer to improve productivity. These investments also improve women's chances for advancement and consolidate their independence. When the woman no longer works alone on the family plot under her husband's authority, when other institutions provide for the needs traditionally met by women, then women have the opportunity to increase their political participation and power in the society.

However, such changes do not evolve automatically or even smoothly. After generations of dreaming of owning their own land, peasants are sceptical about the benefits of collectivization. In Hai Van Commune, in the North, for example, the land reform programme parcelled out land to the peasants as early as 1954. But it was not until 1960 that they pooled their tools and organized mutual aid teams. And until 1964 they did not have enough confidence to collectivize the land and diversify the crops. In 1970, government cadres introduced new electric pumps and irrigation procedures, which required a new division of labour and more collective facilities. Twenty-five years after the initial land reform, some peasants were still confused and sometimes took back their land to cultivate it on an individual basis – which invariably meant a renewal of women's subordination. Now, however, such resistance to collectivization in Hai Van is extremely rare.[6]

In the newly liberated areas of the South, peasants still require assurance before they embrace co-operativization. In U Minh, and other parts of the Mekong Delta, for example, people had been supporters of the revolution since the days of fighting for independence from the French.[7] The peasants of U Minh had paid their dues. They knew their local cadres well and did not hesitate to speak their minds. While they contributed substantial amounts of grain to pay their taxes, they resisted joining co-operatives. Two-thirds of them had been forced off their land, into 'refugee camps', during the war and the other third went to liberated areas deep in the forest. When the war ended, their first concern was to

John Spragens Jr.

return to their old homes and to try to rebuild their private lives – presumably in the patriarchal tradition.

By 1980, only 20% of the peasants in the Mekong Delta had joined co-operatives. Cadres, pushing too hard to sign people up, created resentment in some areas. As a result, the government readjusted its plans for co-operativization and put renewed emphasis on the three basic principles of co-operatives: they must be voluntary; they must be mutually advantageous; and they must have democratic management. Successful pilot projects – taking advantage of co-operative organization and more productive farming methods – serve as models for others. Co-ops have priority in receiving scarce fertilizer, oil, machinery and technical assistance from the state – another reason why as Viet Nam develops its economy, socialist changes will accelerate.

In 1979, the party decided to stimulate economic development by giving both workers and peasants more financial incentive to increase productivity and join co-operatives. They found that they could no longer rely on patriotic fervour, generated by US occupation, to motivate high productivity. Since 1979, various bonus systems, more allowance for local initiative and other reforms have buoyed the economy. One spokesperson explained the continuing debate on a strategy for socialist development:

> The problem is to prepare each step carefully . . . . But if the process takes too long – 20 years – that's too slow. If we move too slowly, the rich peasants will make more and buy up land from the poor peasants. If you are rich and have a tiller and if I am old and my buffalo was killed in the war, I may have to sell you my land and hire out my labor. We cannot allow that.[8]

By 1980, in all of the South, some 50% of the peasants had joined co-operatives covering 36% of the land.[9]

That figure does not include New Economic Zones (NEZ). Almost immediately after liberation, the new government took concrete measures to encourage those living in the bloated southern cities, especially those without jobs, to resettle in NEZs. This Return to the Village Programme accomplishes two essential tasks: it provides jobs and a chance to build a new life for people who had been uprooted by forced urbanization. And it provides a labour force to reclaim uncultivated and war-damaged land and increase agricultural output. There are also NEZs to relieve over-population in certain northern areas. The work in the NEZs is organized co-operatively.

Under the Return to the Village Programme, the government allots a ration of cash and rice to each household member – enough to sustain them until the first harvest comes in. The government also supports non-peasants while they learn a trade. Most NEZs have agricultural technicians to advise the settlers, and mechanics to repair machinery. By 1977, about a million people had 'Returned to the Villages'.

The goal is for another four million to join them. But progress towards achieving this goal has been hampered by the wars with Pol Pot and China and by poor planning. After planners underestimated how long it would take for an NEZ to become self-sufficient, disillusioned, hungry settlers returned to the city. Transforming barren land without the benefit of technology or conveniences like plumbing and electricity requires enormous stamina.

Equal Pay for Comparable Work
Once co-operatives are established, women's rights are not automatically guaranteed. Co-operativization provides certain conditions for freeing women in the countryside, but does not ensure their emancipation. For example, the director of Xuan Phuong co-operative reported how she and other Women's Union members fought the tendency for men to earn more than women. The men had been able to supplement their agricultural income with earnings from bricklaying, carpentry and the like. The women had no such skills. So the director, Vu Thi Cuc, who was also President of the local Women's Union branch, brought the problem to the local party cell and the managing board of the co-op. They decided to help women to learn new trades to supplement their incomes. Subsequently, the women earned as much as the men and also made a greater contribution to the prosperity of the co-op as a whole.[10]

The Women's Union also wages a constant struggle against the tendency to undervalue the work women do. Traditionally, for example, men plough and women plant the rice fields. Following patriarchal tradition, management committees of co-operatives invariably decided that the men's work was more difficult and should be paid more. A leader of the Women's Union reported,

> We demonstrated that technique was more important than whether or not one used a plough. So after a lot of struggle and investigation, led by the Women's Union, the co-ops began evaluating work according to skill, intensity and quality. Since then, ploughing and planting receive equal pay. But we still struggle for equality in salaries in other areas. It is one reason why we work hard to elect women to management boards. We've noticed that when husbands earn more than their wives, they tend to be lazy in sharing housework. With new methods of calculating wages, the more equal the earnings, the more housework the husbands do.[11]

No statistics are available to allow overall comparisons of earnings by women and men in Viet Nam, only some examples. Machinists, many of whom are women, but the majority of whom are men, earn about 30% more than childcare workers, all of whom are women. But a skilled childcare worker earns as much as an unskilled machinist. In the US a skilled machinist earns at least 300% more than a childcare worker.

Moreover, the gross inequalities in earnings that are routine in capitalist economies are very rare in Viet Nam. Only illegal speculators' and large traders' earnings are substantially larger than average. The highest paid worker in Viet Nam, for example, the President of the nation, earns only 4.3 times more than the lowest paid worker, an unskilled, barely productive apprentice. In most enterprises the differential is even narrower. For example, at My Duc Silkweaving Factory, the director earns only twice as much as an average worker; and a highly skilled worker who exceeds production quotas earns about a third more than the director.

Economic reforms instituted in 1979 place more emphasis on material incentives. There is no evidence, however, that rewarding workers for increased productivity will widen the gap between earnings by women and men. Also, government subsidies of rationed food and other necessities, free medical care, education and rent pegged to a tiny percentage of the workers' wages all have an equalizing effect on the wage differential. Roughly 10% of the earnings of most factories are set aside for a welfare fund. The workers themselves decide how these funds should be spent. At the Hanoi Rice-Husking Mill, for instance, they spend the money on improving workers' housing, toilet facilities at the plant, providing a canteen lunch and free paper and pens so women workers can take complementary education classes at no cost to themselves.

Taking the Profit out of Women's Oppression

Nguyen Thi Thap, former President of the Women's Union, concluded from Vietnamese women's experience that more jobs do not necessarily ensure women's equality. As long as a man is an employer who owns the factories and shops, he will always be richer and more powerful than his workers. Thap insisted: 'There can never be equality between exploiter and exploited. When the oppressing class still dominates, the true equal rights of women cannot exist.'[12] Thap speaks from experience.

Under the Thieu regime, those women who did work outside the home were brutally exploited, particularly by corporations owned by foreigners. Rachel Grossman, a journalist based in the US, did an in-depth study of how multinational corporations, particularly in the electronics industry, locate in South East Asia so that they can take advantage of a pool of cheap female labour made docile by patriarchal traditions. The personnel manager of Itel Corporation in Malaysia told her, 'We hire girls because they have less energy, are more disciplined and easier to control.' The manager at Fairchild's in Indonesia was more precise:

> What we are doing here resembles the family system in which I am not just the manager, but also the father to all those here at Fairchild's. This conforms to an important Indonesian principle, that of family. For the women, brought up in families in which the father's word is law, the image is compelling.[13]

These companies, and those like them under the Thieu regime, motivate women workers by organizing beauty contests and cosmetic classes. Actual work conditions are deadly: the average working life is only three or four years because workers lose their eyesight after peering through a microscope, bonding wires the size of human hairs. Chemicals used in the work cause cancer. No talking is allowed on the work floor. Many women are laid off each week for failing to meet production quotas. There is no opportunity for advancement, because only the most menial labour processes for each corporation are located in South East Asia. The workers earn barely enough to cover their room and board. On pay day, the factories arrange for jewellery and cosmetic salespeople to ply their wares during the lunch break. Management seduces workers by making them 'feel part of a global culture where they have a choice between Avon and Revlon . . . where their dormitory rooms are decorated with pictures of John Travolta and Farah Fawcett and music from "Saturday Night Fever" is played on the factory PA system,' according to Grossman.

At the same time, the governments of Malaysia and the Philippines, like the Thieu regime of the old South Viet Nam, lure multinational corporations by rejecting protective labour laws, maternity benefits and other measures to ensure workers' rights. They fiercely repress all labour unions. The corporations reap enormous profits from this super-exploitation, enabling them to drive less exploitative enterprises into bankruptcy. In the capitalist's terms, the most successful business is one which 'gets the most from its workers'.

In the Socialist Republic of Viet Nam, on the other hand, there is no factory owner who makes a profit from exploiting women's labour. Nor does anyone profit from the kind of predicament women find themselves in under capitalism where vast pools of unemployed housewives and other women compete with each other for those relatively few jobs available to them, thus keeping women's wages and working conditions permanently depressed.

A woman in a Vietnamese textile factory wrote this song for her work team's cultural group:

'The cloth which comes out of my loom tonight
will be the national red flag and the scarves of our children
going to school in the morning.'[14]

Women in Viet Nam's factories work hard, for long hours, often with archaic, broken-down machinery and inadequate raw materials. Scarcity of electric power means factories are usually poorly lit. Women walk or bicycle for miles to get to work. While their work and sacrifice may resemble the work women did in the US and England during World War II, the situation is actually very different. During World War II, national enthusiasm for defeating Hitler blinded women to the fact that industry was making huge war profits from their labour. The profit-makers' political power was also consolidated. Employers and the government considered working women as 'temporary understudies'. They renamed job

Textile worker.
Viet Nam News Agency

categories so that women in manufacturing in the US earned 65% of what men earned for doing exactly the same work. Thousands of women had to leave their children in locked cars in the factory parking lot. There were an estimated two million children needing federally sponsored childcare; but, at their peak, only 100,000 children benefited from federally funded programmes. Then, the programmes ended in 1946.[15]

In Viet Nam, as the song says, the cloth they weave is for the country and the children. If there is a surplus, some of it may be reinvested in technology needed by society, but no individual will make a personal gain. Workers, not profit makers, control the government that decides how to use the nation's resources. The workers in each factory elect a management committee to run it. Committee members usually spend a lot of time working along with the rest of the workers, not behind desks,

After March 1978, capitalist control of finance, commerce and industry became a thing of the past in the South as it had been in the North. After much persuasion and struggle, factory owners choosing to co-operate with the revolution sold their inventories to the state or co-op and often became supervisors following principles of democratic management. By 1982 nearly all women in the North and 50% of the women in the South participated in collective forms of production.[16]

However, the transition to socialism in Viet Nam, especially in the South, is in its embryonic stage. The past is still influential. The black market thrives. The poverty of the country is a fertile ground for the growth of corruption, especially among those who became accustomed to US consumerism. Government workers earning subsistence wages, inexperienced managers and technicians sometimes succumb to the pressure of bribes. Corruption and ineptitude may be a danger to the fragile structure of socialism.

From Paternalism to Collective Mastery
In April 1977, the Women's Union in Sadec, south of Ho Chi Minh City, began a campaign to get women to join the Dong Tien Tailoring Co-op. 'We mainly had to struggle against the habit of women being just good housewives, dependent on their husband's wages,' the Women's Union reported.[17] The Women's Union also had to convince some women to give up their small market businesses, which rarely yielded an income large enough to make the owners independent or secure. Nguyen Thi Bach welcomed the chance to join a co-op:

> I used to sell beans in the market and it sure was a hard job. I had to get myself behind the stall every day, rain or shine. Even when I felt sick, I didn't dare stay home for fear I might lose a customer. Now things are a lot better. I've got a steady job, a stable monthly pay, sick leave and other benefits.[18]

As the co-op is able to buy more machines, it can train new women to be members. The Cua Long Handicraft Co-op, described in Chapter 6, is typical of how co-ops operate in Viet Nam. Management is elected by the workers and subject to review and criticism on a regular basis. The workers decide how to spend any surplus the co-op earns: whether on childcare, improved housing or time off for classes. By 1982, more than 2,000 markets in the South were reorganized on a co-operative basis.[19]

Workers with experience under capitalism enjoy the transformation of the South Vietnamese economy. Du Hue Lien, a woman of Chinese ethnic background, used to work as a weaver in a textile factory owned by a rich Taiwanese. She recalled,

> We were super-exploited and always ready to strike. We could not really afford to live on our wage and the boss was always harassing us. A friend of mine committed suicide because of the boss's harassment . . . . Now we have the right to a month's holiday. Now workers can go anywhere. We can eat in the best restaurants. Now, the trade union in the factory makes sure we have apartments. I spent two years in prison because I represented the other workers in a strike. I was very happy when the city was liberated. Our boss fled to the United States and now we run the factory. In spite of our many difficulties, we are no longer humiliated. We have our spirit.[20]

151

Despite the poverty of the Vietnamese economy, women there enjoy a greater degree of legal protection in their jobs than in most industrialized countries. In Viet Nam, women cannot be required to work in jobs dangerous to their health. Since women working in French factories sometimes gave birth by their machines, for fear of losing their jobs; today, they welcome their guaranteed two months' paid maternity leave. The Ministry of Labour provides for enterprises employing women to hire extra workers to fill in for absent mothers, rather than discriminating against women workers because they require extra protections. Other protective labour legislation for women provides time off for illness, including menstruation, without reduction in pay; and prohibition against compulsory overtime for women more than six months pregnant or for nursing mothers. Nursing mothers receive one hour per day paid to nurse their children. Women also receive 15 days' paid leave each year, in addition to normal holiday time, if needed to care for sick children.

According to Confucian tradition, 'manual labour is not worthy of a man.' Vietnamese women have always performed heavy labour. Even after the revolution, they shouldered heavy manual jobs because the wars and the survival of the nation demanded it. They, therefore, welcome labour laws which forbid women from working with strong poisons, in extremely high temperatures, in mining or other heavy labour. Mrs Huong, a former coal miner who became the head of the Women's Commission of the Hong Gai Trade Union Federation, explained, 'As men return from the front, they will take over doing heavier work. Women will do other jobs. There is so much work to be done. Formerly, women had to work twice as hard. Now we will have less work and more time to study and do other things.'[21] The movement to enter 'non-traditional employment', usually heavy blue-collar jobs, in Western industrialized countries has little attraction for Vietnamese women, especially because pay scales in Viet Nam are relatively egalitarian. For women street sweepers, for example, an occupation traditionally dominated by women, it was a progressive step to receive the right to be pensioned five years earlier than the usual retirement age. Furthermore, they receive an extra 5% bonus for working outside and another 30% for the difficulty of the work and the inconvenient hours.[22] They look forward to the day when Viet Nam will be able to afford mechanical street sweepers and they will be encouraged to study skills to take on less strenuous jobs.

Moving up the Job Ladder

In 1945, you could count on two hands the number of women doctors and engineers in all of Viet Nam. By 1975, there were more than 5,000 women holding these jobs in the North. In 1945, there were no women teaching at the university or college level. By 1975, there were 2,000 in the North. In

Students at the Agricultural University.   Viet Nam News Agency

Saigon, under the US-controlled regime, as late as 1960, only ten women had graduated from the School of Medicine, Pharmacy and Dentistry. In 1982, however, 64% of college-trained pharmacists, 47% of medical doctors and 53% of assistant medical doctors were women. And by 1981, in all of Viet Nam, about 35% of scientists, engineers and technical personnel were women.[23]

Dr Vu Thi Phan graduated from the first class of doctors to study in the Democratic Republic of Viet Nam. She smiled as she recalled, 'We studied in the forest under the shade of a tree.' She graduated in 1950 in a liberated area of north-western Viet Nam; and began to work at the Institute for the Study of Malaria, Parasitology and Insectology when it opened in 1957. Within ten years, she was appoined vice-director and in 1975 she replaced the director who was killed in a bombing raid. In addition to designing and executing her own research, Doctor Phan supervises a network of more than 2,000 health workers to prevent malaria. She is proud of their success. When I questioned her in 1981 about traditional hostility faced by women administrators in Viet Nam, she explained her case was different because her co-workers had seen her work since 1957 and knew she was competent.

Dr Hoang Xuan Sinh, one of Viet Nam's top mathematicians, believes women have made enormous strides in taking respected positions in society. 'In my family, both my grandmothers were illiterate. My mother could read a newspaper, but with difficulty. For my generation, there's a chance for women to study anything,' she remarked.[24] In 1970, only about 10% of the students studying to the mathematics teachers at the Pedagogical Institute in Hanoi were women; by 1981, 50% were women. When I asked Dr Sinh if she encountered lack of respect from her colleagues, she laughed, 'Most of my colleagues were once my students, so there is no question about their respect for me.'

Other women who are successful professionals have had more difficulty in proving themselves to sceptical male colleagues. Pham Truong Tho Tho, a doctor of chemistry who now works at the Central Pharmaceutical Institute, recalled:

> In 1962, after graduating from the Hanoi Polytechnic, I was assigned to the Forest Products Chemistry Department of the Forestry Institute . . . . I had no one to rely on . . . the knowledge I had acquired in school remained purely theoretical and general. In fact, I knew almost nothing about botany and natural compounds . . . . Added to these problems were the scornful remarks that reached my ears, 'Let's wait and see what this young engineer is capable of.' . . . I buckled down to my work with a determination to prove that women are in no way inferior to men.[25]

Bui Thi Lang, a doctor of oceanography trained in the US, had to resign from her teaching job at Saigon University in 1972 because she had been too outspoken. Now she heads a team that teaches fishermen how to improve their catch while at the same time protecting the environment. They aim to make shrimping a more profitable export industry. She is also trying to organize the fishermen's wives into co-operatives to mend nets and thus earn an independent income, rather than only mending their husbands' nets at home. Despite the fact that the fishermen are known to be heavy drinkers, Bui Thi Lang insists they have always respected her. They bow to her scientific knowledge, although they are somewhat baffled by her insistence on driving her own jeep. Women drivers are rare in Viet Nam, especially in the South.

Opening the legal profession to women not only provided women with jobs, but also helped to broaden women's political power and protect their gains. Before 1960, there were no women lawyers in Viet Nam. Until the 1960s, it had been taken for granted that only men had the gift for weighty argument, especially for being a judge. Now, when a polygamous husband tries to win his case in court, he must convince a woman judge in an interchange like this: 'My first wife is sterile! I had to have a second wife who would give me children,' he pleaded to a Hanoi Court. 'Did you both consult a specialist?' the judge enquired. 'No? And if it were your fault, you would allow her to take a second husband, would you not?'[26]

The Women's Union recruits women like Nong Thi Trung, once an illiterate highlander, to receive training for work in law and other professions. Trung is now chief judge in her province. There are also two women who serve on Viet Nam's Supreme Court.

On 8 March 1967, the government of the DRV issued a directive to ensure that women would rise in the management of industrial units and agricultural co-operatives. It stipulated that when women constitute 40% of the labour force of a factory or co-op, a woman must serve on the management committee. When the labour force includes 50% women, the assistant manager must be a woman. When the number is 70%, the manager must be a woman. By providing for their training, the directive also encourages women to advance to more skilled positions. The Women's Union helps implement the directive, which reflects the understanding that women managers are better able to understand the strengths and limitations of women workers and are more determined than their male colleagues in the struggle for women's rights.

Mai Thi Tu, co-author of the leading Vietnamese book on the women's movement, told me, 'In factories where women are managers, the working conditions are better than where the management is all men.'[27] Generally, there has been more success in implementing the 1967 directive in agricultural co-ops than in factories. There is at least one woman on the management board, usually out of a total of five, in nearly all agricultural co-ops. Nationally, 18% of the management boards are women. At the March 8th Weaving Mill, named in honour of International Women's Day, there are continuous courses which enable women to train to become heads of production teams and supervisors. By 1974, 200 women replaced men in those jobs; and by 1976, about half the board of directors, heads and vice-heads of departments were women. But the March 8th Weaving Mill is an exception, as the following table indicates.

Table 3
Women in Management Positions

The position	*1965*	*1972*	*1981**
Directors and deputy directors of factories	58	130	160 (3.4%)
Directors of public institutes	21	65	97 (3.9%)
Directors of central level government bureaux	125	183	na

*Data for 1965 and 1972 is for Democratic Republic of Viet Nam only. 1981 data is for the entire country.

Source: Documents from Fourth and Fifth National Congresses of Viet Nam Women's Union, 1974 and 1981 respectively (unpublished mimeos).

The Women's Union is self-critical:

> We must concentrate more on training women to take leadership. We especially must train young cadres, so they replace old ones. There's a generation of women who were veterans of the August Revolution (1945)

who have taken leadership positions, but now need to be relieved by younger women.[28]

In addition to lack of managerial skills among women, there are other reasons for the sluggish promotion of women. At the My Duc Silkweaving Factory, for example, where 450 out of 540, or 83%, of the workers are women, the director is a man. He has been the director since the factory opened in 1968. Two out of three members of the management board are also men. When I asked a group of women workers there if it was a problem having a male-dominated management, they laughed and talked among themselves all at once. One emerged from the group to answer,

> Although the director is a man, he pays good attention to the interests of women. We have special facilities for menstruating women, for childcare and a good system that gets our marketing done collectively and cooks hot meals for us . . . . If the Director did not pay enough attention to women's problems, he would be overthrown.

Another added, 'Now the director is a man, but in the near future it will be a woman. We are preparing to take over. She is now being trained by the present director.'[29] Yet no one seemed to feel that replacing the director of 13 years was an urgent issue.

In the South, where most managers have held their positions only since 1975 or even later, there is no entrenched male leadership to replace. Since the state replaced private owners of large-scale enterprises, former production workers have been promoted to lower management positions at a very rapid rate. On the other hand, patriarchal attitudes and lack of trained women pose even bigger problems than they do in the North.

Nguyen Thi Yen, director of a canning factory in Ho Chi Minh City, told me that in light industry women constitute 40% of the management boards and generally factory directors are women. But if her data were representative of all enterprises in the South, Table 3 would look different. Generally, throughout Vietnamese society and industry, there is a shortage of trained personnel. However, because of the deep-rooted traditional contempt for women, there is a double standard at work that prevents women from being promoted to administrative positions with substantial authority. Until 1976, for example, an affirmative action policy in education recognized that women students were handicapped by centuries of patriarchal subordination, and so gave them preferential treatment in evaluating their applications for admission to higher education. In 1976, this preferential treatment was ended because women presumably no longer needed to be compensated for any historically caused handicap. They had achieved educational equality. Yet, in 1981, I was repeatedly told that under-representation of women in management reflected women's relatively inadequate training. The only way I can make sense of the contradiction is to assume that administrative and leadership positions are still a bastion of patriarchal privilege. Women's technical expertise is more easily acknowledged than their ability to make decisions for others and lead. Of course, Viet Nam is no exception. The percentage of women in managerial positions in other countries, particularly Western capitalist countries, is also very low.

Sex Segregation in the Occupational Structure
In the United States, sex segregation in the labour force (like racial segregation) creates a situation where many women are forced to compete for the relatively few jobs available to them, thereby keeping wages and working conditions in the 'women's sector' permanently depressed. As a result of the segregated job market in the US, working outside the home does not guarantee a woman economic independence or security, especially if she must pay childcare expenses from her earnings. However, cheap female labour under capitalism does guarantee enormous profits and flexibility for corporations.

This is not the case in Viet Nam. A high percentage of Vietnamese women work in jobs where the majority of the workforce is female – in health, education and light industry, for example. Yet this segregation still allows women to achieve economic independence and security. And no one profits from it. Vietnamese women themselves do not seem to be preoccupied with this segregation – which may explain some of its persistence. Most of the menial jobs were reserved for women. Now, therefore, most women are relieved when men perform the heaviest tasks in agriculture, industry and mining. In other words, not all sex-segregated jobs are seen as oppressive to women.

Moreover, it seems that the majority of jobs in the Vietnamese economy are open to women. Those women who do achieve in traditionally 'male' domains – like Dr Sinh in mathematics – are celebrated. The demands of war and a shortage of men have pushed women to break down many occupational barriers. Because war conditions still exist in Viet Nam, we can only speculate how many women will return to traditionally female jobs when the men come home from the front for good. On the basis of the relatively slower pace with which women have entered male occupations since 1975, however, it seems that rather than return to their kitchens, Vietnamese women will hold their ground. They will not, however, advance at the spectacular pace witnessed during the height of the anti-US war.

Sex segregation seems more the result of men's refusal to take women's jobs than women's exclusion from men's jobs. While women become engineers, no men become childcare workers. After visiting each childcare centre, I would ask my hosts why there were no men working there. 'Isn't it important that children be exposed to exemplary men as well as exemplary women?' I asked. The replies varied. Some said, 'We are studying the question.' Others said, 'Women are more suited to this work.' And others, perhaps most accurately, admitted, 'We cannot find men willing to do this work.' They might have added that the problem was exacerbated by the lack of social pressure in society to encourage men to teach and nurture children. In 1981, when I visited the Young Pioneer Centre in Hanoi, I found nearly a third of those studying model making and machine tools were girls. But not one boy studied embroidery. At textile and handicraft co-operatives I visited, about 15% of the workers at the looms and sewing tables were men.

Some of the unwritten rules regarding sex segregation seem quite arbitrary and inconsistent. For example, there seem to be no women drivers in Viet Nam. Even the drivers of the Women's Union vans were men. 'The work is too heavy for a woman,' I was told. Yet 20% of the dockworkers and many roadworkers and bricklayers are women. It is a common sight to see a small peasant woman carrying 75 pounds of produce in baskets suspended from a carrying-pole balanced on her shoulder. In other words, heavy work is considered 'men's work' if it is relatively skilled and involves modern machinery. If the heavy work is relatively tedious and not mechanized, it is the kind of menial work the Confucian patriarchy traditionally relegated to women.

While many women join the Women's Union in agreeing that Vietnamese women have to work too hard and hope that economic development will remedy the problem, I spoke to no one who thought that in order to abolish all contempt for women, men had to become childcare workers. Yet it seems that as long as no men perform that job, patriarchal myths that women are best suited to motherhood and that men are best suited to running society will take longer to die. If men were to gain more experience and recognition as childcare workers, perhaps the way would be open for women to gain more experience and recognition as managers.

The one aspect of sex segregation on the job women do recognize and challenge is the relative exclusion of women from managerial and other leadership roles. Jobs involving leadership responsibility are especially significant since they give their holders power over others. We will return to this problem in Chapter 15.

In conclusion, it is important to reiterate the persistence of a degree of sex segregation in Viet Nam does not prevent women from achieving economic independence and security. If we recall that 35% of civil engineers in Viet Nam are women, while fewer than 3% of civil engineers in the US and only 1% of engineers in Israel are women. we maintain a sense of proportion about the magnitude of the problem. While the pace of women's advance into 'men's jobs' may be slackening, it is still the avowed goal of the party, the government and the Women's Union to promote women to all jobs, including those with major leadership responsibilities.

Notes

1. Data on labour force participation from interview by author with Mai Thi Tu (Hanoi, 30 August 1981).
2. Nguyen Thanh Binh, 'Viet Nam after 10 Years: An Exile Returns', *US/Viet Nam Friendship Association Newsletter*, Vol. 4, No. 6, November–December 1982, p. 5.
3. Nguyen Khac Vien, 'Economic and Social Change', *US/Viet Nam Friendship Association Newsletter*, Vol. 5, No. 1, January–February 1983, p. 5.
4. Mai Anh, 'Up from the Mud', *Vietnamese Women* (Vietnamese Studies, No. 10; Hanoi: Foreign Languages Publishing House, 1966), pp. 153–92.
5. Jayne Werner, 'Women, Socialism and the Economy of Wartime North Viet Nam', *Studies in Comparative Communism*, Vol. XIV, Nos. 2–3, Summer/Autumn 1981, pp. 182–4.
6. François Houtart, 'Problems of Social Transition: An Example from Viet Nam', *Ideas and Action Bulletin* (FAO), No. 137, 1980, pp. 2–11.
7. Information on U Minh from John Spragens Jr, 'Looking Ahead', *South East Asia Chronicle*, No. 76, December 1980, pp. 12–13.
8. Ibid., p. 12.
9. Xuan Nam, 'Changes in the Countryside', *Viet Nam Courier*, No. 12, 1980, p. 20.
10. For details on the land reform and the socialist transformation of the Democratic Republic of Viet Nam, see Gerard Chaliand, *The Peasants of North Viet Nam* (London: Penguin, 1969).
11. Interview by author with Tran Thi Hoan (Hanoi, 30 August 1981).
12. Nguyen Thi Thap, 'Women and Revolution', *Viet Nam News and Reports*, No. 14, March 1973, Supplement on Women, p. 8.
13. Rachel Grossman, 'Women's Place Is on the Integrated Circuit', in special issue on changing role of south-east Asian women, *South East Asia Chronicle*, No. 66, January–February 1979, pp. 2–17.
14. 'Let Our Songs Drown Out the Bomb Explosions', *Vietnamese Trade Unions*, No. 2, 1969, p. 12.
15. William Henry Chafe, *The American Woman: Her Changing Social, Political and Economic Roles, 1920–1970* (New York: Oxford University Press, 1972), pp. 158–70.
16. 'Report of the Central Committee of the Viet Nam Women's Union to the Fifth National Congress of Vietnamese Women' (unpublished mimeo), May 1982, p. 8 (hereafter cited as 'Report').
17. Diem Thuy, 'The Dong Tien Tailoring Cooperative', *Women of Viet Nam*, No. 3, 1976, p. 28.
18. Ibid., p. 29.
19. 'Report', p. 10.
20. Interview with Du Hue Lien by author (Ho Chi Minh City, 13 September 1981).
21. Interview with Mrs Huong by Donna Futterman (Hong Gai, July 1975) (unpublished notes).
22. For details on protective labour legislation, see Cecilia Molander, *Women in Viet Nam* (Stockholm: Swedish International Development Authority, 1978), p. 63.
23. Interview by author with Mai Thi Thu (Hanoi, 30 August 1981). Data on

women in health professions from: 'Women in Health Care', *Women of Viet Nam*, No. 3, 1982, p. 5.

24. Interviews by author with Dr Vu Thi Phan and Dr Hoang Xuan Sinh (Hanoi, 2 September 1981).
25. Pham Truong Thi Tho, 'The Path I Have Travelled', *Women of Viet Nam*, No. 3, 1978, p. 12.
26. Mai Thi Tu and Le Thi Nham Tuyet, *Women in Viet Nam* (Hanoi: Foreign Languages Publishing House, 1978), pp. 245–6.
27. Interview with Mai Thi Tu by author (Hanoi, 30 August 1981).
28. Interview by author with Le Thu (Hanoi, 2 September 1981).
29. Information on My Duc from author's visit to Ha Son Binh Province, September 1981.

10. Sharing Childcare and Household Work

Even with all the social services, women are still at a disadvantage, working the double shift both inside and outside the home. Our Women's Union and branches of the government must do research on how to lighten further the burden of housework and women's special tasks.

Tran Thi Hoan, Vice-Director of Foreign Relations, Women's Union

'Women's work is never done,' as the saying goes. Cooking, cleaning, caring for children is a round-the-clock job – a job essential to maintaining and reproducing the work force in any society. In Viet Nam, as in other pre-industrial societies, housework is exceptionally heavy. Water does not come hot and cold out of a tap. It must be carried from a well and then heated. Wood, coal or paraffin must also be carried every day, if there is to be fuel for cooking and heating. All clothes must be washed by hand, often at communal hydrants or wells. Since there is no refrigeration, food must be bought fresh every day, making daily marketing a heavy chore. When food is scarce, long queues make it an even bigger burden. Most clothing is sewn by hand at home. Household gardens, not supermarkets, supply much of the family's food. Electricity is available only intermittently. Children who are ill may require prolonged care because of the scarcity of antibiotics and other medicines. All these constitute 'women's special tasks', although often older children and grandparents help.

The Vietnamese government recently sponsored a survey to assess the extent of women's time spent in household chores. They reported that a Hanoi woman – working for the government, the Party or a mass organization – devotes 87 hours per week to her office work, supplementary income job and household chores, of which 26.2 hours are consumed in housekeeping. Food buying alone, the study found, requires an average of 50 minutes a day on weekdays and 90 minutes on Sundays and holidays. Each day, 82% of the employees go shopping for fresh food, mostly produce, and 16% for rice. On Sundays, these figures rise to 96% and 36% respectively.

The survey writers seemed disturbed to report only 10% of the women could take time out to study and 18.7% to look after their children's schoolwork.[1]

In the industrialized capitalist countries, women's labour in the home is barely recognized as work, although the system profits from it in a variety of ways. When a woman feeds, clothes and comforts her husband, his employer is, in effect, reaping the benefits of the labour of two for the price of one. As a mother, the working-class woman is pressured to teach her children to meet society's demands and thereby trains the next generation of disciplined workers. Also, because in part, her work at home is not respected, she is vulnerable and available to be exploited outside the home as well.

Houseworkers are isolated in their homes, unwaged and unappreciated. No one notices housework until it is left undone. Then complaints are heard about unmade beds, unwashed dishes and neglected children. In Viet Nam, on the other hand, housework is recognized as productive labour. Article 29 of Chapter V of the Law on Marriage and the Family allows women to seek divorce without losing the fruits of their labour. It stipulates that in the event of divorce, common property is divided according to the amount of work each partner put into the family earnings and, 'Housework is considered the equivalent of productive labour,' even though most Vietnamese women work outside the home as well.[2] This law makes Viet Nam the only revolutionary country to join a few relatively small women's organizations in the West in recognizing that housework is labour that should be compensated. The same law establishes legal equality between husband and wife and affirms women's right to choose a profession freely and to earn an income independent of their husbands.

Men Share Some Housework

Acknowledgement of the fact that women perform a double shift in Viet Nam, working both inside and outside the home, is a significant step towards easing their labours. One strategy for easing the burden on women is to convince men to share it. The emulation movement for a 'new cultured family', sponsored by the Women's Union, rewards families in which the husband shares in the household tasks. Trade unions and other organizations co-operate with the Women's Union in publicizing the importance of men sharing in household work. Rewards include social recognition and token payments. Nguyen Thi Binh, Women's Union Vice-President and Minister of Education, evaluated the effectiveness of this movement:

> I want to inform you that the division of work in the Vietnamese family has progressed a lot. The husband recognizes his duty to care for the family and children. He has to cook and go to market *when his wife is busy or away*. But

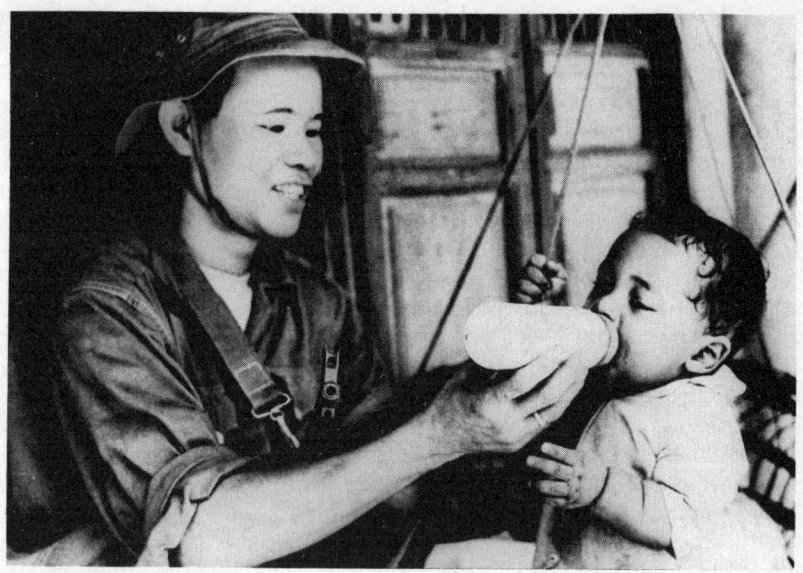

The law requires democracy within the family   Viet Nam News Agency

in spite of all our rules, we cannot oblige men to give birth to children.[3] (my emphasis)

Thus, we see that even a spokesperson for the Women's Union assumes that women have primary responsibility for the home and must, by implication, make special arrangements for the husband to assume her tasks. Madame Binh also implies that the labour of giving birth and the labour of raising children are inextricably tied. It is not surprising, then, that a careful reading of the literature on the 'new cultured family', as well as other official statements on the tasks of housekeeping and childrearing, indicates that there is not enough social pressure put on men to alter significantly the division of labour within the family. Most statements on 'new cultured families' stress the importance of harmony within the family and training children to be 'new socialist women and men', rather than the importance of men sharing the work.

Rather than assigning men equal responsibility, most propaganda encourages men to come to women's aid when the tasks become too great for them to accomplish alone. Some people cite Ho Chi Minh to support their arguments that women are the primary housekeepers:

Many people think that the problem of equality between the sexes is a simple one. One day it is the husband who prepares the meals, does the washing and sweeps up the floor; and the next day the wife will sweep the floor, prepare the meals and do the washing. And that is equality! A serious mistake![4]

But this is only part of the message Ho Chi Minh sent to the Vietnamese people on International Women's Day, 8 March 1952. Those who cite only part of the statement may be misinterpreting it. The next paragraph indicates that Ho Chi Minh did not oppose abolishing the division of labour in the home: rather, he thought that equality for women required a further change as well:

> What equality really means is a thorough-going and difficult revolution because contempt for women dates back thousands of years . . . . If this large-scale revolution is to be successful, progress will have to be made in every field: political, economic, cultural and legal.[5]

Invariably, biographies of exemplary women – women who have excelled as professionals after devoting most of their time to their studies – will include a reference to a husband who cared for the children while the woman was studying. Le Thu, Director of Education of the Women's Union, told me, 'Most of our women professors say it is thanks to our husbands that we can study and raise our educational level.'[6] Also, during surveys, women will often mention the importance of men sharing housework. For example, when asked, 'What should women do to exercise their right to collective mastery?' Nguyen Thi Bich Hue, who is director of a textile mill in Ho Chi Minh City, responded,

> Women must first of all be masters of themselves. They must strive to become skilled workers . . . and, at the same time, they must strictly observe family planning. Another major question is the responsibility of husbands to help their wives look after children and other housework . . . .[7]

In other words, an evaluation of the progress Viet Nam has made toward having men share housework would have to note that while this goal is considered socially desirable, especially by women, its fulfilment is not considered socially urgent. A struggle to make it more urgent is probably being waged by a minority within the Women's Union. Progress is more marked in the cities, among intellectuals and young couples, than in the countryside. But even in the cities, friends told me that it is still the rule that men do not shoulder anywhere near their share of household tasks. One Women's Union official's attempted explanation blames the victim for the problem rather than those with power to resolve it. Tran Thi Hoan wrote, 'Women of Viet Nam still have the burden of family responsibilities because they do not trust men to do the household chores.'[8]

The Women's Union and the overall leadership of the society prefer a second strategy: rather than abolishing the division of labour in the home that requires women to work a double shift, they are socializing house-hold responsibilities. A Women's Union official put it like this:

> It is not intrinsically important for men to wash dishes, but it is essential to have daycare centres, kindergartens, hospitals, canteens, community service teams and welfare measures to reduce the domestic work of women, to free them to work outside the home, give them the leisure to enjoy education and participate in politics and culture.[9]

In March 1982, at the party congress, Le Duan affirmed the party's commitment to women's liberation and then specified the relationship between the individual woman and society concerning responsibility for childcare and housework. He said,

> Special attention is required to provide better maternity and childcare . . . . We shall gradually broaden society's assuming the task of catering to and educating children. However, this in no way relieves the mother's role in bringing up healthy and well-educated children. The highest happiness of a young child is to be fostered and grow up in its mother's love . . . .[10]

Given the sanctity of motherhood in Vietnamese culture and also the anguish of thousands of mothers who were forced by war conditions to live separately from their children for many years, Le Duan's affirmation of women's role as mothers is probably meant partly to reassure people, especially in the South, that the Communist Party does not aim to 'expropriate children'.

Childcare: Lifting the Burden

Motherhood can be an enormously creative job, full of joy and love. Nevertheless, regardless of political commitment and legal rights, if a woman takes care of children *on her own*, there is no way she can study in order to advance herself or participate in political life. A mother, particularly a mother of young children, needs help if she is to have time to read a book, let alone attend meetings or take on professional and leadership responsibilities. Peasant women have traditionally worked up to 18 hours a day at home and in the fields. The lack of childcare facilities not only guaranteed women's subordinate status in the community; it also posed a threat to the children. Dinh Thi Can, Chairperson of the Central Committee for Protection of Mothers and Children, responsible for the national system of childcare in Viet Nam, drew this portrait of the days before childcare became a right.

> Highland women went to work with large baskets on their backs and children tied to their chests . . . the fields were very far from their houses

and they had to walk over rough country before beginning work. Once there, the mother would put the baby on the ground, or, at best, in a bamboo basket, but had no means of protecting her child from bad weather . . . mosquitoes, ants, leeches and wild animals.[11]

And in 1974, Le Duan told the fourth national Women's Union congress:

> In the old society, giving birth to children and rearing them were considered the private tasks of each mother and each family. Therefore, among the oppressed and exploited classes, the mother had to suffer a lot as a servant giving birth to, rearing and educating her children. Such a situation no longer exists . . . .[12]

Article 63 of the 1980 Constitution states, 'The state and society ensure the development of maternity homes, creches (childcare centres for infants and toddlers), kindergartens, community dining halls and other social amenities to create favourable conditions for women to produce, work, study and rest.' Article 65 adds, 'The state and society are responsible for the protection, care and educaton of children and assume an increasing share of the responsibility to raise and educate children in order to improve their social life, study and development.'

Of all the social arrangements designed to lay the foundation for women's equality in the family and in society, childcare has the highest priority. Before 1971, in the North and in liberated areas of the South, there was a social commitment to childcare, but no central agency had responsibility for it. Sometimes the Women's Union took responsibility, sometimes an agricultural co-op, sometimes a factory, trade union or health service. The Women's Union was efficient in organizing women to support childcare centres, but did not have the technical knowledge or resources to fulfil the needs of the centres themselves. An agency of the state was needed, with its own budget, able to do scientific research on children's health and education. Therefore, the Committee for Protection of Mothers and Children was formed in 1971 and given the power to solicit the support of other state agencies in developing a national system of childcare to serve all women working outside the home. The President of the committee has the status of Minister and is a member of the Council of Ministers.

Despite Viet Nam's scarce resources and devastated economy, facilities are found for childcare. During any discussion of childcare, people often refer to a quote from Premier Pham Van Dong to demonstrate the priority childcare holds in society. Premier Dong said, 'If we cannot have socialism for everyone, at least we can have it for the children.'[13] So, for example, shortly after the liberation of Saigon, the People's Committee of the city – the governing body – issued the following instructions on building allocation:

Various administrative units, government bodies, factories, and schools should reserve the most comfortable and best-equipped houses for child-care . . . . In case of a contradiction between the requirements of the offices and that of childcare, it is necessary to encourage cadres, office workers and parents to undergo difficulties and reserve the good and beautiful houses for the children.[14]

Likewise, in Dakla, a village in the Central Highlands where there was no childcare available before 1975, the first brick building in the reconstructed village was a childcare centre. These examples are repeated over and over in Women's Union reports.[15]

Buildings are not the only requirement for childcare that receives priority. The Bac Thanh Plastic Goods Co-operative in Hai Phong, the major port city in the North, was recently commended by the Ministry of Light Industry for working and to meet the needs of children. The co-op manufactures children's sandals and toys. The director explained:

If we only thought of profits we would not take up this line of production because the production of such tiny articles requires too much time and attention and brings in small profits. Costs are higher because of the need for variations which entail the frequent replacement of molds. But this trouble is negligible compared to the satisfaction derived from providing good service to our little customers.[16]

Childcare Workers
The most important condition for childcare is the availability of trained workers, committed to the children. The Committee for Protection of Mothers and Children has responsibility for training. Between 1976 and 1980, some 125,000 went to school to learn how to be 'good mothers, good doctors and good teachers' in their work at childcare centres throughout the country. There are two central schools, one in Hanoi and one in Ho Chi Minh City, each offering full-time study programmes lasting from nine months to three years, where students are paid while they study. There are also smaller schools in districts and provinces, usually offering shorter courses.

When the first school was built in a Hanoi suburb in 1972, it did not get much public support. Traditional contempt for childcare became obvious in comments by people when they saw the new sign at the gate, 'Central Childcare Attendant School'. They joked, 'What's this, a babysitting school for grannies!' and 'Now you have to be an engineer to be allowed to carry babies around!' Within recent memory, only the poorest women hired themselves out to look after rich people's children. These wet nurses were despised. The rare childcare centres in the old days had neither toys nor furniture, but only a few mats laid out on the floor. An older woman would attempt to keep the children from fighting and screaming until their mothers returned.

Opening a school for childcare workers dramatized a new understanding that childcare centres should not be 'warehouses for children', but rather the first step in a process of socialist education. Recruiting competent students for the training school was difficult in the early years. For example, Pham Thi Diem, aged 19, was an excellent student about to graduate from the Vietnamese equivalent of high school. Her mother expected her to continue her studies to become a doctor or engineer, but since she liked children very much, she was attracted by the announcement that the new Childcare Attendant School was opening. She wanted to give it a try. But she had difficulty in convincing her mother to abandon her prejudice against 'babysitters'. Diem tried to reason with her mother, 'This cannot be a low profession, otherwise the state would not require three more years' study after general education in school before starting the work.' Diem also recalled:

> In the first weeks at the school, many students still suffered from an 'inferiority complex', and dared not tell their friends and relatives what kind of school they were attending. During classes, curious peasants would peer through the windows to watch the 'babysitters' at their lessons . . . . But little by little, people have come to understand and support us . . . . The more my classmates and I learn, the more we find that bringing up children and educating them is not so simple. It is both an art and a science.[17]

The future of childcare in the US, on the other hand, looks less hopeful. The President of the National Association for the Education of Young Children, who is also a professor and a director of a childcare centre, wrote,

> I am very concerned about the negative attitudes about childcare in this country . . . . People still view it as 'just babysitting'. . . . And with President Reagan saying this is so, it is no wonder that we are not making progress . . . . I am not optimistic in recommending this profession to graduates. I cannot be confident that within the immediate future their efforts will be respected or that they will be adequately compensated.[18]

The School for Childcare Workers in Ho Chi Minh City was opened in 1977. It has since trained some 2,500 women, of whom many were recruited from high school and some had already worked at childcare centres. Their training emphasizes that childcare is 'a noble profession'. The curriculum at the school includes courses in anatomy and physiology; microbiology (especially parasitology); hygiene; physical exercise; pathology and pharmacology; nutrition; political orientation; drawing, sculpture and model making; cooking and sewing; child psychology; early childhood education; toys and games; language development; music; dance; and childcare administration.

The political orientation course teaches the importance of childcare in socialist society: in freeing mothers to work, study and relax and in teaching children socialist values. The course emphasizes the heavy responsibilities the worker assumes as second mother, doctor and teacher. During a visit I made to the school in Ho Chi Minh City, where I watched several classes, I was impressed by the students' dedication. They seemed honoured to be chosen for training in such important tasks.

The quality of the care is high in childcare centres where workers have been trained by one of these schools. Only teachers who have proved their commitment and competency are assigned after graduation. Perhaps the most important skill they have developed in school is respect for children. During their training, role playing – including acting out the part of the baby crawling on the floor – teaches them new ways to talk to children. Exercising the imagination is central to their training, especially since they cannot rely on expensive equipment and toys once they are assigned to work.

Old Age is Accountable to Youth
In Viet Nam free childcare is available for more than half the children whose mothers work outside the home in the cities and 45% of those whose mothers work in the countryside. In Sweden, childcare is available for only one child in seven. In the US, federally subsidized childcare is available for only 2% of working mothers. The government and the Committee for the Protection of Mothers and Children plan that by 1985, 80% of women who work or study outside the home will have access to free childcare.[19] Also, in addition to holidays and sick leave, when a worker has children under seven years of age, she is entitled to 15 days a year paid leave to care for her children when they are ill. If appropriate, fathers may also receive this benefit. Workers in state and some co-operative enterprises also receive a special allowance to hire someone to do childcare, if no childcare centres are available, but usually a grandparent or older sister will look after the younger children in such cases.

While the childcare movement began in Viet Nam during the war against the US, since 1976, the number of children enrolled in childcare centres has more than doubled. This increase, despite problems of scarcity, floods and war, was only possible because the government and the Committee for Protection of Mothers and Children and the Women's Union and other organizations were able to mobilize masses of people to support the childcare movement. They appeal to people's desire to educate their children as well as women's need to be freed from their household responsibilities. Uncle Ham, a member of the Older People's Union in Phu Dong village in northern Viet Nam, explained why he joined the campaign to grow vegetables and breed pigs to supply the childcare centre in their village: 'Under the skies of Indochina, on this land bathed with courage and so much blood, it is a good thing to establish as supreme, a balance of thought and seniority. That is why fire meets rain and old age is accountable to youth.'[20]

During an emulation movement in My Tho, south of Ho Chi Minh City, the Women's Union decided to celebrate the forthcoming party congress by pledging to open five new childcare centres and train the teachers to staff them.

In Dien Chau District in central Viet Nam, the percentage of children attending childcare centres grew from 22% in 1972, to 71% in 1979. A mass movement made this growth possible. The Youth Organization made the toys, decorations and gardens for the centres. Old people advised on construction and maintenance. The Women's Union encouraged parents to send their children to the centres and also launched a movement for each family to plant one tree and to raise one chicken to support the centre. The co-operatives in the district voted to pay childcare workers the same wage earned by 'category A farmers', the top wage scale available. Freed from much of the burden of childcare, women in Dien Chau District have taken on more leadership positions in the community. Seventeen women work as leaders of party branches, chairpeople of villages and co-op presidents. Some 300 are heads of labour teams and assume the main responsibilities in the economic and technical management of the co-ops.[21]

In a speech greeting the International Year of the Child, To Huu, a member of the Central Committee of the Viet Nam Communist Party, again underlined the importance of the childcare movement and implied that its progress was not yet adequate. He urged that the experience of Dien Chau be applied nation-wide. He reiterated the government's commitment to increase its contribution to maintaining childcare centres so as to ease the burden on community and mass organizations. He suggested ways in which each ministry might contribute to the childcare movement. For example, he proposed that the Ministry of Light Industry arrange for the production of more equipment and toys, particularly dolls with Vietnamese features since the few available were usually imported from Europe.[22]

Table 4 illustrates how the childcare movement has blossomed between 1975 and 1981.

Table 4
Progress in the Childcare Movement

Kindergartens (pre-school: 3−5 years)	*1975*	*1981*
Class rooms	22,300	57,500
Children enrolled	683,100	1,597,000
Creches (infants and toddlers: 2 months to 3 years)		
Class rooms	30,899	46,644
Children enrolled	563,700	1,229,886

Source: 'Appendix to Report by Central Committee of Viet Nam Women's Union to Fifth National Congress of Vietnamese Women' (unpublished mimeo), May 1982, p. 64.

Childcare centres open before working hours and close late to give working mothers time to travel from work and do marketing before they take their children home. There is also childcare available for women taking adult education courses or engaged in other night-time responsibilities. Some childcare centres operate night shifts; others have boarding facilities for children whose mothers are in hospital or out of town on work assignments. Larger centres have special rooms or infirmaries for sick children.

Educating the New Generation
When I visited the May 19th Childcare Centre in Ho Chi Minh City, story telling, singing, dancing and imaginative games seemed to be the main activities, even for children who had not yet learned to talk. Although the centre cares for 300 children and is housed in the former mansion of Emperor Bao Dai's wife, its stock of toys and equipment is scantier than what is available at an average childcare centre for 30 children in the United States. The May 19th Centre divides the children by age into groups of no more than 15, with at least two workers assigned to each group. The staff includes 60 workers; 40 of them teach, the rest are administrative and maintenance personnel. They use a manual published by the Committee for Protection of Mothers and Children that specifies programmes for children of each age group. In the nursery, children from two to six months learn gestures, and learn to grasp, crawl and recognize their surroundings. When I visited, only six of the 14 cribs were occupied.

Children at May 19th Childcare Centre sing about Ho Chi Minh
Arlene Eisen

171

The infants wore no diapers; rather a childcare worker made the rounds every 15 minutes to change mats if necessary. There were two women massaging and singing to the children. A group of children between 24 and 30 months old were sitting in a circle when I arrived. There were ten children and three teachers. One of the teachers was holding a drawing of a pig. The group responded when she asked what the pig ate, what noise it made and what it was good for. Later they sang a series of songs, accompanied by a tambourine. They sang:

'Yesterday I dreamed I met Uncle Ho.
I tenderly kissed our Uncle Ho.
I smiled. He smiled.
He told me I was wise.'

When they finished the song, all the children clapped. Then they sang another song about how wise children always sleep under mosquito nets and if a mosquito manages to fly inside the net, the children should smash it.

The manual specifies that during the month of September, children of 20 to 24 months old should learn how to draw a line, wipe their noses and talk about chickens. During the same month, the next oldest age group will get a more complicated natural science lesson about various animals. But the teachers apply the manual with a great deal of flexibility. One childcare worker explained:

> It is the children who teach us all. We first learn by just reading their looks, their laughs and their cries. That's the key for us all. To be attentive to every moment of their young lives. The children are for us the most interesting and complete fact of our instruction manuals.[23]

Ho Chi Minh's five principles of education (see Chapter 13) provide the foundation for the content of education at the childcare centre. The Director of Education at the May 19th Centre explained,

> We do not actually mention the five principles. We try to introduce the spirit of them in each lesson. To teach courage, for example, we tell a story about how a wolf was chasing a chicken and a dog rescued the chicken by letting the chicken swim on its back. This story also teaches the children to help their friends and love their compatriots. In teaching the children to practise hygiene, we make poems about washing hands, wiping noses and staying out of the hot sun. The teachers must also be models for the children in putting these principles into practice. This is why the work is very complicated.
>
> We also award the children. But each time we give an award, we explain the reasons for the award to all the children. There is no problem with favouritism or competition because we make sure nearly all the children receive awards sooner or later. We mainly use awards to encourage the quiet ones. The staff pay particular attention to the weaker ones, sitting

near them during free games, guiding them and encouraging the more active ones to co-operate with the shy ones.[24]

At another childcare centre in Ho Chi Minh City, a teacher decided to alleviate the toy shortage by making toys herself from empty cans and other scraps. When the children broke the toys as quickly as she made them, she decided to try to teach the children to make their own toys. In the process, they learned a new respect for labour – a cornerstone of socialist ethics. After understanding how much work was required to produce toys, they took care not to break them.

Since my own 15-month-old son accompanied me on my visit to Viet Nam in 1981, I had the opportunity to enjoy a first-hand experience of the childcare system. Although wherever I went I received lavish praise for bringing my child, 'just like a Vietnamese woman cadre,' they would say; they also made clear they understood I would need help with childcare if I was to do the research I had planned. Thoa, a graduate of one of the training centres for childcare workers, accompanied us wherever we went, to look after my son when necessary. She told me about one way she taught children socialist ethics: 'Whenever a child makes a mistake, we teach that child to make a sincere apology. Then all the other children applaud her. We try not to punish children, rather we reward them for good behaviour and stimulate them to improve.'

Yet, not all childcare centres in Viet Nam are staffed by people trained in sophisticated methods of child development. Many centres, perhaps a majority, also lack facilities and the resources to provide an adequate diet for the children. Toys, paper and books are precious, rare items. Dinh Thi Can, President of the Committee for Protection of Mothers and Children, pointed to another problem rooted in Viet Nam's weak economy:

> We would like not to have to take children in childcare centres before they are one year old. Then they could have maximum advantage of their mothers' milk and home care. But let us return to realities. . . . To build our economy up out of the ruins, women . . . contribute by working (outside the home). And they work hard because work is still done mainly by hand. Our living standards are very low in general and the rate of population growth is alarming. The state is not yet in a position to prolong paid maternity leave beyond two months . . . . We are therefore obliged to look after two-month old babies in our creches . . . .[25]

As the Vietnamese economy develops, it is certain that the childcare network will be strengthened. There will be more trained teachers and improved facilities. Not only will there be greater access to quality childcare, but mothers will also have the option of longer maternity leave, if they wish.

Publications for the Children

The Committee for Protection of Mothers and Children provides other services to mothers in addition to childcare centres. For example, the Committee published a booklet on how the school, family and society could co-operate to improve a child's development. One theme in the booklet was a challenge to traditional authoritarian approaches to childrearing. It advises parents to use reason and persuasion in teaching children, not force. The Committee explains that it is more effective to praise good behaviour than to humiliate a child for bad behaviour, especially in public. Behaviour that is praiseworthy includes respecting other children, generosity and making requests rather than demands.

In order to create new socialist women and men, the Committee hopes to stimulate discussion on the best way to teach children four basic principles: collective mastery, love of work, love of socialism and proletarian internationalism. Women's Union chapters all over the country set aside time to discuss the issues raised by the booklet. How to teach children the principle of collective mastery provokes some of the liveliest discussion because, traditionally, Vietnamese children learn obedience and passivity in the face of authority. Now parents are being urged to teach children to take initiatives, to be aggressive in fighting for what is good and to think of themselves as makers of history.

A children's publishing house and film institute both produce materials to assist in children's education. The books published by the Kim Dong House focus on two main topics: education in socialism and national traditions. One-quarter of all children's books are devoted to introducing the rich folk literature of Viet Nam's ethnic minorities and to translating the best stories from other countries. One children's book features poetry written by the children themselves. Nguyen Thi Thanh Tam, aged seven, expressed her respect for labour in the following poem:

The House Painter

Out there in the street,
High up on a ladder,
A housepainter, a woman!
Skyward she climbs
Clothing the house
In new garments.
If one meets her
On her way home,
No need to ask,
'What's your job?'
Just look at the splotches
On her jacket!
How I love you, housepainter!

How I love your job!
Sure, I'll paint houses
When I grow up.
I'll be going everywhere
Painting houses and factories.
The walls I'll paint white as cotton,
The windows pink
And the doors blue.
Every building will don a new coat
And say, 'Thank you, housepainter!'[26]

Animated cartoons and slide shows for children are always very colourful, usually featuring animals or legendary heroes. Often, they aim to teach a moral lesson. For example, a cat suffers as a result of accepting gifts while guarding the co-operative's rice store. A recent feature film for and about children, *Chom and Sa*, is based on a true story about a sister and brother who lost both parents in the war against French colonialism. They survived alone in a cave and years after they were rescued, one became an engineer and the other an actress. A thriving youth theatre produces plays; it travels to the most remote regions of the country.

Every city and town has a Young Pioneer Centre for children older than five or six. In Ho Chi Minh CIty, the palace of Thieu's Vice-President is now the Young Pioneer Centre. One mother in Ho Chi Minh City expressed the relief of many when it opened:

> Now children have a place to go after school. My daughter is learning a lot about science there. She also loves the sculpture class and the books in the library. I don't have to worry about her being influenced by that decadent American culture any more. And everything at the centre is free. [27]

Centres in the major cities are well-equipped: for example, the one in Hanoi is a five-storey building, complete with machine shop and astronomy laboratory. There are six such major centres in 24 cities and hundreds more at the city, ward and commune level. [28] All centres give children the opportunity to pursue hobbies, sports, crafts, special talents and vocational training, ranging from airplane modelling to violin lessons. Libraries at the Young Pioneer Centres offer the children not only books, but also writing workshops and a chance to meet and criticize the authors they have read.

Youth organizations – the Pioneers and Children's Brigades – also assist in childcare, educate and mobilize children to aid in reconstructing the country. Pioneer organizations at Vung Tau and other southern cities, for example, replanted trees on the roadsides to replace the ones US soldiers had bulldozed. Other groups take responsibility for keeping neighbourhoods clean and recycling paper. The proceeds from one national campaign to recycle paper paid for building a new set of railway carriages to make the journey from Hanoi to Ho Chi Minh City.

Community Service Teams and Consumer Co-operatives

Marketing can be a very time-consuming daily routine in Viet Nam. A friend estimated that women in cities may spend three or four hours a day buying food and preparing family meals. In the countryside less time is needed for shopping, since most of the food is home grown. In the cities, the Women's Union and neighbourhood organizations sponsor community service teams that deliver food, both prepared and unprepared, to workers' homes. In addition to shopping, if a family member is ill, the service team spends the day at the house, doing chores, cooking and nursing the sick. My friend joked, 'In the past, only rich people had household servants. Now, all people can get help in the home.' The Women's Union distributes household tasks on a rational basis by organizing teams of people who are unable to perform heavy work but who can sew or cook. They free women who work in other areas from the burdens of working a second shift at home. Members of service teams are usually older women who have experience of housework, but few other skills. Participation in the teams allows them to use their skills, earn a wage and participate in a collective. The teams are organized on the same principles as co-operatives.

In 1960, the Women's Union congress first instituted community service teams. There they resolved 'to gradually organize housework so as to help women concentrate all their time, energy and mind in production and in social activities, so that they have time for study and proper rest. That is our standpoint on the complete liberation of women of the working class.'[29] Each succeeding Women's Union congress resolved to extend the community service teams. The Women's Union also encourages family councils to discuss how household tasks will be shared among the teams, mothers, fathers and children. In practice, it seems children perform a substantial share of the housework if the mother has a job outside the home.

Community service teams multiply as women's work-force participation expands. But they are still not very common in Ho Chi Minh City. There, consumer co-operatives ease some of the burdens of shopping. The main store of the consumer co-operative in Ward 18 of the 8th District, for example, received awards in three successive years because of its devotion to meeting the needs of its customers. Every morning, a worker from the co-op loads vegetables, spices and other necessities on to a cart and tours the ward. She knows the needs of each household, so she packages goods in the amounts desired by her customers, rather than in units that would facilitate bookkeeping. The co-op tries to operate as many sales outlets as possible and to keep them opened at convenient hours. One co-op worker explained, 'A sick man may need menthol balm at midnight, dockers may want some fish sauce very early in the morning to take along with their lunches. Even on my days off, I used to be ready to serve the customers.'[30] What the co-op lacks in stock, which is substantial, it tries to compensate for in fair distribution and service. This helps to make the black market less appealing as well as to cut the time people spend on shopping. However, the co-op in Ward 18 is probably an exception. As late as 1981, the private and semi-legal market still sprawled in Ho Chi Minh City. One Vietnamese remarked, 'We have more experience and success in fighting US tanks than in fighting the black market.' As the economy grows and organization improves, co-ops like the one in Ward 18 will become more common. The government was distressed to learn from a recent survey, that women spend nearly one hour daily shopping for food. The State Trading Services studied the problem and recommended the following measures to relieve women's household burden: 1) increase the number of food stalls in residential quarters to avoid long lines at state stores; 2) have more shop assistants and goods on hand at store counters during rush hours – the end of office hours – when 80% of women workers do their shopping; 3) have mobile counters sent to factories and offices *so that men can also buy necessary provisions*; 4) market semi-processed foods, which will help reduce cooking time.[31] (Author's emphasis.)

To summarize: both the state and the Women's Union are firmly committed to socializing childcare and housework, with the understanding that the complete liberation of women requires the elimination of the double shift. Childcare centres, other arrangements for children's education, and community service teams now enable millions of women to work outside the home without carrying the full weight of the double shift. As the economy develops, the overwhelming majority of women will be freed from most household tasks so that they can participate on a more equal footing with men in developing their capacities and in assuming leadership roles. The remaining obstacles will be maintained more by the tenacity of patriarchal contempt for women: society does not expect women to continue working the double shift.

Notes

1. 'How Much Time Is Devoted to Household Chores by Women State Employees?' *Information Documents by Viet Nam Courier*, No. 26, 16 March 1983, pp. 18–19.
2. Cuba's family code and Nicaragua's laws require both partners to 'care for the family they have created', but does not recognize household work as productive labour. See *Cuba Family Code* (New York: Center for Cuba Studies, 1975), p. 8, and 'Una Revolucion que Comienza: La de la Muier', *Envío*, ano 3, No. 25, Instituto Historico Centro Americano (Managua), p. 5f.
3. Interview by author with Nguyen Thi Binh (Hanoi, 2 September 1981).
4. Ho Chi Minh is quoted by Mai Thi Tu and Le Thi Nham Tuyet, *Women in Viet Nam* (Hanoi: Foreign Languages Publishing House, 1978), p. 171.
5. Ibid., p. 172.
6. Interview by author with Le Thu (Hanoi, 2 September 1981).
7. 'What Should Women Do to Exercise Their Right of Collective Mastery?', *Women of Viet Nam*, No. 3, 1977, p. 6.
8. Tran Thi Hoan. Personal correspondence with author, 3 November 1982.
9. Le Thu, quoted by Kathleen Gough, *Ten Times More Beautiful* (New York: Monthly Review Press, 1977), pp. 91–2.
10. Le Duan, 'Political Report to the Fifth Congress of the Viet Nam Communist Party', Foreign Broadcast Information Service, March 1982.

11. Dinh Thi Can, 'Interview', *Mother and Infant Welfare in Viet Nam* (Hanoi: Foreign Languages Publishing House, 1979), p. 17.

12. Le Duan, 'Role and Tasks of Vietnamese Women in the New Revolutionary Stage', *Some Present Tasks* (Hanoi: Foreign Languages Publishing House, 1974), pp. 67–8.

13. Maxine Molyneux, a member of the Feminist Review collective, speaks of the 'permanent deficiencies' of socialist countries in her evaluation of their progress towards women's emancipation. She consistently generalizes on the basis of scanty evidence. The weakness of her argument is most evident when we compare the priority childcare enjoys in Viet Nam with what Molyneux writes about the same subject. Regarding Third-World countries, she concludes: 'The provision of nurseries is even less likely than schools to be a state priority where there is an overall pressure on resources and where older female kin are available as substitutes for the State.' ('Socialist Societies Old and New: Progress Towards Women's Emancipation?', *Monthly Review*, Vol. 34, No. 3, July–August 1982, p. 59.

14. Phuong Thuy, 'Priority to Our Children', *Women of Viet Nam*, No. 2, 1977, p. 4.

15. My Lan, 'The Changes in Dak La', *Women of Viet Nam*, No. 4, 1980, pp. 6–9.

16. Le An, 'In the Interests of the Little Customers', *Women of Viet Nam*, No. 3, 1979, p. 25.

17. The account of the first school for childcare workers is from Phuong An, 'A New Profession', *Viet Nam Courier*, No. 58, March 1977, pp. 20–3.

18. Betty M. Caldwell, 'Confronting the Realities of Childcare', *Childcare Information Exchange*, No. 28, November–December 1982, p. 13.

19. Cecilia Molander, *Women in Viet Nam* (Stockholm: Swedish International Development Authority, 1978), p. 33; and interviews by author with Mai Thi Tu (Hanoi, 2 September 1981). The 1982 Women's Union congress reported that childcare was available for 27% of creche-age and 32% of pre-school-age children. (The report did not state if these percentages include all children or only the children of mothers who work outside the home.)

20. Quoted by Jacques Danois, *A Good Start* (Bangkok: UNICEF, n.d.), p. 11.

21. Le Hung Quan, 'Dieng Chau District and its Nurseries', in *Mother and Infant Welfare in Viet Nam*, pp. 23–6; and Nguyen Luong Phan, 'the Most Advanced District in the Nursery Movement', *Women of Viet Nam*, No. 4, 1979, p. 28. In the countryside, it seems general policy to pay childcare workers the highest wage available to co-op workers. See Phan Quang, 'Wealth from Acid Soil', *Viet Nam Courier*, No. 10, 1982, p. 7.

22. To Huu, 'The Formation of the New Man Must Start at His Birth', *Women of Viet Nam*, No. 1, 1979, pp. 6–8.

23. Danois, op. cit., p. 48.

24. Interview by author with Director Huong (Ho Chi Minh City, 10 September 1981).

25. Dinh Thi Can, op. cit., p. 16.

26. Van Hong, 'Kim Dong Books for Children', *Women of Viet Nam*, No. 1, 1979, pp. 11–12.

27. Conversation by author with woman on street (Ho Chi Minh City, 11 September 1981).

28. Hoang Whu and Duc Lan, 'The Children's Cultural House and Extra Curricular Education, *Viet Nam Courier*, No. 1, 1983.

29. 'The Vietnamese Women and Their Tasks in the New Stage of Socialist Building', *Speeches from the Second National Congress of Viet Nam Women's Union* (Hanoi, mimeo, 1960), p. 19.
30. Pham Bao An, 'At the Consumers' Service', *Women of Viet Nam*, No. 4, 1979, pp. 14–15.
31. These recommendations were published in 'How Much Time Is Devoted to Household Chores by Women Employees?' *Information Documents by Viet Nam Courier*, No. 26, 16 March 1983, p. 19.

11. The Family in Transition

> The greater the contribution women make to society, the higher their status in the family and the more they enjoy their constitutional and legal rights.
>
> *Editors,* Women of Viet Nam

> You may be the boss of the co-operative, but at home, I'm the boss. Even a woodcutter is master in his own home.
>
> *Example of husband's intransigence quoted by Mai Thi Tu and Le Thi Nham Tuyet in* Women in Viet Nam

In 1930, some of the founders of the Indochinese Communist Party, anxious to build a society free from all 'mystical ties', urged the adoption of the slogan *tam vo*, or 'the three no's': no religion, no family, no fatherland. The slogan never became popular with the Vietnamese people. The ICP soon dropped it because it neither reflected the aspirations of the people, nor helped in the struggle against feudalism and French colonialism.[1] According to a leader of the Women's Union, 'to the Vietnamese people, family relations have always been sacred and very close.'[2] Proverbs, still repeated after centuries, express the importance and permanence of the family as an institution. One proverb states: 'Man has his parents and grandparents, just as a tree has its trunk and a river has its source.' And a folk-song insists,

> 'An unmarried woman cannot help but run around worried and insecure.
>
> Sisters, it is miserable not to have a husband.'[3]

In an often-quoted talk Ho Chi Minh gave to a meeting debating the Draft Law on Marriage and the Family in 1959, he tried to combine Vietnamese love of family – minus the patriarchal structure – with new notions about equality within the family. He gave a revolutionary interpretation of family life:

> There are people who think that as a bachelor I may not have a perfect knowledge of this question. Though I have no family of my own, yet I have a very big family: the working class throughout the world and the Vietnamese

people . . . . 'Living in harmony, husband and wife may empty the East Sea,' the proverb runs. To enjoy concord in matrimonial life, marriage must be based on genuine love . . . . The Law on Marriage and the Family aims at emancipating women, that is freeing half of society. The emancipation of women must be carried out simultaneously with the extirpation of feudal and bourgeois thinking in men.[4]

Ho Chi Minh assumed that the subordination of women in the family is the norm only in feudal and capitalist societies. We have seen how the patriarchal family was the cornerstone of more than two thousand years of feudalism in Viet Nam. Under capitalism, employers profit from keeping women trapped in a cycle of marital dependency, leaving husbands with more power and forcing wives to work under less favourable conditions for lower pay. Under socialism, the goal is to eliminate all inequalities based on exploitation and injustice. Ideally, socialist conditions make it possible for women and men to unite as companions, each maintaining her or his independence, strength and commitment to building a revolutionary society. Le Duan elaborated, 'In socialist society the family is built on equal relations and genuine love. The family is no longer an economic unit.'[5]

In practice, while the importance of the family in Vietnamese society has remained the same, the nature of the family, particularly power relations within it, has changed. Yet few would argue that full equality within the family has been achieved.

The Abolition of Polygamy

The most significant change has been women's right to free choice in marriage and the abolition of polygamy – the most oppressive family institution. In North Viet Nam, the 1946 Constitution and later decrees laid the foundation for outlawing polygamy and forced marriage. Between 1951 and 1958, the ratio of childhood marriages fell from 25 to 8%, while the ratio of free-choice marriages rose from 27 to 63%. But the Law on Marriage and the Family, which explicitly outlaws polygamy, was not passed in the Democratic Republic of Viet Nam until 1960. The state policy has been not to pass a law until it reflects the attitudes of the majority of the people. For 15 years, cadres from the Women's Union and the party struggled to educate the people to overcome centuries of tradition that favoured polygamy. Not all opposition to the new law came from men. For example, some women – fearful of their husbands taking concubines – opposed the provision of the Marriage Law that grants equal rights to children born inside and outside marriage.

The Women's Union proposed the content of the Law; the Ministry of Justice provided the language. The 1960 Law on Marriage and the Family not only bans polygamy; it also outlaws forced marriage, child marriage,

Family shares the work

Peggy Herod

bride price, dowry and wife beating. The law requires democracy within the family, allowing neither spouse to exercise more power than the other. Under the old Saigon regime, Law I/50 'On the Family' made the husband the legal head of the household and forbade divorce unless it was especially authorized by the 'Head of State'. In the US today, there is still no federal guarantee affirming equal rights for women and in many states it is legally assumed that a husband has the power to force his wife to obey him.[6]

In Viet Nam, on the other hand, the law not only requires democracy within the family, it also guarantees the right of each partner to freely choose an occupation, and the right of daughters and sons to equal treatment within the family. Children of parents who are not married have the same rights as children whose parents are married. Both women and men have equal right to divorce; but a man is not allowed to divorce a pregnant woman until a year after she has given birth, unless the woman demands the divorce. The law also overturns patriarchal codes forbidding widows to remarry and protects women's rights to child custody and communal property.

The government and the Women's Union have worked hard to enforce the law. Shortly after it was enacted, a directive from the party Central Committee noted, 'To ensure a correct application of the Law on Marriage and the Family, permanent and long-term propaganda and educational work are necessary among cadres, Party members and people.' Vo Thi The, a retired member of the Central Committee of the Women's Union, told me how she led a group of Women's Union cadres in a campaign that brought the law to the rural strongholds of patriarchy:

> We found young women who were married to boys eight or nine years old. The women would work in the fields and the boys would go to school. They had no sexual relations. The boys were too young to understand anything . . . . We would organize study meetings to discuss the new law – separate meetings for the youth and parents. At first, young brides would not dare to take the initiative in asking for enforcement of the law. But we used these meetings to stimulate their consciousness. After the meetings, they would approach us privately and cry and recount the details of their hard lives . . . . There were so many who were miserable as victims of forced marriage and polygamy.
>
> Sometimes we would have a fierce struggle with the boys' parents, who had already given gifts and paid for their sons' brides. We would explain why they should let the young women be free – how their marriage was a form of servitude – that it was unjust . . . . Those who continued to flout the new law were fined . . . but there were not many . . . . Now, in 1974, we have virtually abolished polygamy and forced marriage (in the North).[7]

While polygamy was officially illegal under the old Saigon regime, it was still common. Some government officials flaunted three or four wives. In a 1980 editorial, the Women's Union national magazine pointed to the problems of enforcing the law in the South:

> These backward habits have not disappeared completely and they are often skilfully camouflaged. But if the authorities hear of such breaches and proof can be found, the guilty parties are severely dealt with . . . . In the southern provinces, nearly five years after liberation, the Law on Marriage and the Family, thanks to the experience of twenty years of application in the North, has had some effect . . . . Now, if a husband beats or abandons his wife, takes a concubine, beats his children, shirks his family responsibilities or spends time on illicit love affairs, the wife can have recourse to the law and get support from the Women's Union to defend her rights and happiness and those of her children. Many second wives of already-married men, after learning of the new law, have not hesitated to seek divorce at the tribunals. Many have set up new families. In the family, new progressive and democratic relations . . . are appearing and have been welcomed by public opinion . . . .
>
> However, in the last 20 years, as our government and people were busy fighting the long war against the imperialists, not enough effort was put into applying this law . . . . Where state control and supervision has been lax, old-fashioned habits have re-emerged. Breaches of the law often occur among working people, even among State employees . . . .[8]

In 1981, the Women's Union began the work of drafting a new law to strengthen the importance of the existing one. They expected the necessary discussions and struggles to enact that law would be complete by 1984. However, before any law can be effective, women must understand their rights. Women's Union cadres often say, 'We cannot force a woman to divorce her husband – even if he's a polygamist – she must do it voluntarily.'

As part of an effort to popularize women's rights, newspapers frequently carry stories like Bich Hoa's. Her husband wanted a second wife because after several years of trying, she had not given birth to a son. Persisting traditions requiring sons for ancestor worship still pressure women to bear children until they produce a son. Rather than lose her husband altogether, Bich Hoa was prepared to give in to her husband's demand that she propose a second wife for him. When the Women's Union heard about the dilemma, they sent cadres to talk to the three parties involved. After some struggle, they convinced the husband that his feudal ways were unacceptable and he abandoned his plan to take a second wife.[9]

Divorce Court in Hanoi

In the Law on Marriage and the Family, the principle of free choice in marriage includes freedom to divorce. The night before I was to visit a divorce trial, Vo Thi The explained to me,

> The law encourages matrimonial happiness, solidarity and unity within the family . . . but divorce is no longer a humiliation for women. It is a kind of liberation from the yoke of an oppressive man. The law and the courts always defend the interests of women and children. The aim of divorce is to defend the rights of women against feudal male supremacy – no matter who initiates the divorce.[10]

Victims of forced marriages are always granted speedy divorces. But in other cases, they try to encourage reconciliation. One aim of reconciliation is to ensure the happiness of the children. The court may assign neighbours or co-workers from the trade union or Women's Union to serve as a reconciliation team. 'To try to reconcile is not to gloss over faults, it is rather to make a persevering criticism of the defects and errors and to stress and encourage what is good and inculcate in both parties a correct conception of marriage and the family.'[11]

If the conflict sharpens, then a divorce is granted. The property is divided according to who earned it, with the recognition that housework is 'earning work'. If the needy party requests it, the court will ask the other party to pay child support according to his or her means. They entrust the children to whichever spouse is best able to care for them. A divorce trial in

Viet Nam can be a dramatic struggle between 'feudal hangovers' and women's rights. As I sat in on one trial in Hanoi, I was struck by the strength of the Women's Union and the advantages women gain from living within a legal system committed to women's liberation. In the court itself, there were three judges, two of whom were women. The defence attorney for the wife was a woman, as was the investigator responsible to the judges for researching the case. All the women were members of the Women's Union. There is no charge for divorce proceedings or for attorneys' services. In this case, however, the husband had not requested the services of an attorney. The issue of contention was classic. The wife, Nguyet, wanted a divorce because her husband, Hung, had been harassing her for a long time. A lower court had granted the divorce, but Hung was appealing against it. The husband and wife each spoke for themselves, giving their version of the story, responding to each other's testimony:

Hung: 'Neighbours tell me she continues to relate to other men. But I am a good husband and want to keep the marriage . . . .'
Nguyet: 'Now, after living together, I have found that matrimonial happiness is impossible. We have conflict about everything: what food to buy, clothes, everything . . . . He even beat me and gambled . . . . All his words about my flirtations are lies . . . .'
Defence Attorney: 'Nguyet, why does your husband accuse you of child neglect?'
Nguyet: 'I went to evening classes for vocational education. He was very jealous. He has insulted me and spreads rumours about me to my friends. He says I was with other men . . . . I insist on an investigation. Go to my school. It is called "Tay Son" and check to see if I was there . . . . It's my right to have friends and go to classes . . . . He said he would take care of our daughter while I was in class, but he left her alone. Sometimes he would agree with my complaints and criticisms of him, but he always behaves differently and never puts promises into practice.'
Investigator: 'Mr Hung, how do you respond to what your wife says?'
Hung: 'She was too young when we got married – 17 years old . . . . She's fickle. I've been more steady. Because of her relationships with other students, she has lost interest in me . . . . They have made her extravagant . . . .'
Investigator: 'Your wife wants a divorce because she has no love for you. How do you respond?'
Hung: 'Our parents agreed to our marriage. It is her fault that there is no happiness in our family . . . . I never forced marriage . . . .'
Investigator: 'But how can you live together if she doesn't want to? What is your real motive for saying you want reconciliation?'
Hung: 'I think it is possible.'
Judge: 'And what about the child?'
Hung: 'I insist on having *my* child with me. My mother and sister will help.'
Defence Attorney: 'You want reconciliation and the child. Is it true? Do you want reconciliation because you love your wife or because you want to maintain the child?'
Hung: 'For the sake of my child, I want reconciliation . . .'
Investigator: 'Nguyet, how do you respond to your neighbours' reports of your flirtations?'

Nguyet: 'They are mistaken. I have many men friends, but they are not my lovers . . . also, my husband's family made life so miserable for me, that I liked to be away with friends.'

Investigator: 'There may have been some flirtation, but we have abolished feudalism and it is fine for you to have male friends.'

After nearly an hour of testimony, the defence attorney spoke on behalf of Nguyet:

> Do not consider me subjective because I am also a woman. I am defending her because of the principles involved, not because of her sex. Nguyet certainly has faults . . . . But there is a strong ideological conflict in this relationship . . . . Once he even got his brother to hold her down while he cut her hair as a revenge for her spending time with her own friends. That was feudal and that is why she has no feeling left for him . . . . According to Article 34 of the Marriage Law, a husband and wife must have mutual respect. He has constantly violated this article. We must consider this case on the basis of her happiness and the principles of mutual support and respect . . . . We think the child should stay with the mother as she requests.

Then the investigator spoke:

> We defeated the French, liberated the North and restored peace. But remnants of feudalism remain, especially in matters concerning marriage and the family . . . . We do our best to put the new law into practice in our lives. In this case, we object to the early age of Nguyet's marriage. She wanted to annul the marriage, but gave into her parents' pressure to stay married. After some time, the contradictions between the couple increased to the point where we witness this bitter session today. People, even young people, must make their own decisions and not be bent by family pressures . . . .

The judges left the court-room and deliberated for less than five minutes. They ruled in favour of the wife on every issue. Then, one of them addressed the husband:

> We must drive away all ideology left from feudalism. You cannot force your wife to live with you if she does not want to. She also has the right to her own friends. Lack of love is the basic grounds for divorce . . . . In the future, Mr Hung, you may have another wife and you must learn to treat women properly. The Marriage Law says that there must be democracy within the family. The family is part of society and for the sake of society, there must be mutual respect and support . . . also, according to the law, both parties must share in the housework . . . . The wife has insisted on divorce. The couple has many contradictions in daily life. That is why we allow divorce . . . . The child should stay with Nguyet because Nguyet has a better job and can take better care of her.'

Both Hung and Nguyet left the court-room without looking at each other again. After the proceedings, I asked the judges why they allowed the husband so much time repeating his side and why they thought his accusations against his wife were relevant. The judges explained that in order to avoid post-trial bitterness, both parties were encouraged to say everything that was on their minds. They did not want the husband to leave the court grumbling that his point of view was not heard. It was important for him to speak fully so that the truth of the situation would emerge. Also, the judges viewed the trial as only one step in a long process of re-education that would continue after the trial. Most of the spectators in the court-room were friends and co-workers of Nguyet and Hung. It was their responsibility to continue Hung's education – to teach him how to transform his feudal, authoritarian ways. Hearing his full testimony would make their task easier.[12]

While divorce in Viet Nam becomes less common as time passes and the legacy of feudal patriarchy becomes less influential, it is still fairly frequent, especially among young, childless couples.

Women's Independence Brings Democracy to the Family

In traditional Viet Nam, an unmarried woman owed unconditional obedience to her father. During the long war against the US invaders, daughters sometimes had to choose between the demands of filial piety and the demands of the liberation struggle. For example, one father complained to his daughter:

> You are my girl. Because you have left this house day and night and abandoned your home chores, one half of our land has not been fully cultivated and weeds have grown up everywhere . . . . Many persons can work for the revolution, but I can find nobody like you! People who make the revolution don't receive salaries . . . . I cannot stop you from working for the revolution, but you should at least take pity on me and not compel me to cook your daily meals. Unfortunately, if you are killed . . . , I will have to bury you . . . . According to the heavenly law, as our ancestors said, children should bury their parents.
>
> If you continue to go out day and night to make contacts . . . and attend meetings with those cadres, you might be led into a loose life. You might lose your virginity and get pregnant. In that case, I think it would be better for me to kill myself than endure the shame . . . . If you take your family so lightly and only think of your organization, do whatever you want. But don't tell your cadres to come here to warn or try to motivate me![13]

The women who endured harangues like this one received support from their comrades. They understood in the long run that even their fathers' best interests would be served if they helped strengthen the revolution. The daughters, of course, emerged with new strength and independence. Changes like these were systematically encouraged by stories broadcast on liberated radio. The following story, initially written for radio, was printed in *South Viet Nam in Struggle*, the official newspaper of the National Liberation Front of South Viet Nam. Pham Hoa, a member of the Liberation Army, returned home unexpectedly after three years' absence. When he walked into his house, he noticed a knapsack on the bed and an American-made belt with two grenades fastened to it. No one was at home. He asked himself:

> Has my wife become a guerrilla? Her timidity was well-known throughout the village. Nobody was as white-livered as she. She would shut her eyes at the sight of anyone cutting the throat of a chicken . . . . What pained me most was her fear of the enemy . . . even when they were a half day's walk away, she would fly into her secret underground shelter. What has made my wife change?

That night, the reunited couple lay in bed together without speaking. Gunfire interrupted their embrace. The woman sat up immediately, but not out of fear. She explained to her husband what was happening, told him to get some rest, grabbed her rifle and left. He followed her out of the door and met an older woman who scolded: 'Don't take her away from us.' He replied, 'I wouldn't dare.' The older woman continued, 'All right! You are a reasonable man. She is an élite fighter, don't you know that? You should not underrate her.' Hoa joined his wife in the trench. He reminisced: 'Without the comfort of a room . . . but standing in a trench of muddy water behind two sub-machine guns, we spent the happiest moments together since our wedding day.'[14]

While not all women became élite fighters during the war, it was very unusual for wives and husbands to live together. Once women gained experience in being on their own, the days of the 'Three Obediences' were numbered. Women had learned that if they did not need their husband's permission to join the revolution, they did not need it for other decisions as well. When I spoke to two Vietnamese men about the issue shortly before the war ended, one admitted that his friends were worried: 'The men think it is natural for the women to have high political rank. But inside the family, it is something else. When my friends return home, there will be struggles and the husbands will learn that the days of "home rule" are over.'[15]

Years of encouragement to put the needs of the country before personal needs gave women new confidence to defy patriarchal tradition. Minh Khai, perhaps the most famous and revered revolutionary woman in Viet Nam, had to forsake motherhood in order to assume her responsibilities in the anti-colonial struggle. Colonial authorities tried to slander women like Minh Khai as immoral, but a popular song at the time defended her decision:

'Our young partisan . . . graceful and small.
. . . and if anyone asks her about marriage
Gently she will say, "Fight the French" first!'[16]

After liberation, in 1975, revolutionary media continued to encourage women to defy patriarchal family pressures that might prevent them from maintaining their hard-won leadership positions. For example, *Viet Nam Courier* reprinted the true story of Thep, the daughter of a poverty-stricken illiterate woman who became the head of the village of Tien Tien, Van Lam District, Hai Hung Province. When she was first appointed, her husband's family were her most militant opposition. The article explained:

> Loath to see their daughter-in-law with more power than their son, they attacked the woman's most sacred feeling. They attacked her faithfulness to her husband. As village head, Thep met with many people . . . so they spread the news that she had committed adultery when her husband was away in the army.
> . . . Thep could not sleep for nights, but the rational and energetic woman held out and behaved with everyone and with her husband's family as if nothing happened, devoting herself heart and soul to her work.

The years passed, and Thep provided outstanding leadership in defending her village against US bombers and in repairing the damage to the irrigation system. 'In her ardour, there was a spirit of responsibility and love for her native place, but also a secret challenge against those who made light of women and had doubts about their abilities.' After the war ended, she led the village in modernizing its agriculture. The article continued to describe Thep's determination in the face of old peasants' disrespect:

> These struggles often seemed to be an uphill task, sometimes more difficult than a task in wartime. In fact, the enemy was not a person in the flesh, nor bombs sowing death. It was in the peasants' mind and had been there for a long time immemorial, and consequently at times, beyond the young village head's reach, much to her anxiety.

Throughout this time, in addition to her job as village head, Thep also cared for her two children and went to school. After he was demobilized, her husband returned to the village and became an accountant at the village store.

> The first days after he came home from the army, he was staggered to hear some people say, 'After only a few years' absence, he comes home henpecked,' or 'He will be led by the nose!' But he managed to ignore this nonsense and lives in harmony with his wife, helping her with her work.[17]

However, a conversation I had with a group of women at the Women's Union headquarters in Hanoi in 1981 indicates that Thep's husband may be exceptional in his willingness to support his wife's leadership. Amid much laughter, the women agreed,

> When men come home and women are no longer meek, the husbands may be upset; for instance, if his wife is the head of a co-op and he is only the head of a work group. But women are flexible. We will be very delicate and diplomatic at home. When the man says, 'You are the head of the co-op, but at home, I am the master,' the wife will be wise and very diplomatic. She will not contradict him directly. She may be silent. But the important thing is the husband cannot be violent towards his wife, if he feels threatened that she is his social superior. Vietnamese women are flexible, we avoid confrontation. We are confident that after a while, the husband will get used to being with a stronger wife. It is better to unite than to divorce.

In other marriages, where women played no special role during the war, there may still be more respect for the wife when the husband returns home. There are many stories told by women in southern provinces about husbands who were tyrannical towards their wives before liberation – husbands who had served in Thieu's army. But after spending some time in a re-education camp, they returned home more humble and more willing to accept their wives' bids for equality.

Women without Husbands

During the 20 years of US occupation of South Viet Nam, millions of families were separated. Living apart became a way of life – so that as late as 1981, when I asked my hosts from the Women's Union if they missed being with their families during the mid-autumn festival, they seemed surprised by the question. 'We're used to it,' one answered, while the other nodded. 'We haven't been able to share holidays with our families for many years.'

To meet the requirements of war, media encouraged the 'Three Postponements': if a couple fell in love, they postponed engagement; if they were engaged, they postponed marriage; and if they were married, they postponed having children. The ideal was for separated lovers to be faithful and celibate. Both women and men wore aluminium 'fidelity rings' made from downed US planes. After the US was defeated, many couples married or had children to celebrate the victory and the end of the 'Three Postponements'. But not all married.

I met Du Hue Lien in Ho Chi Minh City in 1981. She had been a textile worker and also a leader of the clandestine trade union movement in Saigon under the Thieu regime. She was in her early forties and had never married. Her sadness was evident as she explained, 'My lover died during

Widow supports herself as market vendor on roadside   Arlene Eisen

the war. We never had a chance to marry. I would never marry a US puppet and did not have the chance to meet anyone else. Now I am too busy and it is too late.' In addition to being a leader of the Women's Union and of the Hoa community in Ho Chi Minh City, Lien is also a member of the National Assembly. While Vietnamese society respects women like Lien, they also pity her. As a Swedish researcher observed, 'To marry, have children and build a family appear to be the self evident goals of every Vietnamese woman. If a woman were to prefer to live alone, devote her life to work . . . , she can count on being regarded with wonder, lack of understanding and compassion.'[18]

If women like Lien are the exception in Viet Nam, it would be only a slight exaggeration to say that widows are the rule. Nguyen Thi Ngoc Yen is a particularly celebrated widow, although she modestly claims, 'I am only one of millions of mothers.'[19] Her son became the first Vietnamese cosmonaut and she was given a great deal of credit for his achievements.

Today, she is in her mid-fifties and manages a factory. She has been a widow since her husband died fighting the French in 1950. She was left with two small children. According to government policy, she could have sent her children to a special boarding school for the children of fallen soldiers, but she wanted to live with them. Also, she feared the school for heroes' children would spoil her daughter and son. She wanted to teach them humility without giving them special privileges. Her mother cared for the children, while Yen went to work; but those were very lean years.

While travelling in An Giang Province, I was accompanied by a group of peasant women, most of whom were widows. I asked them what helped them cope with the loss of their husbands. Chon answered:

> The loss of our husbands affects us very much. But we live in a community and we have our work. There are many like us and we find joy in fulfilling our tasks. Of course, we never forget our loss. He died for the country. We say to ourselves, 'We must follow his example and devote ourselves to the cause for which he died.' That is the source of our energy.

Chon was one of many peasant women who assumed major responsibilities in defending her village against invasion by Pol Pot's army.

Widows receive material as well as moral support from society. Wives of dead revolutionary soldiers receive a special pension from the government. All widows receive support from the social welfare committee of their co-operative, factory, office or residential district. The Women's Union also organizes mutual aid groups to assist widows and women whose husbands are absent during critical times – during childbirth, illness or other times of need. If a widow's pension is delayed because of poor communication or bureaucracy, the Women's Union will help her for as long as necessary.

A recent story published in *Viet Nam Courier* portrayed a widow in anguish over a decision to remarry. Confucian tradition severely punished widows who remarried, but this story encouraged remarriage for the sake of the woman's happiness. Nevertheless, most widows do not remarry, partly because of the relative scarcity of men and partly because of their own preferences. Participation in Vietnamese social life does not require a woman to be accompanied by a husband. On the contrary, there is little pressure on a widow to remarry. Chon and some of her friends in An Giang who are widows joked about how they did not want to remarry because remarriage would redouble their work, by giving them two sets of children to care for. While they laughed, I had the distinct impression that their desire to remain independent was serious.

On the other hand, most divorced women do remarry, especially if their first marriage was youthful or arranged. Women's magazines often carry stories about women victims of polygamy or child marriage, who, freed from their feudal bonds, are now enjoying socialist marriages based on mutual respect and love.

A team of Vietnamese sociologists studied the changes which war and post-war reconstruction brought to rural family life. They reported in 1980, at An Binh Commune in the Red River Delta, only 14% of families lived with grandparents or in-laws. They believed the trend towards smaller households liberated women from old feudal bonds and reduced the long-standing exploitation of the wife by the in-laws. The study concluded that because the family is no longer a unit of economic production, its members can enjoy more independence and equality. Some 60% of the households are headed by women and women control finances in 76% of the households. A majority of the women whose husbands are gone have been able to save enough money to build brick houses. Out of more than 6,000 people, in 1979, there were only seven divorces. [20]

Struggle for Democracy within the Family Continues

It is a delicate struggle to maintain the form of the family – the last bastion of feudal ideology – but to transform its internal relations. The new family ideally is based on 'unity, equality, on mutual affection and on wife and husband helping each other to work and study so that both make progress, and share the responsibilities of family life and the education of the children.' [21]

In practice, especially in the South, the ideal is far from being achieved. It is still scandalous for a woman to be chief of a co-operative or of a platoon in the militia with a number of men under her authority, among them her own husband or elder brothers. People wait for such women to blunder. to prove the so-called 'in-born' incapacity of women. The authors of a Vietnamese book on women observe,

> Some people prophesize that women who run social affairs will neglect those of their families, and will lose their gentleness and femininity. This is one of the more subtle feudalist reactions. The gentleness and femininity referred to have, in the past, been expressions of submissiveness and passivity. [22]

By the same token, there is particular resistance to men sharing housework. The Women's Union counters this resistance in its meetings, publications and broadcasts. In one such story, called 'A Simple Happiness', a husband encourages his wife to go away to college to study. He receives childcare leave from his work-place. His wife is gone for five years; meanwhile he becomes a model worker and is admitted into the party. [23] Another story severely criticizes a lazy husband who plays chess and chats with his friends while his wife does all the work around the house. It congratulates a neighbour who finally intervenes on his wife's behalf. The neighbour convinces the husband that if he does not share the housework, his wife will not do it either, because she also has more important things to do.[24] In a third story, a man named Hai opposes his wife's going to meetings, until he spies on a meeting, or a 'hen party', as he contemptuously calls it. Then he discovers the Women's Union meetings are discussing serious business to benefit the entire community. After his discovery, he encourages his wife to attend meetings and takes the initiative in sharing housework, so his wife also has time to relax after a full day's work at the co-operative.[25]

The tendency to resist revolutionary changes in the family, however, is strengthened by people's desire to get back to normal, after the trauma and upheaval of decades of war. Party leadership and the Women's Union must organize carefully to assure people that a new respect for women will include a respect for family traditions. The Campaign for a New Cultured Family places particular emphasis on supporting families so as to restore harmony and raise well-educated children. At the same time, it reminds people of the importance of men sharing housework. This double-edged campaign is one strategy designed to wage the delicate struggle for democracy within the family. It is probably too soon to evaluate its effectiveness in meeting people's desires for stability and women's demands for equality. But some progress is evident.

The Women's Union magazine reported in 1977 that more women joined the movement to build a New Cultured Family when they realized it was a practical way to contribute to the complete emancipation of women. In one district, 13 out of 15 'disharmonious' families reunited; nine out of 11 small traders joined production co-operatives and 17 out of 20 'naughty' children improved their behaviour.[26] The article did not mention how harmony was restored to the reunited families and if women in them now enjoyed more respect.

In Thanh Hoa Province, as part of the Movement for New Cultured Families, the Women's Union investigated complaints about rulings by a local divorce court. They found the court negligent in enforcing its rulings that men pay alimony, and was also weak in preventing polygamy and other abuses of women. As a result of the investigation, the court redressed its errors and now the court, the prosecutor's office and the Women's Union plan to co-ordinate their work more effectively.

Love and Sexuality
Even after the war with the US, *Viet Nam Courier* published a story glorifying Bich Thuy, a woman engineer who refused both a marriage proposal and a comfortable job in Hanoi so that she could work at a rural construction site.

> Some years ago, she was in love with a classmate who asked her to leave the plant and live with him in Hanoi. She was torn apart by contradictory feelings. On the one hand, she was 30 and aware it was time to get married. But how could she let down the power station and her companions? If he

could not understand that, how could she be sure that they would be happy together? She made up her mind to stay in Viet Tri . . . .

Each time she goes to Hanoi for a meeting or a visit, her friends – some happy with husbands and children, others working in research centers or scientific departments, chide her: 'You've become just like a worker, are you going to spend the rest of your life in those hills?'

Once she gets back home, this makes her ponder deeply. It gives her difficult moments, but she gets over them. For the workers have adopted her . . . . One of her best friends is My Ngoc, a woman electrician. They are always together and it is not easy to tell who is the worker and who is the engineer.[27]

Bich Tuy's choice was celebrated as a sacrifice required by wartime conditions, rather than as a desirable alternative to marriage.

With the exception of Du Hue Lien, who was over 40, all the single women I met in Viet Nam were sure they would marry some day. But few seemed preoccupied with romance or anxious to marry soon. Married women rarely expressed a preoccupation with their husbands. Tuyen, for example, was accustomed to being separated from her husband for long periods of time, but she could not conceive of being unmarried:

It is only natural to marry. If a woman does not meet someone she loves soon – it will be later. Everyone here works for a common cause, so it is easy to fall in love . . . . I got married in the liberated zones in a collective ceremony with three other couples. It was September 2, Independence Day, in 1953. After the leader of our group pronounced us married and congratulated us, he reminded us to maintain our dedication to the revolution. Three days later, our political assignments sent me and my husband in different directions.[28]

Now that the Three Postponements are no longer necessary, most women marry in their mid-twenties, after they have completed their studies. If an ummarried woman becomes pregnant, her co-operative, the Women's Union or trade union will try to find her a husband or insist the father take some financial responsibility for the child. Rarely do such women remain single.

Today, the ideal in society is for both women and men to practise pre-marital chastity, monogamy and fidelity. But there is obviously some double standard. Remember, Confucian codes recommend an unfaithful wife be trampled by elephants, while there was no mention of a punishment for men who were unfaithful. The women's press frequently publishes stories critical of husbands with polygamous tendencies. Bui Thi Me, retired Vice-Minister of Health of the PRG and long-time party leader, pointed to the persistence of feudal ideology as the source of today's double standard:

> When we admit new party members, it is easier to admit men, because people are more critical of women. We must struggle militantly to clearly define women's merits. If a woman is good in her office work, she may neglect the housework, so her husband will oppose her party membership. We send someone who is his friend to struggle with him so he sees the importance of his wife's office work. But feudalism still has a deep influence. It is a lot easier to pardon a man for his love mistakes than a woman. Of course, we prefer for it not to happen with anyone. But we must struggle to make people less severe in their criticism of women. If a man does the same thing, it is considered OK.[29]

While the Vietnamese double standard may resemble our experience in the West, centuries of polygamy, arranged marriages, Confucianism and Buddhism have had a profound effect on the meaning and ideals of sexuality in Viet Nam. For example, when parents arranged nearly all marriages, men did not have to win a wife to enhance their social status. Pressure to display women as sex objects was alleviated by the universal assumption that parents' wishes would prevail over sons' desires. Today, as in the past, peasant families living in one-room huts cannot mystify sexual relations.

The connotation of physical intimacy is different in Viet Nam, except in areas strongly influenced by US occupation, from in the West. Western visitors to Viet Nam invariably remark about members of the same sex holding hands, hugging and fondling each other in public with no self-consciousness. On the other hand, there seems to be little public concern for sexuality, sexual relations or sexiness. When Westerners raise the issue of sexual freedom, Vietnamese women invariably respond by recalling their sexual victimization. Their experience with 'sexual freedom' has been as victims of rape by landlords or foreign soldiers; or as victims of the degradation of concubinage and brothels catering to French or American soldiers. This is why the demand for monogamy is considered a cornerstone of women's liberation in Viet Nam, not a source of repression.

In the West, much of the public fixation on sexuality is encouraged by an advertising industry which exists primarily because of its effectiveness in encouraging wasteful consumption. In addition, pornography is a multi-billion dollar industry. In the United States, more people read *Playboy* and *Penthouse*, the most popular magazines featuring pornography, than *Time* and *Newsweek* combined.[30] No such phenomena exist in Viet Nam. On the contrary, all organs of propaganda have focused on mobilizing people to concentrate on meeting the demands of defence and national reconstruction. And socialist morality rewards people for devotion to work for the benefit of the whole society, not for immediate personal gratification. In this context, the issues of sexuality and sexual relations appear to be eclipsed.

The absence of any cult of sex, however, does not mean Vietnamese people are indifferent to romance and love. 'A Heart-to-Heart Talk' is the most popular feature of the Women's Union weekly magazine. Readers ask for advice in resolving their questions about love and romance. The editor told me, however, her policy is to encourage a woman to postpone romance and learn a profession, so she can be 'master of herself, the society and the nation'. At other times, the column discusses questions such as how to persuade a boyfriend who has lived in old Saigon, under US influence, to become a productive member of society; or how to choose between two potential husbands, each with different virtues. The Vietnamese press also often features romantic poetry and songs. Love stories are frequently published but they include no discussion of sexual relations and usually end in marriage or in a heroic tragedy that prevents marriage.

In 1981, however, the literary weekly *Van Nghe* published a short story that portrayed a pre-marital love affair in a non-critical light. The story, 'An Old Path, New Events', implied that the couple's parents should respect their love and accept their child.[31] This story is one of the rare examples of muted public discussion of sexuality.

There seems to be no public discussion of women's alternatives to monogamous heterosexuality – either having more than one lover, or bisexuality or lesbianism. I never met a woman or man in Viet Nam who acknowledged the existence of homosexuality in their country. One Vietnamese scholar residing in the US claims, off the record, that lesbians can be found in villages, especially when the men are away. He maintains they meet social disapproval, but no legal persecution.

Groups within the women's movements of many Western countries have demanded that women be free to choose bisexuality, lesbianism or open relationships. Many offer an analysis that links capitalism, the patriarchal family and sexual repression of women. Requirements that women be virgins until their wedding night and that women's sexuality serve men, are part of a system of inequality in which women's bodies are considered the property of men. This analysis begins from women's experience in the West, struggling against an advanced capitalist system. I have tried to indicate why sexuality and sexual repression may have another definition and significance to Vietnamese women. Ideals of heterosexual monogamy and fidelity do not seem to have hindered women's progress towards independence, nor have they interfered with women's solidarity with each other. Women in Viet Nam express affection towards one another freely and openly. In the past, polygamy and economic dependence kept some women divided and especially fostered hostility between mothers and daughters-in-law. Now, a new solidarity has grown among women, created by the shared hardships and joys of those who joined together to fight feudalism and foreign domination. This solidarity thrives in Viet Nam where they have gone a long way towards abolishing the institutional sources of competition among women.

The solidarity among women in Viet Nam is visible and beautiful. I rarely recall sitting among a group of women – especially in the countryside – where they did not have their arms round each other, expressing a sisterly and comradely love. There seems to be no social barrier to women kissing and touching each other. While travelling on the road with four women for ten days in 1974 and again in 1981, I never noticed any sign of jealousy, competitiveness or hostility among them. Kindness seemed natural, but it was never taken for granted.

The strength of their solidarity became more evident when two of the women I was travelling with disagreed among themselves. They argued over the best age to teach a young woman about her body's relation to reproduction. One felt it was a feudal hangover not to teach a girl everything about sex before she began menstruating. The possibility of a child being thoroughly informed about sex before she was 17 or 18 was very disturbing to the other woman. The debate was heated. Both women had daughters. It was not an abstract issue for them. Both were adamant, but after some hours, when it was obvious they would not convince each other, they shelved the argument. Neither had questioned the morality or integrity of the other. Their mutual respect stayed strong and, in the days that followed, I noticed no trace of grudge or hostility. Solidarity and love among Vietnamese people emerges from mutual respect, concern and the experience that teaches they must identify with one another and sacrifice for one another in order to survive. Nguyen Dinh Thi, a writer and political leader in the army, explained more about this issue. He told a European,

> Many people who learned to read and write as adults and who were not well-acquainted with foreign words thought when they heard the term 'individualist' that it meant 'cannibal'. They associated the unintelligible concept of individualism with something dangerous . . . . They themselves had never had time to feel unique or singular. They shared work together, lived together and since time immemorial had made common cause against natural calamity and enemy attack. A joy, a sorrow, a difficulty had seldom been experienced alone.[32]

While Thi's statement, made during the height of US occupation of South Viet Nam, may be somewhat exaggerated, we cite it because it is an eloquent reminder that different historical experience creates varying ideals and expectations. There is nothing inherently oppressive to women in an abstract notion of family. The problem for women arises with a particular weaving of historical developments that create a patriarchal family.

At this stage in their history, most Vietnamese women have embraced the ideal of a revolutionary family in which there is mutual respect, love and democracy. The foundations for democracy within the family are strong: economic independence and the possibility of women earning more than their husbands; political and legal equality; social recognition of women's strength and importance in society at large; as well as specific support from the government and the Women's Union in their daily struggles for equality. Vietnamese women will continue to struggle against the traditions and practices that interfere with the achievement of their ideal. Yet generations of struggle will probably be needed to root out all vestiges of patriarchy from the Vietnamese family, so, rather than being a family in transition, it can be a truly revolutionary family.

Notes

1. Huyn Kim Thanh, *Vietnamese Communism: the Pre-War Phase (1925–1945)* (University of Western Ontario: PhD Dissertation in Political Science, 1972), p. 438.
2. Unpublished correspondence from Viet Nam Women's Union, 29 October 1973, p. 27.
3. Nha Trang, *The Traditional Roles of Women As Reflected in the Oral and Written Vietnamese Literature* (Berkeley: University of California: PhD Dissertation, Department of Anthropology, 1973), pp. 14 (proverb) and 27 (folk-song).
4. Ho Chi Minh, *On Revolution*, ed. Bernard Fall (New York: Signet, 1968), pp. 304–5.
5. Le Duan, 'Role and Tasks of the Vietnamese Woman in the New Revolutionary Stage', *Some Present Tasks* (Hanoi: Foreign Languages Publishing House, 1974), p. 62.
6. 'Women's Rights in the Democratic Republic of Viet Nam', *Viet Nam Courier*, No. 35, April 1975, p. 12. For details about patriarchal laws in the US, see Leo Kanowitz, *Women and the Law* (Albuquerque: University of New Mexico Press, 1969), pp. 88–91; and Karen DeCrow, *Sexist Justice* (New York: Random House, 1974).
7. Interview by author with Vo Thi The (Hanoi, September 1974).
8. 'The Application of the Law on Marriage and the Family in Viet Nam over the Past Twenty Years', *Women of Viet Nam*, No. 2, 1980, pp. 11–12.
9. Chiem T. Kiem, *Women in Viet Nam* (Honolulu: East West Center, 1967), pp. 55–7.
10. Discussion with Vo Thi The (Hanoi, September 1974).
11. 'Implementation of the Policies of the Women's Union in Various Services', *Women of Viet Nam*, Nos 3–4, 1971, p. 21. For details on the Family Law and its implementation, see *An Outline of the Institutions of the Democratic Republic of Viet Nam* (Hanoi: Foreign Languages Publishing House, 1974), pp. 156–84.
12. I attended this divorce trial in 1974. When I questioned Women's Union officials in 1981, they agreed that today's divorce proceedings have not changed.
13. Quoted by David Hunt, 'Organization for Revolution in Viet Nam', *Radical America*, Vol. 8, Nos 1–2, 1974, pp. 143–5.
14. *South Viet Nam in Struggle*, No. 163, 4 September 1972, p. 5.
15. Discussion with economist on his way to Peking in train (October 1974).
16. Mai Thi Tu and Le Thi Nham Tuyet, *Women in Viet Nam* (Hanoi: Foreign Languages Publishing House, 1978), pp. 130–3 and p. 153.

17. Phuong Anh, 'A Village Head', *Viet Nam Courier*, No. 46, March 1976, pp. 7–9, 29.
18. Cecilia Molander, *Women in Viet Nam* (Stockholm: Swedish International Development Authority, 1978), p. 52.
19. Interview by author with Nguyen Thi Ngoc Yen (Hanoi, 2 September 1981).
20. Duc Uy and Vu Van Thao, 'The New Features of the Family Structure in Viet Nam's Rural Areas', *Viet Nam Courier*, No. 8, 1980, pp. 12–13. A slightly different version of the same study appeared in *Women in Viet Nam*, No. 1, 1981, pp. 16–18.
21. Tu and Tuyet, op. cit., identifies the family as the 'last bastion of feudal ideology', on p. 240 and defines the ideal revolutionary family on p. 250.
22. Ibid., p. 246.
23. 'A Simple Happiness', *Women of Viet Nam*, No. 2, 1980, pp. 13–14.
24. Ton Ai Nhan, 'The Magic Bread Fruit Tree', *Women of Viet Nam*, No. 4, 1977, pp. 3–5.
25. Vu Thanh, 'Story on Marriage and the Family at a Woman's Meeting', *Women of Viet Nam*, No. 2, 1977, pp. 18–19.
26. 'The Building of a Civilized Way of Life and the New Cultured Family', *Women of Viet Nam*, No. 4, 1977, pp. 1, 3.
27. Phuong Anh, 'Sketch of a Woman Far From Hanoi', *Viet Nam Courier*, No. 36, May 1975, pp. 28–30.
28. Discussion with Tran Thanh Tuyen by author (Hanoi, September 1974).
29. Discussion with Bui Thi Me by author (Ho Chi Minh City, 13 September 1981).
30. Script of slide show on pornography by Women Against Violence and Pornography in the Media (San Francisco, 1981).
31. Thanks to John Spragens Jr for calling my attention to: Le Truong Thanh, 'Ngo Cu Chuyen Moi', *Van Nghe*, No. 47, 21 November 1981.
32. Peter Weiss, *Notes on the Cultural Life of the Democratic Republic of Viet Nam* (New York: Delta, 1970), pp. 67–9.

12. Ensuring Her Health, Controlling Her Body

> We must work for women to be collective masters in three fields: the nation, society and the self . . . . To be collective master of oneself means to have full control over your body, the right and possibility to decide when and if you will have children and what kind of career to pursue.
>
> Le Thi Xuyen, former Vice-President of the Viet Nam Women's Union

Health care in Viet Nam is free – the right of all people. The emphasis in the health-care system is on prevention, and women's health receives special priority. No doctor, hospital or drug company makes a profit in Viet Nam. Article 47 of the 1980 Constitution states,

> The state is responsible for the protection and improvement of people's health; develops preventative medicine; combines modern and traditional medical and pharmaceutical practices; combines the techniques of prevention and cure with the emphasis on prevention; and combines state-run health services with people's health services at the grass roots level.[1]

Given these policies, women's health and reproductive rights have made enormous progress in recent years, despite serious obstacles. There is a scarcity of drugs and medical equipment. Premature babies must share incubators; intra-uterine devices must be imported from Sweden and antibiotics are precious. What the medical system lacks in supplies and equipment, it tries to make up for in preventive measures and social organization. The Health Ministry, the Committee for Protection of Mothers and Children and the various mass organizations all work to make the public highly literate in medical education, sanitation and immunization. However, since good nutrition is the foundation of preventive medicine, even preventive measures are severely handicapped by food shortages. Malnutrition is the most serious health problem in Viet Nam, especially for children.

The anti-malarial campaign is an example of the progress made in preventive medicine, relying on mass mobilization, rather than sophisti-cated medical technology. Viet Nam still imports most anti-malarial drugs, many of which are ineffective against the particularly virulent strain of the disease found in Viet Nam. Before 1960, malaria was endemic in three-quarters of the North, afflicting 56 out of every 10,000 people. Today, in the North, only 0.4 out of 10,000 contract the disease. In the South, before 1975, an average of 100 out of 10,000 suffered from malaria. By 1981, the number had been reduced to 30. This success in controlling malaria is a result of the Institute for the Study of Malaria's training of nearly 80,000 part-time health workers to take books, films and exhibits to remote areas, to teach people basic hygiene and simple methods of eliminating mosquitoes. Professor Vu Thi Phan, Director of the Institute, predicts this mobilization will eliminate malaria entirely within ten or 15 years.[2]

Since the early 1970s, the population of the North has been totally immunized against cholera, typhoid, smallpox and polio; but these dis-eases still took their toll of thousands of lives in the South as late as 1975. After liberation of the South, massive innoculation campaigns were at the top of the agenda. By 1976, 80% of the population had been innoculated against cholera and smallpox and 95% of the children were innoculated against polio, tetanus, typhoid and diphtheria.[3]

Reorganization of the pharmaceutical industry in the South facilitated the massive innoculation campaign. Within a year after liberation, for

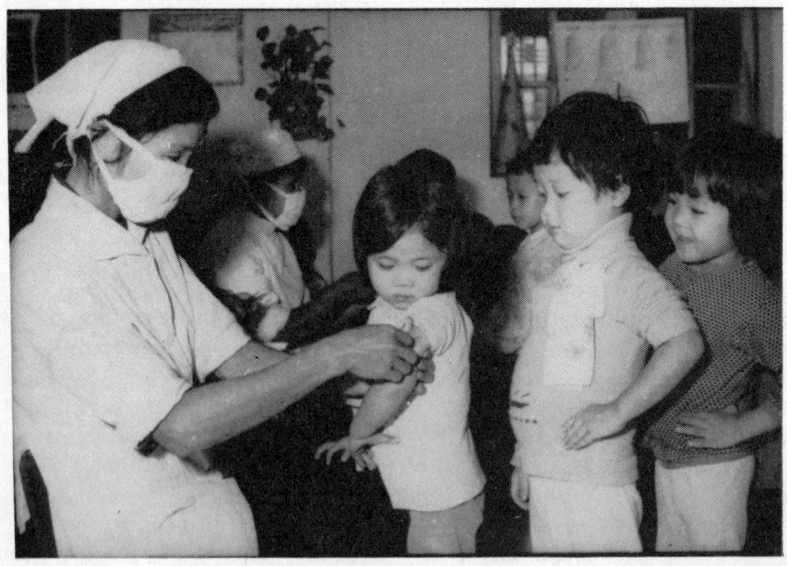

Viet Nam News Agency

example, the Pasteur Institute in Nha Trang tripled its production of vaccine and also developed several new products. Tran Thi An, a pharmacist at the Institute, attributes the change, in part, to a new attitude among the workers: 'In the past we worked like machines. Now we've learned the real aim of science is to serve the people.'[4]

The following statistics summarize Viet Nam's medical achievements. In 1945, average life expectancy was 32 years and there was one doctor for every 180,000 people. In 1982, life expectancy was 55 years in the South and 60 in the North with eight doctors for every 10,000 people.[5]

Doctors There to Serve

When I thanked a doctor in Hanoi for examining my coughing baby, he seemed embarrassed by my gratitude. 'We are here to serve,' he reminded me. Seven years before, when I visited the new hospital in Quang Tri, the northernmost province of South Viet Nam, the doctors were proud to say, 'The wars have trained our doctors to be close to the people. Their ideological convictions prepare them to suffer hardships like any peasant. There is no trace of Paris left in our doctors.' Those practising in the cities under the Saigon regime had a great deal to learn from their colleagues who had been working in liberated territory. Doctors who did not flee to Paris and Los Angeles had to close down their private clinics and work full time in non-profit-making hospitals and clinics. A doctor who had practised in old Saigon wrote to her friend about how 'the revolution recovered the beautiful qualities of a doctor':

> A change in the style of work here, 'collective diagnosis', has moved all of us . . . . In the past, we overestimated our position and set too much store by our contributions and in consequence, belittled the nurses and the cooks. Now we have come to know that every link in an unbreakable chain of medical treatment is important.[6]

However, since the economic reforms of 1979, the state permits doctors in the South to treat private patients, after they have served their full shifts in public clinics. Mass organizations will have to guard against deterioration in the quality of service at public clinics.

A US medical worker who had served for two years as a physical therapist in South Viet Nam before liberation, had the opportunity to see the hospital where she had worked after liberation. After her 1976 visit, she reported:

> The changes in attitude, morale, conditions and approach to medicine are evident everywhere . . . . Under the old Saigon regime, morale was low . . . hospital buildings were left uncleaned and unrepaired and lab work was inaccurate if it existed at all. In the past year, many doctors, nurses, lab

technicians and pharmacists from the liberated areas and from the North moved to cities and villages in the South to assist in the development of a new health care system. For the first time, the hospitals are clean and the emphasis is on prevention, nutrition and sanitation. [7]

Now, in every town or village there is an organized network of trained medical personnel, ranging from paramedics, nurses and midwives to assistant doctors and doctors. In selecting people for medical training, priority is given to daughters and sons of peasants, so that they will be able to establish better rapport with their patients. Midwives receive a year's training, assistant doctors study for four years and doctors study for six. Although sometimes transportation may be difficult, anyone who is ill has access to a district hospital where a doctor or medical council decides on the optimum treatment.

The number of doctors has doubled since 1974, and 60% to 70% of the students in medical school are women. About half the medical students in Ho Chi Minh City, for example, are from rural areas and will return there when they have completed their studies. In other words, medical training does not create a privileged group who prefer a comfortable urban life. [8]

Revolutionary medical training prepares health workers to meet the emotional as well as physical needs of the patients. Nurses routinely stay up all night with patients, comforting them, reading to them or visiting their families. Western doctors have been particularly impressed with Viet Nam's psychiatric techniques which rely a great deal on 'mothering', nurturing support, rather than using isolation or confinement. [9]

Medical workers belong to a trade union that defends their interests. The medical trade union also takes the initiative in criticizing hospital staff if a patient is not receiving adequate treatment. There are daily self-criticism/criticism sessions at the time when medical teams receive their assignments from the previous shift. There are also weekly meetings in which the staff in each ward evaluates the week's work. Discussions are often heated, when a medical worker trained in the old way clings to his own privileges and prerogatives.

Liberation also transformed the traditional Red Cross in Saigon from a charity organization to a mass organization of 300,000 members, trained in basic first aid. Revolutionary cadres worked particularly hard to recruit pedi-cab drivers, so that now every cab driver in Ho Chi Minh City knows how to administer first aid and where to find the hospitals and clinics in his district.

The Disabled: Their Right to Independence

There are so many disabled people in Viet Nam that a special Ministry was created to be responsible for helping them to achieve health and dignity. The staff of the Ministry itself includes many disabled people. An estimated 1.5 million people – 2.5% of the population – are seriously disabled. More than three-quarters of these people are disabled as a result of wounds received in fighting, bombings, police raids, torture and explosion of mines. Victims of poison gas and babies born with genetic abnormalities as a result of US use of toxic chemicals are not included in these numbers. Some 40% of disabled people are women.

Traditionally, disabled people whose families could not afford to support them survived by begging. During the Thieu regime, people dreaded the charitable institutions where the disabled were warehoused in sub-human conditions. Since liberation, disabled people who remain in institutions administer them democratically. The goal of those institutions and other programmes is to help the disabled to become as independent as possible.

By 1981, some 30% of the country's disabled people had been helped to find homes and jobs so they could live independently. A member of the Association for the Blind who helped establish a model work-place, explained,

> All disabled people voiced one desire: not to be a burden on their families or on society; not to attract contempt or pity. Life is not just eating and getting dressed. We wanted to live fully and, above all, communicate with others and be useful . . . . Only work could bring equality and love of a creative life to the blind.

His understanding of the feelings of disabled people pervades the work of the Ministry.

Mobile health teams were specifically organized to serve the needs of the disabled in rural areas. The teams include specialists in physiotherapy and orthopaedics. They are equipped to examine, restore and replace prothesis, although a shortage of araldite for the construction of new limbs severely limits their work. The teams are also plagued by inadequate transportation.[10]

Reproductive Rights

Abolishing Forced Motherhood

Reproductive self-determination, or, as the Vietnamese call it, 'collective mastery of oneself', is a basic condition for women's liberation. More crudely: without birth control, biology is destiny, trapping women on a treadmill of childbearing and dependency. Before liberation, Vietnamese women had virtually no right to choose. Under feudalism, large families provided more labour power to increase the wealth of the patriarch. Since infant mortality was high, women often stayed pregnant to ensure that at least some of their children would survive. The preference for sons pressured women to continue bearing children until they gave birth to the male who could perform the rites of ancestor worship. Also, patriarchal demands for fidelity were more easily enforced when women did not have access to birth control. All these factors combined to create a collective consciousness that valued very large families. Fear of poverty and famine rarely discouraged large families. A popular proverb among peasants held, 'As heaven creates the elephant, it will create the grass (to feed it).' Despite the availability of birth control today, one still hears sayings that reflect the continued pressure on women to bear children: 'Bear as many children as you can.' 'Bear children in a series while you are young.' 'You have something when you have a son, you have nothing, even if you have ten daughters.'[11] In some areas, the ideal peasant family still includes eight to ten children.

In addition to social pressure, ignorance of birth control methods and scarcity of birth control devices, the patriarchal abuses of concubinage and rape have also prevented women from exercising their reproductive rights. Poverty-stricken peasants were often forced to sell their daughters into concubinage. Concubines, as well as first wives, were not only exploited as labourers in the fields, they were also victims of the sexual demands of their husbands. Moreover, a peasant had virtually no defence against rape by her landlord; a worker no defence against rape by her supervisor. Ho Chi Minh called public attention to this violence against women in an article that denounced the French for degrading Vietnamese women, treating them as prostitutes and raping them with impunity.

Then rape reached astronomical proportions during the US occupation of Viet Nam. For the GIs, rape and murder seemed easier when they thought their victims were not quite human: 'gooks, dinks, slopes', they said, with slanted eyes and perhaps 'slanted pussies'. Few spoke of the Vietnamese as people. They were numbers in body counts. Corporal John Getmann, 3rd Marine Division, explained the racism of the system: 'When somebody asks, "Why do you do this to people?" your answer is . . . "It doesn't make any difference what you do to them; they're not human." And this thing is built into you from the moment you wake up in boot camp . . . .'[12]

When a GI tried to stop several others from raping a Vietnamese woman, they brushed him aside with, 'What are you worrying about? She is only a gook!' The jargon of army lawyers cynically expressed the same conspiracy of racism and sexism. The MGR – 'Mere Gook Rule' – was the unwritten legal precedent that nearly guaranteed an American soldier his freedom if he was charged with raping a Vietnamese woman.[13] By contrast, thousands of children fathered by GIs are products of this rape – painful evidence of the most gross denial of women's reproductive rights. In revolutionary Viet Nam, rape is so rare that it is not considered a social problem.

The main factor promoting women's reproductive rights, however, is the mobilization of the resources of the state and the Women's Union to counter the millennial pressures on women to produce large families.

Family planning is not only a goal stated in the Constitution, it is also a priority policy incorporated into the plans of various ministries, the Women's Union, the Committee for Protection of Mothers and Children, the trade unions and youth organizations.

The Committee for Protection of Mothers and Children takes responsibility for co-ordinating the family planning movement. Its goals are to 1) protect the health of mothers and children; 2) free women from the burdens of childbirth and childcare so they can achieve equality with men in the family and in society; and 3) reduce and stabilize population growth to strengthen the nation's economy. The aim is to halve the birth rate between 1981 and 1985, except in regions where there are ethnic minorities.[14]

Launching the family planning movement in Viet Nam has been difficult. Because of the tenacity of feudal and patriarchal ideals, birth control could not become official policy in the North until 1963. The 'Three Postponements' during the anti-US war encouraged couples to postpone having children. But in the spring of 1973, the family planning movement was not very popular because many people wanted to celebrate the signing of the Paris Peace Agreements with the birth of a child. In the South, there was no family planning movement until 1975, and even then it was weak. Vietnamese census takers were shocked to learn the nation's population was 50 million in 1975. It was then that a new impetus was given to the movement in the North. Nevertheless, the population grew to 55 million by 1980. Although the birth rate had been reduced from 3 to 2.6%, it was still unacceptably high.

The family planning movement has been most effective where Women's Union chapters are strongest and can make people aware of the advantages and urgency of family planning. Local Women's Union chapters lay the political foundation for mobile teams that perform gynaecological examinations and insert intra-uterine devices (IUDs), the favoured method of birth control in the countryside. These teams include assistant doctors or trained midwives who have received additional training in family planning. IUD insertion is treated as a serious medical procedure. Medical teams carefully screen women to make sure there is no infection before they insert the IUD. After insertion, they instruct the woman to refrain from sexual intercourse, strenuous work and bicycle riding for one month. As a result of the care taken, the incidence of harmful side-effects is relatively low: 1.4% of women with IUDs experience menstrual disorders and 0.4% suffer other complications.[15] The incidence of complications accompanying IUD use in the US is substantially higher due to the cavalier approach of medical practitioners.

One woman from the US who visited Hanoi had the opportunity to compare Vietnamese and US approaches to IUD complications. During her visit, she had severe menstrual cramps. Her guides insisted on taking her to the hospitals. The hospital had modern X-ray equipment but no flush toilets. They X-rayed her pelvis to make sure the IUD was not causing her problem. To prevent infection, they gave her vitamin C, iron pills and antibiotics. A nurse bathed her before the doctor gave a pelvic examination, which she said was very gentle. All this was standard procedure. They told her if they had decided to remove the IUD, she would have remained in hospital for two days to make sure there were no complications. Also standard procedure. She also learned that they used acupuncture to regularize menstruation and reduce cramps. She found no hint of the contempt for women's bodies so prevalent among gynaecologists in the US.

When I asked Women's Union officials if there was any coercion used to promote family planning, they laughed, 'Oh, no, we do not have regulations like in China.' There are incentives, however. After IUD insertion, a woman receives a two-week fully paid holiday, which also answers her medical requirement for rest. She receives extra medicine and food rations for a month. In factories, workers may sign contracts not to bear children for a given number of years. If they break the contract, they may lose their honorary titles and no longer be considered 'advanced workers'. In other work-places, a woman who spaces her first two children five years apart and has no more after that, will receive a small bonus. In 1979, however, only 600 women received such material rewards.[16]

In addition to mobile medical teams and district health centres in cities and villages, clinics and hospitals in large factories and other work-sites also dispense contraceptives. All contraceptives are free. By 1978, some 909,300 women were using IUDs – an estimated 27% of married women of childbearing age.[17] The system discourages oral contraception because of its harmful side-effects and high cost. Only about 2,000 women use the pill in all of Viet Nam. Condoms are popular in the cities, especially among office workers. The Committee for Protection of Mothers and Children distributes some seven million condoms annually.

When preventive measures fail, women may choose abortion. Abortion is free and available to any woman on demand. There is no 'right to life movement'. In fact, propaganda opposing contraception or abortion is censored. About 50,000 women choose abortion each year. The number of unauthorized abortions, performed out of hospitals, has been reduced to practically nil.

Sterilization, either by vasectomy or tubal ligation, is not common. There is no programme of massive sterilization, either involuntary or voluntary. Women under 35 or with fewer than three children cannot be legally sterilized unless there are special circumstances. When I spoke to doctors at the Ob-Gyn Hospital in Ho Chi Minh City about how forced sterilization is used in the US to limit the growth of Black and other populations of colour, they were horrified. 'But if they do not inform the women they have had a serious surgical procedure and do not have their consent, how can there be proper medical follow-up?' they asked incredulously. At Tu Du Hospital, the largest one of its kind in Ho Chi Minh City, only 14,975 tubal ligations were performed in the four years between

1976 and 1980. Fewer women chose tubal ligations in 1980 than in 1979. The corresponding figure for vasectomies was only 925.

Dr Phuong, the director of obstetrics at Tu Du Hospital, writes a weekly newspaper column about hygiene, birth control and pre-natal care. The hospital also co-operates with the Women's Union and the Youth Union in organizing classes on reproduction, family planning and basic anatomy. Unmarried people aged 18 and over are encouraged to attend as well as married people. However, clearly much more education is required among the population, even in Ho Chi Minh City, the most sophisticated city in Viet Nam. While the number of IUD insertions increased ten times at Tu Du Hospital between 1976 and 1980, from 800 to 8,000, the increase certainly does not match the increase in births, which rose to 12,000 in 1980.

One obstacle to a more effective family planning movement was noted by the former President of the Viet Nam Women's Union in her speech to the Fourth Party Congress:

> Not until recently did many places pay attention to mobilizing women and take effective measures to educate men. If a wife wants family planning while her husband does not, then contradiction would arise within the family. The raising of consciousness on the revolutionary significance of this problem, the dissemination of scientific knowledge on this matter, coupled with the most active measures will make family planning become a life-style in our society.[18]

As long as pressures from in-laws and husbands prevent women from taking advantage of the available birth control network – and their resistance to birth control seems formidable – women's reproductive rights will be limited. The government and the Women's Union recognize this problem and plan to accelerate an educational campaign in favour of family planning so that by 1985, birth rates will be sharply reduced to 1.7%.

Reproductive Rights: The Right to Motherhood without Fear
In 1945, the 300 hospital beds provided for maternity care in all of Viet Nam were reserved for a small élite. Now, every co-operative, the larger factories, and the local administrative units in towns and some villages have their own maternity clinics, staffed by doctors, assistant doctors and midwives. Some 90% of Vietnamese women give birth in these clinics.

In 1945, the infant mortality rate – death before the age of one year – was 40%. In North Viet Nam, in 1972, it was 1.2% and by 1980, it had dropped to 0.7%. At Tu Du Hospital – the hospital where all the most complicated deliveries are performed – in 1980, out of 12,000 births, only two mothers died and the infant mortality rate was 17 per thousand, including premature births. It is significant that in the state of California in 1978, the average infant death rate for all races was 12 per thousand;

but for Black infants, it was 21 per thousand.[19]

Dinh Thi Can, Chairperson of the Committee for Protection of Mothers and Children, recalled the old days:

> In the course of my revolutionary work, I saw many women, workers and peasants give birth to babies near their machines or in the fields. Pregnant women were never entitled to rest before or after delivery . . . . The only law concerning mother and infant welfare was the law of natural selection.[20]

Now standard protection for pregnant women includes free pre-natal care, maternity care and obstetrical surgery, if needed; fully paid maternity leave for 60 to 75 days; extra rations, milk and allowances for baby clothes; longer leave and additional rations for mothers with twins; time off to nurse at work; and fully paid leave to care for sick children. The Committee for Protection of Mothers and Children includes a hospital and research institute devoted to developing improved methods of pre-natal, maternity and childcare.

Since 1975, the changes for pregnant and birthing mothers in the South have been significant. Between 1975 and 1980, 1,000 new hospitals were built and the number of rural maternity homes increased from 6,565 to 9,034.[21] Mobile health teams and rural clinics have been organized to teach people elementary hygiene and to fight harmful practices, such as the tradition that pregnant women drink the urine of male infants to gain strength. Before liberation of the South, women who could not afford to go to private maternity homes were often brutalized in public wards. Mrs Nguyen Thi Lien, a basket seller in O-Mon District, for example, was confined in the public ward for the birth of all seven of her children. She recalled,

> Whenever I came here for confinement, I felt so ashamed. Yet I came here because I could not afford the fees of private maternity homes. Since we were given free services, we were treated like beggars. We had to endure the pangs of childbirth silently, because groaning would invite scolding and even torrents of insults from nurses. Relatives were not allowed to visit patients and we had to go out to meet them at the gate to get our food. Since there were too many patients, I had to lie on the floor. The floor was wet and dirty. I had no other way.[22]

After liberation, the nurses who had worked in O-Mon and other clinics were obliged to attend a special re-education course, teaching them the virtues and responsibilities of people's medical workers. Gradually, after much struggle, those who used to be harsh with their patients developed a new approach to their duties, based on respect for their patients, and won their affection. The O-Mon maternity unit has been cleaned and expanded to meet the needs of all the women in the district.

There have been similar changes at Tu Du Hospital. When it was a charity ward under the Thieu regime, patients were treated with contempt. Now, pregnant women are encouraged to attend childbirth preparation classes – a series of six – 'so they can be masters of their own pregnancies,' Dr Phuong told me. Although Tu Du treats women whose pregnancies are considered risky by district maternity clinics, only 5% of the live births require Caesarian section. In the US, 17% of all deliveries are by Caesarian section. [23] The dramatic difference is the result of the respect and patience Vietnamese medical staff practise with their patients. Dr Phuong elaborated:

> My old director, who fled the country after liberation, did not like to wait for a woman to deliver naturally. He was always in a rush to get to his private clinic. He did not care how these poor women might suffer from surgery. Now, we always wait, unless it is obviously dangerous. We use acupuncture to stimulate contractions. And we have found tea made from sunflower petals can also ease labour pains. [24]

The problems faced by expectant mothers and new mothers are not caused by lack of official concern or medical respect for their right to motherhood without fear. As in the area of childcare, the main obstacle to progress is the country's poverty. Pre-natal classes, for example, cannot counteract the dangerous effects of malnutrition. There is still a shortage of doctors and medicine. Equipment like breast pumps and incubators – taken for granted in industrialized countries – are precious in Viet Nam. The Committee for Protection of Mothers and Children has issued special appeals to women's organizations all over the world to aid it in its work by donating equipment and medicine.

Ageing with Respect and Security

One measure of a society's respect for women is its treatment of older women. In societies where women are valued primarily for their sex appeal and child-producing capacities, they become objects of scorn, burdens to their families and the community, when they are 'past their prime'. In the US, for example, it often seems that older women must apologize for their survival. They face perpetual fear of poverty, rejection and loneliness. In Viet Nam, on the other hand, older women are respected members of the community and take leadership roles more often than their younger counterparts. I always found older women, particularly peasants, to be more self-confident and aggressive than younger women and often more so than men.

Women have the right to retire at 55, men at 60. Retirement is not compulsory. If a woman or her co-workers believe she is healthy enough to continue, and she prefers to remain on the job, she may do so. At retirement, workers receive 80% of their wage as pension. If they work at

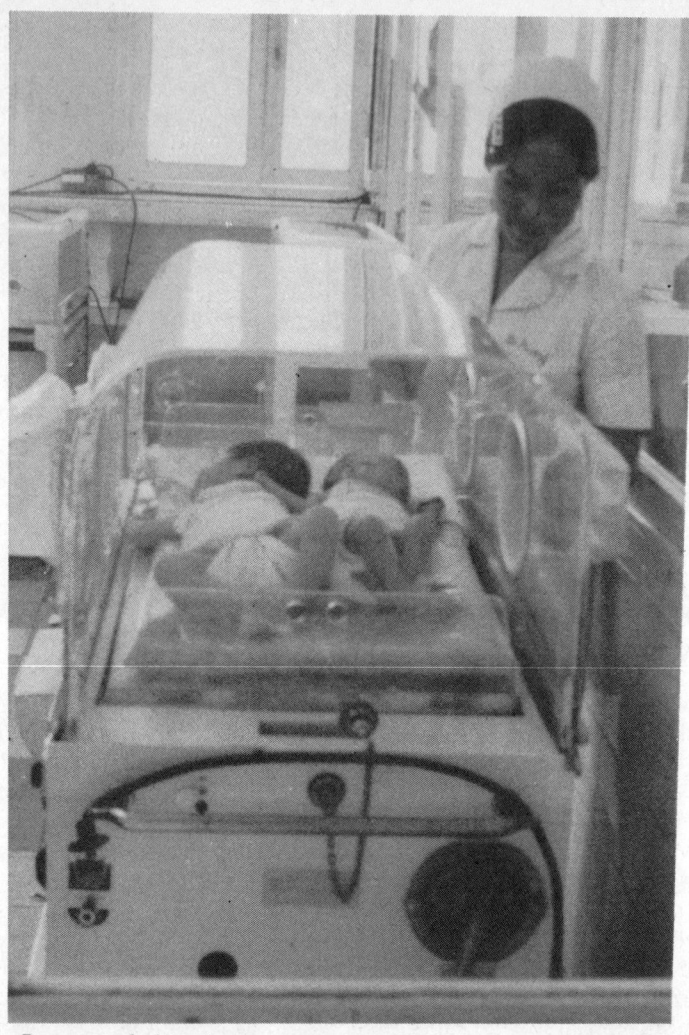

Premature babies share incubator at Tu Du Hospital, Ho Chi Minh City. Doctor Ngoc Phuong checks them.   Arlene Eisen

a part-time job after beginning to receive a pension, nothing is deducted from it. Many women retire to care for their grandchildren or to become full-time activists in the Women's Union or other political organizations. The Women's Union welcomes the leadership of older women. Their experience and understanding of their communities is valued. Older women are in the leadership of the Women's Union at every level, from the local branch to the national Central Committee. Many of them are veterans of the August Revolution of 1945. Now the concern of the

Women's Union is to train younger women to replace those whose health does not allow them to continue working.

Of course, since many older women are not cadres or have not worked outside the home, not all necessarily receive an adequate pension. Social welfare committees in all districts provide for the aged who have no other means of support. In the southern provinces, where the war severely disrupted daily life, older people face additional problems when they are disabled or separated from their families. Within months of liberation, the revolutionary administration set up centres for old and disabled people who had formerly been vagrants. Residents of these centres spend the day doing light manual labour. After work, they sit in the sun or in their rooms visiting one another. Members of the centres are encouraged to feel 'like a great family of older people returning home after years of unstable and vagrant life.' Sometimes former vagrants felt uncomfortable at the centres and time was required to make them feel secure. One reported:

> In the early days, I dared not eat all the meals brought to me by the woman in charge. I always set aside part of them for fear of having nothing to eat afterward. This was a habit I acquired from my former life as a beggar. In those days, none of us believed we would ever have three meals a day. The revolution is really very considerate.[25]

Centres like the one in Ho Chi Minh City are provided for vagrants in other cities and towns where they are needed. Mutual aid teams, organized by the Women's Union and other organizations, also function in the towns and the countryside to help older people with their daily problems as well as with special needs.

In Viet Nam, the progress made in rural hygiene, in mass immunization, in programmes to guarantee women's health and reproductive rights, and in programmes to heal the worst wounds of war – such as drug addiction and venereal disease – although important, are only the first steps in a long and complex campaign. Food shortages make malnutrition the number one health hazard. The shortage of experienced personnel, equipment and medicine, and medical ignorance among the population will continue to damage the health of the people for some time to come. And, as industrialization proceeds, new health problems will arise. The Ministry of Public Health, recognizing these problems, elaborated a programme of action that gives priority to: 1) healing war wounds and their complications; 2) preserving and improving the health of the population, especially that of women and children.[26] Given these priorities, women's health is bound to improve and with the attention given to women's right to control their own bodies, reproductive rights will be expanded.

Notes

1. While official policies may not always be put into practice, they do represent the shared goals of society. By comparing official statements from opposing systems, one may appreciate their significance. For example, Israel makes childbearing a national duty. David Ben-Gurion, Israel's founding President, wrote, 'Increasing the Jewish birth rate is a vital need for the existence of Israel, and the Jewish woman who does not bring at least four children into the world . . . is defrauding the Jewish mission.' Contraception and abortion are expensive in Israel. For the Ben-Gurion quote and an Israeli woman's rebuttal, see Lesley Hazelton, *Israeli Women* (New York: Simon and Schuster, 1977), p. 63.
2. Interview by author with Vu Thi Phan (Hanoi, 2 September 1981); and 'Anti-Malaria Campaign in Dac Lac Province', *Viet Nam Courier*, No. 79, December 1978, p. 19.
3. 'Una Mirada Sobre la Medicina Moderna de la RSVN', *Boletin Informativo*, Viet Nam News Agency (Havana), No. 98, 15 February 1981, p. 14.
4. Xuan Ha, 'The Pasteur Institute of Nha Trang', *Viet Nam* (pictorial), No. 228, December 1977, pp. 8–9.
5. 'Health Care in Viet Nam: Politically Defined Priorities', *South East Asia Chronicle*, No. 84, June 1982, pp. 23–4.
6. Nguyen Thi Hien, 'A Letter from a Children's Hospital in Ho Chi Minh City', *Women of Viet Nam*, No. 1, 1977, pp. 13–14.
7. Heidi Kuglin, 'Impressions of Viet Nam', *US/Indochina Report*, June 1976, p. 6.
8. Data from Vo The Quang, MD, 'Talk to US/Viet Nam Friendship Association' (San Francisco, California, 15 April 1983).
9. See Chapter 21, 'Psychiatry in Viet Nam', in Joan K. McMichael (ed.), *Health in the Third World: Studies from Viet Nam* (Nottingham: Spokesman Books, 1976), pp. 322–7.
10. This section on treatment of the disabled in Viet Nam sumarizes *The Disabled: Their Right to Life* (Vietnamese Studies, No. 64; Hanoi: Foreign Languages Publishing House, 1981); quote on p. 64.
11. Thu Ba, 'The Family Planning Movement', *Women of Viet Nam*, No. 4, 1980, pp. 15–16.
12. Viet Nam Veterans Against the War, *Winter Soldier Investigations* (Boston: Beacon, 1972), p. 5.
13. 'This World', *San Francisco Chronicle/Examiner*, Sunday 21 March 1971, p. 7. For a more complete analysis of the 'Politics of Rape' in Viet Nam, see Arlene Eisen Bergman, *Women of Viet Nam* (San Francisco: Peoples Press, 1975), Chapter 4.
14. Dr Nguyen Thi Xiem, 'Fifteen Years' Birth Control by Contraceptive', *Mother and Infant Welfare in Viet Nam* (Hanoi: Foreign Languages Publishing House, 1979), p. 59.
15. Ibid., p. 62.
16. Thu Ba, op. cit., p. 18.
17. Xiem, op. cit., p. 62. Thu Ba, however, gives a much higher number: 1,456,276, for the same year (op. cit., p. 17).
18. Ha Thi Que, 'Speech at the Fourth Party Congress', Special Supplement of *Women of Viet Nam*, No. 4, 1976, p. 7.

19. California data from 'Health Goals Met – But not for Blacks', *San Francisco Chronicle*, 23 June 1982, p. 46. Data on mother and infant mortality in Viet Nam from unpublished correspondence from Viet Nam Women's Union, 1974 and 1982, and 'Interview with Dinh Thi Can', *Mother and Infant Welfare in Viet Nam*, p. 11.
20. Ibid., pp. 10–11.
21. 'Cultural and Social Achievements in the Last Five Years', *Viet Nam Courier*, No. 3, 1982, p. 6.
22. Do Quyen, 'The Maternity Ward of O-Man District', *Women of Viet Nam*, No. 1, 1976, pp. 24–5.
23. Center for Health Statistics, 'Data Matters', California Department of Health Services Files, February 1982.
24. Interview by author with Dr Ngoc Phuong (Ho Chi Minh City, 12 September 1981).
25. Phuong Thuy, 'The Great Family of Vagrants', *Women of Viet Nam*, No. 3, 1977, pp. 18–20.
26. Chapter 22, 'Medicine in the Viet Nam of the Future', in McMichael, op. cit., pp. 333–4.

13. Education for Emancipation

Equality for women is an important goal of our educational system. In the old days, the percentage of women in school was very low. Many families allowed their girls to attend the first grade and after that kept their daughters home to work and care for the younger children, and then married them off. Now sons and daughters have an equal right to attend school. Fifty percent of the students in general education are women. In general, the pupil who is head of the class is a girl.

Nguyen Thi Binh, Minister of Education and Vice-President of the Viet Nam Women's Union

Confucian patriarchs considered women unworthy of an education. For centuries, the few women who attended school did so disguised as men. In 1975 then, if 75% of the people living in the countryside under Thieu's regime were illiterate, we must assume that probably 90% or more of the women in those regions could not read or write. Without literacy, women remain prisoners of patriarchal feudal traditions, lacking the intellectual weapons to fight dogma, superstition, the pervasive contempt which they encounter or occupational discrimination.

Education, particularly higher education, is a basic requirement for women to achieve equality. And, as society focuses increasingly on economic development and technology, education takes on an even greater importance. Educational advancement, in fact, is the cornerstone of the Women's Union strategy for women's emancipation. They believe that only when women have reached the same 'cultural level' as men, can they be emancipated. The concept, cultural level, combines educational achievement with political consciousness, with the emphasis on educational achievement. The state and society take responsibility for resolving the problems of poverty and feudal ideology which obstruct women's liberation. Education is women's responsibility. In her summing up of a recent teach-in devoted to making recommendations for improving women's status, Nguyen Thi Dinh, the Women's Union President, concluded,

As for us women, in order to meet the requirements of our times, we must learn to improve our cultural and professional standard and our skills. That is the firmest basis for the implementation of the policy regarding promotion and liberation of women.[1]

Nearly every woman I talked to in Viet Nam about problems impeding women's liberation, pointed to the same need: to increase women's competence.

However, sometimes it appears that holding women's relatively low cultural level responsible for their under-representation in leadership and higher-status occupations is more a reflection of traditional Confucian contempt for women's intellectual capacities than a scientific evaluation of women's current abilities and potentials. Also, more recognition must be given to the fact that the burdens of the double shift have to be equalized before women have the same opportunity as men to participate in social and political life, and thereby gain the necessary experience and self-confidence to assert themselves. Yet, whether one agrees with the Women's Union that education is the firmest basis for women's liberation or simply a necessary weapon for women in their continuing struggle, education remains an essential condition for women's emancipation.

Learning under Fire

During the war against the US, schools in the city had to be evacuated to the countryside. They were open for 24 hours a day, with three shifts per day, to compensate for the lack of facilities. Because large concentrations of people would attract bombers, university classes, even those in which hundreds of students were enrolled, were subdivided into groups of no more than 30 students each. Dr Sinh, a mathematics professor, told me how she repeated each lecture ten times, running from one group to the next. Of course they also lacked library facilities and light for study at night. Nevertheless, between 1970 and 1981, the proportion of women studying to be maths teachers grew from 10 to 50%.[2] Invasion in the north by China and in the west by Pol Pot's troops put new strains on the educational system. Chinese troops, for example, destroyed every school building in the six provinces they invaded.

Economic underdevelopment creates additional problems in education. These problems are, perhaps, best illustrated by Huong, a teacher who lives in the suburbs of Hanoi. She gets up every morning at 4.30 to haul water to her fourth-floor apartment, cook breakfast and prepare lunch to take to work. Then she bicycles for an hour to reach her school. On her way home in the late afternoon, every day, she goes to market. Then she cooks supper and stays awake until 11 every night, correcting papers, preparing classes and doing her own research. 'By the time I get to school in the morning, I am exhausted,' she laments. 'No matter how

217

much talent I may have, how great my potential as a teacher, I just don't have the energy by the time I get to class to be a good teacher.'[3] She is confident, however, that in the future, teaching conditions will improve.

Despite pressures of war and economic underdevelopment, Viet Nam's achievements in education are impressive. Consider the pre-revolutionary educational situation: 1) after 100 years of French colonialism, in 1945, 90–95% of all Vietnamese people were illiterate; 2) in 1938–39, the years in which the colonial administration invested the most in education, there were only 567,000 children in school, 17% of whom were girls; 3) in 1945, there were only 600 Vietnamese enrolled in higher education with less than 10 women known to be university students; 4) in the South, under the Thieu regime, as late as 1975, 50% of city dwellers and 75% of rural people were illiterate.[4]

And after liberation: 1) by 1958 in the North and by 1978 in the South, a mass mobilization had eradicated illiteracy; 2) by 1981, some 16 million people were enrolled in some type of class: that is, one out of every three children and adults were attending primary school, complementary adult education or an institution of higher education;[5] 3) women comprise 50% of the students in primary and general education and 51% of the students in secondary and vocational education; they comprise between 38 and 40% of the students in technical schools and universities, depending on the area of specialization;[6] 4) all education is free, including costs of room, board and supplies for those enrolled in higher education.

Literacy and Adult Education Campaigns

When a reporter visited an agricultural co-op, a 60-year-old co-op member emerged from the crowd and spontaneously recited this verse:
'Yes, I used to be a poor illiterate woman,
Living a dog's life in the darkest of times.
But now, thanks to the Party, I've known a new life.
I can read and write and am no longer blind.'[7]
The literacy campaign that enabled this and every other woman in Viet Nam to learn to read required a massive mobilization of those who were already literate. The literacy campaign in Quang Tri Province, for example, began in 1973, shortly after it was liberated. When I visited Trieu Phong District School in the autumn of 1974, I found 23 women and two men studying maths at a fourth-grade level. All of them had been illiterate the year before. Their rapid advance was motivated by a militant understanding that once they had political power, only lack of education prevented them from controlling their lives or being full 'collective masters'. The same school organized classes to train an army of teachers. In a six-week course, those who already had a primary school education were learning to teach others. In 1973, about 85% of the people of Quang Tri were illiterate. By 1975, literacy there was virtually unknown.

An adult education class   Viet Nam News Agency

When the rest of the South was liberated, other provinces followed the example of Quang Tri. Often, the literacy campaign continued in people's homes on a one-to-one basis. A very large network of patient and sensitive teachers was required. For example, for weeks, every time Chi, the village teacher, went to Mrs Lam's house, the illiterate woman's child would tell the teacher her mother was not at home. Finally, one day when Chi arrived with four of her younger students, Mrs Lam could no longer avoid her. Chi first praised her weaving. 'What a beautiful mattress! Teach me how to weave, will you?' Chi asked. But before Mrs Lam could demonstrate her weaving techniques, one of her children demanded to be fed. Chi motioned to the students who accompanied her and they immediately began preparing the meal, while keeping the children occupied. Once the children were out of earshot, Chi assured Mrs Lam that she could teach her to read and make sure the children were taken care of at the same time. Mrs Lam hesitated, 'I've lived nearly half my life without knowing even half a word. My head is just blank and seems to be stuffed with cotton. What's the good of learning? I have enough trouble with the kids. How could I find time to study?' But Chi persisted in her promise to help and finally Lam agreed to try. Chi wrote big and clear letters in the copy book she had brought for Lam: 'A, B, C.' Mrs Lam kept repeating every sound, very awkwardly at first. She wrote and erased the first few letters until the table was covered with a carpet of chalk dust. After seven evenings, Mrs Lam could write her name, her children's names and the name of her village. She could also read newspaper headlines. After 18 days of hard work, Mrs Lam had learned to read and write, and was eager to enroll in a group class where she could continue her education.[8]

The Women's Union has played an essential role in the literacy campaign, encouraging women to attend classes and organizing special classes for them and special teams to take over household tasks and childcare for those occupied with their studies. The Ministry of Education also had a special department to meet the needs of the literacy campaign. They issued textbooks, but in An Giang and other provinces, local teachers rewrote the texts so they would be more relevant to local conditions. After a woman achieves literacy – which includes, according to the Vietnamese definition, the ability to take dictation, read and comprehend newspapers and magazines and add, subtract, multiply and divide – she is encouraged to continue her education in an elaborate network of adult education classes.

Every year millions of women and men attend complementary education classes from the general education level to the university level. More than half the students in these classes are women. Some of the classes are organized in residential neighbourhoods. For example, I visited an evening complementary education class in Ho Chi Minh City where 12 women met in someone's home to improve their reading and maths skills. A few of the women were in their twenties. One was 83. She said she was attending the class so she would be able to read novels. The teacher was a volunteer from the Educational Service who met with this group for two hours per night, three nights per week. She volunteered after working all day at her regular teaching job. The local Women's Union chapter and other mass organizations chipped in to pay for the notebooks the women used. They also organized childcare for the women who needed it.

The teacher had written a paragraph on the blackboard about a Vietnamese historic monument. She explained the meaning of the text and then urged the group to read it in unison. Then each woman read it individually. The students were enthusiastic in their reading. Next, the teacher asked questions, testing the students' comprehension and spelling. After about a half hour of work on the text, she switched to maths exercises. Some of the women who excelled at reading were halting in their understanding of arithmetic symbols. They talked a lot among themselves, helping one another to solve the problems. In this district of Ho Chi Minh City, 88 such classes meet every night. The same is true for the 17 other districts of Ho Chi Minh City.

Co-operatives and factories also organize classes for their workers or help them go to classes in central vocational and technical schools. Classes for workers are available in three shifts when necessary. Some workers, like Minh, director of the Cua Long Handicraft Co-op, study French and English in evening classes. She encourages all members of her co-op to study languages and other courses to improve their cultural levels. Many workers also take correspondence courses. After five years on the job, workers in state enterprises have the right to go to school, either part or full time, while retaining their salary, in order to develop their skills or advance their careers. In most hospitals, for example, the best nurses have the opportunity to study secondary-school courses after work. When they complete these courses, they receive two months' paid leave of absence to prepare for medical school entrance exams. If they fail, they can take another paid leave to prepare again, if their chances for succeeding are considered good. Some 60% of the students in medical school are women.[9]

The Ministry of Education plans to expand the availability of adult education. With the co-operation of the Women's Union, trade unions and other organizations, women are able to count on assistance in child-care and educational expenses, so most women will have the opportunity to increase their skills, raise their cultural levels and even embark on new careers at various stages in their life.

Educating New Socialist Women and Men

By 1982, some 12,510,000 young people were enrolled in general educa-tion. In the North, most children go to school for nine years, while facilities in the South only allow children to attend school for four or five years. The Ministry of Education expects that by 1990, all Vietnamese children will be able to complete secondary school.[10] Not only access to education, but also the content of education has changed drastically over the years. The Minister of Education explained:

> During the period from 1945–75 in the North, we completely transformed the former colonial school system, first into a national system, then into a socialist system. In the South, under the US puppet regime, the school system was modelled according to US neo-colonialist designs. Immediately after the complete liberation of the South, we took over all the schools there, public and private, and began converting them, little by little, into national schools, to proceed to integrate them into a unified socialist school system.[11]

Rather than learn to read with texts like *Dick and Jane*, made in the US, Vietnamese children learn with stories like this one:

> Little Buoi has a very important task of carrying messages for the National Liberation Front. Little Buoi was never late in taking messages to their destinations, and she has never let the enemy find out what she is doing. Nor has she let a message fall into the hands of the enemy.

They learn maths with exercises like this one: 'The enemy entered the village and arrested 12 youths. The people of the village demonstrated against this arrest and forced the release of 8 youths. How many more youths' releases do they still need to demonstrate for?'[12]

The school system is designed to encourage every child to develop to his or her maximum potential and, at the same time, meet society's need

Boys and girls are treated equally in school   Viet Nam News Agency

for trained personnel. Students come from all social classes and those from traditionally disadvantaged backgrounds – from ethnic minorities, for example – may enroll in special classes. Everyone learns language, maths, chemistry, physics, literature, cooking, painting and carpentry. Beginning in the fifth grade, students learn English, French or Russian. There is no special tracking* for boys and girls. Officially, boys and girls learn to sew in the first grade, and all children learn cooking in the fifth and sixth grades. There may, however, be some inconsistency in the application of this policy because one can only find photos of boys doing woodwork and girls doing needlework illustrating magazine articles.[13]

Ho Chi Minh's five principles of education set the guidelines for the education of the next generation. They teach: 1) love your country and your compatriots; 2) improve, work and study constantly; 3) be modest, frank and courageous and observe discipline; 4) practise hygiene; 5) strengthen unity. When Vietnamese speak of promoting a national and a socialist education, they usually have these five principles in mind.

Schools also aim to combine work and study. Younger as well as older children do productive work. An official from the Ministry of Education explained the motivation for the policy of combining mental and manual study:

*Tracking (a US system) entails not only courses but also special projects and varied differential treatments.

Our education is not a privilege for the rich. Our students do not study irrelevant things, but rather develop needed skills in science, technology, art and literature . . . . When students live and work among the people, they understand the needs of the people and improve their political consciousness.[14]

A teacher, who had taught English in Saigon under the Thieu regime and now teaches at the Agricultural University, noted how this policy affected her students: 'Before, they expected to be killed and could not see any point in studying when they had no future. Now they work hard. They feel they have important work to do in rebuilding the country and it is exciting to teach them.'[15]

The Ministry of Education instituted a series of educational reforms, beginning in September 1981. The reforms are expected to improve the quality of maths and language instruction and ensure that a graduate of general education can be a productive member of society without necessarily going on to higher education. Work study programmes acquainting students with the major trades are given more emphasis. The reforms also aim to increase co-operation between schools and work-places. The last major goal of the reform is to 'discover the gift and professional vocation of each student to encourage, guide and foster the professional skills most suitable to their ability.'[16]

After the fifth grade, students who have demonstrated particular aptitudes may attend special classes encouraging their development in that area. There are special classes for those gifted in maths, literature, science, foreign languages and music. Every year, any child can ask to take an exam testing her qualifications to enter a special class. One teacher observed that while there is a tendency for more of the special students to come from urban families, particularly from those with cadre parents, peasant children in special classes tend to be the most gifted.[17]

Schools in the South have developed flexible programmes to meet the needs of children there. For example, particularly in the poorer districts of Ho Chi Minh City, children have difficulty attending day classes because their parents require them to work or care for younger sisters and brothers. To remedy this problem, the city's Educational Service opened evening claseess for children. In 1981, some 7,300 children in District 11 attended these evening classes which include grades one to five. The Women's Union, along with other organizations, worked with the Educational Service to mobilize people in the district to support the schools. They canvassed door to door, recruiting students for the school and persuading reluctant parents to allow their children to attend. The Educational Service planned to incorporate some 200,000 formerly unenrolled children into evening schools in 1983.[18] Such programmes are particularly significant for girls because under the old regime, daughters of poor families had no educational opportunities.

Higher Education

It is difficult to present comparable statistics on the percentage of women students in higher education because the base for tabulation has changed. In 1972–73, in North Viet Nam, nearly 44% of all students in technical schools, colleges and universities were women: an impressive change from the days when there were virtually no women in higher education. But few of that 44% may have been university students. A 1982 Women's Union report noted: 1) 26% of students in universities in the entire country were women; 2) 25% of professors of higher education, including secondary schools, were women; 3) only 8.1% of those holding Masters' and doctorate degrees were women.[19]

Until 1976, there was a kind of affirmative action policy that favoured women and national minorities for university admission. Young women needed only 14 points to pass from one class to the next, while young men needed 15. Likewise, women's passing scores on entrance exams to trade schools and secondary schools were lower than men's. Women also received preference for study abroad. Some officials explain the special treatment was a way of overcoming centuries of discrimination against women and claim that after 1976, these provisions were no longer necessary.

However, a Women's Union cadre reported that the affirmative action policy was designed to offset the handicap to young women students of greater responsibilities at home. They do not have the same opportunity to concentrate on their studies because they are expected to help look after the family.[20] Other parents told me they expected the same amount of co-operation in housework from their sons and daughters. If the latter is the case, then the affirmative action policy may no longer be necessary. But it seems more likely young women are still at a disadvantage because of their chores at home. The elimination of affirmative action may prevent them from obtaining the education necessary to assume greater leadership roles in the society.

In any case, the reorganization of the system of higher education in the South has given women important opportunities to advance as they contribute to reconstructing society. After 18 months of intense struggle post-liberation, colleges and universities were transformed from centres for training loyal followers of the 'American way', to schools that teach their students to serve the needs of the new society. Before, higher education was reserved for the privileged few – usually males. Some 80% of the students under the old regime studied law and literature and fewer than 1% studied agriculture. Schools were reorganized and new teaching materials designed, but the most important change had to be in the orientation of the teachers themselves. Nearly 1,200 intellectuals from Ho Chi Minh City attended a basic political course from December 1975 to the end of April 1976. For four months, they studied the history of the Vietnamese revolution and nation and the character of socialist education. They deepened their understanding of lectures by visiting factories

Viet Nam News Agency

A chemistry professor at work in Ho Chi Minh City

and New Economic Zones and by taking part in manual labour.[21] As late as 1981, intellectuals trained before 1975 still attended conferences, forums and classes to teach them to respect their working-class students, productive labour and the goals of socialist education.

Professor Sinh, a mathematician trained in France who teaches in Hanoi, explained why she appreciated the time she spent in the countryside:

> I did not know the situation in the countryside at all. I spent one month a year there helping peasants with their bookkeeping, planning and reckoning . . . . I used this experience to reform my teaching so it was more responsive to my students' needs. For example, I learned that we had to teach scientific concepts more slowly. Also, after spending time in the countryside, we introduced a new branch of maths into our college, 'operational research', designed to aid peasants in planning production and distributing harvests.[22]

Sinh added that spending time in the countryside is not a rigidly imposed requirement. The policy is flexible and only those who understand the relevance of the experience spend time in the countryside. No one is coerced.

Ngo Ba Thanh, a Columbia-educated attorney and member of the National Assembly representing Ho Chi Minh City, is also active in the Intellectuals' Association there. She told me how the party has been realistic and somewhat indulgent in persuading old regime intellectuals to work for the new society. 'Intellectuals get paid twice as much as ordinary cadres. The party is most realistic.' She smiled as she continued, 'They know our political consciousness is not high. They know it is harder for us to adapt to hard work and sacrifice. They understand our weaknesses and the weaknesses of each social class. They educate us step by step.' However, others report that cynical intellectuals scorn cadres who appear to them relatively less sophisticated.

The student body at colleges and universities in the South is also undergoing transformation. In the past, only 15% of the students were from working-class families. Most were the sons of wealthy businessmen and corrupt administrators. They used bribes to pass exams and maintain their student status so as to avoid conscription into Thieu's army. Since 1976, entrance exams test the students' capacity to serve the country and special measures are taken to recruit daughters and sons of workers and peasants. There is no tuition fee and the state pays for the living and academic expenses of all students. Those who were students in the old Saigon University take political education courses before being transferred from studying subjects of interest only to the privileged former élite to useful courses in teacher-training schools and economic institutes.[23]

So as to be effective in equipping students to tackle the tasks of economic development, all higher education is based on the principle of combining study with practice, education with production, and school with social life. Some schools are directly linked to farms and factories. They practise the '4 + 4 + 1 + 3' formula: four hours in the classroom, four hours in productive work, one hour for recreation and three hours for homework, for six days a week.[24] At Can Tho University, agricultural students are only allowed to graduate after they have solved a specific agricultural problem encountered while working with the peasants of that province.[25]

Finally, women in the central highlands are enjoying dramatic changes in their educational opportunities. In the autumn of 1977, the first college in the central highlands opened, welcoming students from the various national minorities of the region. Nearly half the students there are women who, had they been born a generation earlier, would have spent their lives illiterate, working slash and burn agriculture and distilling spirits for their husbands and sons. Now they are studying scientific agriculture, engineering and electricity.[26]

The eradication of illiteracy and the admission of substantial numbers of women into institutions of higher education within one generation testify to the enormous progress women have made in challenging patriarchal assumptions of women's inferiority. As more and more women excel in school and enter the professions, it becomes increasingly difficult to justify excluding them from positions of equal responsibility and power with men. Yet the same obstacle that prevents women from equal participation in economic and political work, also restricts their educational achievements: namely, the double shift. While the pupil at the head of her class in general education is usually a girl, by the time a young woman reaches secondary school, she begins to fall behind her male classmates in her studies. Many teachers attribute this problem to the young women becoming preoccupied with romance. However young men's progress does not seem to be impeded by their love-letter writing activities.[27] It is more likely that women begin to fall behind men in their school work because they are taking care of their families and homes as well as their studies.

Some might speculate that young women also fall behind because they do not receive as much encouragement to achieve as the men and are not motivated by opportunities to excel once they have completed their studies. I do not believe this is true. While sex segregation does exist to some extent in the professions, women who have achieved high-status positions receive a great deal of positive publicity in society. Their celebration is designed to motivate others to follow in the footsteps of exemplary women. If a woman is conscientious and ambitious, and is not over-encumbered by family responsibilities, the educational system will encourage her achievements.

Notes

1. Mai Thi Tu, 'Vietnamese Women in the Eighties', *Viet Nam Courier*, No. 10, 1981, pp. 19–22.
2. Interview by author with Professor Hoang Xuan Sinh (Hanoi, 2 September 1981).
3. Sara Rosner, 'Intellectuals North and South', *South East Asia Chronicle*, No. 76, December 1980, p. 29.
4. On education under the Thieu regime see Ngoc Bao, 'A Rotten Regime', *South Viet Nam in Struggle*, Nos 227–8, 20 December 1973, p. 7; also 'The Development of Education in the DRV', in *Education in the DRV* (Vietnamese Studies, No. 5; Hanoi: Foreign Languages Publishing House, 1965), p. 24. Nancy Wiegersma argues that women's educational opportunities expanded under the French. She may be referring to the 17% of girls attending primary school – no doubt the daughters of the élite – but she gives no data to support her assertion. See her 'Women in Transition to Capitalism: 19th to mid 20th Century Viet Nam', *Research in Political Economy*, Vol. 4, 1981, pp. 1–2.

5. 'Educacion', *Boletin Informativo*, Viet Nam News Agency (Havana), No. 110, August 1981, p. 7.
6. Viet Nam Women's Union, *Women of Viet Nam: Statistical Data* (Hanoi, 1981), p. 31.
7. Viet Hoa, 'Women's Clubs: A New Feature of Rural Life', *Women of Viet Nam*, No. 1, 1971, p. 18.
8. Cecilia Molander, *Women in Viet Nam* (Stockholm: Swedish International Development Authority, 1978), p. 38. Data on percentage of women in medical school from Lucy Forest, interview with Madame Nguyen Thi Binh (unpublished notes), 14 January 1980.
9. T.T., 'I'm Deeply Grateful to You', *Women of Viet Nam*, No. 4, 1977, pp. 15–16.
10. Lam, 'Education in 1982', *Viet Nam Courier*, No. 1, 1982, p. 5; and Lucy Forest, op. cit.
11. Nguyen Thi Binh, 'Rapid Renovation of Our Schools', *Cultural Problems*, Vol. I (Vietnamese Studies, No. 49; Hanoi: Foreign Languages Publishing House, 1976), pp. 119–20.
12. The first text is from Katsuichi Honda, *A Voice from the Village* (Tokyo: Committee for English Publication, 1967), p. 10; the second text is from John Spragens Jr, *Education in Viet Nam* (Japan: Looking Back Publications, 1971), p. 49.
13. Viet Hoa, 'A Boarding School for Children of War Martyrs', *Women of Viet Nam*, Nos 1–2, 1973, pp. 28–9.
14. Interview at Ministry of Education by author (Hanoi, September 1974).
15. Martha Winnacker, 'Lives in Transition', *South East Asia Chronicle*, Nos 56–57, May–July 1977, p. 4.
16. Mai Thi Tu, 'The Professional Orientation for General School Students', *Viet Nam Courier*, No. 2, 1982, p. 23. Also Dr Nguyen Khac Vien discussed these educational reforms in an interview with this author (Hanoi, 1 September 1981).
17. Interview by author with Professor Hoang Xuan Sinh (Hanoi, 2 September 1981).
18. From interviews during visit by author to evening class (District 11, Ho Chi Minh City, 12 September 1981).
19. Data from unpublished Women's Union reports, and Molander, op. cit., pp. 36 and 97.
20. Molander, p. 39.
21. Hoang Nhan and Phong Hien, 'The New System of Higher Education in Ho Chi Minh City', *Viet Nam Courier*, No. 54, November 1976, pp. 16–18.
22. Sinh interview.
23. Phong Hien, 'Metamorphosis of Saigon University', *Viet Nam Courier*, No. 46, March 1976, pp. 16–18.
24. Vu Huyen, 'The Study and Work School', *Viet Nam* (pictorial), No. 22, June 1977, pp. 2–5.
25. 'The Real Viet Nam: Two Scientists Visit Boston', *Indochina Newsletter*, No. 14, January–February 1982, pp. 2–4.
26. Tran Ngo, 'The Spring Flowers on Dar Lac Highlands', *Women of Viet Nam*, No. 3, 1978, pp. 19–20.
27. Both in 1974 and 1981, I often heard this explanation for the relative reversal of young women's progress in school. So did Molander (op. cit., p. 39).

14. Restoring Women's Dignity

> After fifteen years in the liberated zone, when I first returned to Saigon, I was overwhelmed by all the prostitutes, drug addicts, unemployed, widows, disabled, orphans, beggars and the cultural intoxication of the people. At first, it seemed like a sea you could drown in. But as we mobilized the people – especially the women – we all learned to swim together.
>
> *Bui Thi Me, retired Vice-Minister of Public Health, Provisional Revolutionary Government of South Viet Nam*

Many Vietnamese viewed the half-million GIs in Viet Nam not as defenders of freedom but as consumers. Sex was the biggest product. At the height of US occupation, there were nearly half a million prostitutes in South Viet Nam. These prostitutes were the end product of a process begun when Diem first rounded up his opponents and forced them into concentration camps in 1956. By 1973, as a result of forced urbanization, bombings and defoliation, peasants had swollen the population of Saigon to over four million – ten times the city's size in 1954. The primary means for these displaced women to survive was prostitution. Saigon became one huge American brothel, mass producing prostitutes by the thousand.[1]

According to Sister Françoise Vandermeersch, a nun with years of experience in working with prostitutes in Europe who assisted the Vietnamese Ministry of Social Services in 1976, documents discovered at the abandoned US Embassy revealed that 300,000 women were registered to work at official 'Centers of Leisure'. These were brothels constructed and maintained by the US-sponsored Saigon regime.[2] These documents record high-level meetings of the representatives of the various ministries in the Saigon regime: Justice, Health, Public Works, Interior, Social Action and Finance. During one of these interministerial meetings in October 1965, plans were laid to establish 'Centers of Leisure' in the suburbs of South Viet Nam's 12 major cities.

Those officials initiated construction of the centres after consultation with provincial chiefs on the most discreet, secure locations. They agreed to keep central government involvement in the centres secret and blame provincial officials if there was any publicity. Prostitution was, after all, officially illegal. But Saigon officials were greedy for the American dollars which the brothels would bring. Once the centres were operating, 80% of the revenue went to the central government and 20% stayed at the brothels to maintain the women and the establishment.

The Centers of Leisure were under strict military management by Thieu's troops. They ran the establishments with an iron hand according to rules agreed on at the ministerial meeting. The centres were constructed according to the specifications of ministry blueprints, which called for special prayer rooms as well as dormitories for the prostitutes. The women were permitted one day off a week and were allowed to leave the centre for a maximum of ten hours. The documents specified that women under 18 years of age were not be employed, but this rule was often broken.

Putting Government Pimps out of Business

The 1960 programme of the National Liberation Front and the Programme of Action of the Provisional Revolutionary Government of South Viet Nam adopted in 1968 both affirmed the commitment to 'combat the US-imported slavish and depraved culture and education, which impaired our people's fine cultural traditions.' On 1 April 1975, as the campaign to liberate the South neared final victory, the PRG issued a ten-point policy for administering newly liberated areas. The policy banned all agencies that 'promoted the alien culture which degraded women'.

As soon as Saigon was liberated, prostitution was banned and the Women's Union, along with the Youth Organization, launched a campaign to find housing, food and new skills for thousands of unemployed women. Most of the former prostitutes, who had been peasants forced to flee their land during the war, welcomed the chance to return to their homes and rejoin village life. Others settled in New Economic Zones, to reclaim devastated land and rebuild their lives in communities where their past was unknown. A July 1976 survey indicated the original prostitute population had been reduced to 50,000. Other sources say it was 100,000 in 1976.[3]

But enormous problems persisted. With the economy in shambles, it was not easy to find jobs for the women who remained in the cities. Socialist food distribution prevented mass starvation, but for women accustomed to US standards of glitter and consumption, the possibility of soliciting the dwindling flow of foreign visitors remained appealing. Of those women who were not yet incorporated into the Programme for the Restoration of Women's Dignity in 1976, 60% were illiterate, 64% were infected with syphilis and 30% had gonorrhea.

In 1981, of the 600 women at the 'New Women's School', one of the few remaining schools needed for retraining former prostitutes, 15% of the students were under 17 years of age.[4] Nguyen Thi Thanh, President of the Women's Union in Ho Chi Minh City and member of the Standing Committee of the party in Ho Chi Minh City, believes that 'New prostitutes are still victims of the neo-colonial regime. Younger women simply follow the bad example of the old . . . people with bad habits who don't want to work.'[5]

The testimony of young women who worked as prostitutes after 1975 indicates that they are victims not only of neo-colonial values, but also of poverty and lack of job opportunities. Ha, a woman who had been tricked into prostitution shortly before liberation, returned to her native village in 1976 and planned to sell vegetables in the market. But her father became ill and all their money evaporated.

> At this time I met up with a fellow. He worked on the docks. We lived together. We were happy but one day he left without saying where he was going. This was in 1978. My father wanted me to marry a young orphaned man . . . . Only he was a drug addict and squandered my money on drugs. Then I returned to Saigon and 'did it again'. I was arrested and transferred here (the New Women's School).

The interviewer asks if she ever wants to run away.

> Oh yes! We all dream of escaping at first. But now I have joined several organizations at the school, I sing and have a job, . . . I will stay here a little longer . . . . Life is so hard outside!

Another student at the school, since 1980, admitted,

> I don't feel confident enough (to return home). I am afraid of doing it again . . . because of the high cost of living, unemployment, the women who entice you, the men who watch you and above all, alas! the habit.[6]

Women who turned to prostitution after 1975 are rare. If they are 15% of the estimated 30,000 remaining prostitutes, then perhaps only 4,500 women have turned to the streets since liberation. It is interesting to compare this number with the avalanche of new recruits to the sex industry in Thailand, estimated at between a half-million and one million. The reason for the contrast is Thailand's neo-colonial economy, which makes young peasant women one of the main resources to be exploited for the sake of the balance of payments and urban growth. Sexual tourism – trips to Thailand with 'exotic pleasures' included in the packaged price – provides a decisive share of Bangkok's foreign exchange earnings.[7]

'Reason and Love Movement'
While prostitution is sponsored by corrupt regimes, like Thieu's and the current administration in Thailand, it is actively discouraged by the

Chau, Mai and Dau at Dong Nai School for New Life. Chau had a child when she was 12
Sara Rosner

Vietnamese government and the Women's Union. However, prostitutes are not viewed as criminals or sick people. In trying to convince prostitutes to give up their trade, Women's Union cadres remember, 'It wasn't the fault of the woman. It was the fault of the old regime, which fostered such bad behaviour among women. And bad habits are not easy to cast off.'[8]

In 1977, when the Women's Union launched the 'Reason and Love Movement' in Ho Chi Minh City to help the relatively few remaining prostitutes to change their lives, they applied the principle of treating prostitutes as victims rather than criminals. The campaign was especially active in District 1, the former heart of Saigon's 'red light district'.

The Women's Union special group of 21 aimed to educate the prostitutes and some of the other street hustlers in the district so that they themselves would choose to change their lives. Within a short period, using reason and love, they persuaded more than 200 women to join work brigades and go to the New Economic Zones.[9] Tens of thousands of women have received on-the-spot re-education from mobile education teams like the 'Reason and Love Movement'. These teams have had the most success with women who were relatively new to prostitution.

By 1981, most prostitutes who remained in the trade were relatively seasoned and required more systematic re-education than mobile teams could offer. These are the women who board at the Centres for the Restoration of Women's Dignity or the 'New Women's School'.

In North Viet Nam, within several years of the French defeat, the 30,000 women who had been prostitutes were trained and integrated into productive jobs in the new society. For 20 years, prostitution was virtually unknown in the Democratic Republic of Viet Nam. However, when I visited Hanoi in 1981, outside my hotel I met a couple of young women wearing make-up and dressed in printed slacks and shirts – unusual for Hanoi women. A third woman who was huddling with us under the eaves in the rain took me aside and told me the other two were prostitutes. She explained rather matter-of-factly: 'Our standard of living is very low and these women don't have hope things will get better. Life is very hard in Viet Nam now and they don't know another way to improve their condition.'

Later, when I questioned my Women's Union hosts about the incident, they were surprised. They thought my informant was, perhaps, misjudging the women because of their dress. They thought the hotel security would not have permitted the women to work near the hotel. But they did not eliminate the possibility altogether:

> There are free relations now between the North and the South and not all the influence of the South on the North is good. There are no full-time prostitutes in the North, but some women do it part time, to supplement their incomes. There are very few of them, but if we don't eliminate the problem quickly, it will become bigger. We don't punish women who prostitute themselves. We meet with their families and friends and ask them

to help re-educate the women. In most cases the family doesn't know what their daughter is doing. Parents can often control the problem, once they know about it because children have great respect for their parents and usually will not disobey them.

The Centres for the Restoration of Women's Dignity

The Ministry of Social Services, in co-operation with the Women's Union, administered four Centres for the Restoration of Women's Dignity. Sister Vandermeersch visited one centre which housed 600 women. She was impressed by the respect shown for the women being trained there.

Duy Lien, who supervises the centres in the area of Ho Chi Minh City, defined their tasks: first, to cure venereal disease; second, to provide education including literacy and Vietnamese history and culture, so the women regain some pride in themselves and their country; third, to teach women skills so they can get a job and play an active role in reconstructing society. And finally, Lien explained: 'We work for them to become genuine Vietnamese women who love their country, love their customs, their children, their homes and the people around them.'[10] The primary task is the restoration of the women's health. Doctors use acupuncture at the centres, as well as herbs, to help detoxify women who had become drug addicts.

Nearly all the former prostitutes have children and other relatives to support. So the state subsidizes the support of their dependants while the women are living in the centres.

The former prostitutes elect their own representatives to administer the centre where their live, work and study. Revolutionary cadres, usually from the Women's Union, provide leadership, but Vandermeersch could find no trace of authoritarianism or paternalism. Everyone is addressed as sister, and the cadres sleep in the same dormitories as the former prostitutes. They share responsibility for coping with the women's problems in adapting to their new lives off the streets. They also publish a weekly hand-written newspaper.

Vandermeersch described their daily routine. After a period of gymnastics and breakfast, the women spend their mornings learning a skill, either by practising a craft or an agricultural task. The noon meal is more nutritious than most peasants eat. After the traditional midday rest, the women attend literacy and elementary education classes three afternoons a week and political education and history classes another three afternoons a week. In the evening, they spend their time in cultural activities.

Political education includes such topics as 'Why is it necessary to study?', 'The origins of prostitution', and 'The new woman in the new society'. After a lecture, the class breaks into discussion groups to debate the topic, and then reassembles for a question and answer session.

Sister Vandermeersch emphasized the programme for the Restoration of the Dignity of Women is severely restricted by Viet Nam's economic problems. There are not enough antibiotics to treat all the venereal disease. And, 'Learning to sew is a matter of survival,' responded Vandermeersch when asked about the former prostitutes learning sex-stereotyped skills. 'Their only clothes are patchwork.' In the centre that trained 600 women, there were only three sewing machines and they were not being used because fabric and thread had run out. At the same centre, there was no radio, tape recorder, or record player, although this equipment might have been useful for the women's education, as well as for recreation. There was one pen for 20 students and with the paper shortage, a scrap of paper was a precious gift for someone learning to read and write.

In 1980 Duy Lien, Director of the War Invalids and Social Affairs Service in Ho Chi Minh City, summed up the lessons they had learned:

1. Mental poisoning should not be underestimated. Patience and perseverance is the watchword . . . . Thus not only the reformees but also the reformers must undergo a process of education and enlightenment.
2. Most of our wards are people who have lost self-confidence and self-respect, lack will, are full of complexes and badly in need of affection.
3. There are favorable factors for their recovery, first their origin in the poorer, working social strata; then their youth. These positive elements will develop if given the proper environment.
4. Positive elements must be discovered and fostered in each individual . . . . We recognize and commend good points, even when they relate to trivial matters, but they must be concrete, visible and accepted by all . . . if a person has committed some wrong action the day before, we don't make the slightest reference to it.
5. Labor is a means to reform people . . . . They feel legitimate pride when selling vegetables they have grown or sitting in classrooms on benches they have built . . . .
6. To remedy the problem of personnel shortage we have picked the best elements from among the students themselves and appointed them to managerial posts.[11]

Lien estimated it would be 1986 before prostitution is eliminated in Viet Nam and the women are entirely integrated into the new society. It takes three or four years to make sure the women with the worst cases of syphilis are no longer infectious. Nguyen Thi Thanh, President of the Women's Union in Ho Chi Minh City, thought it would take dozens of years before all the social and cultural effects of neo-colonialism were eliminated.

Regardless of the timetable, it is certain that prostitution and its companions – drugs and pornography – are no longer sponsored by those in power in Viet Nam. Rather, the government and society provide progressive alternatives in the form of job training, acupuncture and physical and emotional therapy as well as new forms of culture. As the sex industry in Viet Nam dies, all women – not just former prostitutes – recover their dignity.

Notes

1. For more information on the mass production of prostitutes during the US occupation of South Viet Nam, see Chapter 5, *Women of Viet Nam*, by Arlene Eisen Bergman (San Francisco: Peoples Press, 1975), pp. 82–91.
2. Sister Françoise Vandermeersch interviewed by author (November 1976); material from interview published in Arlene Eisen, 'Women's Dignity Restored in Viet Nam', *The Guardian*, 8 December 1976, p. 15.
3. Ibid.; and Cecilia Molander, *Women in Viet Nam* (Stockholm: Swedish International Development Authority, 1978), p. 85.
4. Françoise Correze and Huu Ngoc, 'A School . . . A Family', *Viet Nam Courier*, No. 4, 1981, p. 15.
5. Interview by author with Nguyen Thi Thanh (Ho Chi Minh City, 5 September 1981).
6. Correze and Ngoc, op. cit., p. 16.
7. For details, see excellent article by Pasuk Phongpaichit, 'The Bangkok Masseuses: Holding Up the Family Sky', *South East Asia Chronicle*, No. 78, April 1981, pp. 15–23.
8. Duong Ky Anh, 'The Road She Chose', *Women of Viet Nam*, No. 3, 1980, p. 21.
9. Doan Thanh, 'Reason and Love', *Women of Viet Nam*, No. 4, 1977, pp. 11–12.
10. This material and Vandermeersch in Eisen, op. cit., p. 15.
11. Do Thi Duy Lien, 'Feelings of Love and a Sense of Responsibility', *Women of Viet Nam*, No. 4, 1980, pp. 11–13.

15. Women's Leadership: The Revolution Within the Revolution

> The promotion of women was the real revolution which upset the old social order founded on male hegemony and contempt·for women . . . . Cadres opposed the promotion of women colleagues, husbands hampered the progress of their wives, worrying lest the latter overtake them. Women needed as much courage as in armed struggle to assert themselves in their new role. They themselves had to battle to get free of the traditional oppression exerted by the old morality over generations of women, which was echoed over in themselves.
>
> *Mai Thi Tu and Le Thi Nham Tuyet in their book,* Women in Viet Nam

The ranks of women leaders have grown by fits and starts. First, years of very slow progress, then as the entire society was mobilized for defence against US invasion, women assumed leadership positions at a spectacular rate. Although it may be premature to conclude the trend has been reversed, since 1976 the percentage of women in leadership has not increased. In some areas it has fallen. This chapter is devoted to understanding this uneven progress – its history, causes and prospects.

Mai Thi Tu and Le Thi Nham Tuyet are not isolated feminists in Viet Nam; they do not face a hostile government or organized opposition. The statement quoted above comes from their recent book, which is considered a definitive work about women in Viet Nam. The book was so much respected that it is one of the few titles to be translated into several foreign languages by the official Foreign Languages Publishing House in Hanoi.

In other words, many Vietnamese officials and the Women's Union recognize women's struggle for leadership in society as a struggle involving power: 'a revolution within the revolution'. They affirm the importance of that revolution and do not underestimate the obstacles in the way of promoting and accepting women in leadership. They understand that if women are not represented at leadership levels in proportion to their contributions to production, defence and the rearing of future generations, they cannot be completely liberated. For example, Nguyen Thi Dinh, then President of the Union of Women for the Liberation of South Viet Nam, wrote an article underlining the importance of electing women to leadership. The article appeared in April 1976, during the election campaign for the first reunified National Assembly, in Saigon's daily newspaper, *Saigon Giai Phong*:

> To join the National Assembly and the administration is for women the most basic political right. It is also a very strong political encouragement to the women's movement. The women deputies will make substantial reports on the life and aspirations of women of various social strata and join in the elaboration of laws and policies. They will be able to use all means and materials afforded by the State machinery to look after the legitimate interests of women and children. The presence of women in the National Assembly and administration and in all spheres of activity will effect a tremendous influence on the emancipation of women.[1]

Since the founding of the Indochinese Communist party in 1930, there has been a constant struggle between those aiming to promote women's leadership on the one hand, and the people, institutions and traditions opposing women's leadership on the other. Despite progress, the forces restraining women still had the upper hand as late as 1954. Tu and Tuyet write:

> In the countryside, although the August Revolution toppled the power of the ruling class, and its most prominent, tyrannical representatives – the mandarins and the colonialists – feudal relations of production still persisted. (Land Reform did not begin until 1954.) Women peasants, though emancipated by law, remained subject to a patriarchal power that administrative measures could not fully eradicate. Meanwhile, the national danger (French invasion) relegated these internal contradictions (women's oppression and the persistence of landlordism) to second place.[2]

Tu and Tuyet note substantial but inadequate progress for women in the years 1954–60:

> Contempt for women still prevailed, as was evident in wage scales, certain statutes and discrimination against women in promotion. As a result, although they constituted an important work force, women played only a secondary role in the management of production and in state organs.[3]

In December 1960, a conference of political women cadres passed a resolution, which was later approved by the leadership of the party, that in order to mobilize women and develop their capabilities, a new policy of bold promotion and rapid training of women for management positions was required. It is significant to note that this policy was adopted before the general mobilization against the US invasion.

238

Preparing for Leadership

In the course of protracted struggle for independence, women learned to use automatic weapons and anti-aircraft artillery. The experience of shooting down a plane helped overcome centuries of indoctrination in women's inferiority. The new experience of repairing her own machine helped to convince a factory worker that she could be self-sufficient. Cam Thanh, a writer who toured the fighting front often, remarked: 'At first, women do not think they can do such things. But the truth is a convincing answer.'[4]

The Vietnamese call this process *tu giai phong* or self-liberation. By participating in new activities, people begin to question and reject old, oppressive ways. Women also found new pride in the transformation of traditional roles. For example, when a woman supplies meals to the Liberation Army, she feels a pride and sense of purpose that she could not feel when she served meals to a landlord or a husband she had been forced to marry. Each woman who learned to fight or drive a tractor became a model and inspiration for the next. For example, Ut Tich, the local guerrilla commander who became a national hero, became a morale booster and model for other women. Ut Tich fought in the South.[5] In Hanoi, a group of women tractor drivers who worked at the pier unloading ships, named their work team after her. Thuoc, one of the drivers, described how Ut Tich's example helped her to learn to manoeuvre pulling a long line of trailers.

> The day I began to work at the wharves, I was scared to death . . . . An accident could happen so easily. When I was at driving school, we drove light tractors over good roads . . . . (This was very different.) During the years of American air raids, we often worked at night. The trailers were heavily loaded, the lanes were poorly lit . . . . Sometimes the tractors broke down or brushed against each other causing goods to fall all over. But we stood fast. Our team bears the name of Sister Ut Tich, hero of the South. In 1967, when our all-woman team was formed . . . many of us were hampered by a kind of inferiority complex: no one knew about labor management, engine maintenance and especially about leadership work . . . . But we strove to learn from the example of Sister Ut Tich.[6]

Thuoc herself became an example for others after learning engine repair and designing a new starting method that saved tons of fuel. As news of her achievements spread, other women were encouraged to take on new responsibilities, including leadership, which had previously been reserved for men.

Emulation movements, especially the 'Three Responsibilities Movement', also encouraged women to take special responsibilities and leadership in production, defence and family work. After the air war against the North ended in 1973, the content of the Three Responsibilities changed to: 1) take responsibility for production and political leadership in carrying out 'duties to our country'; 2) ensure effective organization of the family for the growth of future generations; 3) struggle for equality between women and men. Local chapters decided on the most appropriate ways for their members to fulfil these responsibilities. At the end of each six-month period, the collective evaluated their work and gave awards to those women who had achieved the most. The discussions surrounding the awards also provided women with suggestions and new understandings of how to improve their leadership.

Years of struggle reinforced these lessons. As time passed, there were fewer bystanders. Novels, short stories, poems, songs, plays, newspaper articles, movies, paintings and sculptures all presented examples of heroines who inspired increased confidence on the part of still more women. It seems that the majority of leading characters in the art and literature of revolutionary Viet Nam are women. Mostly they are heroines who have overcome enormous obstacles to make either productive, political or military contributions to the revolution. While they may be somewhat romanticized, their status challenges male hegemony. The Vietnamese have a saying, 'Women are the greatest victims of the war, but they are also its greatest heroes.'

A new generation of women grew up, learning from heroes like Ut Tich and Minh Khai. They learned from paintings and woodcuts that show sturdy women with strong arms, backs and shoulders. Girls in the liberated zones of the South, during the 1960s and 1970s, learned to read with stories about Sister Phuong who set booby traps while her mother was away from the village on an army assignment. One of the favourite children's books, 'In Mom's Absence', provided an effective lesson in the abolition of sex roles.

> To Anh, her mother meant glittering cartridges with which her mother taught her to count . . . . Bé, for her part, did not mind her mother's absence. To climb to the top of the coconut tree was her habit. She climbed it every day, acting as an observer, informing the rest of the village of the places under enemy aircraft attack . . . . Bé leaned the ruler against the coconut tee, and in doing so, she recalled the picture of her mother leaning her rifle against a pillar in the house.[7]

Towards the end of the story the reader learns that Bé's mother is the famous commander, Ut Tich.

Unfortunately, people who lived under the Thieu regime until 1975, and many of those who did not, were unaffected by stories about Ut Tich. Some never heard of her. Others may have had no idea of how to apply the lessons of such exemplary women to the realities of their own lives, especially when they were still dominated by the all-consuming tasks of childrearing and earning a living. More systematic leadership training was needed.

The 1960 conference that resolved to promote women to management positions also established the first cadre-training school for women. Le Thu, the director of the Women's Union cadre-training school in Hanoi, talked about the specific importance of training women to be leaders: '. . . in order to develop a strong women's movement, we must have women cadres because women understand each other more clearly.'[8] The curricula of the cadre-training schools are discussed in Chapter 8. By 1981, the two central schools had trained 3,311 women as cadres. They are proud that many of their graduates not only work for the Women's Union, but also take leadership positions in the party and government.[9]

The Women's Union also brings opportunities in leadership training to remote areas. For example, in 1975, Dar Lac Province in the central highlands had only four cadres in charge of the women's movement and none of them were from the national minorities who lived in the region. There was no grass-roots organization from the district to the village level; women therefore had little support for assuming any kind of leadership role in that province. The Women's Union remedy was to begin a cadre-training course for the national minority women of the province. Eighteen women attended the first course. After two months of theoretical study and heated discussions, the class returned to the villages to do four months' practical work. The women worked day and night in the fields, fetching water and pounding rice. While working, they talked about state policies and the Women's Union. This work laid the foundation for the organization of the Women's Union in that province.

After this success, the Women's Union initiated more cadre-training courses for national minority women. By 1978, almost 1,500 women had received some leadership training and 87 villages in Dar Lac had Women's Union chapters. They, in turn, organized meetings in which 120,000 women were able to begin their political education.[10] Table 5 summarizes the Women's Union's success in training new cadres throughout the country.

Table 5
Women's Union Cadre Training, 1975–80

Level	Number of Classes	Number of Women Trained
National	9	1,370
Provincial	899	47,495
District	1,854	207,513
Village	11,247	1,183,098
Totals	*14,009*	*1,439,476*

Source: 'Appendix to the Report to the Fifth National Congress of Vietnamese Women' (unpublished mimeo), May 1982, p. 64.

'Frogs Jumping on the Altar'

When women become village leaders – when they take jobs with authority which were previously reserved for men – they are like 'frogs jumping on the altar'. That is how people perceived the earliest challengers to male hegemony in social and political affairs. People waited for the new leaders to blunder so that they could reaffirm the 'in-born incapacity of women'.

By 1965, despite party resolutions urging the promotion of women to leading positions, only 11% of all leading posts were held by women.[11] Tu and Tuyet attribute the slow progress to 'several causes, but it was basically due to narrow-mindedness and lack of confidence in women among male executive cadres.' In most cases there was no question of women unseating men in power. The men's fears were less tangible. For example, a male director and a representative of a woman's committee were debating her proposal that the post of office manager be filled by a young woman. The director was flabbergasted:

> That girl? But she's too young; we have older comrades, haven't we?
> But isn't youth an important criterion, comrade director?
> I know, I know, but that's only theory. Old comrades have been tried and tested in the struggle and their loyalty to the revolution is unquestionable.
> Well, are not the excellent results of our colleague's work sufficient to prove her loyalty and revolutionary ardour?
> I don't deny it. But . . . she is too young to be a leader!
> We have confidence in her. She is still inexperienced, but she must be allowed to exercise such a function if she is to make progress!

That was enough for the director. He could contain himself no longer.

> I will not argue anymore. I just don't agree with you. Why make a fuss about her? Even my wife, who is old enough to be her aunt, is not yet head of a department![12]

It was in this sort of atmosphere that the first chairwomen, women chiefs of office, women's team and brigade leaders, and section chiefs were nominated. They were few and each of them had to perform competently, as well as convince patriarchal die-hards that it was normal for a woman to do so.

The Vietnamese press still features stories praising a 'feminine style of leadership' that emerged in the 1960s. Women leaders became known for their dedication, hard work, their sensitivity to the needs of their constituents, their competence and integrity. Cases of corruption were almost unknown among women cadres. 'They did not drink, smoke or indulge their stomachs as men did.' When the party began a review of its membership in 1976, in order to expel those who had been bureaucratic or corrupt or had not fulfilled its ideals in other ways, not one woman lost her membership, while hundreds of men were expelled.[13]

Trends in Women's Political Power

Since the 1960s, the political strength of women in Viet Nam has grown dramatically. While women are still under-represented in leading positions, by international standards they are far better represented than most of the women in the world. While there are still no women among the very top members of the party, the Politburo, their numbers in the Central Committee have grown. Women's absence from the Politburo is probably best explained by the fact that virtually all those posts are held by the generation who led the 1945 August Revolution. That group emerged at a time when only men went to school. The women of that generation – with the possible exception of Minh Khai whom the French executed – were not only educationally handicapped, but everyone was also raised to believe there was no alternative to male domination.

Nevertheless, between 1965 and 1975, the number of women holding ministerial or vice-ministerial positions in North Viet Nam grew from five

Woman cadre collects arms from Thieu's soldiers   Viet Nam News Agency

to 12. By the end of 1981, there were 23 women out of a total of 100 who were ministers or vice-ministers in reunified Viet Nam.[14] Women who were ministers before 1975 expanded their areas of responsibility after the country was reunified. As Madame Binh told me, 'Being Minister of Education for the whole country is more responsibility than being Foreign Minister for half a country.' The Women's Union is proud of these leaders. They do not view them as 'tokens' or women who have compromised their commitment to women's rights. In celebrating their achievements in 1975, the editors of *Women of Viet Nam* magazine wrote:

> One may say that the majority of women officials at all levels have sprung from the women's movement, from work in the Union. Outstanding instances of this are the Foreign Minister of the PRG and four Vice Ministers of government in the DRV. Their deep understanding of the masses and their close ties with the women's movement have allowed them to fulfil their role as representatives of women's right to be mistresses of the land and to enhance the democratic character of state organs.[15]

Also at the national level, women's representation in the National Assembly is significant because it results from general elections for which lists of candidates are proposed by various mass organizations, including the Women's Union. Women's sharp rise, then declining representation after 1975, may indicate a disturbing trend.

Table 6
Women in the National Assembly

Year	Number of Women	Percentage of Total
1946*	10	2.5
1960	53	11.6
1965	66	18.2
1972	125	29.7
1975	137	32.3
1976*	132	26.8
1981*	108	21.8

*These sessions included representatives for all of Viet Nam. During the intervening years, the National Assembly represented the North only.

Source: Viet Nam Women's Union, *Women of Viet Nam: Statistical Data* (Hanoi, 1981), p. 13.

The women elected to the National Assembly include representatives of national minorities, political cadres, members of the army, workers, peasants, intellectuals and Women's Union cadres. Le Thi Thieu, one of the women elected from Ho Chi Minh City in 1976, perhaps best symbolizes the phenomenal rise of women from marginal to central roles in society. She is a mother of six and worked as a street sweeper before liberation. Thieu explained,

> It was a job no one else wanted because we were considered social outcasts. As I was illiterate and my husband was unemployed, I considered myself lucky to have such a job. I had heard that the communists were very cruel people who would kill anybody who worked for the old regime . . . . I was terribly scared on the eve of liberation. But I kept sweeping up garbage. Then, as we public workers were invited to hear some explanations from the revolutionaries, many of us, including myself, were terrified. But we found the kindest, most reasonable and human people who told us our work was very important and to do our best. Our working conditions would be improved. So I worked harder than ever.

She began literacy classes and when it was time to nominate candidates for the National Assembly, her neighbours and fellow workers nominated her. She was elected.

> Before I did not even know what the National Assembly was or what a deputy did. Now I know and speak up in committee meetings for the working class of my precinct. I have regular meetings with the people who elected me and carefully listen to their troubles so I can help solve them.[16]

Yet the declining percentage of women elected after 1975 – a reversal of a 30-year trend of increasing women's representation – is disturbing. In the 1976 elections, despite Nguyen Thi Dinh's urging (quoted on p. 238), voters seemed to be more willing to reject women candidates than men; 26% of the women candidates were not elected compared with 18% of the male candidates.[17] There are no comparable numbers available for the 1981 elections, but it would appear that an even higher percentage of women candidates were rejected.

Some of the women I questioned were not particularly concerned about the decline in women's representation in the National Assembly. A number of Women's Union officials explained the election results as an indication that the latest National Assembly required more intellectuals and technical experts to meet the country's demands for economic development: although fewer women were elected, those who were elected were 'higher quality'. In fact, in 1976, 22 out of 132 women elected, or 17%, were intellectuals. In 1981, 44 out of 108 women elected were intellectuals – a leap to 41%.[18] The implication of this argument is that there were more qualified men than women intellectuals available to serve – an assumption not proved.

Nguyen Thi Binh explained the decline in women's representation in terms of the relatively stronger influence of feudal thinking in the South:

> In the liberated zones, the consciousness of the people was very high and supported women's equality. But in the occupied zones, especially in the cities and town, the consciousness was lower . . . . Everybody recognizes women can work, but it is more difficult to accept that a woman can govern. The Women's Union has not fulfilled its duty to explain to people that this conception is wrong.[19]

Data from the 1976 election support Binh's explanation: that is, 32% of the nominees from the North and 23% of the nominees from the South were women. Data are not available to ascertain whether women who had been elected to the 1975 Assembly in the North lost their seats in 1976 or 1981. In other words, we cannot establish whether the trend towards growing women's representation was reversed in the North or whether it was simply held back in the South. But the further erosion of women's representation in the 1981 National Assembly represents an overall loss for women, North and South.

A similar trend appears to be emerging in women's political power at the provincial, district and village levels. The People's Provincial Councils are just below the National Assembly in the government structure. They are elected once every three years by secret ballot. Again, the various mass organizations propose candidates to ensure that the various sectors of society are represented. District and Village Councils implement national laws at their respective levels. They also have responsibility for planning economic and public works, construction and cultural activities. They examine and approve local budgets, maintain public order and security and protect the rights of citizens in their areas. For example, Village Councils decide whether to allocate public funds to childcare facilities.

Table 7
Women Serving on People's Councils

Type of Council	Percentage of Council Members Who Are Women			
	1965	1975	1979*	1981*
Provincial	17	33	na	23
District	25	38	29	22
Village	21	41	29	23

*Percentages are for reunified Viet Nam, others are only for the North.

Sources: Cecilia Molander, *Women in Viet Nam* (Stockholm: Swedish International Development Authority, 1978), p. 95; Jayne Werner, 'Women, Socialism and the Economy of Wartime North Viet Nam', *Studies in Comparative Communism*, Vol. XIV, Nos 2–3, Summer/Autumn 1981, p. 173; Viet Nam Women's Union, *Women of Viet Nam: Statistical Data* (Hanoi, 1981), pp. 15–16, and 'Appendix to Report to the Fifth Congress of Vietnamese Women', May 1982, unpublished mimeo, p. 64; and unpublished correspondence.

The decrease in women's representation between 1979 and 1981 at all levels of the political structure is an alarming trend, which cannot be explained by the incorporation of relatively more chauvinist southern voters. It is probably too soon to analyse the dynamics of this trend: whether it represents backsliding on the part of the party, government and Women's Union or simply the re-emergence of feudal patriarchal traditions which are no longer suppressed by the urgent demands of war.

Women in Management

On 8 March 1967, the government issued a directive to strengthen the trend towards women's leadership in the economy as well as in government. To ensure that women would rise in the management of industrial and agricultural enterprises, the government stipulated quotas for a designated number of women managers, according to the percentage of women in the work force of that enterprise (see Chapter 9, pp. 155–7 for details).

Nguyen Thi Hoi, a young peasant woman and militia member, talked about the success of the policy's implementation within the first year of its announcement:

> After the coop was set up, I became Deputy Chief of a production group. I do the same jobs as the other cooperators: ploughing, harrowing, pricking, harvesting . . . . In August 1967, I became a Party member. I have authority over women and men, and they do as I ask because it is they who elected me to lead them.[20]

Vietnamese studies have shown that in co-operatives with women leaders, production has generally exceeded the norm. For example at Phuc Le co-op on the outskirts of Haiphong city, 109 of 182 party members, including the party secretary, are women. Women also comprise half the administrative and management committees. In the years since women have taken a more active role in its management, the co-op has been transformed from one which could not grow enough food to feed its own members to one which was able to sell a substantial surplus to the state.[21]

In Yen So co-op, south of Hanoi, a woman has been deputy manager for 13 years. Jayne Werner, a US scholar, visited it in 1980. She found two other top posts – the party secretary of the village and the chairperson of the people's committee – were also held by women. Women comprised 35% of the party members of the village. During the time that women assumed leading roles, 1965–75, productivity increases brought a substantial improvement in people's standard of living. The manager expected that male villagers returning to Yen So were unlikely to undermine this female authority because women had demonstrated their leadership brings great progress.[22] Werner also cites other studies published in the party journal concluding that the districts which had been most successful in promoting women's leadership also enjoyed the most impressive harvests.

But the promotion of women to management does not yet reflect the importance of women's labour-force participation. After the flurry of promotions between 1967 and 1973, progress in enforcing the directive has been very slow. For example, in 1966, only 3% of co-op presidents were women. Fifteen years later, in 1981, for all of Viet Nam, the figure was only 5.1%, although the number of deputy presidents was 18.3%.

On the other hand, the percentage of women managers in selected industries has increased substantially in recent years, since reunification. For example, the number of women directors and assistant directors of enterprises in light industry more than doubled between 1976 and 1980, from 23 to 54. The number of women managing handicraft co-operatives nearly doubled during the same years.[24] It would seem, then, that women are encouraged as leaders of other women, but women's leadership meets with stubborn resistance when it entails exercising authority over men.

Why the Frogs Move at a Snail's Pace

Despite party directives and studies, Women's Union exhortations and the evident competence of women, more time — perhaps generations – will clearly be required for women to overturn the contempt for them inherited over the centuries. Resistance to women's leadership is, perhaps, the most telling barometer of continuing disrespect for women. In 1973, Bui Thi Cam, one of Viet Nam's first women lawyers and a Women's Union leader, told a US visitor, 'We have equality but we are not yet equal.'[25] Eight years later, Ngo Ba Thanh, also a lawyer, a Vice-President of the Women's Union and an author of the 1980 Constitution, reiterated the same idea:

> The heritage of Confucianism, feudalism and capitalism runs deep. No generation could have changed as much as we have. We have been pushed by history. But we still do not have full equality. We have one of the most progressive wonderful constitutions in the world; but we cannot liberate women by the stroke of a pen. It is much harder to fight against obsolete customs than against the enemy. [She spent years in Thieu's prisons.] . . . . Men and women cannot be made equal in a mechanical way. We must take into account that women are mothers and teachers, so we must liberate them from the home.[26]

The obsolete customs Thanh referred to have been recognized as stumbling blocks by an impressive array of women whose capacities are beyond question. Nguyen Thi Dinh is the general who, in January 1960,

General Nguyen Thi Dinh at work   Viet Nam News Agency

led the insurrection of Ben Tre Province – the model for the general uprising against Diem later that year. Now President of the Women's Union, Dinh admitted that even she had to contend with age-old contempt for women:

> When I was appointed Vice-Commander in Chief of the People's Liberation Armed Forces, some people thought it was only for propaganda. But when I succeeded, they realized the appointment was correct. Men have this psychology: they are not confident when a woman is leader (over them) – it is their complex. Women must be superior to show their capacity because when men and women are equal, a man will always choose a man.[27]

In 1981 President Dinh chaired a conference devoted to exploring women's work, aspirations and difficulties in fulfilling them. Outstanding workers, managers and professionals testified. In addition to the burdens of the double shift, the main problem they pointed to was 'the feudal concept of making light of women'. Le Thi Kim, aged 38, acting director of the Mai Linh Sericulture (silkworm cultivation) Centre, detailed progress there in family planning and childcare. Then she detailed women's struggle for acceptance as leaders:

> The only remaining obstacle is the feudal concept of making light of women. While we were concentrating on the fight against grasserie [a disease that destroys silkworms] disease, more than a few of our male colleagues showed their skepticism and indifference to our efforts. When the Women's Union magazine publicized our success and mentioned my contribution as sponsor of the project, some of our male colleagues reacted angrily and they set about discrediting our work as 'unworthy of such praise'. Their reaction reached its climax when the Ministry of Agriculture named me acting director of the center. They sent written protests to the Council of Ministers,

so the Ministry had to send an investigation team to our center and organize an opinion poll. The result was that more than 90% of the people polled agreed to my appointment. Some of our male colleagues still openly declared their objection, but they are a small minority.

We propose that all levels of the administration take firmer steps to enforce the policy (to promote women to responsible posts) and initiate a powerful movement of public condemnation of any tendency to play down the role of women . . . . We women must have self-confidence and should not waver before the reaction of those confused by feudal ideology.

Then Do Thi Ngot, aged 38, President of the Minh Tan commune, testified to similar problems in a rural setting:

I am one of millions of Vietnamese women who matured in the Three Responsibilities Movement, taking charge of the families, social work and defense of our villages when our husbands and sons were at the front. But the lingering vestiges of feudal ideology place a serious hurdle in our way. (I have been president for 11 years.) But even today, some of my villagers stubbornly refuse to come to me, but instead go to the deputy president, a man, whenever they need a signature from the commune authorities.

My husband, who fought in the liberation army in the south, was killed in action in 1975. I was left with a daughter and was thus disadvantaged in two ways – in the family of my husband because I had no son; and in the commune, because I had become a widow. Some jeered at me: 'Look at the widow looking after court affairs!' Even the women did not hide their jealousy.

But I was too concerned with my work to busy myself with such back-biting. (She described her many tasks.) . . . . At times I have felt exhausted and wished to resign . . . . But I was encouraged by the trust some showed in me . . . . I don't think any man in my condition could work so hard. (She enumerates the significant responsibilities of women leaders in her commune.) Practice has shown women can do any job in the commune . . . .[28]

These women testify to the courage and strength needed for all women to take on leadership responsibilities. They also indicate the potential for the development of a militant movement that might remove patriarchal obstructions to the expansion of women's leadership in the future.

The Party's Responsibility

While the Women's Union continues to defend women's right to leading positions, several high-level party officials hold the party responsible for the continued failure to accept women's leadership and promote their potential. Ha Thi Que, member of the Central Committee of the Viet Nam Communist Party, former Women's Union President and organizer of the first brigade of armed women in 1945, wrote an important article in the party's theoretical journal, *Communist Review*, in November 1978.

She implied that women who took leadership roles during the war are now being replaced by men. She cited patriarchal thinking as the fundamental cause of the problem, but was more pointed in holding the party responsible for not finding more effective ways of resolving it. She drew attention to the party's 'unscientific attitudes towards training women cadres', noting that women were put into leadership positions during the 1960s without the proper training. She wrote:

> In a patronizing way, women were brought in at this level, in that branch, so there would be enough to fill the number requirements . . . . In our country, conservative, slow-moving influences, various backward ideas and customs remaining from the old society still have a frightening strength . . . . (As a result) not enough attention has been paid to women's particular problems of morale and so within a few years' time, quite a few women have been dropped from responsible positions.

She explained that women who take on leadership responsibilities can be easily discouraged because of family pressures, backward thinking that does not acknowledge their contributions, and patriarchal indoctrination that undermine women's self-confidence. Ha Thi Que recommended women be given special political and material support, especially during the times when they are most vulnerable: courtship, childbearing and menopause.[29]

In my own experience in Viet Nam, while it is difficult for a foreigner to be sure of her impressions when interpreting innuendo across language and cultural differences, men representing the party sometimes impressed me as patronizing towards women. When I arrived in a village, I was usually welcomed and given a background briefing by a gathering of Women's Union officials, other representatives of women in the community and party leaders. Often, the party leaders were men, and they sometimes gave speeches like the one I heard in My Chau District, Ha Son Binh Province:

> I want to express the party's appreciation for the women of this province . . . . We make sure that representatives of women are present in every branch of our activities . . . . In all the communes, we celebrate 8 March, International Women's Day, and 20 October, the founding date of the Women's Union . . . . As one of the leaders of the party in this district, I want to emphasize the importance we place on the women's movement. Women in our district have become self-sufficient in clothing, cotton, threads and blankets . . . they make beautiful handicrafts . . . .

Once, when I asked my travelling companions from the Women's Union – who were party members themselves – why the party representative at our meetings was invariably a man, Hoan, Deputy Head of Foreign Relations of the Women's Union, responded, 'They could send a woman, but they send a man to express the breadth of your welcome.'

The percentage of women in the party has not increased within the last ten years. In 1965, the percentage of women in the party was only 5.4. After a 1967 resolution urging the recruitment of women into the party, the number jumped to 25% in 1973. Hoan did not think the percentage of women had increased since then, although the abolute number of party members has nearly doubled from one million in 1975 to about 1.7 million in 1982.[30] At the 1976 party congress only 14% of the 1,008 delegates were women, despite a recommendation from the Central Committee to provincial party committees to ensure that at least 25% of the delegates were women.[31] It does not appear that women were any better represented at the Fifth Party Congress in 1982.

In a speech to the fifth party congress, Le Duc Tho, representing the Politburo or top leadership, urged the participants to strengthen the party by overcoming problems that prevent the emergence of women's leadership:

> The training of workers to be cadres for southern and mountain localities and for women has been carried out without the appropriate programs, plans, measures and curricula. Some party members have been rightist, bureaucratic and conservative . . . . No small number have succumbed to bourgeois and neo-colonial lifestyles. They have displayed mediocre, degenerate and deviant tastes . . . . In the machinery of our Party and State, arbitrariness, despotism and feudalistic paternalism still prevail and stifle challenge and struggle.[32]

Bui Thi Me, a party leader, former minister in the PRG and Vice-President of the Women's Union in the South, thinks that before women will be able to advance in the society as a whole, they must be able to advance more within the party. She expects it to be a long struggle, although she is proud of the progress women have made in the party in Ho Chi Minh City. While the absolute numbers are smaller, Bui Thi Me estimates the percentage of women in the party in Ho Chi Minh City is greater than in the North – approaching one-third. When I asked her which strategy she thought was most decisive in promoting women's leadership – raising their cultural levels or combating feudal ideology – she replied,

> We think the process of raising the technical level of women has been institutionalized. *The Constitution, socialist law and organization all support raising their cultural level. So increasing the capabilities of women is certain.* To struggle against feudal ideology is more difficult because it deals with the deep feelings of people. The two strategies must be implemented at the same time . . . . When we encounter double standards within the party, for example making it easier to admit men than women, we must struggle to define women's merits clearly.[33] (my emphasis)

Many women in the West, impressed by the leadership women had achieved in Viet Nam during the war, expected them to lose their hard-won positions when men returned from the front. Their expectation was based on fear that the socialist government was not sincerely committed to women's liberation. I have not found substantive evidence to confirm this fear. Once a socialist government is in power, it is possible to *begin* the socialist transformation of society, including the liquidation of patriarchy. But no government can change millennial traditions by fiat.

The greatest promotion of women to leadership occurred in the North in the years 1968–73. The development of socialist institutions, not simply the war (because there was war in 1945 against the French and again in 1960 against the US), gave the greatest impetus to women's advancement. Since 1975, that advancement has slowed – even halted in some areas – for a variety of reasons: 1) As Ha Thi Que explained, the war forced the careless promotion to leadership of some unqualified women who have since resigned. 2) Once men were available for leadership, when the upheavals of war subsided and the crisis mentality cooled, some people wanted to return to more normal, that is patriarchal, ways with men heading their households. They pressured women to abandon their positions of authority or to give up plans for achieving such positions. Also, patriarchal tradition created resistance to women assuming authority over men. 3) Since 1975, the lack of socialist development and commitment in the South has meant greater resistance to women's leadership there than in the North. Therefore in statistical averages, the problems of women in the South offset the progress of women in the North where there has been longer experience of socialist transformation. 4) Individual men do not fear losing their public positions of power to women because, (see p. 242) the men who often reject women's promotions are already secure in their leading positions. Rather, patriarchal beliefs rooted in hundreds of years of feudalism are tenacious in both North and South. The patriarchal beliefs that seem particularly virulent in blocking women's leadership are men's fear of losing their dominance in their homes and a generalized disrespect for women's capabilities and blindness to their achievements. 5) The party and the Women's Union have not found methods of combating these patriarchal beliefs, especially in their more subtle forms. While the party, state and Women's Union are all clearly committed to this struggle; the demands of war, poverty and the damage done by bureaucratic malaise have prevented a more effective implementation of this commitment.

Despite the disappointing data on women's promotion within the last few years, Vietnamese women's record in assuming leadership responsibilities is still impressive. It is hardly conceivable that the structure of leadership could return to that of pre-war days. Many men, moreover, are still away at the front in the state of semi-war with China. It seems that the longer women assume the leading roles once held by men, the more likely they are to retain them when the men finally return.

If the persistence of feudal patriarchal ideology is the most trouble-some obstacle to women's advancement, then a closer look at the cultural aspects of women's struggle is imperative.

Notes

1. Nguyen Thi Dinh, 'South Vietnamese Leader on General Elections' (translated by Viet Nam Women's Union), *Information Bulletin* (mimeo), 28 April 1976, pp. 5–6.
2. Mai Thi Tu and Le Thi Nham Tuyet, *Women in Viet Nam* (Hanoi: Foreign Languages Publishing House, 1978), pp. 153–4.
3. Ibid., pp. 227–8.
4. Interview by author with Cam Thanh (Hanoi, 30 August 1974).
5. For more information on Ut Tich, see Nguyen Thi, 'A Fighting Mother or the Story of Nguyen Thi Ut', *Vietnamese Women* (Vietnamese Studies, No. 10; Hanoi: Foreign Languages Publishing House, 1966), pp. 85–6.
6. Minh Ha, 'Ut Tich's Adopted Sister', *Women of Viet Nam*, No. 1, 1971, pp. 11–12.
7. Nguyen Thi, 'In Mom's Absence', in *The Little Shoeblack of Saigon* (South Viet Nam: Giai Phong Publishing House, 1972), pp. 9–37.
8. Unpublished correspondence with Women's Union, December 1981.
9. Dai Minh Tinh, 'Twenty Years' Development of the Central School for Women Cadres', *Women of Viet Nam*, No. 1, 1981, pp. 7–8.
10. Nguyen Thi Lan, 'Cadre Training: An Urgent Task', *Women of Viet Nam*, No. 2, 1979, p. 27.
11. Tu and Tuyet, op. cit., pp. 240–1.
12. Ibid., pp. 241–2.
13. Interview by author with Le Thu (Hanoi, 2 September 1981).
14. These data from Cecilia Molander, *Women in Viet Nam* (Stockholm: Swedish International Development Authority, 1978), p. 95; Arlene Eisen Bergman, *Women of Viet Nam* (San Francisco: Peoples Press, 1975), p. 187; and Mai Thi Tu, 'Vietnamese Women in the Eighties', *Viet Nam Courier*, No. 10, 1981, p. 19.
15. 'Growing Mature in Combat', *Women of Viet Nam*, No. 4, 1975, p. 6.
16. Wilfred Burchett, 'Viet Nam Moves Forward', *Guardian*, 13 April 1977, p. 14.
17. Viet Nam Women's Union, *Information Bulletin* (mimeo), 12 May 1976, pp. 3–4.
18. Viet Nam Women's Union, *Women of Viet Nam: Statistical Data* (Hanoi, 1981), pp. 13–14; and unpublished Women's Union correspondence.
19. Interview by author with Nguyen Thi Binh (Hanoi, 2 September 1981).
20. Gerard Chaliand, *The Peasants of North Viet Nam* (London: Penguin, 1969), p. 239.
21. 'Women's Role in a Commune', *Women of Viet Nam*, No. 4, 1975, pp. 9–12, 19.
22. Jayne Werner, 'Women, Socialism and the Economy of Wartime North Viet Nam: 1960–75', *Studies in Comparative Communism*, Vol. XIV, Nos 2–3, Summer/Autumn 1981, pp. 182–3.

23. Data for 1966 from ibid., p. 178; and for 1981 from Duong Hong Dat, 'Women in Agricultural Science and Technique', *Women of Viet Nam*, No. 1, 1981, p. 11.
24. *Viet Nam Women's Union*, 1981, op. cit., pp. 24, 26.
25. From the unpublished notes of Deirdre Donovan who visited Viet Nam in June 1973.
26. Interview by author with Ngo Ba Thanh (Ho Chi Minh City, 8 September 1981).
27. Interview by author with Nguyen Thi Dinh (Hanoi, 4 September 1981).
28. Mai Thi Tu, op. cit., pp. 21–2.
29. Ha Thi Que, 'Overcoming Erroneous Opinions to Push Forward the Work of Women Cadres', Tap Chi Cong San (*Communist Review*), November 1978. Summary translation provided by unpublished paper by Sophie Quinn-Judge (Bangkok, 1981). An article published in 1979, probably by Politburo member Le Duc Tho, also criticized the failure of the party to promote women and youth to leadership (*Communist Review*, No. 9, 1979, pp. 74–5).
30. Available data on party membership are not consistent. The ones I use come from unpublished correspondence with the Women's Union, 29 October 1973; from discussion with Tran Thi Hoan by author (Ho Chi Minh City, 12 September 1981); and from Le Duc Tho, 'On Party Building' (speech to fifth party congress of Viet Nam Communist Party), 27 March 1982, translated by Foreign Broadcast Information Service, US Department of Commerce (8 April 1982). Douglas Pike, *History of Vietnamese Communism* (Stanford: Hoover Institution Press, 1978), p. 97, gives a higher percentage of women in the party; so does Molander (op. cit.).
31. Ibid., p. 26.
32. Le Duc Tho, op. cit., p. 9.
33. Interview by author with Bui Thi Me (Ho Chi Minh City, 13 September 1981).

16. Riding the Tempest or Breaking the Bonds of Patriarchal Culture

A rosy-cheeked woman, here I am fighting side by side
    with you men!
On my shoulders weighs the hatred that is common to
us.
The prison is my school, its mates my friends,
The sword is my child, the gun my husband.
*Poem by Minh Khai, written on her prison wall with
her own blood shortly before the French executed her
in 1941*

While patriarchy is the dominant theme in Vietnamese cultural history, it is not the only one. When women gather their cultural weapons, they not only draw on contemporary experience and ideals, but also on a history of women's resistance to patriarchy and foreign domination. For centuries, two themes, contempt for women, on the one hand, and respect for women, on the other, have competed for authority in defining the consciousness of the Vietnamese people. The Confucian way of life, embedded in centuries of feudalism, was a model of patriarchy. The principle 'men are respected and women are despised', laid the foundation for the division of labour between women and men. A proverb observed, 'An officer is one who commands soldiers; a husband is one who commands wives.'[1] Men lived outside the home in society; women lived only in the home in the family.

French colonialism superimposed its rule on this patriarchal foundation. Vietnamese men became the slaves of French men and Vietnamese women became the slaves' slaves. US occupation added another layer to the wall of contempt that imprisoned women, bringing mass rape, prostitution and pornography. It also brought a series of values that convinced many women that happiness could be bought with US dollars, regardless of the price paid for those dollars. This is the legacy the Vietnamese refer to when they speak of vestiges of feudal, patriarchal, colonial and neocolonial ideology.

Vietnamese women readily admit the persistence of this ideology. But an important line of defence against patriarchal ideology is a heritage that pre-dates the establishment of patriarchy in Viet Nam.

A Proud Woman's Heritage

The most important book on women published in Viet Nam begins with a detailed account of ancient Vietnamese times when women may have ruled.[2] The authors cite many legends and folk-tales implying the existence of a matriarchal society and crediting women with advancing civilization by discovering agriculture. Lady Sao Cai introduced rice cultivation and irrigation. Ancient temples honoured the contributions of women and goddesses responsible for the survival of a people. Sculptures of women with large hips and breasts indicate the early Vietnamese also worshipped women's fertility. Legends celebrate women's strength, like the tale of Nu Oa, the mountain builder, cited in Chapter 2. Another legend praises Lady Sao Cai for discovering fire. In many regions, Lady Fire was worshipped in the form of an older woman. Also, the goddess of carpentry invented the saw and taught men to build houses and canoes.

Annals written by early Chinese invaders express their horror at finding women freely choosing their mates in marriage. In many popular songs – still sung by the ethnic groups in Viet Nam who have retained some of the pre-patriarchal heritage – the woman is the one who proposes marriage. This is still the custom among the Ede, Jarai, Hre and Mnong national minorities. Ancient Vietnamese marriage was matrilocal: that is, the bride remained with her clan and the husband left his clan to join his wife. Chinese annals also noted, 'The Lac Viet do not know the name of their fathers and do not respect their marital duties.' Chinese historians were amazed to find, 'When a Lac Viet woman delivers a child, she leaves her bed and her husband takes her place: like a confined woman, he has to observe certain restrictions in his daily food and take care of the new-born baby.'

A thousand years after this was written, fathers in some villages in northern and central Viet Nam lie in bed and re-enact labour pains to ease those of the mothers. Another custom requires the father to climb on to the roof, so as to risk his life, as his wife does in childbed. These practices, known as couvade, are found in patrilineal as well as matrilineal societies. However, it is one of the few customs in which the man is encouraged to do woman's work. In prehistoric Viet Nam, among some tribes, the oldest woman was the head of the communal family. On the plateaux of southern Viet Nam, older women mediated in inter-tribal conflict. They were village chiefs, judges and presided over ceremonies.

A proud woman's heritage also influenced Buddhism, which was introduced into Viet Nam about 2,000 years ago. Some town and village pagodas bear the names of female Buddhas: Lady *Dau* (Mulberry), Lady *Da* (Stone), Lady *Truong* (the General). Another temple is named after Mother Bodhisatva who saved her village from floods. In short, women were credited with the early taming of Viet Nam's natural environment. They were responsible for clearing forests, carving mountains, beginning agriculture and controlling floods – the foundation of the Vietnamese nation.

Two hundred years before the Chinese arrived, during the Hung period, private property enabled the development of different social classes and the emergence of patriarchy. But its consolidation took a long time, despite the military and political power which the Chinese exerted to enforce Confucian codes. Elements of matriarchy persisted until the 1400s, especially in the more remote villages. Echoes of the proud women founders of Viet Nam never entirely faded away. They remain in folksongs, stories and legends. One contemporary folk-song reminds us that women were not always subordinate:

'We all have to pay someone the debt of life.
But where formerly it was paid to one's wife,
Today it is paid to one's husband.'[3]

One of the authors of the book that publicized what she regards as Viet Nam's matriarchal past hopes this history will 'make a bridge between past and present, to show that despite women's oppression, the ideals of women's liberation are not new, that women's inferiority is not ordained since the beginning of time.'[4]

Women Who Would Not Bow Their Heads
The tradition of women's resistance in Viet Nam continues with the earliest attempts to drive out the Chinese invaders. Two sisters led the first national insurrection, 40 years after Christ was born. At that time, the one million people who lived in Viet Nam suffered under the harsh rule of the Chinese governor, To Dinh. After To Dinh executed her husband, Trung Trac and her sister, Trung Nhi, called on the people to follow them in an insurrection. However, before the people would follow women as military leaders, the Trung sisters had to gain their confidence. Legend says that Trung Trac killed a tiger and used its skin to write an anti-Chinese proclamation. Trung Trac became known as the strategist and Trung Nhi earned respect as a fearless warrior. They trained 36 other women to be generals of their people's army of 80,000. They drove the Chinese out of Viet Nam in AD 40.

Today, stories, poems, plays, postage stamps, posters and monuments still glorify the heroism and patriotism of the Trung sisters. A Women's Union official explained, 'We view the Trung rebellion as an all-people's movement under the leadership of women.' Every year, with the return of spring, on the 16th day of the second moon, Vietnamese people celebrate the anniversary of the death of the Trung sisters – which often coincides with International Women's Day, 8 March.[5]

Some two hundred years later, a peasant woman named Trieu Thi Trinh again took the initiative in leading thousands of people – women and men – in a campaign to expel the Chinese army of occupation. In the course of an argument with her brother, she made a pledge which is still heard in Viet Nam today:

'My wish is to ride the tempest, tame the waves, kill the sharks.
I want to drive the enemy away to save our people.

258

I will not resign myself the usual lot of women
who bow their heads and become concubines.'

Before her 21st birthday, she had led 30 battles and Viet Nam was independent again. But independence was short-lived. After six months, Trieu Thi Trinh's army was defeated. Like the Trung sisters, Trinh committed suicide rather than return to serfdom. After her defeat, the Chinese tried to discredit Trinh, depicting her as a monster. Chinese portraits show Trinh with huge breasts, three metres long, flying over her shoulder as she rides on an elephant and grimly charges an unseen enemy. To the Chinese patriarchs, the ideal woman was docile, modest and flat-chested. Nevertheless, the Vietnamese continued to tell the legend of Trinh with pride.

Vietnamese male patriots, despite their privileges over women, have maintained an ideal of women as fighters against foreign domination. Invariably, foreign domination was totally intertwined with patriarchy itself. The saying, 'When the enemy comes, even the women should fight,'[6] encouraged many anonymous women to follow the examples of the Trung sisters, Trinh and other famous women heroes.

While the Vietnamese women's place in the home kept them subordinate to men, it also helped them to play a special role in maintaining Vietnamese national identity, because in the home they were isolated from foreign influence. For example, while invaders forced Vietnamese men to join the Chinese army, women passed Vietnamese culture on

Today, at the Temple of the Trung Sisters in Hanoi   Arlene Eisen

from one generation to the next in songs they sang as they worked the rice fields and in lullabies to their children. In addition to fighting for independence, women also led peasant uprisings against Vietnamese feudal lords. Towards the end of the 18th Century, Bui Thi Xuan became famous as one of the generals in a wave of peasant rebellions that established the reformist Tay Son dynasty. She continued to fight, even after the Tay Sons fell. When the new emperor, Gia Long, finally captured her, he ordered that she be trampled to death by elephants – the traditional punishment for women who had committed adultery. He fed her heart, arms, liver and lungs to his troops, believing that the remains of this exceptional woman would imbue his troops with courage. Today, in Hanoi, there is a major boulevard named after Bui Thi Xuan.

Her Story: Women's Culture of Resistance
Most of Viet Nam's early records were kept by Confucian scholars. The histories they wrote implied that all women were content to live their lives guided by the rules of chastity and the Three Obediences. Written histories hardly ever mention women, much less that they may have been dissatisfied with child marriage, polygamy and other patriarchal bonds. But the record of Viet Nam passed on in Vietnamese folk-songs tells a different story – her story. Hundreds of songs composed by women as they worked in the fields echo strong protests. This song ridiculed assumptions of male superiority and demands for obedience:
>'We honorable sisters are like a mass of boulders in heaven.
>How could you youngsters as small as mice think of disturbing us?
>Cursed be you bunch of mice.
>When this rock falls down, your bones will be crushed.'[7]

They also protested against arranged marriages:
>'A young girl is like a piece of silk in the market.
>She doesn't know into whose hands she is going to fall.'[8]

And they challenged the practice of forcing adult women to marry young boys in order to provide cheap labour for the boys' families:
>'Bump! Bump! I took a walk with my husband on my back.
>Crossing a shallow spot, I dropped him by mistake.
>Hey fellow sisters! Lend me a scoop,
>I'll scoop the water and get my husband out!'[9]

Other songs rejected polygamy:
>'If hungry, you would be better off eating a bunch of sycamore leaves;
>Marry a monogamous man, stay away from sharing a husband with
>   other women.'[10]

There were other songs against sexual repression designed to maintain women as men's property:
>'Chastity is truly worth a thousand gold coins:
>Counting from my ex-husband to you, I have had five men.
>As for lovers that I have had in secret,

A hundred of them have gathered on my belly as they would in a
    market.'

And:

'Even if I am faithful to my husband, when I am dead I am not spared
    from being a ghost.
Being a loose woman, when dead I will be buried in the field, just the
    same.'

And some songs expressed the protests of widows:

'Giving me three cows as an offering later, when I am dead, my son,
Is not as kind as allowing me to remarry now when I am alive.'[11]

In the 19th Century, a woman poet, Ho Xuan Huong, became famous
for her attack on the corruption and hypocrisy of feudal patriarchy. Her
poetry escaped the Chinese influence more than any other because she
composed her poems in *chu nom* – the script for the Vietnamese language
considered vulgar by Confucian scholars. She played with words, reversing
letters in a way that gave a double meaning, one legitimate and one socially
subversive, to many of her lines. Lower-class women must have loved her
poetry, because her poems survived for more than a hundred years in the
memories of three generations, before they were first published in 1914.[12]
Ho Xuan Huong was the daughter of a concubine belonging to a middle-
level official. She herself was forced into concubinage, but after she was
widowed, she wrote a poem denouncing polygamy:

One wife is covered by a quilted blanket, while one is left in the cold.
Cursed be this fate of sharing a common husband.
Seldom do you have occasion to possess your husband, not even twice a
    month.
You toil and endure hardships in order to earn your steamed rice,
     and then the rice is cold and tasteless.
It is like renting your services for hire, and then receiving no wages.
How is it that I have turned out this way!
I would rather suffer the fate of remaining unmarried and live alone by
    myself.

She also dared to defend unwed mothers:

'To marry and have a child, how banal!
But to be pregnant without the help of a husband, what merit!'

While feudal nobles presented themselves as honourable gentlemen, she
mocked their privilege and expressed her contempt:

'If only I could change my destiny and be a man,
I would not content myself with such feats of valor.'[13]

Women like Ho Xuan Huong and the Trung sisters were clearly
exceptional. But the common women throughout Vietnamese history
passed on their legends and ideals with pride. Peasant women were not
only sorrowful victims of feudal patriarchy. Their songs expressed their
anger and also gave strength to their resistance. While polygamy forced

women to compete among themselves, songs of women's solidarity indicate that some learned to join together in the face of oppression:
'Let's leave loyalty to the King for our father,
And filial piety for our mother,
And keep love for ourselves.'[14]
Cultural images of women reflect their experience and reinforce it. Revolutionary culture creates images of women that draw on threads of resistance in their history, and reinforce them to encourage further change.

In the Context of Revolutionary Culture

Socialist ethics, an important component of revolutionary culture, encourage all Vietnamese people to resist oppression; to practise co-operation, solidarity, self-sacrifice and altruism; to respect others and to respect labour. Both women and men embrace these values. In the West, nearly every popular image of manhood includes 'owning a woman'.[15] In Viet Nam, the ideal man is a patriot who fights selflessly for his country, a worker and, perhaps, a party member.

An elaborate cultural network promotes these values: the mass organizations and their publications, emulation campaigns, cultural clubs, mobile song groups, theatre groups, musicians, poets, dancers, painters, sculptors, amateur cultural groups in schools and work-places, Young Pioneer Centres, films, libraries, exhibitions, museums, radio and television. Every branch of the arts has its own organization that sponsors these cultural workers whose work meets revolutionary standards. Anh Tho, one of Viet Nam's best-known poets and former President of the Writers' Union, explained more about cultural standards in Viet Nam today:

> We say that art should be national, popular and scientific. In practice, these three criteria can be interpreted in many ways. For example, a healthy, revolutionary love song would encourage people to work, practise solidarity, to get joy from love. A decadent love song would encourage sadness, jealousy, worry, feelings that sadden people . . . .
>
> The older generation of poets who wrote under the Thieu regime write about the moon, the wind, the flowers – but always from a very sad, melancholy perspective. They describe their personal feelings, stay in their ivory towers and seem proud that very few people can understand what they write – sometimes not even the poets themselves. I wrote a poem urging them to be more responsible in their writing:
>
>> 'Dear friend, our poetry must be like a rice seedling,
>> when we transplant it, we can change minds.
>> The young moon you love shall send its shining rays to the people,
>> And with a new life, begins joy.'
>
> Cultural reform will require a long time. Sometimes I invite some of

these élitist poets to an adult complementary education class at night. To get them out of their ivory towers, to shake them a little. It is difficult. But we are optimistic about the young generation . . . . They understand that poetry is something very broad. All that we love and can feel is poetry. Poetry will make us close to other people.

I wrote a poem about bomb craters that were transformed into places to grow fruit and ducks. Even people who like romantic poetry like that poem because it is about a 'green reality'. It talks about overcoming death with life.

Creation happens when people work. Some poems made by workers are better than those made by poets. Poetry and folk-songs are the richest part of our culture. We all receive it from our mothers in the form of lullabies. Often, when I go to read poems in the countryside, a woman will come up to me afterwards and make a suggestion that improves my poem.

Since 1975, I have written about the joyous atmosphere in Ban Me Thuot after liberation, about the return of my husband to his native land and about the new life that begins after destruction. In my latest work, I do not criticize male chauvinism directly, but I do talk about the strongest, best women – which, I believe, is a way of increasing respect for women.[16]

Revolutionary Images of Women

Recent films and books feature respect for women as a central theme to replace the degradation of women featured in what they call the 'yellow culture' imported from the US. Between 1954 and 1974, the Saigon regime received US subsidies to import more than 7,500 films from the US. They amounted to 96% of all films shown in Viet Nam. Those imported films waged psychological war against the Vietnamese people. Certain themes recurred: glorification of the alleged military invincibility of the US; encouragement of superstition and mysticism; pornography; disrespect for women; lust for money and wanton violence; and disrespect for labour.[17]

On the other hand, *Star of August*, perhaps the most popular award-winning film made since liberation, features a woman hero. It is set during the August Revolution of 1945. The hero leaves her baby in the care of neighbours so that she can lead a peasant uprising.[18] Three major 1980 films feature women heroes: *That Day on Lam River* stars a boatwoman who becomes a liaison agent for the party and demonstrates her gradual awakening to revolutionary ideals. *Homeland* stars a woman working in a forestry site and her heroism when the Chinese invade. *The Unachieved Plan* portrays a woman who takes leadership on a cattle-breeding farm.[19] Another popular film focuses on a beautiful, bright Hanoi student who volunteers to work at a hydroelectric construction site. She falls in love with a co-worker but he dies in a flood. She continues working, despite her grief, and is chosen to attend engineering school. Later she returns to the hydroelectric site as an engineer, defends it against US bombs and is then assigned to direct the construction of a new plant.[20]

Popular art in Viet Nam today

The film *First Love* tackles some of the problematic issues created by US occupation. Duy becomes cynical and joins a gang after the woman he loved, Huong, married an American. Duy's eldest sister is an urban guerrilla who tries to convince him to join the struggle. She proves to Duy that Huong sold herself to the American to save her father from a frame-up engineered by the American. Duy also learns the American murdered Huong when she discovered he was profiting from the sale of Vietnamese orphans. But Duy's conversion to the revolution is not automatic or smooth. The film's ending is ambiguous.

Women's contribution to the nation's defence and reconstruction is a recurrent theme of travelling cultural groups as well. For example, the Ballet Troupe of the Ka Tu transform a traditional national minority dance into a re-enactment of a wartime episode in which the Ka Tu people released thousands of angry hornets to attack ambushed GIs. Most of the members of the dance troupe are women who were illiterate before 1975, living in US-controlled strategic hamlets. Some participated in the actual ambush portrayed by the dance.[21]

The image of a woman with a rifle is still a very popular one in the revolutionary culture of Viet Nam. Whether she has captured a US bomber pilot or a Chinese foot soldier, she is a symbol of the relatively weak Vietnamese nation, overcoming all obstacles to defeat a more powerful aggressor. Perhaps the image is not meant to encourage women's liberation, but only to raise the morale of people who must win against tremendous odds. Nevertheless, the picture of the woman winning a battle against a man with superior arms and numbers is a challenge to patriarchal assumptions. The image of the woman warrior has been etched in the consciousness of masses of people. A missionary from the US met two male guerrillas shortly after the liberation of their province in 1975. Without any prompting, they presented their theory explaining the revolution's success:

> It is this way. All superior nations of the world are like men, masculine. Viet Nam is like a woman, feminine. But what do you know, the woman who is supposed to be weak defeated the man! That is because our women are strong. Like Chi Huong, you know, the sister who has been serving you your meals. She is not afraid of anything. Our army even has women commanders.[22]

While Vietnamese women may be somewhat patronized by the men, revolutionary culture never treats them as sex objects. A well-known male poet recalled, 'Earlier we wrote poetry about loving beautiful girls who lived in well-tended rooms. In 1953, for the first time, I wrote about an old woman.'[23] The media contain nothing to suggest women's problems are caused by their being ugly, smelly, pimply or sexually unappealing in any way. There is no trace of the notion that women should spend their time making themselves physically appealing to men.

Every Western woman who has visited Hanoi agrees that the streets feel safe at any hour. People stare because we are foreigners, but their stares have no sexual or aggressive content. I remained a bit sceptical until my own first visit when our group of six women walked through a crowd of more than 200 male soldiers who had been milling around, without the slightest hint of harrassment. Except in the southern cities, most of the women dress alike. Every day they wear loose black trousers, a white or sometimes pastel print blouse and sandals. On special occasions, they may wear the traditional *ao dai* dress. Most women wear their hair long, pinned back with a clasp. In the South, one sees more short hair-styles, but few are artificially curled. In the market of Ho Chi Minh City, a woman still waits for customers whose toe-nails she can polish. Hardly any women wear make-up and few wear jewellery except for wedding rings. On the other hand, a visible minority of women in Ho Chi Minh City and other major urban areas in the South maintain the appearance of being consumers of Western styles – despite the need to import them. There seems to be no public pressure to conform to traditional styles. An occasional disapproving glance from a more sheltered northern visitor is ignored by the short skirted woman wearing make-up on the streets of Ho Chi Minh City.

Cadres from the Women's Union in Ho Chi Minh City, although they tend to be more stylishly groomed by Western standards than their northern counterparts, expect that appreciation of Western styles will gradually fade. They are more concerned with the revival of clandestine pornography – an important component of yellow culture – than with a short skirt or patch of rouge. In fact, enclaves of the old Saigon persist within Ho Chi Minh City. While perhaps the majority of the population of the city is working and is incorporated into one or another revolutionary organization, a substantial minority attempts to continue the street life to which they grew accustomed during US occupation. Groups of relatively long-haired young men, on motorcycles and bikes, or loitering around a coffee shop, stand in sharp contrast to the typical Vietnamese youth. Their appearance is sometimes menacing, and although I was told that rape is so rare that no statistics are available, these young men ogle women in a way I had never experienced in the North.

When I was in Ho Chi Minh City in 1981, the Women's Union and other organizations were accelerating a campaign against music and other cultural expressions which they felt corrupted young people. A poster celebrating the campaign against yellow culture featured a traditionally dressed woman, in *ao dai*, not work clothes, appearing demure and pure. In other words, not all images of women in the contemporary culture portray them as warriors or tractor drivers.

Embracing Motherhood: A Constant Theme in Vietnamese Culture
General Dinh represented the women who fought for liberation in the South. Her biography tells of her transformation from an illiterate peasant to one of the most important leaders of the armed forces that defeated the US Army. She is an inspiration for any woman fighting for emancipation. In Viet Nam, she is loved and respected as a political and military leader, and also as a warm, motherly woman. She gave birth to a son, but did not raise him herself so she could devote all her energy to the resistance. However, during the war, the Vietnamese sometimes spoke of her as if she were the mother of the entire People's Liberation Armed Forces.

These lines from a poem by a famous male poet, Luu Truong Lu, express a tension between women's challenge to patriarchy and the persistence of traditional sex roles. They also show that women's strength is the overriding aspect of this continuing contradiction.

Nguyen Thi Dinh

In the assault you command a hundred squads.
Night returns, you sit mending fighters' clothes.
Woman general of the South, descended from Trac and Nhi [Trung Sisters]
You have shaken the brass and steel of the white house.

One wonders if, in fact, a general would have to mend fighters' clothes after commanding a hundred squads; and if she did, why romanticize it? Is this not a glorification of the same double shift that makes it very difficult for all but the most exceptional women to assume leadership roles and achieve high-status positions equal to men?

Preparation for assuming the double shift begins early. While official childrearing manuals may not distinguish between methods of raising daughters and sons, parents still make serious distinctions which lay the foundations for the different sex roles assumed later in life. For example, Dinh Thi Khoa, the President of the Mai Chau District Branch of the Women's Union in Ha Son Binh Province, was explaining the various projects of the Women's Union: 'We have just started discussing the best methods of educating our children. I have only two daughters so my experience is limited. Boys and girls are different and require different methods.'[24] The librarian at the Young Pioneer Centre in Hanoi remarked on the different tastes of the young readers she served:

> Boys like adventure stories and histories of battles. Girls like traditional stories, psychological fiction and stories of daily life. I think boys and girls have different tastes because of the influence of daily life. Boys play out adventure stories in the yard of the Centre here. Girls stay at the table reading quietly and think; they don't express their feelings in action.[25]

While the librarian understood that the girls were not born quiet, she expressed no concern that the influences making girls contemplative and boys adventurous might make women too timid to be accepted as leaders in society.

Postage stamp depicting mother leading a protest

Without doing a systematic content analysis of a representative sample of Vietnamese art and literature, it is difficult to conclude confidently which themes are really dominant in Vietnamese media – the woman defying traditional roles that oppress her or the woman embracing those roles. It would seem revolutionary themes predominate, but they often incorporate patriarchal assumptions about women. Also, the affirmation of woman fulfilling her role exclusively as mother is frequent enough to pose serious questions.

For example, one story praised Mrs Lam's devotion to caring for her paralysed husband and five children, especially the eldest son who could not hear or speak. She taught him to read and write and use sign language. The young man grew to be unusually nurturing:

> The eldest son became something like an eldest daughter in the family. As a matter of fact, Tien saw to everything, looked after his brothers and had a special love for his mother because only mother and son could 'talk' to each other. He attended her most devotedly when she was ill.[26]

Two poems by young girls, published in the Women's Union magazine in 1980, reflect the different roles they see performed by their mothers and fathers:

Poem

O friends
How I love Pa!
In the evening
He tells me beautiful stories
And gives me candies
When I get good marks.
The girl who lives next door
Is not so lucky:
Her parents quarrelled
And her father left.
And since then she never smiles
At work or at play
Even when she got top marks.
Ah, if her father knew!
And if he would return
So that smiles
Would come back to her lips.

by Nguyen Thi Mai Anh, Tam Hop Primary School, Tam Dao, Vinh Phu

Ma's Hands

A plot lay idle and you touched it
And vegetables grew lush and green.
The roof leaked and I couldn't sleep.
You touched it,
Repose came to me.
As I laze in bed in the early hours of the morning,
Your hands touch the rice and vegetables
And a tasty meal is ready.
Whenever I sit dozing over my homework.

A loving touch of your hand and things are set right again.
Should a drizzle fall and make the step slippery,
It takes you just a moment to make me walk in safety.
Summer makes water scarce, but we don't have to worry,
It doesn't take your fairy's hands very long to fill buckets and vessels.
At the mill, night or day, your hands touch the loom
And yarn is turned into precious fabric.
That's the way your hands are: simple and wonderful.
A lesson that will be with me all my life.

by Nguyen Thanh, 7th Form, Khuong Thuong School, Hanoi[27]

There were four winners in a poetry contest to honour International Women's Day, 8 March 1982. Their poems appeared in *Van Nghe*, the literary weekly. None reflected revolutionary images of women. Two were traditional love poems, one was about the stars and the fourth spoke of a grown daughter's desire to see her distant mother.

The leading actress of Viet Nam, Tra Giang, in a speech to the 1979 session of the National Assembly, noted the dual role of women:

> There are many themes for us artists to reflect: heroes and heroines in fighting and in work, loyal wives, valiant mothers . . .'. Personally I think in the period to come, the exploits of our heroic fighters in both the southwest and northern border fronts must be well reflected on the screens.[28]

Did her failure to mention 'loyal husbands' or 'valiant fathers' reflect a patriarchal double standard? Probably.

While there is a clear and consistent public stand taken on many issues in Viet Nam, against US imperialism for example, there does not appear to be a consistent posture censoring images that may belittle women, especially if those images are part of the country's folkloric heritage. For example, the Foreign Languages Publishing House recently published a series of pamphlets, each comprising a collection of 'Tales, legends and stories from Viet Nam, past and present'. Within the same volume, one finds a story promoting equality between wife and husband, effectively criticizing the husband for treating his wife as if she were a child; and another story – a legend – explaining the origin of the first mosquito: an unfaithful, greedy (bloodsucking) wife.[29]

Finally, while women are never portrayed as sex objects in officially sponsored literature, remarks about their appearance do sometimes reinforce Confucian standards of beauty – both physically and morally. These standards discourage women who are aggressive or develop muscles or a suntan from hard work in the sun: 'She was not outstandingly pretty. A slightly swarthy complexion and rather plump. But she was a sweet girl.'[30]

Xuan Thuy, a leading member of the Viet Nam Communist Party, noted as recently as 1980 that one form of patriarchal ideology – that women are only good for motherhood and cooking (see Chapter 2) – is a significant obstacle to women's liberation. Two aspects of patriarchal ideology reinforce the idea that women are only good for motherhood. First, the government and the Women's Union are committed to making the burdens of motherhood and housework lighter, yet no official in the Women's Union or any other woman I spoke to question the role of mother in itself. Women like Minh Khai, Nguyen Thi Dinh and the thousands of anonymous mothers who devoted their energies to the national liberation movement are honoured for sacrificing the joys of motherhood. But rejecting motherhood is not seen as a strategy or goal for women's liberation in Viet Nam.

Free accessible birth control, education and job opportunities provide the necessary conditions for women's independence and voluntary motherhood. But an entirely free choice would also require visible, socially accepted – if not applauded – alternatives to the role of mother for women. We have no way of knowing if the government and Women's Union's failure to promote these alternatives is based on an ideological principle or on a pragmatic recognition that it will take the general public a long time to embrace a notion so challenging to patriarchal traditions.

While most Vietnamese are not blind to the reality of women working in many roles besides mothering, as long as motherhood is seen as women's primary role, women will be at a disadvantage in fulfilling other roles, especially those requiring time-consuming training, professional expertise and leadership. While childcare centres and other arrangements that socialize the household components of the double shift are enormously significant, it is difficult to imagine a situation in which the double shift itself is no longer an obstacle to women's full emancipation. In Viet Nam, the double shift persists because of the physical limitations of an underdeveloped, war-torn economy; because of the tenacity of patriarchal tradition that legitimizes men's resistance to sharing equally in the tasks of childrearing and housework. Therefore, the second aspect of patriarchal ideology that reinforces the idea that women are *only* good for motherhood is the idea that only *women* are good for motherhood. We noted earlier Madame Binh's statement, 'In spite of all our rules, we cannot oblige men to give birth children',[31] as an explanation for men not sharing equally in household responsibilities. Yet childbearing and childrearing need not be performed by the same person.

Madame Binh and other Women's Union representatives may be reflecting the general sentiment in society by accepting a modified version of the 'biology-is-destiny' assumption. For example, at the May 19th Childcare Centre, the vice-director thought women should staff the centre because they had more ability in caring for children than men. Ironically, as she spoke, our driver, the father of seven children, distracted my 15-month-old son and kept him from crying with far more affection, skill and success than a young woman who was a professional childcare worker.

Dang Thi Ngoc, vice-director of the school to train childcare workers in Ho Chi Minh City, gave this response when I asked her why they did not train men: 'There have been times when training men has been mentioned, but never seriously discussed. We cannot find men who want to do the work. Our work is very tiring. Men do not want to change diapers . . . .' When I asked if men would be more willing to change diapers if society gave more respect to such tasks, her answer seemed to contradict her first statement: 'Men are required at the front and in heavy construction. This work is lighter, so more suited to women. You should not conclude men refuse the work because of lack of respect for it.'

Most men, in fact, may be required for heavier tasks, especially in an economy that relies on muscles rather than machines. But since women also perform extremely heavy tasks – they became famous, for example, for their 'bronze shoulders' in carrying tons of supplies to the front – it is difficult to understand why some men cannot be spared for lighter tasks. And while one frequently sees images of women with rifles or working with heavy machines – traditionally male occupations – it is quite rare to see an image of a man caring for a baby or doing embroidery. Men's absence from women's work is not limited to childcare. Nguyen Thi Yen, a Women's Union cadre in Ho Chi Minh City and director of a consortium of canning factories, believes, 'Women contribute to light industry because they have special merits in food production . . . . Women's hands are more clever than men's in separating parts of fruit for canning.'[32] Only her own patriarchal conditioning blinds Mrs Yen to the fact that chefs at Ho Chi Minh City's finest hotels are men trained by the French.

The Struggle Continues

The pages of the Women's Union magazine reflect a cultural struggle over sex-role definitions and sexual division of labour. The story about Mrs Lam reinforces the patriarchal idea that women's primary responsibility – and perhaps their exclusive responsibility – is as mothers. Other stories challenge that idea. For example, a story by Le Thu, the Director of Education of the Women's Union, describes a family with three daughters. One studies at technical school and so 'a man is not needed in the house to repair a broken fan or bike.' When the father returns home, he proudly announces, 'Well, we now have an engineer, an army doctor and a teacher in the house. I have nothing to envy those of my friends with crowds of male descendants.'[33] A column called, 'A Laugh with Children', satirizes sex roles that subordinate women. One was pointedly subtitled, 'The Roles He Will Act':

> Little Khoa, aged four, likes to pretend.
> 'Well,' Pa once said, 'suppose you are me. What will you do?'
> 'I'll smoke, read papers, teach . . . .'
> 'Now suppose you're me,' Ma joined in the conversation. 'What will you do?'
> 'Oh, I will go to market, I'll go to work, cook, wash, I'll . . . .' Little Khoa stopped, not looking very enthusiastic. 'But I'd rather be Pa.'[34]

This is one of the few cultural expressions I have seen which implies that patriarchal ideology is not simply a remnant of a feudal, colonialist or neo-colonialist past. Clearly, Pa enjoys a relative privilege today. The patriarchal division of labour allows him to relax and study precisely because of the additional work shift shouldered by Ma. However, in general, the Women's Union is silent on the issue of male privilege and avoids analysing 'lack of democracy within the family', as male power present in the structure of contemporary society.

Rather, the Women's Union and revolutionary cultural workers concentrate on promoting images that enhance society's respect for women without addressing the issue of men's status and power directly. For example, the following poem reinforces women in maintaining the new roles they assumed during the war and implies that women continue in men's jobs during peacetime:

> 'I remember the days when you held a gun in your hands
> Fighting against the US/Thieu army to defend the homeland.
> Today you stand in a boat with an outboard motor
> Going out fishing on the high seas with your co-villagers.'[35]

The Women's Union understands that presenting images of strong women 'on high seas' is essential in promoting women's contribution to society as well as in promoting women's liberation. They have been bold in portraying women leading armies – ancient and modern – capturing enemy soldiers and driving tractors. They feature and praise women like Minh Khai who defied patriarchal restrictions in order to defend the nation. But they are relatively timid in encouraging men to take up certain women's roles and in suggesting alternatives to women's traditional role as mother. This timidity acts as a brake in freeing women from their traditional oppression.

The Vietnamese conception of women's emancipation is an evolving one, neither abstract nor fixed. It reflects their struggles, both internal and external, priorities, resources, needs and experiences. And, their approach may change.

Notes

1. Richard Coughlin, 'The Position of Women in South East Asia' (mimeo: Yale Asian Cultural Report Series, 1949), p. 3.
2. The following discussion draws on Mai Thi Tu and Le Thi Nham Tuyet, *Women in Viet Nam* (Hanoi: Foreign Languages Publishing House, 1978), pp. 12–30.
3. Ibid., p. 24.
4. Interview by author with Mai Thi Tu (Hanoi, 30 August 1981).
5. This account of the Trung Sisters is condensed from Arlene Eisen Bergman, *Women of Viet Nam* (San Francisco: Peoples Press, 1975), pp. 30–1.
6. Mai Thi Tu, 'The Vietnamese Woman Yesterday and Today', in *Vietnamese Women* (Vietnamese Studies, No. 10; Hanoi: Foreign Languages Publishing House, 1966), pp. 17–18.
7. Nha Trang, *The Traditional Roles of Women as Reflected in the Oral and Written Vietnamese Literature* (Berkeley: University of California, Asian Studies, PhD Dissertation, 1973), p. 217.
8. *Viet Nam Advances* (Hanoi), No. 3, March–July 1969, p. 15.
9. Xuan Dieu, 'Folksongs of Viet Nam', *Viet Nam Advances*, Vol. 3, No. 3, March 1958, p. 20.
10. Nha Trang, op. cit., p. 232.
11. Ibid., p. 228.
12. ibid., p. 206.
13. This poem is found in 'Supplement on Women of Viet Nam', *Viet Nam News and Reports*, No. 14, March 1973, p. 4. Others by Ho Xuan Huong are found there or in Nha Trang, op. cit.
14. Mai Thi Tu, 1966, op. cit., p. 19.
15. Kalamu ya Salaam, 'Rape: A Radical Analysis from an African-American Perspective', *Our Women Keep Our Skies from Falling* (New Orleans: Nkombo, 1980), p. 30.
16. Interview with Anh Tho by author (Ho Chi Minh City, 13 September 1981).
17. 'Cinema in the Hands of Neo-Colonialism: A Means of Psychological Warfare', *Viet Nam Courier*, No. 64, September 1977, p. 10.
18. Reviews of *Star of August* by Van Hanh in *Viet Nam* (pictorial), No. 227, November 1977, and *Women of Viet Nam*, No. 2, 1980, p. 18.
19. Le Son, 'Among Many Artists', *Viet Nam* (pictorial), No. 287, March 1981.
20. 'Echoes Across the River', *Women of Viet Nam*, No. 1, 1977, pp. 26–7.
21. Ho Hai, 'The Girls Dancing the Ballet of the Hornets', *Viet Nam* (pictorial), No. 227, November 1977, pp. 12–13.
22. Earl Martin, *Reaching the Other Side* (New York: Crown, 1978), p. 220.
23. Xuan Dieu cited by Peter Weiss, *Notes on the Cultural Life of the Democratic Republic of Viet Nam* (New York: Delta, 1970), p. 57.
24. Interview by author with Dinh Thi Khoa (Mai Chau District, Ha Son Binh Province, 3 September 1981).
25. Interview by author with librarian at Young Pioneer Centre (Hanoi, 30 August 1981).
26. Bach Van, 'Love and Responsibility', *Women of Viet Nam*, No. 1, 1977, pp. 20–2.
27. 'Poems', *Women of Viet Nam*, No. 4, 1980, p. 16.
28. Tra Giang, 'Unity and Victory', *Viet Nam* (pictorial), No. 246, June 1979, p. 19.

29. Ngo Thi Kim Cuc, 'The Sweetness of Peace', and Mai Hoa, 'The First Mosquito', both in *The Sweetness of Peace* (Hibiscus Series; Hanoi: Foreign Languages Publishing House, 1981), pp. 5f and 44f.
30. Sy Hong, 'Story Told at a Border Post', *Women of Viet Nam*, No. 3, 1979, p. 19. There is a tradition in Viet Nam that favours light complexions, but it is not based on racism as much as on feudal values which hold peasants, whose skin is bronzed by years of toil in the sun, in contempt.
31. Interview by author with Nguyen Thi Binh (Hanoi, 2 September 1981).
32. Interview by author with Nguyen Thi Yen (Ho Chi Minh City, 5 September 1981).
33. Le Thu, 'The Third Daughter', *Women of Viet Nam*, No. 4, 1980, pp. 18–19.
34. 'Roles He Will Act', *Women of Viet Nam*, No. 2, 1981, pp. 5–6.
35. 'The New Vietnamese Women as Seen by Poets', *Women of Viet Nam*, No. 3, 1977, p. 12.

17. The Steps Get Shorter

> When I first met you in 1974, we had only liberated Quang Tri Province. Now we are welcoming you to Saigon, which, for some time now, we have called Ho Chi Minh City. There is a big difference. The struggle gets easier and each step made by the revolution gets shorter.
>
> *Bui Thi Me, retired Vice-Minister of Health of the PRG and Vice-President of the Union of Women for the Liberation of South Viet Nam*

The great majority of women joined in the revolutionary struggles in Viet Nam because they saw their own survival and liberation depended on reaching the two interrelated goals: securing the country against foreign domination and launching the socialist transformation of their country. The Vietnamese people won complete independence in 1975 and reunified their nation in 1976. It was what they had been fighting for since 1945. But peace was short-lived. People who had scarcely finished rebuilding homes destroyed by US tanks were forced to live again in thatched huts after Pol Pot's troops invaded the south-western provinces. Then Chinese troops invaded the northern provinces.

Now there is a fragile peace. Troops are mobilized to face the continued threat of invasion from the north, while the rest of the population mobilize to avert famine. They, particularly the women, turn towards rebuilding their war-ravaged country using socialist principles to transform power relationships in the society; and expanding the gains they made during the liberation wars.

In this context, Vietnamese women have made dramatic strides towards their emancipation They have won reproductive rights; their right to respectful health care and education is limited primarily by the appalling poverty of the country as a whole. They have overthrown feudal patriarchal family institutions such as polygamy and child marriage. They are wrestling with ways of creating a revolutionary family, armed with a law requiring democracy within the family. Vietnamese women can now be economically independent of their fathers and husbands; and they enjoy

275

access to nearly all jobs and leadership positions in society. And the government recognizes society's responsibility for lifting women's burdens in the home – what we have called 'socializing the double shift'. Each of these victories was not simply granted by fiat by the socialist state. Rather, they were won after complicated struggle and must be defended and expanded by thousands of women mobilized for action.

A particular combination of circumstances has empowered Vietnamese women and made these achievements possible: 1) the liberation of Viet Nam from colonialism and all other foreign domination; 2) the reunification and early budding of socialist institutions; 3) the political commitment of the government and leading party to women's emancipation; 4) women's extraordinary participation in production and political and military struggles during the long wars of national liberation; 5) the unity

Celebrating liberation, 1975.

Viet Nam News Agency

and organization of the women themselves: the Viet Nam Women's Union.

National liberation and socialism are intertwined. As long as France or the United States dominated Viet Nam, no socialist change was possible. However, if Viet Nam had won its independence, but rejected socialism – preserving class oppression, patriarchy and other inequalities – the government would have been unpopular and, therefore, easy prey to imperialist designs for reconquest. National liberation, reunification and socialist commitment created the foundation for women's emancipation. Alone, they did not guarantee it. Whether one compares the status of Vietnamese women now with their pre-revolutionary status or with the status of women in non-revolutionary societies, the results are dramatic.

The history of Vietnamese women was one of constant misery; they were prisoners of arranged marriages, Confucian patriarchal dogma and

Celebrating liberation, 1975   Viet Nam News Agency

endless labour. Colonialism and then US occupation only added to the burdens that women carried. But the history of women in Viet Nam became a hotbed of challenge and change as the people began to fight for their independence. At the same time, as socialist transformation proceeded, so did progress for women. Early steps towards socialism made the difference in the northern part of Viet Nam after it had won independence from France in 1954.[1] Land reform paved the way for women's economic independence and freed them from the bonds of the patriarchal family. Collectivization of agriculture and reorganization of industry were fertile fields for challenging the traditional sexual division of labour. Also, whatever surplus was produced could be spent on improving women's health, childcare facilities and the life of society as a whole, rather than enhancing the personal wealth of the landlord or factory owner.

While socialism pointed the direction of change towards women's liberation, the war with the US accelerated the pace of that change. Policies encouraging the promotion of women to leadership roles had been 'on the books' for several years before the war escalated. But once men left the villages to fight, women were urged to take leadership responsibilities at an unprecedented rate. The continuing commitment of the country's leadership, women's participation in the nation's struggles and the Women's Union have been determining factors in Vietnamese women's irrevocable advances.

The Women's Union – nearly ten million strong – includes mostly peasant and working-class women. Rather than facing a hostile state, as do women's movements in capitalist countries, the Women's Union enjoys state support. In fact, the state holds the Women's Union responsible for representing the aspirations of Vietnamese women. It is well organized and its leaders, many of whom are women in their sixties, have been strengthened by experience that spans two revolutions.

If the gains women have made are only partly rooted in the role they played during the wars Viet Nam was forced to fight, the logical conclusion is that once peace is secure, women will maintain their gains. While peace has been too short-lived to reach a definitive conclusion, I believe the facts presented in the preceding chapters demonstrate the validity of this theory. Women's rights to health care, childcare, education and economic independence have expanded since 1975. While once only women in the North enjoyed emancipation from patriarchal marriages, since 1975, women in the South also have the right to democracy within the family.

We know that throughout most of recorded history, women have been subordinate to men. Yet that fact does not imply some universal patriarchy – a constant that has endured throughout the ages. Barbara Ehrenreich, a leading feminist writer in the US, pointed out that there is a difference between a patriarchy that practices female infanticide and a socialist society in which women are under-represented on the central committee of the ruling party; 'and the difference is worth dying for.'[2] The Vietnamese women would surely agree.

'This Is Liberation, It Offers a Future, But Right Now It Makes Great Demands'

The relative pace of change, especially in the realm of women's leadership, has slowed significantly since the war's end in 1975. Some commentators draw the wrong conclusion from this observation. Christine White, from the University of Sussex, for example, states, 'The lesson that politically active Vietnamese women have learned is that "only women care about women".'[3] No politically active women I spoke with in Viet Nam or those whose writing is available, said anything of the kind. Rather they point to economic and educational strictures and remnants of patriarchal feudalism in people's consciousness to explain the slowing pace of change. These strictures are a legacy of the past which were eclipsed by the pressures of war.

Batya Weinbaum, a radical feminist theoretician in the US, labels the idea that disrespect for women is a holdover from the feudal past as 'intellectual buckpassing'.[4] The implication is that Viet Nam's leaders will not accelerate their attack on the sexual division of labour 'because it

Celebrating liberation, 1975   Viet Nam News Agency

279

would create chaos throughout the social order.'[5] A closer look at the Vietnamese experience demonstrates that no patriarchal buck is being passed. Because this book is about women, we have not documented the oppression of the vast majority of Vietnamese men. As a colonized people and as poor peasants, Vietnamese men have also had an enormous stake in revolutionary change or 'creating chaos in the social order'. Patriarchy is not the only remnant from Viet Nam's feudal and colonial past. Confucian mandarins required unconditional deference from peasant men as well as women. Passivity in the face of authority, particularly in the form of bureaucratic excesses, continues to plague Vietnamese society.

President Ho Chi Minh visiting an evening class   Viet Nam News Agency

When Bui Thi Me speaks of the difficulty of uprooting feudal ideology because it is interwoven with 'people's deepest feelings', she is realistically assessing the problem and acknowledging the party's responsibility for transforming these emotions. But she also understands it would be futile to demand an immediate intellectual confrontation with time-worn emotions. Recognizing the lengthy struggle required to uproot all forms of male chauvinism is not the same as giving up on the struggle or putting it on the back burner. Whether in encouraging women to develop new skills or in recognizing the burdens of the double shift, Viet Nam's national leadership has been exemplary among governments in its commitment to overthrow patriarchy.

There have been enormous changes in the sexual division of labour in Viet Nam: the women who were once ruled by the code of the Three Obediences are now directing co-operatives and engineering hydroelectric plants. These changes have not, as Weinbaum predicted, 'provoked chaos in the social order'. Rather, enlightened Vietnamese leadership, both male and female, including the highest levels of the Communist Party, have noted how beneficial these changes have been to the entire society. Ho Chi Minh pioneered in promoting the understanding that the socialist revolution could not succeed without the emancipation of women. The Viet Nam Communist Party and the state have been committed to incorporating women into the struggle and to securing the benefits of that struggle for women (see Chapter 6). Resistance to women's liberation comes rather from those guided by feudal patriarchal traditions, so deeply etched in their consciousness that they may respond with an automatic cry of no to any thought of women's equality.

The Vietnamese experience challenges those who fear 'socialist betrayal of feminism'. From Viet Nam, we learn that changing consciousness – a consciousness inextricably linked with people's deepest emotions – is probably the most difficult task faced by revolutionaries. Cadre training, self-criticism/criticism, mass organization and education – all the resources of society – will be mobilized for generations before the last vestiges of feudal and capitalist thinking disappear.

In fact, feudal and capitalist insitutions still exist in Viet Nam. Socialism itself is still embryonic in Viet Nam. This point cannot be emphasized enough. The war with the US forced North Viet Nam to interrupt its development of socialist institutions and the South has only been governed by socialist policies since 1976. Moreover, socialism cannot be created by an act of will by those with state power. It requires a technical foundation for its socialized industry and agriculture and enormous political struggles. Nguyen Khac Vien, editor of *Vietnamese Studies*, estimated it would take ten or 15 years to change the social structure so as to provide the foundation for new ways of thinking:

> By then the State and the collective sector will have expanded; management will be more experienced, modernized and the inertia of the older genera-

tion will be done away with. A new generation, new technology and supply base, including energy, will be achieved. . . . Three days by train to Ho Chi Minh City is not socialism. It will take ten to 15 years to become fully fledged. And we can only achieve this goal with peace.[6]

Struggles over Priorities

We have cited many self-criticisms by the Women's Union as well as by men in the party, exposing the tenacity of patriarchal contempt for women and urging the promotion of women's leadership and the development of more effective strategies to achieve women's full emancipation. A 1981 teach-in, organized by General Dinh, the President of the Women's Union, was explicit and militant in calling for 'a powerful movement of public condemnation of any tendency to play down the role of women.' Many testified that the main obstacle to women assuming leadership was the 'feudal concept of making light of women'. They suggested specific ways of encouraging and remunerating women in the discharge of their two 'equally important tasks: their jobs at home and in the factory'. It is significant that a transcript of their criticisms was translated and published in the official international publication of the Socialist Republic of Viet Nam, *Viet Nam Courier*.[7] Yet it seems those making these criticisms have yet to win a struggle to grant top priority to the total overthrow of these patriarchal holdovers. That struggle continues inside the party and the Women's Union. The campaign to make family planning and childcare available to all women is a priority. But neither the fifth party congress, nor the fifth national congress of Vietnamese women, both held in the spring of 1982, emphasized the importance of the struggle against patriarchal ideology.

The Women's Union congress noted the problem, but only made a muted recommendation subordinate to the general tasks of 'raising women's socialist consciousness':

> Our Congress wishes that the Party's stance and views on the problems of women's liberation and women's equal rights with men will be more clearly manifested in books and newspapers, on the screens and stage and on radio and television, so that women's problems will become more and more the common concern of the whole society.[8]

Understandably, priorities are determined by the requirements of the nation's survival: to develop an economy capable of meeting the basic needs of the people and to defend the nation against foreign aggression. While women like Ha Thi Que, Bui Thi Me and other high-level party members have lobbied for a struggle to promote women's leadership, the main thrust of the internal party struggles is aimed at designing a strategy for economic development that utilizes material incentives and local initiative without undermining the nation's socialist potential. The struggle to unify the party and to recognize and counter Chinese aggression has also taken its toll of political resources.

Even if the requirements of the nation's survival were not so consuming, there would still be the problem of bureaucracy. Abusive bureaucrats can sabotage all people's efforts to achieve thorough liberation – but especially women's opportunities to achieve leadership positions (see Chapter 6). In fact, women's advancement to leading positions may be Viet Nam's most reliable measure of success in combating bureaucracy in general. Just as the women's movement in the past was an essential component of the national liberation struggle, today's women's movement continues to be part of a struggle to liberate all people from the élitism, corruption and bureaucracy rooted in Viet Nam's lingering feudal and neo-colonial institutions.

The political programme adopted at the 1982 Women's Union congress, which focuses on the urgent contributions women can make to the nation's economic development, reflects the priority the Women's Union sets. It may, in fact, be objectively impossible to abolish the double shift and its resulting political handicaps for women while Viet Nam faces the dangers of invasion and the deprivations of a backward economy.

This does not mean, however, that voices calling for a militant struggle to transform patriarchal thinking have been silenced. They have a formidable arsenal to draw upon. The 1981 teach-in was well publicized. Not only the publications of the Women's Union, but also national organizations of writers, artists and other cultural workers, as well as the trade unions, are mobilized to give dignity and respect to women in the mass consciousness.

But what, more specifically, do they mean when they speak of overthrowing 'feudal contempt for women'? Usually they mean challenging a disrespect that insists women can only excel in domestic tasks and are incapable of raising their cultural level enough to hold high-status jobs. They demand recognition of women's capacity to perform domestic and all public roles. This, perhaps, is where the political consensus ends.[9]

Some Women's Union spokespeople interpret the policy on democracy within the family – a cornerstone of a larger struggle for respect for women – as a call for men to help when their wives become too encumbered by housework. A few see it as a call for women to share the same opportunities as men to relax and study, and therefore for men to share equally in household tasks. Some interpret Ho Chi Minh's statement that women's equality requires a 'thorough-going and difficult revolution' as an invitation to question power relations within the family; others do not. Mai Thi Tu and Le Thi Nham Tuyet criticized subtle patriarchal reactions that equate femininity with passivity and submissiveness (p. 193 of this book). Other Women's Union members, perhaps the majority, still believe passivity is a virtue in women.

At this stage, we hear no Vietnamese women talking about men assuming women's jobs, only about women assuming men's jobs, when they discuss eliminating the sexual division of labour. It may be possible to achieve women's liberation without eliminating all division of labour based on sex. As Kalamu ya Salaam understood, 'women are not men, nor is it necessary for them to become men-like in order to self-determine, self-respect and self-defend . . . .'[10] The problem arises when the real differences between women and men are assumed to be a basis for denying power to women. As long as the division of labour reserves a disproportionate number of leading positions for men and assumes that domestic tasks are exclusively women's work, then, given the historic traditions of downgrading women's work, full women's liberation will be difficult to achieve.

I think there is a correlation between the assumption that men should not do women's work and the assumption that women do not make good leaders. The correlation may be rooted in two ancient Confucian dogmas: 1) 'Men live outside the house in society, women live inside the family.' 2) 'An officer is one who commands soldiers, a husband is one who commands wives.' These proverbs eloquently articulate the subordination of women to men's power and authority in the feudal family and society. As long as these influences prevail in Viet Nam today, few women with authority over men will be accepted. Chapters 9 to 14 inclusive, detailed the progress women have made in creating institutions to end their subordination. As these institutions are consolidated, as socialism develops and gathers strength, we anticipate women's ideological struggle will reflect that progress.

Bringing It Home

The Vietnamese defeat of US imperialism brought lasting changes to the lives of women all over the world. The US government tried to export its control and its culture. The people of Viet Nam resisted. The US war machine, built and fuelled by five presidents, strained US society to its limits. The war returned to the US in the form of crisis: the deaths of husbands, sons and brothers; Watergate; inflation, unemployment, recession; heroin addiction and delayed stress syndrome; cynicism.

After much controversy, a national monument bearing the names of the 57,939 Americans who died in Viet Nam was finally opened to the public in November 1982. Unlike other war memorials, it only lists the names. There is no inscription about the war, nor the usual pledge that 'they shall not have died in vain'. Moreover, the claims of 10,000 veterans for compensation for their dioxin-induced symptoms remain unanswered.

The US defeat in Viet Nam was a warning to future administrations. Not in Angola, Mozambique, Zimbabwe, Nicaragua or El Salvador – nowhere – would the US commit its military might without fear of suffering 'another Viet Nam'. Viet Nam became synomymous with defeat for imperialist venture. So the women of Mozambique could proceed with their struggle against polygamy, after having won their independence from Portugal, without having to devote precious resources to a fight against direct US intervention. And the US government continues to search for the means to dominate without committing thousands of US troops.

Vietnamese women are proud of their contribution to the liberation of others. General Dinh told me, 'We have led our struggle not only to liberate women in our country, but to help liberate women all over the world; because we know women are the most oppressed everywhere, no matter what country they are in.'[11] Vietnamese women have helped to liberate others not only by joining in the defeat of French colonialism, US imperialism and Chinese invasion; not only by providing an image and inspiration for change and the infinite possibilities of human resistance, but also by allowing us to learn from their costly experience.

The people of Viet Nam, especially the women, would be the first to remind us that they have found no universal formula for liberation. No one strategy could be applied to other countries whose size, people and history are so different. We have seen many ways in which the experience of Vietnamese women is unlike that of women who live in colonizing countries, except perhaps the women of the internal colonies – Black women inside the US, for example.

Yet the system that attempted genocide in Viet Nam is responsible for the forced sterilization of women inside the US – particularly of women of colour. The pesticide used by the men who defoliated Viet Nam caused cancer. As they raped in Viet Nam, they rape here. They exported pornography to Viet Nam, while pornography remains a multi-million dollar industry inside the US. They dropped the equivalent of two Hiroshima-sized atomic bombs per week on Viet Nam; and they continue to threaten nuclear destruction of Europe and the rest of the world. As the US maintains an economic blockade against Viet Nam, attempting to starve the country into submission, we in capitalist countries in the West strain under record unemployment, cutbacks in health care, childcare and other social services, and unpredictable inflation.

Vietnamese women endured the worst US society has to offer. They learned the war against Viet Nam was not the mistaken policy of some misguided presidents. It was the deliberate strategic outcome of a system that had to attempt to destroy a liberation movement that defied it. In resisting this system of imperialism, Vietnamese people led the way in demonstrating how thorough our own revolution must be inside the US and other Western countries. For example, women fighting against rape by GIs in Viet Nam never considered relying exclusively on the system's police department for help, nor did they target Vietnamese men who were also victims of male chauvinist violence. (Many Vietnamese men were brutalized by homophobic GIs who assumed that they were homosexuals because they held hands with other men.) The Women's Committee to Defend the Right to Live, organized in response to a particularly atrocious rape, understood that their primary target had to be their most powerful enemy: US imperialism, represented by its government and armed forces.

Vietnamese women were able to build a strong movement because they focused their energies. Their strategy could unify the majority of active women because it reflected the felt experience and aspirations of millions of peasants and working-class women. As we begin to fight for change and our own movement advances, what we can learn from Viet Nam will take on richer meaning. Bui Thi Me spoke of the 'worldwide family of militant women', when she welcomed me to liberated Quang Tri in 1974. Her vision and confidence in solidarity are eloquent antidotes to the cynicism of our bureaucratic, high tech, bloated societies. Their strength, organization and determination have shown that a united people, confident that their cause is just, certain of their eventual victory, can defeat the most formidable military arsenal in the world.

Vietnamese women have shown that women's liberation is not an isolated battle: it is interwoven into the fabric of people's struggles everywhere. Our success in winning our own demands for women's liberation partially depends on the effectiveness of our solidarity with those leading the struggles to defeat imperialism.

The victories of the people of Viet Nam are also the victories of the overwhelming majority of people in the US, France or England. We can strengthen our common victories by participating in campaigns to help rebuild Viet Nam and counter the continued attempts to sabotage its achievements. We can share experiences with the women in Viet Nam; learn from their example of unity; feel sure that liberation movements will grow and become stronger. As the momentum and revolutionary power grow, the steps we have to climb get shorter.

Vietnamese women are proud of being women: they are as proud of their endurance as mothers as they are of their heroism in military battle. Their pride includes identifying with the victories of women in other countries. They invite all women to share their women's pride.

Notes

1. Jayne Werner makes a similar point in her article, 'Women, Socialism and the Economy of Wartime North Viet Nam, 1960–1975', *Studies in Comparative Communism*, Vol. XIV, Nos 2–3, Summer/Autumn 1981, pp. 165–90.
2. Barbara Ehrenreich, National Conference of Socialist Feminists, July 1975. Quote by Batya Weinbaum, *The Curious Courtship of Women's Liberation and Socialism* (Boston: South End Press, 1978).
3. Christine White, 'Viet Nam and the Politics of Gender' (mimeo: University of Sussex, 1981), p. 11.
4. Weinbaum, op. cit., p. 60.
5. Ibid., p. 114.

6. Nguyen Khac Vien, 'Economics and Social Change', *US/Viet Nam Friendship Association Newsletter*, Vol. 5, No. 1, January–February 1983, p. 6.
7. Mai Thi Tu, 'Vietnamese Women in the Eighties', *Viet Nam Courier*, No. 10, 1981, pp. 19–23.
8. 'Report of the Central Committee of the Viet Nam Women's Union to the Fifth National Congress of Vietnamese Women' (unpublished mimeo), May 1982, p. 32.
9. Some critics of socialist societies' progress towards women's emancipation mistakenly assert the existence of an immutable 'official line' on women. Molyneux goes further and denies the possibility of even beginning a struggle to change it. Her racist arrogance blinds her to the integrity of political struggle in countries like Viet Nam. She wrote, 'Even less critical distance [from her notion of the codified theory on the woman question] can be expected in Third World countries that are now closely linked to and dependent on the Soviet Union and which lack the historical background and cultural resources with which to evaluate and criticize this part of what they are assured is orthodox Marxism.' Quoted from 'Socialist Societies Old and New: Progress Towards Women's Emancipation', *Monthly Review*, Vol. 34, No. 3, July–August 1982, p. 67.
10. Kalamu ya Salaam, 'The Struggle to Smash Sexism Is a Struggle to Develop Women', in *Our Women Keep Our Skies from Falling* (New Orleans: Nkombo, 1980), p. 41.
11. Interview by author with Nguyen Thi Dinh (Hanoi, 4 September 1981).

Chronology

5000 BC: Relics found from this date mark the beginning of Vietnamese history.

300–200 BC: Emergence of patriarchy in Viet Nam.

111 BC: Chinese first conquer Viet Nam.

40 AD: Trung sisters lead the first national insurrection against the Chinese.

981 AD: Chinese expelled from Viet Nam.

1847: French first invade Viet Nam.

1930: Indochinese Communist Party and the Viet Nam Women's Union are founded.

1944–45: Famine years. The first unit of the Viet Nam People's Army is organized and general insurrection sweeps the country. Also known as the August Revolution, 1945.

2 September 1945: Ho Chi Minh reads Vietnamese Declaration of Independence from France. Days later, French launch war of reconquest.

1946: Constitution of the Democratic Republic of Viet Nam ratified.

8 May 1954: Viet Minh defeat the French at Dien Bien Phu.

20 July 1954: Geneva Accords recognize Viet Nam as one, independent nation; but designate the 17th parallel as temporary military demarcation line to facilitate troop withdrawal. General elections for new government for reunified Viet Nam scheduled for 1956.

1955–56: Diem begins reign of terror against Viet Minh and possible sympathizers in South Viet Nam. First US military advisers arrive. No elections allowed.

20 December 1959: National Liberation Front formed. Calls for general insurrection against Diem and for reunification of the country.

1960: Law on Marriage and the Family passed in the Democratic Republic of Viet Nam; outlaws polygamy, forced marriage and calls for democracy within the family.

1961: Union of Women for the Liberation of South Viet Nam is formed.

1 November 1963: Coup topples Diem. Also in that year, NLF scores major victories.

1964–65: US begins bombing and sending large numbers of troops to Viet Nam.

1967: 535,000 US troops arrive by the end of the year.

January–February 1968: Tet offensive launched by the NLF.

May 1968: First session of Paris Peace talks.

June 1969: Provisional Revolutionary Government of the Republic of South Viet Nam founded at Congress of Representatives of the People of South Viet Nam.

March 1970: Prince Sihanouk overthrown. US troops invade Cambodia.

May 1972: Quang Tri liberated, the first province of South Viet Nam to be governed by the PRG. President Nixon orders bombing escalation.

December 1972: Christmas bombing of Hanoi and other densely populated areas. One-third of all US Air Force's operative B-52s are shot down.

27 January 1973: US, Thieu regime, PRG and DRV sign the Paris Peace Agreement.

1973–74: Fighting continues after US and Thieu regime violate Peace Agreement.

March 1974: Fourth national congress of Vietnamese women meets in Hanoi.

Autumn 1974: Mass demonstrations in South Vietnamese cities, including Catholic and Buddhist forces, call for Thieu's resignation.

March 1975: Liberation army begins spring offensive in central highlands.

30 April 1975: Flag of the PRG raised over the Presidential Palace in Saigon. US Ambassador flees hours before.

April 1976: Elections held throughout Viet Nam for reunified National Assembly.

June 1976: Viet Nam officially reunified and renamed Socialist Republic of Viet Nam. Women's Unions from North and South are also reunified.

January 1979: After Viet Nam People's Army's decisive aid to FUNSK, Pol Pot flees Phnom Penh. People's Republic of Kampuchea formed.

February 1979: Six hundred thousand Chinese troops invade Viet Nam, take heavy losses and retreat within three weeks.

May 1982: Fifth national congress of Vietnamese women includes representatives of women from all over Viet Nam.

Recommended Reading and Resource Centres

Books

I. Since Liberation

Mark Baker. *Nam: The Viet Nam War in the Words of the Men and Woman Who Fought there*. (New York: William Morrow and Company, 1981.)

Wilfred Burchett. *The China, Cambodia, Viet Nam Triangle*. (London: Zed Press, 1981.)

Arlene Eisen-Bergman. *Women of Viet Nam*. (San Francisco: People's Press, 1975.)

Fifty years of Activity of the Communist Party of Viet Nam. (Hanoi: Foreign Languages Publishing House, 1980.)

Stanley Goff, Robert Sanders and Clark Smith. *Brothers: Black Soldiers in the Nam*. (Novato, California: Presidio Press, 1982.)

Kathleen Gough Aberle. *Ten Times More Beautiful*. (New York: Monthly Review Press, 1977.)

Ben Kiernan and Chantou Boua (eds). *Peasants and Politics in Kampuchea (1942–1981)*. (London: Zed Press, 1982.)

Mai Thi Tu and Le Thi Nham Tuyet. *Women in Viet Nam*. (Hanoi: Foreign Languages Publishing House, 1978.)

Cecilia Molander. *Women in Viet Nam*. (Stockholm: Swedish International Development Agency, 1981.)

Mother and Infant Welfare. (Hanoi: Foreign Languages Publishing House, 1979.)

Dileep Padgaonkar. *Kampuchean Chronicles*. Tokyo: National Federation of UNESCO Associations in Japan, 1980.)

John Pilger and Anthony Barnett. *Aftermath*. (London: New Statesman, 1982.)

Nguyen Khac Vien. *Contemporary Viet Nam (1858–1980)*. (Hanoi: Red River Publications, Foreign Languages Publishing House, 1981.)

Nguyen Minh Kien. *Understanding China*. (Hanoi: Viet Nam Courier, 1981.)

William Shawcross. *Sideshow*. (New York: Simon and Schuster, 1979.)

Vietnamese Studies. These are a series of books published by Viet Nam Courier in Hanoi. Each volume is devoted to a specific theme: *The*

Disabled: Their Right to Live (no. 64, 1981); *Handicrafts* (no. 62, 1980). For a listing of those available in the US, write to Book Center, 518 Valencia Street, San Francisco, California 94110.

Viet Nam Women's Union. *Fifth Congress of Vietnamese Women: Basic Documents.* (Hanoi: 1982.)

Viet Nam Women's Union. *Statistical Data.* (Hanoi: 1981.)

II. Pre-1975, Background Reading

Wilfred Burchett. *North of the Seventeenth Parallel.* (Hanoi: Red River Publishing House, 1957.)

Wilfred Burchett. *Inside Story of Guerrilla War.* (New York: International Publishers, 1966.)

Wilfred Burchett. *Viet Nam North.* (New York: International Publishers, 1967.)

Wilfred Burchett. *Viet Nam Will Win.* (New York: Guardian, 1970.)

Gerard Chaliand. *The Peasants of North Viet Nam.* (Baltimore: Penguin, 1969.)

Jean Chesnaux, Georges Boudarel and Daniel Hemery. *Tradition et Révolution au Viet Nam.* (Paris: éditions anthropos, 1971.)

Ho Chi Minh. *On Revolution.* Bernard Fall (editor). (New York: Signet, 1968.)

Ho Chi Minh. *Selected Writings.* (Hanoi: Foreign Languages Publishing House, 1977.) Pages 371–409 on women.

Joan K. McMichael (ed.). *Health in the Third World: Studies from Viet Nam.* (Nottingham: Spokesman Books, 1976.)

Ngo Vinh Long. *Before the Revolution.* (Cambridge: MIT Press, 1973.)

Nguyen Thi Dinh. *No Other Road to Take.* Mai V. Elliott translator. (Ithaca, New York: South East Asai Program, Department of Asia Studies, Cornell University, 1976.)

Archimedes Patti. *Why Viet Nam?* (Berkeley: University of California Press, 1980.)

Pentagon Papers. New York Times Edition. (New York: Bantam, 1972.)

Pham Van Dong. *Selected Writings.* (Hanoi: Foreign Languages Publishing House, 1977.)

Clyde Taylor (ed.). *Viet Nam and Black America.* (New York: Anchor, 1973.)

Truong Chinh. *Selected Writings.* (Hanoi: Foreign Languages Publishing House, 1977.)

Viet Nam Veterans Against the War. *Winter Soldier Investigation.* (Boston: Beacon Press, 1972.)

Vietnames Studies No. 10 On Women. (Hanoi: Foreign Languages Publishing House, 1966.)

Vo Nguyen Giap. *The Military Art of People's War.* (New York: Monthly Review Press, 1970.)

Peter Weiss. *Notes on the Cultural Life of the Democratic Republic of Viet-Nam.* (New York: Delta, 1970.)

Articles and Pamphlets

Chantou Boua. 'Women in Today's Cambodia'. *New Left Review*. No. 131 (January–February 1982) pp. 45–61.

Rachel Grossman. 'Women's Place Is on the Integrated Circuit'. *South East Asia Chronicle*. No. 66 (January–February 1979) pp. 2–17.

Hibiscus Series. *Tales, Legends and Stories from Viet Nam*. (Hanoi: Foreign Languages Publishing House, 1981.)

Francois Houtart. 'Viet Nam'. *Ideas and Action Bulletin: FAO*. No. 137 (1980) pp. 2–11.

Ministry of Foreign Affairs. *On the Question of Americans Missing in the Viet Nam War*. (Hanoi: Department of Press and Information, 1980.)

Ministry of Foreign Affairs. *The Truth About Viet Nam_China Relations over the Last 30 Years*. (Hanoi: Department of Press and Information, 1979.)

Nguyen Khac Vien. *Viet Nam '80: Conversations with the Medisch Committee of Holland*. (Hanoi: Viet Nam Courier, 1980.)

The Reunification of Viet Nam: Documents of the Political Consultative Conference on National Reunification. (Hanoi: Foreign Languages Publishing House, 1975.)

Those Who Leave. (Hanoi: Viet Nam Courier, 1979.) Reprinted by US/Viet Nam Friendship Association, Box 5043, San Francisco, California 94101.

Viet Nam: Which Human Rights? (Hanoi: Viet Nam Courier, 1980.)

Jayne Werner. 'Women, Socialism and the Economy of Wartime North Viet Nam.' *Studies in Comparative Communism*. Vol. xiv, No. 2–3 Summer/Autumn 1981) pp. 165–190.

Resource Centres and Periodicals

Association of Vietnamese Patriots in the US, Box 4495, Berkeley, California 94704, publishes *Announcements* in English and a monthly newsletter in Vietnamese.

Far Eastern Economic Review, Hong Kong, publishes a weekly magazine with frequent coverage of Viet Nam.

Foreign Broadcast Information Service, US Department of Commerce, Washington DC, publishes transcripts of translations of Vietnamese radio broadcasts.

Center for International Policy, 120 Maryland Avenue NE, Washington DC, publishes *Indochina Issues*.

Friends of Vietnam, Box 129, Dorchester, Massachusetts 02122, publishes *The Indochina Newsletter* and distributes other publications about Viet Nam.

South East Asia Resource Center, Box 4000 D, Berkeley, California 94704, publishes *South East Asia Chronicle* and distributes a variety of other publications.

US/Viet Nam Friendship Association, Box 5043, San Francisco, California 94101, publishes a *Newsletter* and also distributes *Viet Nam Courier* and other publications from Viet Nam.

US/Viet Nam Friendship Association of Southern California, 3600 Wilshire Blvd No. 2200, Los Angeles, California 90010, published 'Viet Nam and Human Rights' and distributes other publications about Viet Nam.

US Committee for Scientific Cooperation with Viet Nam, c/o Professor Edward Cooperman, Department of Physics, California State University at Fullerton, Fullerton, California 92634, publishes a *Bulletin* and also distributes other papers concerning scientific developments in Viet Nam.

XUNASABA, 32 Hai Ba Truong, Hanoi, Viet Nam, distributes all Vietnamese publications, including *Vietnames Studies*, *Vietnamese Courier*, *Viet Nam* (pictorial) and *Viet Nam Women*. Write to them for complete catalogue of publications available in English, French, Spanish and other languages.

ASIA TITLES FROM ZED PRESS

POLITICAL ECONOMY

BEN KIERNAN AND CHANTHOU BOUA
Peasants and Politics in Kampuchea, 1942-1981
Hb and Pb

DAVID SELBOURNE
Through the Indian Looking Glass
Pb

HASSAN GARDEZI AND JAMIL RASHID (EDITORS)
Pakistan: The Roots of Dictatorship
The Political Economy of a Praetorian State
Hb and Pb

STEFAN DE VYLDER
Agriculture in Chains
Bangladesh — A Case Study in Contradictions and Constraints
Hb

REHMAN SOBHAN AND MUZAFFER AHMAD
Public Enterprise in an Intermediate Regime:
A Study in the Political Economy of Bangladesh
Hb

SATCHI PONNAMBALAM
Dependent Capitalism in Crisis:
The Sri Lankan Economy, 1948-1980
Hb

DAVID ELLIOT
Thailand: Origins of Military Rule
Hb and Pb

A. RUDRA, T. SHANIN AND J. BANAJI ET AL.
Studies in the Development of Capitalism in India
Hb and Pb

BULLETIN OF CONCERNED ASIAN SCHOLARS
China: From Mao to Deng
The Politics and Economics of Socialist Development
Hb and Pb

HUA WU YIN
Malaysia: The Politics of Imperialist Domination
Hb and Pb

RUTH AND VICTOR SIDEL
The Health of China:
Current Conflicts in Medical and Human Services for
One Billion People
Hb and Pb

BETSY HARTMANN and JAMES K. BOYCE
A Quiet Violence:
View from a Bangladesh Village
Hb and Pb

REHMAN SOBHAN
The Crisis of External Dependence
Hb and Pb

ELISABETH CROLL
The Family Rice Bowl
Food and the Domestic Economy in China
Hb and Pb

W.F. WERTHEIM AND MATTHIAS STIEFEL
Production, Equality and Participation in Rural China
Pb

SRIKANT DUTT
India and the Third World:
Altruism or Hegemony
Hb and Pb

CONTEMPORARY HISTORY/REVOLUTIONARY STRUGGLES

SUMANTA BANERJEE
India's Simmering Revolution:
The Naxalite Uprising
Pb

WILFRED BURCHETT
The China, Cambodia, Vietnam Triangle
Pb

SELIG HARRISON
In Afghanistan's Shadow:
Baluch Nationalism and Soviet Temptation
Hb and Pb

MUSIMGRAFIK
Where Monsoons Meet:
History of Malaya
Pb

LAWRENCE LIFSCHULTZ
Bangladesh: The Unfinished Revolution
Pb

SATCHI PONNAMBALAM
The Tamil Question
Hb and Pb

HUMAN RIGHTS

PERMANENT PEOPLE'S TRIBUNAL
Philippines: Repression and Resistance
Pb

JULIE SOUTHWOOD AND PATRICK FLANAGAN
Indonesia: Law, Propaganda and Terror
Hb and Pb

RELIGION

KIM YONGBOCK
Minjung Theology:
People as the Subjects of History

WOMEN

BOBBY SIU
Women of China:
Imperialism and Women's Resistance, 1900–1949
Hb and Pb

ELSE SKJONSBERG
A Special Caste?
Tamil Women in Sri Lanka
Pb

GAIL OMVEDT
We Will Smash this Prison!
Indian Women in Struggle
Hb and Pb

AGNES SMEDLEY
Portraits of Chinese Women in Revolution
Pb

MARIA MIES
The Lacemakers of Narsapur:
Indian Housewives Produce for the World Market
Pb

ARLENE EISEN
Women in the New Vietnam
Hb and Pb

ELISABETH CROLL
Chinese Women
Hb and Pb

PATRICIA JEFFREY
Frogs in a Well:
Indian Women in Purdah
Hb and Pb

Zed press titles cover Africa, Asia, Latin America and the Middle East, as well as general issues affecting the Third World's relations with the rest of the world. Our Series embrace: Imperialism, Women, Political Economy, History, Labour, Voices of Struggle, Human Rights and other areas pertinent to the Third World.

You can order Zed titles direct from Zed Press, 57 Caledonian Road, London, N1 9DN, U.K.

WOMEN IN THE THIRD WORLD: TITLES FROM ZED PRESS

BOBBY SIU
Women of China:
Imperialism and Women's Resistance, 1900–1949
Hb and Pb

INGELA BENDT AND JAMES DOWNING
We Shall Return:
Women of Palestine
Hb and Pb

MIRANDA DAVIES (EDITOR)
Third World — Second Sex:
Women's Struggles and National Liberation
Hb and Pb

JULIETTE MINCES
The House of Obedience:
Women in Arab Society
Hb and Pb

MARGARET RANDALL
Sandino's Daughters:
Testimonies of Nicaraguan Women in Struggle
Pb

MARIA MIES
The Lacemakers of Narsapur:
Indian Housewives Produce for the World Market
Pb

ASMA EL DAREER
Woman, Why do you Weep?
Circumcision and Its Consequences
Hb and Pb

RAQIYA HAJI DUALEH ABDALLA
Sisters in Affliction:
Circumcision and Infibulation of Women in Africa
Hb and Pb

MARIA ROSE CUTRUFELLI
Women of Africa:
Roots of Oppression
Hb and Pb

AGNES SMEDLEY
Portraits of Chinese Women in Revolution
Pb

RAYMONDA TAWIL
My Home, My Prison
Pb

NAWAL EL SAADAWI
Woman at Zero Point
Hb and Pb

ELISABETH CROLL
Chinese Women
Hb and Pb

ARLENE EISEN
Women in the New Vietnam
Hb and Pb

Zed press titles cover Africa, Asia, Latin America and the Middle East, as well as general issues affecting the Third World's relations with the rest of the world. Our Series embrace: Imperialism, Women, Political Economy, History, Labour, Voices of Struggle, Human Rights and other areas pertinent to the Third World.

You can order Zed titles direct from Zed Press, 57 Caledonian Road, London, N1 9DN, U.K.